ROUTLEDGE LIBRARY EDITIONS:
HUMAN RESOURCE MANAGEMENT

Volume 25

PERFORMANCE MEASUREMENT AND THEORY

T0384405

PERFORMANCE MEASUREMENT AND THEORY

Edited by
FRANK LANDY, SHELDON ZEDECK
AND JEANETTE CLEVELAND

Routledge
Taylor & Francis Group

LONDON AND NEW YORK

First published in 1983 by Lawrence Erlbaum Associates, Inc.

This edition first published in 2017
by Routledge
2 Park Square, Milton Park, Abingdon, Oxon OX14 4RN

and by Routledge
711 Third Avenue, New York, NY 10017

Routledge is an imprint of the Taylor & Francis Group, an informa business

© 1983 Lawrence Erlbaum Associates, Inc.

All rights reserved. No part of this book may be reprinted or reproduced or utilised
in any form or by any electronic, mechanical, or other means, now known or
hereafter invented, including photocopying and recording, or in any information
storage or retrieval system, without permission in writing from the publishers.

Trademark notice: Product or corporate names may be trademarks or registered
trademarks, and are used only for identification and explanation without intent to
infringe.

British Library Cataloguing in Publication Data
A catalogue record for this book is available from the British Library

ISBN: 978-1-138-80870-6 (Set)
ISBN: 978-1-315-18006-9 (Set) (ebk)
ISBN: 978-0-415-79207-3 (Volume 25) (hbk)
ISBN: 978-0-415-79209-7 (Volume 25) (pbk)
ISBN: 978-1-315-21194-7 (Volume 25) (ebk)

Publisher's Note
The publisher has gone to great lengths to ensure the quality of this reprint but
points out that some imperfections in the original copies may be apparent.

Disclaimer
The publisher has made every effort to trace copyright holders and would welcome
correspondence from those they have been unable to trace.

PERFORMANCE
MEASUREMENT
AND
THEORY

EDITED BY

Frank Landy

Sheldon Zedeck

Jeanette Cleveland

TECHNICAL EDITOR

Ann Landy

LAWRENCE ERLBAUM ASSOCIATES PUBLISHERS
1983   Hillsdale, New Jersey   London

Copyright © 1983 by Lawrence Erlbaum Associates, Inc.
All rights reserved. No part of this book may be reproduced in
any form, by photostat, microform, retrieval system, or any other
means, without the prior written permission of the publisher.

Lawrence Erlbaum Associates, Inc., Publishers
365 Broadway
Hillsdale, New Jersey 07642

Library of Congress Cataloging in Publication Data

Performance measurement and theory.

Bibliography: p.
Includes index.
1. Employees, Rating of—Addresses, essays, lectures.
I. Landy, Frank, J. II. Zedeck, Sheldon. III. Cleveland,
Jan.
HF5549.5.R3P476 1983   658.3'125   83-968
ISBN 0-89859-246-1

Printed in the United States of America
10 9 8 7 6 5 4 3 2 1

Contents

PART II: INDIVIDUAL CONSIDERATIONS

PART III: METHODOLOGICAL AND MEASUREMENT CONSIDERATIONS

COMMENTS

COMMENTS

PART IV: SOCIOPOLITICAL CONSIDERATIONS

COMMENTS

REPLY

Preface

Performance is the Holy Grail of the applied psychologist. The Educational Psychologist examines the impact of instruction methods on the acquisition of knowledge and skill. The Personnel Psychologist studies the effect of training on job performance. The Human Engineer designs environments which yield optimum performance. An understanding of performance is the prize we seek in this volume as well. We will approach the topic from a theoretical perspective.

Research in performance has been conducted explicitly for over 40 years (and implicitly since the time of Aristotle). We know lots of little things about the topic. A major obstacle to increasing our understanding of the bigger issues in performance theory seems to be the absence of a clear agenda for research and thinking. We have been bogged down in the technology of performance assessment and have paid little attention to the theory which must support this technology. Our intention in this volume is to begin to construct such an agenda.

Research, theory, and application are hardly independent of one another. As Kurt Lewin used to say, the most practical thing is a good theory. As a result, we think that the papers presented in this volume will not only spur research, but will also provide an opportunity for some careful considerations of how performance is currently measured in various applied settings. The breadth and depth of the presentations require two characteristics in the reader—a desire to give serious thought to the problems of understanding performance and a willingness to take the various papers and discussions as a point of departure rather than a point of arrival. We hope that the reader is left with many questions when the volume has been read. If all of the questions which the reader might have had are answered in the various presentations, then there was probably no need for the volume in the first place.

To our knowledge, there is no other similar book on performance research and theory. To be sure, there are an increasing number of ''how to do it'' books. This book might be considered more a ''why to do it'' manual. Certainly, ''how to'' cannot exist without ''why to.'' As you will see, the chapters present positions, not reviews. Each contributor has been asked to take a point and present a coherent discussion of it. In addition, each position paper is examined by an independent scholar who comments on the value of the position presented. Since such an approach necessarily relies more heavily on logic than data, it should be easier for nonpsychologists to read than the usual ''research'' paper.

The book is divided into four major areas. Each area treats a somewhat different aspect of performance theory. One area concerns intraindividual issues. Another addresses interindividual or organizational dynamics. The third section takes up the topic of methodology. A fourth section deals with philosophies, which may underlie performance theories and measurement techniques. These four areas represent examples of needed research and thinking. They hardly *define* the research agenda. The transitions between and among areas is not always smooth. This may simply be the legacy of several decades of technological concentration, but we must begin to catch up somewhere.

We are grateful to the many individuals who helped us carry off the performance conference which provided the occasion for these papers. These individuals include our colleagues in the Society of Organization Behaviorists who made suggestions for structure, Joy Creeger who helped coordinate both the conference and the manuscript preparation as well as transcribe the discussions which followed the conference presentations, and various graduate students at Penn State who helped with conference arrangements and details, particularly Wendy Becker. The first chapter describes in some detail, the specific supporting agencies and their roles in this effort. Nevertheless, it is appropriate at this point to acknowledge our gratitude to both Jeff Kane and Bert King for their moral and logistic support.

Frank Landy

PERFORMANCE
MEASUREMENT
AND
THEORY

1 Introduction

Frank Landy

Sheldon Zedeck

Performance and its measurement are playing increasingly greater roles in the conduct of human affairs. There are as many kinds of performance as there are occasions for performance. The occasion might be a classroom and the performance that of a teacher or student. The occasion might be a satellite launching and the performance might be the transmission of pictures back to earth. The occasion might be a session of love making and performance might be sexual gymnastics. The occasion might be a work setting and the performance might be the productivity of a single worker. Each of these is an instance of a stiuationally defined expectation of ''superior'' performance.

Although we might have no problem counting units of production or quality of picture transmission, it might be somewhat more difficult to agree on the definition and measurement of sexual or classroom performance. Thus, in the latter two instances we are faced with a need to interpret what may be ambiguous information. We may even be placed in a position of negotiating a definition of performance. In either case, measuring the performance in question presents some problems.

This book deals with problems in performance measurement. You may have encountered some of these problems before—problems like bias in instruments, bias in evaluators, unreliability, changing definitions of ''success.'' You may never have considered some of these problems before—problems like the role of capitalism in performance measurement, the effect of ignoring poor performance on the gross national product, and the difficulty of predicting performance levels in situations that have never occurred, and that one hopes will never occur.

You are probably familiar with the traditional reasons for measuring performance. The measurement of individual performance allows for rational administrative decisions at the individual employee level. It also provides the raw data for the evaluation of the effectiveness of such personnel-system components and processes as recruiting policies, training programs, selection rules, promotional strategies, and reward allocations. Finally, it provides the foundation for behaviorally based employee counseling. In this counseling setting, performance information provides the vehicle for increasing satisfaction, commitment, and motivation of the individual. Performance measurement allows the organization to tell employees something about their rates of growth, their competencies, and their potentials. There is little disagreement that if done well, performance measurements and feedback can play a valuable role in effecting the grand compromise between the needs of the individual and the needs of the organization. The key phrase here is "if done well." To do it "well," we need to understand what "it" is. It is this issue—the understanding—that we addressed in the conference "Performance Measurement: Directions for the Future," held from November 6 to 8, 1981, in Dallas, Texas, and that we address in this book. We identify some of the boundary conditions for performance measurement. And we point out some of the obstacles to doing it well.

A LITTLE HISTORY

The measurement of performance has occupied the attention of applied psychologists for several decades. The graphic rating scale was introduced in 1920 as an attempt to capture something of the more "impressionistic" characteristics of energy expenditure and its effectiveness. Frederick W. Taylor was more than complete in defining what performance was for Schmidt, the pig-iron handler. The Gilbreths were quite eloquent in their systematic articulation of the language and units of work measurement.

In the 1930s and 1940s, a good deal of research was devoted to the format, method, and physical characteristics of performance-measurement systems. Questions regarding the nature of anchors, the definitions of areas of performance, the physical layout of rating scales were all very popular. Even at that "early" stage, the issue was not *if* performance would be measured; the only question was *how*.

During this period, there were excursions into psychometric theory but these were usually only indirectly related to the more applied aspect of performance measurement: They generally were concerned with developing new statistical techniques, uncovering interesting characteristics of transformed distributions, or looking at some basic characteristics of sensation or perception. Variations on Thurstone's Law of Comparative Judgement accomplished all of these purposes. But these studies dealt only peripherally with the issue of measuring human performance in work settings.

In 1952, the late Robert Wherry produced some reports for the Army that directly addressed the rating process. He deduced certain logical relationships among various components of the rating sequence. He suggested that these components included observation, storage, retrieval, and judgment. Further, he stated a number of specific corollaries to the basic propositions. These corollaries spelled out the anticipated effects of altering various aspects of the rating process. The corollaries were based to some extent on logical relationships, to some extent on previous psychometric research on these components, and to some extent on classical test theory. To our misfortune, the reports virtually disappeared. The only people aware of them were people who had professional contact with Wherry either through collaborative research or as Ohio State graduate students.

For the next 20 years or so, research on performance assessment continued to wallow in the quagmire of methodology: scales that went up rather than down; scales with the high end on the left rather than on the right; scales with letters rather than numbers. In a sense, if one examined the research conducted in performance evaluation, it seemed that it was just an engineering problem: It would only be a matter of time before a better mousetrap would be found. Just as spirits were flagging, the Behaviorally Anchored Rating Scale arrived to save the day. For more than a decade, researchers luxuriated in developing BARS systems for measuring the performance of everyone from firefighters and police officers to grocery-store packers, providing yet another example of the mission-oriented research so common in applied experimental psychology. These scales were devoted to satisfying a definite need—the measurement of performance in a particular occupational area. Unfortunately, our knowledge of rating and raters did not develop appreciably during this period.

Partly as a result of the changes within psychology as a discipline, and partly as a result of disenchantment with BARS approaches to performance measurement, researchers began examining variables of a more dynamic nature in the hope of understanding the performance-assessment process. This involved reexamining the traditional notions of error; exploring the relevance of information-processing research, models of person perception, attribution, and implicit personality theory; studying individual difference variables that were nontraditional (such as cognitive complexity, perseveration, etc.); and a host of other macro and micro variables that might conceivably help understand the rating process. In the last several years, there have been several review papers that have called for a broader consideration of the phenomena that comprise interpersonal evaluation. These reviews have suggested borrowing from other subdisciplines and other allied fields of behavioral science. There does seem to be some agreement that a moratorium on rating-scale development research might be in order. It was from this historical context that the structure for the "Performance Measurement" conference and the present text emerged.

LOGICAL CONSIDERATIONS IN THE CONFERENCE STRUCTURE

As a result of independent reviews completed by Landy and Zedek, the editors of this volume, several areas had been identified as "underrepresented" in the research literature. Among these areas were the effect of organizational and suborganizational variables on performance definition and assessment, the effect of performance-measurement systems and definitions on organizational health and well-being, the role of motivation in the behavior of evaluators, and the effect of values and attitudes on the nature of measurement and definitional system. It was decided that the conference would be used to sensitize researchers to the areas as yet unexamined rather than to showcase what was already known about performance measurement. In a sense, the conference was to be an attempt to draft a research agenda for the next decade.

Having identified the thrust of the conference, it was now necessary to determine exactly how time would be allocated and topics developed. Preliminary discussions had been held with the Office of Naval Research (ONR) and the Office of Personnel Management (OPM) regarding financial and logistic support for the conference. Both of these agencies were very interested in a conference of this sort for many reasons. The Office of Personnel Management was charged with the responsibility of determining personnel procedures for the massive work force of federal employees. Further, the Civil Service Reform Act had exaggerated the pressure to improve performance-measurement techniques for the federal work force. The Office of Naval Research was, by definition, concerned with the concept of performance readiness in the military context. But in a more general sense, both of these agencies had a long and commendable record of supporting basic research in psychological processes, including performance measurement.

In the early stages of conference planning, a meeting was held to draft a preliminary set of topics for the conference. This meeting was attended by Bert King from ONR; Jeff Kane, Magda Colberg, Marianne Nester, and Frank Schmidt from OPM; C. J. Bartlett; and Landy and Zedek, two editors of this volume. At that meeting, a preliminary list was developed for topical consideration. Subsequently, the editors discussed topics among themselves and with Jeff Kane from OPM. The result of these discussions were twelve broad areas of concentration for the conference. These areas are as follows:

1. Political and philosophical considerations in performance assessment.
2. Power distribution within organizations.
3. The effect of organizational characteristics on performance-measurement systems.
4. The effect of performance-measurement systems on organizational characteristics.

5. The effect of individual performance on organizational structure and process.
6. A cognitive view of performance measurement.
7. A social personality view of performance measurement.
8. The supervisor/subordinate Dyad.
9. Performance evaluation as a motivated event.
10. Performance evaluation and definition in military settings.
11. Objective versus subjective performance measurement.
12. Conceptualizing performance through modeling.

As can be easily seen, this was a list with awe-inspiring scope. It would be virtually impossible to satisfactorily cover even one of these topics in a several-day conference, let alone all of them! It was decided that these headings would be used as labels for conceptual categories. This would allow each contributor to determine how to flesh out the concept. In a sense, the contributors were asked to give papers that were examples of the salient issues in particular conceptual categories. The papers that appear in this volume are these examples. The contributions are grouped into four broad categories: organizational issues, individual-difference issues, methodological issues, and sociopolitical issues.

The contributors were chosen carefully, and they all have certain characteristics in common. First, they are scholars. They have demonstrated through their research and writing that they have the capacity to expand areas for consideration, not simply to fill in holes. In addition, for the most part these contributors had not devoted their major research attention to the issue of performance definition and assessment, at least not in the broad context of suggesting research priorities. Finally, each of the contributors had expressed a willingness to listen and discuss what he or she heard, a rather demanding task for individuals who are more often the subjects than the objects in the communication paradigm.

The contributors were also dissimilar in many respects. In fact, few of them agreed with each other about anything. Each of them brought a unique research history to the task. They represented many different disciplines including anthropology, sociology, law, and psychology. Within the psychology group, there were representatives of various subdisciplines including industrial/organizational, social, cognitive, differential, and personality. It was this broad and heterogeneous mixture that the organizers hoped would produce the bridges that were so obviously absent from much of the earlier research in the area of performance assessment.

STRUCTURE OF THE CONFERENCE AND THE PRESENTATIONS

Because we felt that a structured response to each of the twelve contributions might add considerably to the value of that contribution, and because this effort seemed much too intimidating for us, we identified a discussant for each major contribution. These discussants were chosen on the same basis as were the major contributors. They came from varying disciplines, liked to argue, and were recognized scholars. As a matter of fact, several discussants were originally approached as contributors and declined because of the time commitment required to produce a major theoretical statement in an area with which they were only peripherally involved. Because they expressed an interest, optimism, and curiosity, they were natural choices for the somewhat different role of discussant.

The discussants were given several alternative courses of action to pursue. If they liked, they could present a "minority report" on the topic. In other words, they might agree with what the major contributor said, but still feel that certain other things, which required some discussion, were left unsaid, or they might feel that the contribution was not necessarily "wrong," just irrelevant to the topic at hand. A second possibility was to disagree with the substance of the major contribution and point out weaknesses while suggesting alternative considerations. A final alternative was to take the major contribution as a point of departure and simply extend the comments of the contributor. Examples of all three approaches appear in this text. We leave it to you to determine which discussion represents which alternative. It is not always obvious.

The process of paper and discussion production was rather simple. Major authors forwarded drafts of their papers to discussants prior to the conference. This provided the discussants with some opportunity to prepare formal comments. In some instances, discussants and contributors had interactions of substance about their respective contributions prior to the conference.

After the conference, final drafts were submitted to the volume editors. The papers that appear in this volume are those final postconference drafts. Major presenters were given the option of formally replying in print to discussants if they so wished. Some contributors took advantage of this opportunity and others felt no need to make additional comments. The "Reply" sections of the chapters represent the formal written replies rather than comments made at the conference immediately following the discussants' presentations. Although it must have been tempting for several major contributors to modify their last drafts in an effort to mitigate the effects of their discussants, no one took that unfair advantage.

During the course of the conference presentations, there was a good deal of spontaneous discussion about the various topics. This discussion involved not only presenters and discussants but also members of a motivated, well-prepared, and critical (in the nicest sense of the word) audience. There were approximately 80 "observers" who attended the 2½ day conference. These observers came from research settings, federal agencies, private industry, and academic settings. They added immeasurably to the effort through comments, both in the formal sessions and in more informal conversation. We are grateful to them for their interest and aid.

This volume represents the results of the several-year effort that culminated in the conference held in Dallas, Texas, from November 6 through November 8, 1981. Each chapter includes the major topical presentation, the formal discussion, and any reply from the major contributor to the discussant. The final chapter represents a synthesis, summary, and conclusion through the eyes of the editors. We feel that the conference achieved its purpose. We would very much like this volume to be the first in a series that reports the proceedings of an annual or biannual Performance Assessment Conference. It is clear to us that energy must be expended in developing lines of research that have been ignored in the past. This type of conference is a good way to start such development.

ORGANIZATIONAL CONSIDERATIONS

The three papers that comprise this section are macroscopic in view. They consider performance definition and assessment in the larger context of organizational purpose, structure, and process. Concern for the impact of the organization on the individual is virtually unrepresented in the research literature addressing performance assessment.

Hall considers the relative impact of single individuals on the organizational structure and process. Mitchell looks through the other end of the telescope and considers the impact of organizational, task, and situational variables on individual performance. Steers and Lee move one step further and consider the effect of the strategies that organizations use to evaluate performance on the loyalties and commitment of those being evaluated.

2 The Effect of the Individual on an Organization's Structure, Style, and Process

Douglas T. Hall

Dr. Hall discusses the impact of an individual's performance on an organization's structure, style, and process. He states that the performance of the top-level individual can influence the goals and structure of the organization. The performance of the bottom-level individual can affect the organizational culture and the delivery or distribution of rewards. The performance of middle-level individuals has its impact through the implementation of top-management policies, systems, and so on. The middle-level individual has more methods (power) to block or facilitate change in the organization than either top- or bottom-level people.

In what Hall calls strategic situations, the individual may manipulate the course of organizational events. The effect of aggregated individuals at the bottom level may be one representation of organizational climate. Hall also describes the "new value" or protean employee who contributes to an employee-centered climate.

Hall discusses the implications individual impact has for performance measurement. Briefly, he urges that we guard against overdesigned reward systems (avoid unnecessary complexity) yet reward multiple dimensions of performance. Hall states that individuals should be rewarded for long-term performance and for performance that focuses on obtaining organizational goals.

Staw asserts that Hall vascillates between discussing the impact of the individual and that of the collective group on the organization. Although Hall shows how top managers' actions can be facilitated or inhibited by managers at middle and lower levels, Staw believes that the core issue is to determine how to assess an individual's impact on the organization. To more adequately assess this impact, Staw urges that both proximal and distal effects of the individual's behaviors be examined. An action may appear to be effective in the short run but have some undesirable long-term consequences.

In many organizations today, improving performance is not as difficult as it was in the past. Through programs employing (among other motivators) positive reinforcement (Hamner & Hamner, 1976), goals and objectives (Latham & Locke, 1979), feedback (Nadler, Mirvis, & Cammann, 1976), financial incentives (Larcker, 1981), job redesign (Hackman & Oldham, 1980), and quality-of-work life (Goodman, 1979), technologies for enhancing performance at work have become remarkably effective during the last five or ten years. If anything, performance is now too easy.

A major problem in the area of performance improvement involves what happens next. What are the results of improving performance in one area? Are there unintended negative consequences in other areas? Can an organization be too successful? Is it true that the only thing worse than not achieving your goals is achieving your goals?

In this paper we will examine the effect of the performance of a single person on an organization, on its structure, style, and process. We first examine the different ways a single person might be in a position to exert strong influence on an organization's behavior, making a distinction between formal power and strategic power. Next, we examine systematic differences in the ways a person at top, middle, or lower levels of an organization could have an impact on system functions. And, finally, we examine the implications of individual impact for performance measurement.

SITUATIONS FOR INDIVIDUAL IMPACT

One of the "blind spots" of the literature on organizational behavior is caused by an implicit assumption that the direction of influence in the person–organization relationship is from the organization to the person: that is, the organization influences the person, but the person does not influence the organization.

To organize our discussion, we divide personal-influence situations into two different types: those in which the focal person is in a formal power position (with legitimate expectations of influence), and those in which the person is in a strategic position to manipulate the course of organizational events in some way. Note that the two do not have to be mutually exclusive. In fact, the most effective formal-power figures are probably also those who can develop advantageous strategic situations as well. Further, our purpose is not to be exhaustive, but to examine some of the more important examples of the influences of individual performance.

Formal Power Situation

The most obvious example of the influence of a single individual in a formal power position would be that of the incumbent of a high-level position in an organizational hierarchy. Because organizational structures are generally under the control of senior people—in particular the person at the top (president, chairperson, director, etc.)—this case of one-person influence is self-evident. Further, the leadership style of the person at the top also plays a strong role in shaping the style and process ("climate") of the organization (Hall & Schneider, 1973).

However, it is really not quite that simple. Some "high-powered" people (i.e., some people in "high-powered" positions) in fact exercise more power than others. For example, one Chief Executive Officer (CEO) of a major manufacturing company has extremely strong ideas about changing the style and process of his organization from a traditional, tough-minded "Theory X" style to a much more participative climate, including team management, quality circles, and job redesign as major elements. In terms of tradition and position power (control over budgets, structure, personnel decisions, etc.), the CEO of this company has considerable "clout." However, despite several years of his talking about the need for these organizational changes, years of task forces and management seminars, many visits to Japan and Europe, and several new senior organization development staff people, there has been little real change at the plant level.

Consider another example: the U.S. Military Academy at West Point, the "Harvard Business School" of militarism. West Point is part of the U.S. Army and exists to train and educate future Army officers. It is an Army post, and its structure conforms to the Army structure (98% of the faculty are Army officers, cadets have been sworn into the Army, and they are subject to the Uniform Code of Military Justice). The style and process, however, are different from most Army posts in that West Point is a college, in addition to being a tactical training site, so that the climate is academic and relatively (relative to the "real Army") informal. Geographically bounded by the banks of the Hudson River to the east and by mountains to the north, west, and south, with military police guards at the gates, and with all members (cadets, faculty, faculty families, enlisted support personnel) living and working on post almost year-round, West Point is a total institution, in Goffman's terms. As such, the "inmate culture" (in this case, the cadet culture) is extremely strong.

The superintendent is a former four-star general, a highly respected former NATO commander, who came out of retirement after the 1976 cheating scandal and took a one-star demotion to head the Academy. As a three-star general in a military structure, his position power was extremely high, as was his personal power. A major objective was to modify the cadet culture (although these are my words, not his).

Because the cadet culture within a class is largely set during the first summer of what is formally called Cadet Basic Training, (and what cadets call "Beast Barracks"), a primary target of change was to reform "Beast." Cadet Basic Training (CBT) is a full summer of rigorous physical training and military tactical education: long days, no free time, little or no leave time, no visitors for the first few weeks, and close supervision and demanding assignments from the upper-class "officers" who are in charge. It is considered by new cadets as an initiation-type experience. Upper-class cadets eat with the plebes and can discipline them at the table by requiring them to sit at attention (making eating impossible) for most of the meal. After miles of running and lengthy calisthenics, being deprived of food and water in this way is extremely painful. Demerits are given for infractions, and they have to be "walked off" in the barracks courtyard. What little personal free time there is can be removed for infractions (i.e., being "confined to barracks"). Any time a plebe encounters an upper-class cadet, there exists a possibility of some sort of harassment (being called to attention, spot inspection, being quizzed on "plebe knowledge," etc.) and possible disciplinary action. Because upper-class cadets patrol the halls of the barracks, to avoid a trip to the bathroom, some plebes urinate in the sinks in their rooms.

The superintendent wanted to eliminate the harassment of Beast Barracks and create a "positive leadership style." A highly respected colonel who personally possessed such a style was made commander of CBT. He assembled a team of faculty and tactical officers who also fit this style and were known to be accepted and respected by the cadets. This team appointed cadet officers for Beast who also fit this positive style. Lengthy training and planning sessions, some with psychologist-consultants from the Behavioral Sciences and Leadership Department, were conducted for the faculty and tactical officers. Similar training was held for the cadet officer staff. A strong consensus developed that "this summer will be different." The goal was lower plebe stress and lower attrition.

The result: Stress and attrition were unchanged. Mess hall and barracks harassment continued. It was not until the commanding colonel personally appeared in the mess hall, ordered the cadet officers to let plebes eat, and further stationed numerous tactical officers throughout the hall for enforcement that this form of harassment ceased. Barracks stress remained very high. Result: another example of the weakness of power.

THE INDIVIDUAL AT THREE LEVELS

Why were these two apparently powerful individuals unable to influence the style and process of their organizations in these examples? I propose that one answer is that each organization was in fact not one organization but three: the top of the system, the middle, and the bottom. In each of these cases the person at the top was attempting to change the bottom but was unsuccessful in changing the middle first. In the case of the manufacturing company, "middle" means the plant managers and their staff, accustomed to high autonomy, who were definitely not committed to the reforms of the CEO but whose active support was

TABLE 2.1
Impacts on Organization Design Facets and Individuals at Three
Levels of an Organization

Organization Design Facet	Level That Exerts Most Control		
	Top (Institutional)	Middle (Managerial)	Bottom (Technical)
Goals	x		
Structure	x		
People			
Selection		x	
Promotion		x	
Development	(x)[a]	x	
Culture	(x)	x	x
Information technology	(x)	x	
Rewards			
Type	x	x	
Delivery	(x)	x	x
Tasks	(x)	x	(x)

[a]Parentheses indicate that control can be high or low depending on the motivation and the effectiveness of the agent.

essential to implementation. In the case of West Point, "middle" means the cadet officers, who are the link between the Army officers in charge and the plebes; when it came to the crunch, the "initiation effects" of the cadet officers' socialization experiences in their own Beast Barracks, plus the tradition of 200 years, became manifest, and when their initial attempts at positive leadership were not totally successful, they reverted to the traditional style.

What, then, can the person at the top control? Let us consider this issue in relation to the components of organization design, as described by Galbraith (1977). Let us also consider which design features are under the control of middle-level and lower-level participants. A summary of these relative impacts is shown in Table 2.1.

The major components of the design of an organization are its goals, structure, people, information technology, rewards, and tasks (Galbraith, 1977). The two areas that are almost exclusively in the purview of the top are goals and structure. Although task forces and other participative mechanisms may be used as inputs to these issues, the identification of the organization's goals (or "mission") and structure are usually under the final control of senior executives and/or the board of directors, or another similar body.

What determines the real impact of a person (or a few persons) at the top is the extent to which that person successfully exerts control over the remaining components of the organization's design. If the top person chooses to influence the type of people in the system, through actively changing selection, promotion, and development policies, and through consciously managing the culture through symbols, mass communication, and other uses of the "figurehead" role, that person's impact will be enhanced. If the top person utilizes new information technology (new budget and reporting systems, performance-feedback systems, participative planning systems, etc.), this enhanced communication, monitoring motivation, can also greatly enhance his or her impact. Through information induction, it has been shown that organizational processes can be affected as much by the information people transmit as by that they receive. Thus the information has a dual effect on employee behavior (Prakash & Rappaport, 1977). Often information technology is seen as a technical staff function rather than as a top-management policy tool, which effectively abdicates this power to middle-level management-information systems specialists. The results show at best no impact and, at worse, serious unintended negative consequences.

As a specific example regarding information technology, we are now seeing countless human-resource management systems, designed to link up business planning with human resource and career planning. The most effective seem to be those initiated by top management to meet organizational needs (e.g., succession planning). They may be rather simple and unexciting to MIS experts, but they *are* used, and they have affected the types and flows of people in middle and senior positions. Human resource systems initiated and implemented by middle-level information specialists and managers tend to be more sophisticated and "better," but they are often simply ignored by the line organization. They gain quality at the expense of acceptance. I argue that the product of quality and acceptance is higher for top-initiated information technology if the implementation involves middle- and lower-level participants.

Rewards can also be powerful instruments of top-level individuals for influencing the style and process of the organization. Policies about the type of rewards to be used (pay, stock options, personal recognition, etc.) and about issues such as strengthening the link between performance and rewards are almost the exclusive domain of top management. Because rewarded behavior is repeated, this aspect of organization design can probably yield the most rapid changes in style and process. If performance is rewarded, individual will perform to that criterion that is most strongly rewarded. For example, a recent performance problem in many firms is top executives' focus on short-term performance, which is strongly rewarded (Rapoport, 1978). Larcker (1981) found that organizations with performance plans in which executives were rewarded (with cash or stock) for long-term performance (at least three years) showed greater corporate capital investment than did a set of associated control firms not adopting performance plans. To encourage a corporate climate favoring long-term investments and development, top management need simply create rewards for long-term performance.

The actual delivery of rewards is probably most dependent on the performance of middle- and lower-level individuals. If an organization has a pay-for-performance policy, even if the top-management team receives differential increases, bonuses, or other awards, if middle- and lower-level managers continue to give across-the-board raises to make their lives easier, the basic style and process of the organization will be unchanged. And if the middle does not adopt the new reward system, the bottom will not.

In terms of task activities, these are usually an operational issue, rather than being policy related and are thus the responsibility of the middle level. Through participatory management, it is possible for lower levels to affect tasks as well.

A useful account of the employment of formal and strategic power to affect organizational style and process is found in Biggart's (1981) recent examination of the management style of Governor Ronald Reagan. Organizational goals were clear in Reagan's well-articulated set of conservative Republican principles. Organization structure was based largely on a chief of staff for administration and the cabinet for decision making. He reserved for himself the role of statesperson, spokesperson, and manipulator of symbols (e.g., with the media), setter of standards and criteria for judging issues: in short, at once the symbolic figurehead and the ultimate authority. He did not become involved in active day-to-day management, he forced subordinates to minimize their differences, he encouraged consensus from the cabinet, and he did not tolerate "end runs" and personal supplications. He was highly organized (as one aide reported, according to Biggart (1981), "If he's got two things to do, he makes an outline [p. 300]''), and required intense communication at middle levels. Teamwork was demanded and rewarded. As one former subordinate reported, (Biggart, 1981):

> I remember one day that we got together initially at six o'clock [in the morning] because we had to have a pre-meeting at seven o'clock, in order to be ready for the Cabinet meeting at eight o'clock, and by nine o'clock we had the thing solved [p. 304].

Thus, by use of all the elements of organization design (goals, structure, people, information technology, rewards, and tasks), along with his personal skills as principle spokesperson and symbol, Reagan put his "fingerprints" on the style, structure, and process of the state government (Biggart, 1981).

The Organization's Founder

One person who is often in control of most of these organization design dimensions is the founder of the organization. At least in its early stages, the founder *is* the organization. And then, if the founder is capable of making the organization grow, the personality and style of this person become projected on the culture and style of the organization. Examples here would be the strict controls of a Henry Ford, the creativity of an Edward Land, and the enthusiasm of a Mary Kay.

A critical performance-measurement issue in the case of the founder is that ultimate control often remains with the founder. And if the performance of the organization is highly dependent on that of the founder, there may be no real opportunity for an independent assessment of and feedback about performance. Only if the founder's controls are reduced or if there is a strong Board of Directors of if the founder/owner has a rare ability to foster open upward communication can valid feedback on performance be achieved.

The Middle Manager

If top-level individuals impact the style and process of the organization through policy, systems, symbols, and inspiration, the middle-level person does so through implementation (or lack of same). A simple count of the x's (without parentheses) in Table 2.1 reveals the key role of the middle level: There are more means by which the middle can facilitate or block change than there are for any other level in the organization. Thus, the most effective process for changing organizational style and process is not "top down" or "bottom up": It is "middle out." Case studies of top–down change (Hall, Rabinowitz, Goodale & Morgan, 1978) and bottom–up change (Scheflen, Lawler, & Hackman, 1971) identify one important cause of implementation problems as the failure to involve middle management in the change process. In successful change, top, middle, and bottom are all involved. And the level with the greatest formal and informal power to involve the other two levels in an organization-wide cooperative effort is the middle, because it has the lowest combined structural distance from the other two levels.

Often, however, the middle's influence on style and process is exercised in a negative way, as a source of resistance to change. The middle has the greatest stake in the status quo, because it is charged with responsibility for implementation and end-result achievement, and it needs predictability and stability to achieve objectives in an efficient way. The top and bottom may be dissatisfied with the status quo (probably for different reasons) and are often motivated to push for change (top people, for improved performance, new products, diversification or consolidation, centralization or decentralization, etc., and lower-level people, for improved work conditions or rewards). The Hovey and Beard Company case described by Bavelas and Strauss (1955) is an excellent example of an attempt to produce a change that was supported by the top and bottom, but was opposed by the middle—and that was eventually discontinued.

STRATEGIC INFLUENCE SITUATIONS

We now move from positions of formal power to situations of strategic influence and consider various ways the lower-level member of an organization can influence the style and process of the organization.

The Individual Employee

Let us start by considering another obvious situation: "the employee," or the impact of aggregated individual performance. Obviously, in the final analysis the ultimate performance of the organization is the result of the combined behaviors of individual employees at the "delivery level." Similarly, the style and process of the organization are largely the result of the culture created by the norms, values, and behaviors of individual members.

There are several ways the performance of the lower-level individual can affect the style and process of the organization. Effective performance on a valued task can lead to increased feelings of psychological success, satisfaction, self-esteem, and job involvement (Hall & Foster, 1977). As Schneider (1980) has found in his work with banks, these positive employee attitudes can strongly enhance the climate and performance of an organization. This link between aggregated employer attitudes and organizational performance is especially strong in service organizations, where to a great extent employee behaviors and attitudes and the resulting climate are perceived as dimensions of performance by clients. Positive attitudes resulting from strong performance can also affect cost-related behaviors such as absenteeism, turnover, and work quality. A fascinating method of measuring the financial impact of employee attitudes has been proposed by Mirvis and Lawler (1977).

Effective employee performance also has a feedback effect on managerial behavior, such that the managers of high-performing employees respond by relaxing their supervision and allowing employees more automony and participation in decision making. Thus good individual performance contributes to a management style of increased participation (Farris, 1975).

Combining all of these effects yields the *organizational performance cycle* shown in Fig. 2.1. This cycle can be triggered at any point, but leadership style, employee performance, and perhaps work climate might be the most amenable to direct influence.

The "New Value" Employee

Ten years ago this writer predicted, on the basis of the values and behaviors of the late-1960s to early-1970s cohort of college students, that work organizations would soon receive an influx of a "new breed" of employee, a person who strongly valued personal freedom, meaning and challenge in work, justice and equity, and the commitment to behave according to his or her values. These new-breed values were summarized as follows: (Hall, 1971):

1. There is now more concern about basic goals and values, not just different values per se.
2. Action is more important. Merely talking about one's values is suspect. The cry is "Do it!"

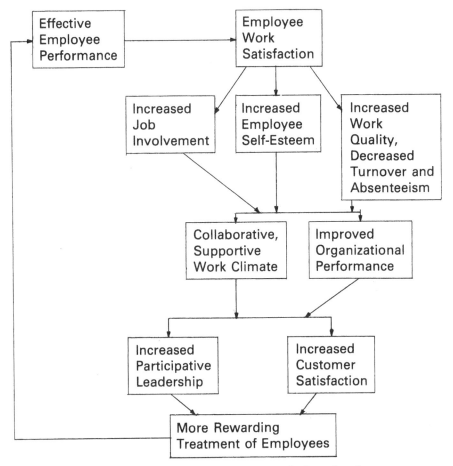

FIG. 2.1.   Effects of employee performance on organization style and process.

3. Personal integrity, honesty, openness, and realness are more important.
4. Many of the "youth" values are humanistic, oriented towards personal fulfillment and psychological success. This reflects a shift away from concerns for extrinsic symbols of success and security. The ultimate meaning and purpose of living are more important.
5. There is increased concern for the ultimate social value of one's work, the *consequences* of that work and not just its content.
6. Authority based on age or position is less highly regarded and the authority of one's expertise, personal style, convictions, or competence carries much more weight with youth. Shared authority is more important than before. (p. 19)

It is clear now that work values in the labor force have shifted in this direction (Renwick & Lawler, 1978; Yankelovich, 1981). We now see increasing numbers of employees concerned about self-fulfillment at work, career rewards commensurate with contributions, information about their futures and that of the organization, more say in career decisions, and freedom on the job as well as freedom *from* the job (leisure).

Performance resulting from these new values contributes to a new style and climate in the organization in the following ways:

More management-contingent behavior. Because participation, meaning, and freedom are more important, employee behavior is more strongly linked to management style in these areas. The new-value employee will work extremely well for a participative management and will make life difficult for a "Theory X" boss. The traditional employee expected less from a boss and thus was less affected by leadership style.

Decreased organizational commitment. The new employee feels more freedom to pursue a "protean" or self-directed career (Hall, 1976). Commitment to an employer is not valued for its own sake. Commitment is also more contingent; it will be high *if* the organization provides the appropriate job challenge, rewards, and future opportunities.

Increased separation of work life and personal life. With the increased concern for leisure time, there is increased unwillingness to let work spill over into personal time. There is less willingness to work overtime (at nights, on weekends), less desire to travel out of town (which requires evenings away from home), and less business socializing.

Sharper definition of the pivotal work role. With the increased desire for leisure, there is greater worker unwillingness to perform "peripheral" tasks, those not part of the formal job expectations. Examples would be secretaries who decline to serve coffee and executives who do not feel obligated to ask spouses to attend company social events or who do not feel obligated to entertain business colleagues at home. (The increase in the number of two-career couples has contributed to this removal of the entertainment function from the perceived work role.)

More calculative employee cooperation. This may sound contradictory. What it means is that there are more employees who are consciously aware of maximizing their own returns from work (be they career opportunities, challenge, recognition, pay, visibility, etc.). Millions of assertiveness programs, stress-management seminars, career self-management workshops, personal power and influence programs, and self-improvement "guerrilla guides" to success have taken their toll on the organization's style and process. People will help others at work to the extent that helping others will help them. This results in much "second guessing" about coworkers' motivations in helping, and, sometimes, lower levels of trust.

Increased flexibility regarding the time and place of work. With more two-career couples, single parents, and employed mothers, there has been a boom in flextime, part time, and leaves of absence. The concept of a part-time, "slow-burn" career has become more accepted. With portable computer terminals, the organization's information system can easily be moved into the employee's home, resulting in "flexplace" as well as flextime in work. These flexible work arrangements, however, can have negative side effects 1)of further weakening the social bonds between organization members, and of 2) letting work intrude further into home life.

Increased legalism and management concern for employee rights. There is increased attention to due process in the work setting. Personnel decisions are increasingly based on openly documented criteria of work performance. This results in a climate of greater freedom and security for employees who are good performers, greater anxiety and motivation for poor performers, and more need for sensitivity, objectivity, and documentation for managers—in sum, a more legalistic work climate.

In short, more "protean" careers. The protean career is (Hall, 1976):

> . . . a process which the person, not the organization, is managing. . . . The protean person's own personal career choices and search for self-fulfillment are the unifying or integrative elements in his or her life. The criterion of success is internal (psychological success), not external [p. 201].

Thus, in a variety of ways, the work behavior and performance of the new-breed employees have put their stamp on the style and process of work organization. Organizations have become more flexible, more person-centered, more autonomous, yet at the same time more legalistic and administratively centralized. This style of organized flexibility contains elements of Warren Bennis' (1966) predictions for the "fate of bureaucracy."

The Informal Peer Leader

As organizations have become more flexible and employee-centered, there is, in more effective organizations, an increased sensitivity to emergent peer leaders in the work force. With activities such as team management, project management, and quality circles, the group is becoming an important building block of organization structure, much as Likert (1961) advocated with his "linking pin" group concept. Although the linking pin is the formal leader (e.g., department manager), the effective group will also encourage and utilize emergent peer leadership as well. To the extent that peer leaders are able to perform productive tasks (i.e., those related to formal work goals), the work group will be more cohesive, cooperative, and successful.

The Technological Gate Keeper

Another lower-level person whose individual performance can be directly related to organizational outcomes is the technological gatekeeper. As the work of Tom Allen and his MIT colleagues shows, the gatekeeper is the person connected to both the external technical environment and to the internal problem-solving environment, and is thus in a key strategic position to enhance organizational innovation and productivity.

The critical issue here is whether the organization consciously attempts to identify, utilize, and reward such gatekeepers. The more this happens, the richer the internal information network will be.

The Person in a Key Visible Position

In some organizations, particularly those with a long-linked technology, some links are more critical than others, either because the skill demands at that point are so great, because it may be a very visible point in the operation (perhaps the delivery point, where the actual service or work is or is not produced), or because the error tolerance (redundancy) at that point is low. An example would be the manager of a professional athletic team. A professional team is a large, complex organization, with many participants whose performance can affect overall organization performance. Poor publicity or unattractive physical plant or unsafe conditions can produce empty seats, even for a winning team, as poor financial management can cause losses even for a winner. Conversely, good promotion (as in the case of Bill Veeck's White Sox) or a long tradition of excellent community relations (as in the case of the Wrigley family's Cubs) can produce financial success even from losing teams.

However, in any given year, organizational success or failure is often attributed to whomever happens to be that year's manager. The manager is in the critical, visible position of being largely responsible for the recruitment, development, and deployment of the talent that either wins or loses ball games.[1] Furthermore, the behavior and performance of this visible person affects the climate of the team and the style of the relationship between the team and the public (i.e., the external environment). Similar "front-line" positions would be the local parish priest or rabbi, the manager of a corporate profit center, the squad leader in an Army unit, the classroom teacher, the project manager of a huge, financially risky project, and the plant supervisor. Not all are externally

---

[1]The fact that the manager or coach may not always have as much impact over team outcomes as others attribute to him or her is illustrated by Arkansas football coach Lou Holtz's statement about disliking road trips: "I play as well on the road as I do at home, but my teams don't" (*Sports Illustrated*, September 21, 1981, p. 16).

visible, but they are all critical in that they form the link between a large organization and the actual production of goods or services.

The Perpetrator of a Major Snafu

The impact of the performance of a single individual can be increased sharply if he or she is the perpetrator of a major organizational snafu. The performance of Lieutenant Calley at My Lai would be an example. Even if the person is one of many who perform similar acts, if one person's performance happens to be noticed and receive publicity, that person's performance will become the focus of further attention. Efforts at organizational reform will be designed in terms of that one person's performance and how it might be prevented in the future.

For example, as described in the *Boston Globe*, July 14, 1981, a Baptist minister in Grand Rapids, Michigan, used a six-volt battery attached to a wire grid in the seat of a stool to administer shocks to bible-school students to "gain the attention and hold the interest of the group [p. 5]" for one class demonstration during 12 1/2 hours of instruction. This demonstration was written up by UPI and aroused national interest and outrage. Headlines about the minister's "electric chair" appeared throughout the country. After some unsuccessful attempts to explain how and why the device was used, the minister discontinued its use and asked for forgiveness from those he offended. This specific aspect of performance swamped all others in importance and generalized to affect the way constituents defined the effectiveness of the organization (*Boston Globe*, July 14, 1981):

> "We aren't a bunch of loonies who are electrocuting kids," said one irate church-goer. "It's really quite frustrating when you think we spent months preparing for Bible school but ended up being portrayed as the church that uses shock therapy" [p. 5].

Another example of the system effects of individual (mis)performance occurred in the West Point cheating scandal, in which hundreds of cadets were found guilty of violating the Military Academy's Code of Honor by collaborating on an electrical engineering take-home exam. Because of the huge number of honor violations and the resulting publicity the incident received, years of self-examination and reform took place. A national study commission, headed by Colonel Frank Borman, conducted a massive inquiry and analysis of the structure and climate of the Academy (The Special Commission on the United States Military Academy, 1976), a new superintendent was brought in, and significant changes in staffing, structure, and curriculum were made. My impression, as a Visiting Professor in 1979 to 1980, was that the climate was still adversely affected, particularly in the form of shaken confidence or "organizational self-esteem."

Because organizations are so vulnerable to individual errors in critical positions, and because individual successes are so rarely rewarded, we are left with the age-old downside risk factor in performance and the resulting "play-it-safe" ethic that emerges. Lower-level decisions are reviewed at several higher levels, and higher-level decisions are previewed at several lower levels, in an attempt to reduce the impact of individual performance. Consider the role of CEO of General Motors, in the view of Thomas Murphy, upon his retirement from that position (*Wall Street Journal,* 1980):

> Mr. Murphy jokes that the main decisions he makes are "what time to get up and whether to go to church." He says that all subjects at scheduled meetings are carefully worked over by staffers and scrutinized by committees beforehand. By the time he sees the material, he says, "the data suggests the decision" and he often just concurs [p. 19].

This completes our discussion of the ways one person can affect the style of an organization, from CEO's to organizational snafu's (have we come full circle?). We have seen how individual performance affects an organization differently at the top, middle, and bottom. Strategic power can interact with formal position power to mitigate the influence of the top and to enhance that of the bottom. Now let us consider what these individual performance effects imply for the measurement of performance.

IMPLICATIONS FOR PERFORMANCE MEASUREMENT

Because we began by considering performance at three different levels of the organization, let us conclude in the same way, starting from the top.

Guard against Overdesigned Reward Systems

The major problem with formal reward systems is that too often they work. And they are often like computer programs, which have the annoying tendency of doing exactly what you tell them to do—even if you (unwittingly) tell them to do something stupid or wrong. Performance-based reward systems, be they incentive pay plans, management by objectives (MBO) systems, or positive-reinforcement programs, tend to produce the behavior that is desired and rewarded. Often, however, they produce other, unwanted behavior (goal displacement) as well, such as an excessive focus on individual (versus collective) performance, on short-term (versus long-term) results, and on tangibles (cost, profit) versus intangibles (such as teamwork, climate, and quality).

One response to these unintended performance consequences is to make the reward system more complex to correct these problems, which usually results in even further negative consequences. We should avoid the temptation to account for every single reward contingency and instead use *simplicity* as an important criterion for reward systems. The fewer controls and safeguards we need, the better. The more we can "design in" trust, self-measurement, and self-control, the more accurate and accepted these systems will be.

Reward Multiple Dimensions of Performance

This may seem to contradict the first point but it really does not. Although we should not try to define dimensions of performance down to the point of counting hairs on the gnat's eyebrow, we should not let any one dimension of performance assume paramount importance. For example, top-level bonus plans that focus heavily on outcomes such as market share or budget performance simply invite neglect of too many other aspects of effectiveness. A balanced set of performance dimensions (balancing task and social, internal and external, and short-term and long-term activities) should be employed.

More Rewards for Long-term Performance

In much the same way as organizations are now being held accountable for long-term impacts of noxious environmental conditions on workers' health (e.g., Agent Orange in Southeast Asia, asbestos in workers' lungs, long-term effects of low-level radiation in nuclear facilities) and on the physical environment, it is possible to measure and reward top-level members for long-term organizational performance. Performance plans are now being used to reward R & D expenditures, investments in employees (e.g., training, education, development), and performance in the future, for example, 3 or 5 years hence. The rewards may take the form of cash, stock options, pension contributions, as well as other payoffs. We could also measure how well a manager's former subordinates perform over the course of their careers, and reward accordingly, to encourage mentoring and other forms of effective people development.

Develop New Rewards Specially for the Middle

In view of the critical importance of middle levels in delivering results, special attention should be given to this group. It is especially important to develop longer-term rewards here, because there is so much pressure now for short-term results. Middle managers should be rewarded for interunit cooperation, for the development of consensus and teamwork. They should be assessed in terms of the quality and completeness of the information they communicate upward, given their critical information-link role. They should be rewarded based on the attitudes and climate in their units as well as on "hard" measures of performance. The use of employee survey data at Sears for developing and evaluating managers is a good example of this approach.

Avoid Excessive Focus on Individual Performance

We may have reached the point of diminishing returns in our measurement of individual performance. Because of present reward systems, and the present ethic of individual careerism and me-ism, perhaps we have become peroccupied with "performance of and for the individual." We know many of the dangers of individual incentive plans at lower levels (Lawler, 1971). We need to find ways at all levels to measure and reward "performance for the organization."

Reward Integration and Pattern Maintenance.

We have also placed too much stress on the task-related dimensions of goal attainment and adaptation and too little on the social dimension of integration and pattern maintenance (cultural latency). We need to find ways to reward managers and executives who can integrate the needs of employees with those of the organization, as well as those who can maintain and develop organizational culture and traditions that provide inspiration, pride, identification, and a sense of community.

Reward Process and Behavior Rather than Output

This is heresy, I realize. However, many of the dysfunctions we have discussed have resulted from an overstress on end results, which produces an "end justifies the means" mentality. So let us reward the means. If we choose the correct means, such as communicating valid information, trust, free choice in decision making, and developing organizational consensus and internal commitment to action (Argyris, 1970), we would move a long way toward achieving positive ends. Hatvany and Pucik (1981) make a strong case for the utility of rewarding behavior rather than output in Japanese organizations.

Reward Ad-Hoc Activity

Part of the reason for many people's risk aversion is that individual behaviors of excellence are not rewarded, but individual errors (snafus) are severely punished. A system of on-the-spot rewards for outstanding specific behaviors could help reward risk taking. For example, one major oil company gives spot cash bonuses for "good jobs." These immediate rewards would also help motivate and sustain those individuals in thankless, high-visibility, high-pressure, key positions. Ironically, the time span of rewards is wrong in two directions: the one-year evaluation period is too long term to reward individual acts and too short term to reward investment behavior. We need to simultaneously decrease and increase the time span of evaluations.

Reward Informal Group Leadership

If organizational processes such as teamwork, consensus, and open communication are to be viewed as important, emergent group leadership will be important. However, rewards such as promotion may be less available in a time of slow economic growth and retrenchment. Therefore, other rewards for informal leaders are necessary: informal recognition by higher management, performance appraisals that explicitly measure peer leadership, formal designations of ''acting manager's'' when managers are absent, and so on.

Employee Peer Measures

Because we are stressing the measurement of process variables such as peer leadership, teamwork, valid information flow, and integration, a logical source of information on such behavior would be the peer group itself. A risk here, of course, is that peer ratings can produce conformity, so these need to be used along with data from other sources.

Rewards for the New-Breed Employee

Because many of the conditions most valued by the new-breed employee are intrinsic, it should be possible to design new-breed rewards that are at once more effective and less expensive. Because personal autonomy is so important, more effective employees could be given more flexibility in work hours, more options for occasional part-time work based on personal and family needs, and more opportunity to work at home. We already see this use of personal autonomy and flexibility as a reward in some well-managed companies, such as Continental Bank. Further, if cafeteria benefit plans (which would be very attractive to new-breed employees) are not feasible, it should not be too difficult to let people trade certain benefits for vacation time, as is done at Continental. It is also possible to increase the commitment of new employees through policies such as assistance with spouse relocation during an employee transfer, support for child care, company-paid overnight child care when travel is required or when the employee's spouse is invited to company conferences in distant locations. Rather than decry these new-breed concerns, the effective organization is the one that can utilize them as motivators.

Downplay Careerism; Reward the Steady State Career

Many of the dysfunctions in present performance systems are caused by an excessive focus on advancement as a major reward. This "carrot" is coming back to haunt the organizations in two ways: (1) it is becoming less available in many situations; and (2) once a person reaches a "terminal" level or career plateau, the carrot is gone. Then executives wonder why employees "don't care" any more!

We may need to reexamine the concept of the "steady-state" career, in Mike Driver's terms. In this model, the career is a particular occupational role, such as engineer or accountant, rather than an upwardly mobile career path. Another form of steady-state career would be that in which the career is defined as membership in a particular organization (e.g., "I spent my career with XYZ Biscuits.").

To do this, it would be necessary to build in more rewards for longevity—for example, a "seniority bonus," independent of salary, so that the organization would not incur a permanent obligation. In fact, the rewards could be "soft" benefits, such as vacation time, as well as money. They could be reviewed each year for effectiveness.

We have gone about as far as we can with our present reward systems. They simultaneously work too well and not well enough. We need to back off and develop simpler, less-expensive rewards for a different facet of organizational functioning. We are fortunate that we cannot afford to continue defining and rewarding individual performance as we have been. Through external competition, through economic conditions, through leander organizational structures, and through new-breed protean employees, we will be forced to develop more effective approaches to managing performance.

REFERENCES

Argyris, C. *Intervention theory and method.* Reading, Mass.: Addison-Wesley, 1970.

Bavelas, A., & Strauss, G. Group dynamics and intergroup reactions. In W. F. Whyte, et al. (Eds), *Money and motivation* New York: Harper & Row, 1955.

Bennis, W. G. *Changing organizations.* New York: McGraw-Hill, 1966.

Beggart, N. W. Management style as strategic interaction: The case of Governor Ronald Reagan. *Journal of Applied Behavioral Science,* 1981, *17,* 291–308.

Boston Globe, *Minister sorry for "electric chair,"* July 14, 1981, p. 5.

Farris, G. F. Chickens, eggs, and productivity. *Organizational Dynamics,* 1975, *3,* 2–15.

Galbraith, J. *Organization design.* Reading, Mass.: Addison-Wesley, 1977.

Goodman, P. S. *Assessing organizational change: The Rushton quality of work experiment.* New York: Wiley-Interscience, 1979.

Hackman, J. R., & Oldham, G. R. *Work redesign.* Reading, Mass.: Addison-Wesley, 1980.

Hall, D. T. Potential for career growth, *Personnel Administration,* 1971, *34,* 18–30.

Hall, D. T. *Careers in organizations.* Santa Monica, Calif.: Goodyear, 1976.

Hall, D. T., & Schneider, B. *Organizational climates and careers.* New York: Academic Press, 1973.

Hall, D. T., & Foster, L. W. A psychological success cycle and goal setting: Goals, performance, and attitudes. *Academy of Management Journal,* 1977, *20,* 282–290.

Hall, D. T., Rabinowitz, S., Goodale, J. G., & Morgan, M. A. Effects of top–down departmental and job change upon perceived employee behavior and attitudes: A natural field experiment. *Journal of Applied Psychology,* 1978, *63,* 62–72.

Hamner, W. C., & Hamner, E. P. Behavior modification on the bottom line. *Organizational Dynamics,* 1976, *4,* 3–21.

Hatvany, N., & Pucik, V. Japanese management and productivity. *Organizational Dynamics,* 1981, *9,* 4–21.

Larcker, D. F. *The association between performance plan adoption and corporate capital investment* (Accounting Research Center Working Paper #81–1). Evanston, Ill.: J. L. Kellogg Graduate School of Management, Northwestern University, January 1981.

Latham, G. P., & Locke, E. A. Goal setting: A motivational technique that works. *Organizational Dynamics,* 1979, *8,* 68–80.

Lawler, E. E., III. *Pay and organizational effectiveness.* New York: McGraw-Hill, 1971.

Likert, R. *New patterns of management.* New York: McGraw-Hill, 1961.

Mirvis, P. H., & Lawler, E. E., III. Measuring the financial impact of employee attitudes. *Journal of Applied Psychology,* 1977, *62,* 1–8.

Nadler, D. A., Mirvis, P. H., & Cammann, C. The ongoing feedback system: Experimenting with a new managerial tool. *Organizational Dynamics,* 1976, *4,* 63–80.

Prakash, P., & Rappaport, A. Information inductance and its significance for accounting. *Accounting, Organization and Society,* 1977, *2,* 29–38.

Rapoport, A. Executive incentives vs. corporate growth. *Harvard Business Review,* July–August 1978, 81–88.

Renwick, P. A., & Lawler, E. E., III What you really want from your job. *Psychology Today,* May 1978, 53–58, 60, 62, 65, 118.

Scheflen, K. Lawler, E. E., III, & Hackman, J. R. Long term impact of employees' participation in development of pay incentive plans. *Journal of Applied Psychology,* 1971, *55,* 182–186.

Schneider, B. The service organization: Climate is crucial. *Organizational Dynamics,* 1980, *9,* 52–65.

"The departing No. 1 dreaded speaking; Feld GM ran him," *Wall Street Journal,* Nov. 4, 1980.

The Special Commission on the United States Military Academy. *Report to the secretary of the Army by the special commission on the United States Military Academy.* Washington, D.C.: Department of the Army, December 1976.

Yankelovich, D. New rules in American life: Searching for self-fulfillment in a world turned upside down. *Psychology Today,* April 1981, 35–91.

Proximal and Distal Measures of Individual Impact: Some Comments on Hall's Performance Evaluation Paper

Barry M. Staw

Douglas T. Hall has set out to solve an extraordinarily difficult problem—that of specifying the effect of a single individual upon the workings and outcomes of an organization. In thinking about this question, I was first struck by the ambiguity of the issue, then by the silliness of even asking such a question, and finally by the centrality of the question for organizational analysis. Each of these reactions will probably also strike the reader as I discuss both the issue as well as Hall's attempt to grapple with it.

If we think of a large, complex, and formal organization on the one hand, and a small, low-power, transitory individual on the other, and then ask how this poor isolate can move the monolith, we must sigh with disbelief. Can Rosie-the-Riveter change Lockheed and Private Jones significantly affect the Army? These questions are scarcely worth answering. Could Henry Ford affect Ford Motors and John D. Rockefeller alter the oil business? These questions are also scarcely worth answering. As we can see, the interesting and more difficult cases lie between these extremes.

One of the things Hall does in his paper is to show how actions of top-level administrators can be frustrated by either inaction or counterbehavior at lower organizational levels. Hall carries this discussion into an analysis of the influence of three levels within organizations. He then shows how each of these levels has leverage upon different aspects of the organization and that these levels face each other in an interdependent network. In his analysis, however, Hall slips between the effect of individuals acting independently and individuals acting as a collective unit. His discussion is interesting, but it moves us closer to a framework of collective influence than it advances the issue of how we can assess an individual's impact. This prompts me to return to the core problem we face.

ASSESSING THE IMPACT OF AN INDIVIDUAL

Assessing individual action presents many of the same problems as program evaluation. In each, one can measure the set of actions or procedures undertaken and test whether anything has been done (just as we do when we conduct a manipulation check in experiments). One can also assess whether the actions undertaken have had larger or more pervasive effects. However, as shown in Fig. 2C.1, the further one moves from an individual's actions the more difficult it is to demonstrate effects. Proximal effects are simple to find if they are conceptually close to the action, are nearby in social space, and are immediate in time perspective. Distal effects that cross conceptual boundaries, affect different groups or organizational space, and are long-term in nature are much harder to find.

Several years ago, I worked with Thomas D. Cook in designing an evaluation system for the U.S. Peace Corps. The Peace Corps wanted to know how to test whether one of their volunteers was contributing to the health system of a developing country. If a volunteer were helping to drain swamplands, the effect of such actions might be to reduce the population of mosquitoes, which in turn might reduce the incidence of malaria, which in turn might affect the country's mortality rate. Given such a causal chain it is clear that you can conclude almost whatever you want depending on how far you move from proximal to distal criteria. Thus, even when a program is widely claimed to be a success, any single volunteer's effect upon the criterion variable is probably immeasurable.

In performance-evaluation systems, our practice is to assess whether people are following procedures that we *assume* are contributors to out comes. Organizations, for example, prefer to reward people who complete their work accurately, produce more than others, help their coworkers, and exhibit some enthusiasm for the organization. Implicitly we have assumed that these factors are positive contributors to subunit, departmental, and organizational performance. Thus, we seem to have as much confidence in our implicit theories of performance as the medical establishment has in causal models such as the standing water $\rightarrow$ mosquitoes $\rightarrow$ malaria $\rightarrow$ mortality sequence of events. However, as Hall and others have noted, we are often surprised to learn that these simple assumptions can be wrong. More work sometimes causes bottlenecks (Weick, 1974); effort in the wrong direction can be worse than no effort at all (Kerr, 1975); absenteeism and turnover can have some positive as well as negative consequences (Staw, 1980; Staw & Oldham, 1978).

We seem to be less surprised when we learn that particular organizational policies (e.g., decentralization, matrix structure, transfer pricing) do not always lead to successful outcomes. In some way, we may be more willing to recognize the vagaries of our theories of organizational effectiveness (those that connect organizational procedures to aggregate measures of organizational outcomes) than we are of our theories of individual performance (those connecting indi-

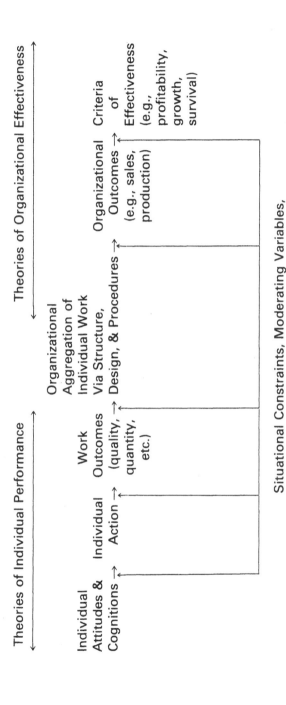

FIG. 2C.1. Individual and Organizational Factors Affecting Performance.

33

vidual action to outcomes). We also may be more willing to accept the strength of competing influences in affecting organizational as opposed to individual outcome measures (see Fig. 2C.1).

TOP-LEVEL IMPACT

In assessing the impact of an organization's leader, we compound the ambiguity of our theories of effectiveness and the meagerness of individual action. Lieberson and O'Connor (1972) have asked empirically if leadership changes explain as much of the variance in corporate profits as general economic conditions and industry trends. Salancik and Pfeffer (1977) have similarly asked of city mayors have had an appreciable effect on municipal budget expenditures. In both of these studies, environmental factors accounted for the bulk of the variance (although it should be mentioned that Weiner and Mahoney [1981] have disputed the methodology used in these studies). In a similar vein, Grusky (1963) and others (Allen, Panian, & Lotz, 1979) have shown that there is a strong correlation between turnover in coaches and the fortunes of baseball teams. But, this turnover research shows more strongly that poor performance leads to firings than it demonstrates that a new coach has any significant effect on a team's win/ loss record. The coach, like a chief executive, is not the one doing the performing for the organization and may therefore have only limited influence on its success. This position is captured well in a quote from Geoffrey Hazard, Acting Dean of Yale's Management School (*Time,* May 4, 1981):

> Every Chief Executive Officer I've ever talked to, once pushed into a corner with two martinis, will tell you that though the myth is that he stands with the reins of power in his hands, his big question is not "How shall I drive this marvelous chariot?" but "How the hell can I get these goddam horses to move their asses at all [p. 61]?"

Against this background of ineffectualness, there are numerous case examples of charismatic political leaders who appear to have shaped the course of their nations as well as organizational leaders who have guided their companies' fortunes. We also have examples of failures in which mistakes by a leader seem to have driven a nation or organization to disaster. The key question, however, is whether we are victims of the fundamental attributional error—observors attributing environmentally determined events to personal causes. Because leaders' actions are so salient to us, we may impute more free will to their decisions than is deserved and we also may ascribe more causal impact to a single leader's strategies or actions than is warranted. Strong economic, social, and political forces may actually determine the consequences for which we credit leaders with achievement and blame them for stupidity.

In finding a way to assess the impact of top-level administrators, we must break organizational outcomes down to a manageable level. This is what Hall has done when he asks whether managers have an effect on goals, structure, reward systems, and organizational culture. These are appropriate questions, just as questions about the delivery of services are useful in program evaluation. However, in evaluating the impact of top management, one must also look at the broader and more distal consequences of a leader's actions. Even if we believe that it is impossible to assess a manager's actions in light of all the exogenous variables and time lag of effects, we must at least question the theory behind his or her behavior. At the extreme, when there is little consensus on criteria for effectiveness (e.g., in educational organizations), the leader's *theory* of effectiveness or philosophy of the enterprise may, in fact, be all there is to evaluate.

IMPACT BY LOWER-LEVEL MEMBERS

Like Mechanic (1962) and others who have written about the power of lower-level participants, Hall has shown how employee behavior can drive the organization. Although Hall considers the impact of lower- and middle-level people as an aggregate, it is also possible to document their individual effects. Individuals build niches around their work lives, influencing the interpersonal fabric as well as the technical sides of their tasks. This stream of influence may not go too far before getting swallowed by larger forces, however. Thus, for lower-level participants we need to measure effects that are immediate in space (e.g., the work group) and time if we are to demonstrate influence.

The most immediate form of measurement, drawing on Fig. 2C.1, is the assessment of individual attitudes and beliefs. It used to be assumed that certain attitudes and personality structures were desirable for particular organizational roles and such assumptions formed the basis for trait-based evaluation. In recent years, we have learned to distrust implicit theories of performance based on attitudinal and personality variables, and we have moved towards behavioral measurement. However, we have not really moved too far. Most current assessments of individual performance simply measure whether proper or legitimized actions have been performed by the actor. By employing a behaviorally anchored rating scale, we ask questions about whether the individual helps customers, cooperates with coworkers, arrives on time, stays late, and so on. With such questions we really do no more than what a manipulation check accomplishes in the experimental paradigm. Something has been done, although it is another question whether anything positive will result.

Much of the difficulty in assessing individual performance comes from trying to measure outcomes rather than behaviors. For many jobs, outcome measures are not readily available and, in some cases, the specification of outcomes for evaluation is counterproductive. The legal staff of an organization, for example, may be motivated to provide good legal services. However, if they are to be evaluated by the proportion of cases won, they may only pursue the sure winners, whereas if they are evaluated by the number of cases defended, they may take every case to court. This is an extreme example, but still representative of the evaluation dilemma. Sometimes professional specification of legitimate behavior, drawing on the professional's own theory of performance, is better than pushing towards outcome measurement.

Hall notes that measurement and reward systems often have dysfunctional side effects. If short-term, tangible, individual behavior is rewarded, something is likely to be extinguished or at least demphasized in the struggle—the likely victims being long-term, intangible, and collective action. In fact, when we look at major organizational disasters, we often find highly motivated, well-monitored, and direct behavior—all moving in concert towards a corporate collapse. Doing well at the wrong thing sometimes only compounds the problem, as Platt (1973) has shown in his analysis of social traps and as Weick (1979) has noted in his evolutionary model of organizational adaptation.

SOME OVERALL RECOMMENDATIONS

Hall recommends that we guard against overdesigned reward systems. He favors simple, self-measured, and self-controlled evaluation systems (e.g., professional standards) rather than the attempt to control every possible contingency. He also recommends that we move measurement out over time so that long-term investments are rewarded and long-term costs (e.g., pollution, destruction of human resources) are accounted for. He calls for multiple measurement in which variables other than concrete outcomes, such as integration, pattern maintenance, informal group leadership, and risk taking, are rewarded. Finally, Hall advocates the legitimization of rewarding *process* rather than achievement and the recognition of steady-state careers rather than simple upward mobility.

Hall's recommendations, I believe, come as a reaction to our current infatuation with organizational control systems. As Hall correctly notes, it is often not so much a problem to control behavior through reward systems as it is to live with what we have paid for. If we analyze current incentive systems, the emphasis is on short-run outcomes, risk-minimizing strategies, and individual as opposed to collective efforts. Hall's recommendations are an effort to set the balance straight.

Although most of Hall's recommendations ring true, they also pose a number of internal contradictions. How do we, for example, reward long-term consequences and risk taking, while at the same time advocate the use of procedural rather than outcome measures? How do we use self-controlled reward systems and at the same time emphasize longer-term and collective products? How do we promote achievement and also emphasize pattern maintenance and steady-state careers? These are important dilemmas for which there may not be general answers.

The measurement and reward system for use at each level and sector of an organization may need to be different. For example, the proper time perspective of evaluation may, as Elliott Jacques suggested long ago, lengthen at increasing levels in the hierarchy. Second, the risk-aversion problem may or may not outweigh the cost of a major organizational snafu, depending on the centrality of a given position in the organization and how loosely coupled (Weick, 1976) is the overall system. A loosely coupled system is much better at absorbing the shock of an innovative but failing behavior than is a highly interdependent network. Third, whether one uses self-designed and self-controlled reward systems depends on the type of work force involved and on who possesses the expertise. Fourth, whether one uses individual versus collective evaluation and rewards may depend on the task interdependency of the organization and on the type of culture one wants to develop. Fifth, whether one relies upon procedural measures or outcome variables depends on the confidence one has in a given theory of performance or effectiveness. It is easier to rely on procedural measures when there is a known technology and when uncertainty in the process is low.

Although it is possible to provide recommendations for evaluation systems in particular instances, there are, as we have noted, few general solutions. What is worse is that even our limited recommendations do not stem from moderated relationships or complex models that can be solved in the traditional sense. Instead, our recommendations must be formed for dilemmas in which tradeoffs are made, with the full knowledge that any solution will be inappropriate to some degree.

The most difficult dilemma for an evaluation system is probably the tradeoff between efficiency and effectiveness criteria. For efficient operations it is important to have short-term, procedural, and localized measures of performance, because without these, individuals may have little or no guidance in their behavior. However, for effective operations, there is really no escape from treating the entire organization as a performance system. The total organization needs to be analyzed regularly on what it currently is and what it intends to become. For example, an emphasis on high-quality, state-of-the-art products implies a very different set of employees and control system than an emphasis on low-priced, high-quantity production. Each strategy can result in an effective organization, even though the evaluation system implied by each would be entirely different.

Once an organization's philosophy or market strategy is formed, it provides a set of constraints and assumptions on which more specific theories of performance and effectiveness can be based. Too often, however, it is simply assumed that a set of evaluation procedures are effective once they are in place. Therefore, whenever organizations seem to be running efficiently on well-accepted theories of performance and effectiveness, it is probably time to engage in some of the following stretching exercises, attempting to move evaluation from proximal to distal criteria:

1. Question the assumptions or implicit theories on which performance is judged.
2. Attempt to move measurement out in organizational time, looking for long-term costs as well as benefits of accepted outcomes and procedures.
3. Attempt to move measurement out in organizational space, asking questions about how one person's work has affected others or the larger system.

In essence, I see the evaluation of performance as a continual but healthy tension between the proximal and distal criteria. At each level in the organization, localized traditions, procedures, and assumptions are important. But, at the same time, it is probably healthy for there to be a periodic review of assumptions, and a stretching of performance measures to a more systemic level. These, I believe, are some of the ingredients of organizational adaptiveness, useful for survival under changing environmental conditions. Thus, treating evaluation as a solvable problem may be less productive than addressing it as a dilemma with which one must continually grapple.

REFERENCES

Allen, M. P., Panian, S. K., & Lotz, R. E. Managerial succession and organizational performance: A recalcitrant problem revisited. *Administrative Science Quarterly,* 1979, *24,* 167–180.

Grusky, O. Managerial succession and organizational effectiveness. *American Journal of Sociology,* 1963, *69,* 21–31.

Kerr, S. On the folly of rewarding A, while hoping for B. *Academy of Management Journal,* 1975, *18,* 769–783.

Lieberson, S., & O'Connor, J. F. Leadership and organizational performance: A study of large corporations. *American Sociological Review,* 1972, *37,* 117–130.

Mechanic, D. Sources of power of lower participants in complex organizatons. *Administrative Science Quarterly,* 1962, *7,* 249–364.

Platt, J. Social traps. *American Psychologist,* 1973, *28,* 641–651.

Salancik, G. R., & Pfeffer, J. Constraints on administrator discretion: The limited influence of mayors on city budgets. *Urban Affairs Quarterly,* 1977, *12,* 475–496.

Staw, B. M. The consequences of turnover. *Journal of Occupational Behavior,* 1980, *1,* 253–273.

Staw, B. M., & Oldham, G. R. Reconsidering our dependent variables: A critique and empirical study. *Academy of Management Journal,* 1978, *21,* 539–559.

Time, May 4, 1981, p. 61.

Weick, K. *Reward concepts: Dice or marbles.* Unpublished paper, Cornell University, 1974.

Weick, K. Educational organizations as loosely coupled systems. *Administrative Science Quarterly,* 1976, *21,* 1–19.

Weick, K. E. *The social psychology of organizing* (2nd ed.), Reading, Mass.: Addison-Wesley, 1979.

Weiner, N., & Mahoney, T. A. A model of corporate performance as a function of environmental, organizational, and leadership influences. *Academy of Management Journal,* 1981, *24,* 453–470.

3

The Effects of Social, Task, and Situational Factors on Motivation, Performance, and Appraisal

Terence R. Mitchell

Dr. Mitchell suggests that psychologists have been too narrow in their focus in research on performance and he presents a performance-model sequence describing links between arousal, motivation, behavior, performance, and the evaluation situation, and the role of task, social, and organizational factors in determining these relationships.

With respect to the arousal–motivation link, factors such as setting goals, tying rewards to behaviors, and treating people equitably may influence motivation. The traditional explanation for the motivation–behavior link is that ability and effort are combined to produce behavior. However, Mitchell states that without considering social, task, and situational factors, it is difficult to determine whether behavior is caused primarily by motivation or ability. He suggests that the interdependence of the group (whether a solution to a problem requires cooperative effort) is an important consideration in defining the nature of this link.

With respect to the behavior–performance link, social and situational factors should be considered because the task or work situation may determine whether group or individual performance measures are selected or whether behavioral/nonbehavioral measures are used. In the performance–appraisal link Mitchell states that the validity of assessing the criterion measure must be ensured. He states that little research has been directed towards determining the impact of position and organizational characteristics on the validity of evaluation.

Drs. Goodman and Fichman raise six points on which they differ from Mitchell. They believe that more precise definitions of arousal, motivation, and performance are needed, do not agree that current theories of motivation do not deal adequately with contextual variables, and state that in Mitchell's performance model, the factors are not conceptually distinct.

In response, Dr. Mitchell states his belief integrating social, task, and situational variables into existing motivation theories would be more harmful than helpful.

There is currently great concern about the levels of productivity in the United States. The great increases in the 1960s were followed by only modest increases in the early 1970s. By the late 1970s and early 1980s, there were even occasional indications of declines in productivity. Obviously, if we wish to maintain our standard of living and full employment, we must attend to this problem.

The explanations for these shifts in productivity levels are numerous. Some people suggest that our rate of technological innovation has dropped off, whereas others cite increased competition from other countries who use less expensive labor. A third reason that is frequently mentioned is that the work force is less motivated and that increasing effort and commitment on the job might turn things around.

The purpose of this paper is to examine the research in the area of motivation, the way in which motivation contributes to performance and the way we appraise that performance. In particular, we concentrate on the social, task, and situational factors that influence motivation, performance, and appraisal. As we will see these factors have in general been underrepresented in current theories of motivation and performance. New work is needed to increase our overall understanding of the causes of effective performance; this paper aims to identify some productive avenues of research.

The foundation for this discussion is shown in Fig. 3.1. The logic is as follows: First, the individual is aroused. Arousal is usually the antecedent to motivated choice and may be caused by a variety of factors. Arousal is followed by intentions to choose some behavior that will reduce the arousal. That is, we *intend* to engage in some action and these intentions represent our motivation to behave in some particular way. The actual actions are our behavior and may or may not be different from our intentions. The behavior itself or behavior in aggregate over settings or times is defined as performance. The performance is appraised or evaluated in some way and then the organization responds to these appraisals by providing feedback, rewards, job assignments, and various other things. This organizational response will in turn have an effect on subsequent arousal.

Now, obviously Fig. 3.1 covers a lot of territory—far more than can be dealt with in this paper. There are numerous theories and research articles on each of these links. The plan of the paper is to limit the focus to a few of the links and to just a few of the factors that influence each link. We first focus on the arousal → motivation → behavior sequence and then we discuss the behavior → performance → appraisal part. Each of these two parts provides a brief overview of the traditional or well-established explanations for the links and then presents some

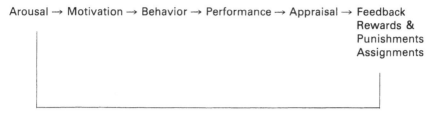

FIG. 3.1   General performance sequence.

recent and divergent perspectives. The major focus of most of these new perspectives is how task, social, and organizational factors influence the relationships diagrammed in Fig. 3.1. They implicate new approaches for theory, research, and practice in the field of motivation and performance appraisal, which we describe.

THE AROUSAL–MOTIVATION LINK

Numerous comprehensive reviews exist that describe the current state of research in the area of motivation (e.g., Campbell & Pritchard, 1976; Korman, Greenhaus, & Badin, 1977; Locke, 1975; Mayes, 1978; Mitchell, 1979, 1980; and Staw, 1977), so we are not concerned with a detailed study-by-study review. Instead, we attempt to present those generalizations with which most researchers seem to agree.

First, we should provide a definition of what we mean by motivation. Many nonacademics would probably describe motivation as the degree to which an individual tries hard to do well at a particular task or job. Dictionary definitions describe motivation as the goad to action. The more technical definitions given by social scientists suggest that motivation is the combination of psychological processes that cause the arousal, direction, and persistence of behavior (e.g., Atkinson, 1964; Campbell, Dunnette, Lawler, & Weick, 1970; Huse & Bowditch, 1977; Kast & Rosenzweig, 1979; Korman, 1974; Luthans, 1977). Many authors add a voluntary component or goal-directed emphasis to that definition (e.g., Hellriegel & Slocum, 1976; Lawler, 1973; Ryan, 1970; Vroom, 1964). Thus, motivation becomes those psychological processes that cause the arousal, direction, and persistence of voluntary actions that are goal directed.

Even though there is some disagreement about the importance of different aspects of this definition (e.g., whether arousal or choice is more important), there is consensus about some of its underlying properties. First, motivation has traditionally been considered as an *individual* phenomenon. Each individual is unique and *all* of the major motivational theories allow for this uniqueness to be demonstrated in one way or another (e.g., different people have different needs, expectations, values, attitudes, reinforcement histories, goals, etc.). Second, motivation is usually described as *intentional*. That is, motivation is supposedly under the person's control. Most behaviors that are seen as influenced by motivation (e.g., effort on the job) are typically viewed as actions the individual has chosen to do.

A third point is that motivation is multifaceted. The two factors of greatest importance have been the arousal (activation, energizers) and direction (choice) of behavior. The question of persistence has been of minor importance partially because the maintenance of behavior (once it is started and directed) has received less attention and partly because some authors have defined persistence simply as the reaffirmation of the initial choice of action (March & Simon, 1958).

The arousal question has focused on what gets people activated. What are the circumstances that arouse people so they want to do well? The second question, that of choice, deals with the force on the individual to engage in desired behavior, which results in an intention to behave in a given way. These distinctions are reflected in much of the writing on motivation.

The fourth point is that the purpose of motivational theories is to predict *behavior*. Motivation is concerned with action and the internal and external forces that influence one's choice of action. Motivation is not the behavior itself and it is not performance. The behavior is the criterion—what is chosen. And in some cases, the chosen action will be a good reflection of both the antecedent (intention) and the consequence (performance). But the psychological processes, the actual behavior, and the performance are all different things and the confusion of the three has frequently caused problems in analysis, interpretation, and application.

Fig. 3.2 presents a representation of these distinctions and outlines those topics that we review in this half of the paper. What we are suggesting is that certain factors cause arousal and other factors cause intentions (motivation). Once the intention is formed, certain personal or situational variables make it easy or difficult to carry out the intention. In general, the factors on the top half of the figure have been studied frequently whereas those on the lower half have emerged as important more recently. Also, these latter factors focus primarily on social, task, and situational variables.

Traditional Theories of Arousal

For many years the most popular theories of arousal have been those that emphasize needs. Theories that emphasize individual needs (e.g., need achievement) or groups of needs (e.g., need hierarchies) all postulate that the arousal process is due to need deficiencies—that is, people want certain things in their jobs and when they are not getting them they will work to fulfill those needs.

The major implications of this research have been twofold. First, these theories clearly recognize and make central the idea of individual differences (Alderfer, 1977). Different people are motivated by different things. The second point that is widely accepted is that organizations have generally overlooked

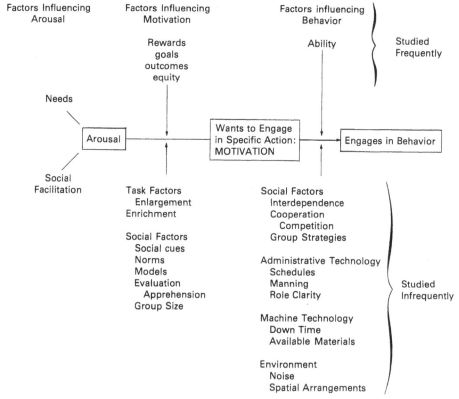

FIG. 3.2.   An overview of the causes of behavior.

upper-level needs. The work of such people as Maslow, McGregor, Herzberg, Alderfer, and others all suggest that, in general, organizations spend much more time being concerned with the fulfillment of lower-level needs (e.g., through motivational systems emphasizing pay, hours of work, the physical setting) than with the fulfillment of upper-level needs (e.g., through systems emphasizing autonomy, recognition, creativity, variety, etc.).

New Approaches Studying Arousal

In recent years there has been a shift away from these need-based theories of arousal (Salancik & Pfeffer, 1977, 1978; Weiner, 1972) to approaches that emphasize processes such as social facilitation or evaluation apprehension (Ferris, Beehr, & Gilmore, 1978). These theories suggest that people are aroused by the presence of others and the knowledge that other people are evaluating them. The social cues in the form of expectations given off by subordinates, coworkers, and supervisors become important causes of arousal.

What almost all of these current theories emphasize in one way or another is that arousal is transitory and highly related to the social or task environment rather than a deep-seated continuous need that resides solely within the individual. Central to almost all of the new approaches is the idea that the individual processes and evaluates a lot of information and that motivation is strongly linked to this information-processing activity.

Traditional Theories of Motivated Choice

The research on theories of arousal has essentially taken a back seat to theories of motivated choice in the last ten years (Mitchell, 1979). The ratio of current research on these approaches is approximately five to one in favor of the choice models. The major theories that we review are goal setting, expectancy theory, operant conditioning, and equity theory. Our focus is on the major principles of application that these theories have generated.

Even though we have described these theories as predicting the force on the individual to engage in some action, we should point out that the criterion used in most of this research is not intention but the behavior itself (usually effort on the job) and in some cases performance success. Although it is true that when the behavior occurs we may infer that motivation was partly the cause, it is important to point out that this does not have to be the case. There are situations and circumstances in which the behavior may be only marginally under the control of intentions or in which the amount of effort exerted is less than intended. We return to this point later.

The research on goal setting provides quite clear results. People work harder with goals than without goals. This is especially true if the goals are specific and difficult to attain, and if feedback is provided (see Locke, 1978; Steers & Porter, 1974; Yukl & Latham, 1978). On-going research emphasizes such issues as whether participative or assigned goal setting works best and whether rewards influence motivation directly or indirectly, by changing the level of the goal.

Expectancy theory and operant conditioning, although very different in underlying philosophy (cognitive versus noncognitive), generate similar principles of application. Both approaches have demonstrated that rewards should be closely tied to behavior, that reward administration should be frequent and consistent, and that people are motivated by outcomes (expected or past).

Review of expectancy theory (e.g., Connolly, 1976; Mitchell, 1980; Schwab, Olian-Gottlieb, & Heneman, 1979) and operant conditioning or social learning (e.g., Babb & Kopp, 1978; Davis & Luthans, 1980) are available. People doing research on both theories are concerned with how rewards are tied to behavior, what sorts of reward schedules to use, how to measure various theoretical components, and so on. But except for some minor disagreements (see Mawhinney & Behling, 1973), the approaches are in agreement about principles of application.

Equity theory research (Carrell & Dittrich, 1978; Goodman, 1977) has demonstrated that people are motivated by a desire for fairness. When they believe that they are being treated unfairly, they behave in ways that they believe will restore their sense of equity. Although overreward (we are getting more than we should) and underreward (we are getting less than we should) are similar from a theoretical perspective, the research suggests otherwise. People are more comfortable (less likely to change their behavior) with overreward than with underreward. When people feel they are underrewarded and can do little about directly influencing their rewards, they are likely to be dissatisfied, work less, and be absent more frequently than when they feel they are being treated equitably.

Without getting into detailed analysis, one can point out some important differences and similarities among the approaches. The most striking difference is the basic underlying motivational mechanism postulated as the cause of the force on the individual to behave in a certain way: intention to reach a goal, expectation of maximum payoff, past reinforcement history, and a desire for fairness. The similarities are that all four approaches define motivation as an individual, intentional process. Also, except for the operant approach, all three of the others focus on relatively current information processing. In this respect, the arousal and choice models seem to be headed in a similar direction. Finally, three of the models define motivation as directly influenced by outcomes (expectancy, operant, and equity approaches) whereas goal setting sees outcomes as indirectly influencing motivation through goal level.

Because of the vast amount of literature currently available on these topics, some sort of summary perspective is needed. These theories have told us a lot about motivation and everyone would probably agree that they all have an element of the truth in them. However, in order to utilize what we have learned from these approaches, one must be able to set specific goals, tie rewards to individual behavior, and treat people fairly and equitably. To do this, however, depends on a number of social, task, and situational conditions' being present, and unfortunately these conditions are often absent.

For example, one major problem is that many jobs involve considerable interdependence (Lawler, 1973). People must frequently work with others in order for the job to be accomplished successfully. This interdependence often makes it difficult to specify or tease out individual contributions (Jewell & Reitz, 1981). To the extent to which there is failure to accurately assess individual behavioral contributions, there will be trouble with individual goal setting and reward administration. Either group goals or rewards may be used.

A second important factor is observability (Kane & Lawler, 1979). Individual feedback and reward administration both depend on the extent to which one knows what employees are doing. In many cases, people work alone, or in relatively isolated situations (e.g., within offices, on the road, etc.). To the extent that there is poor information about what people actually do, there will be difficulty with implementation of reward systems.

A third problem has to do with change. Rapid changes in jobs due to improvements in technology and personnel turnover (Kavanagh, 1981) necessitate changes in the motivation system in the form of different behaviors to observe and different rewards to administer. In fact, some authors (e.g., Hill & Miller, 1981; Katz, 1980) have argued that high performance is dependent on matching the changes in people and jobs throughout a career.

Finally, the heterogeneity of jobs and people causes difficulty as well. Ideally, each type of job requires a different job description, different behaviors, and, therefore, different reward systems. The implication of the problems caused by change or heterogeneity is that implementing motivational principles often requires compromise. In many cases people or jobs are lumped together (over time, jobs, or settings) for appraisal or administrative purposes. When this aggregation occurs it becomes more and more difficult to set individual goals and to provide individual rewards and feedback. In short, deviation from the individual, behavioral conceptualization of motivation will probably reduce the effectiveness of the motivational program and the ability to measure its impact.

Thus, for many jobs, the traditional choice models of motivation may be inappropriate or difficult to apply. Some jobs require work in teams. Individual performance on some tasks may be difficult to specify and measure. Close supervision may not be possible on all jobs. Ambiguity and change may be inherent in some tasks. The question then becomes one of determining what factors control motivation in these circumstances—in short, what prompts people to want to work hard in teams or under conditions of change or ambiguity? The research that has emerged on this question tends to focus either on the task or the social context as causes of motivation.

New Approaches to Motivated Choice: The Task

Although the work on the motivating properties of tasks has been going on for quite a few years, it is only within the last ten years that we have seen a great increase in this research. Turner and Lawrence (1965), Hackman and Lawler (1971), and Hackman and Oldham (1975, 1976, 1980) have described a job-characteristics approach to motivation.

This approach suggests that tasks have motivating properties—that is, certain types of tasks are more fun, interesting, or challenging to do—and that people exert greater effort on these types of tasks than on routine, boring, repetitive ones. The properties that are most frequently cited are variety, an important or significant job, a whole or clearly identifiable task, autonomy, and feedback. To some extent all of these properties can be part of the task itself and therefore some of the problems mentioned with respect to the choice models of motivation are circumvented. Specifically, a task can be enlarged or enriched without demanding close supervision, set goals, managerial (as contrasted with task) feedback, observability, clear behavior-reward links, and so on.

The empirical research on the topic has generated mixed assessments (see Hackman & Oldham, 1980; Roberts & Glick, 1981; Steers & Mowday, 1975). Most authors agree with the basic premise that tasks can be motivating but the specifics of which factors are important and how that information is processed by workers are still unclear. Also, it appears as if the main effect of the task characteristics may be on attitudes like job satisfaction rather than on behaviors like increased effort or performance (Umstot, Bell, & Mitchell, 1976; Umstot, Mitchell, & Bell, 1978). Thus, the research to date on the motivating properties of tasks has left us with many unanswered questions.

The Social Context

In comparison, the research that focuses on the social context has a less unified body of theory but more substantial results. That is, there are a number of different social factors that people have suggested have motivating properties and the research, although not overwhelming in terms of quantity, has demonstrated clear and powerful effects on motivation.

Some of the most important work focusing on the social context evolved out of the work on social facilitation. Zajonc (1965) had demonstrated that the presence of others caused arousal and then Cottrell (1972) suggested that one of the main reasons for this arousal was evaluation apprehension. People in a social context are aware that others are evaluating them and most people want that evaluation to be positive (see Ferris, et al., 1978).

This emphasis on evaluation apprehension pointed out two important social-interaction variables that might influence one's motivation or effort on the job. First, it seems reasonable that if one's performance can be traced to these variables, one should be more motivated to do well than if performance cannot be traced to them. One study that demonstrated this effect (White, Mitchell, & Bell, 1977) had people working on a clerical task in which the finished product was some correctly labeled computer cards. In one condition the workers wrote their names on their completed stacks of cards and threw them in a large bin. In the other condition they simply threw the cards into the bin without their names. All employees were paid by the hour, so there was no additional financial incentive to be productive, but those who thought that their work could be traced to them produced significantly more than those who thought that their quantity of work could not be detected. These data strongly suggest that evaluation apprehension can be a powerful motivator.

The social cue is the second interaction variable of importance. When one is aroused by the presence of others and apprehensive about their evaluation, attention is paid to the cues (information) provided by coworkers about appropriate attitudes or behavior. For example, Salancik and Pfeffer (1977, 1978) suggested that one's attitudes and reactions to a task (remember the job-characteristic approach) may be more a function of what one's coworkers say about the task than the actual task properties themselves. This hypothesis was tested directly and supported in three independent research studies (O'Reilly & Caldwell, 1979; Weiss & Shaw, 1979; White & Mitchell, 1979). The social cues clearly had an effect on attitudes about the job.

These same type of cues have also been shown to affect performance. For example, the classic study by Schachter, Ellertson, McBride, and Gregory (1951) involved coworkers who told the subjects to either slow down or speed up. These coworker cues produced a large difference in performance.

The Schachter et al. (1951) study brings us to the topic of norms. When social cues or information about expected work attitudes or behavior are shared and agreed upon by group members, these expectations are often called norms. Ever since the classic Hawthorne studies we have been aware that norms for productivity can be powerful predictors of actual productivity. Hackman and Morris (1975) and Hackman and Oldham (1980) have reviewed and summarized much of this work in the context of their overall group-performance model. Some current empirical work (e.g., Lichtman, 1980) is available that continues to demonstrate the importance of norms, but in general norms have not been heavily researched in the context of the effects of social variables on motivation.

Two other streams of research that emphasize slightly different variables are social-learning and social-impact approaches. One of the cornerstones of social-learning theory is that people often model the behavior of salient and important people with whom they interact. Modeling is seen as both a learning process as well as a regulating process (see Davis & Luthans, 1980, for a review). That is, people learn new behaviors from models and use them as guides for what is expected in various situations.

The research on the effects of models has been supportive of these ideas. For example, Rakestraw and Weiss (1981) have shown that having a high-effort model results in higher productivity than does having a low-effort model. And Weiss and Nowicki (1981) demonstrated that high-competence models also influence task satisfaction in a positive direction. Thus, another way to increase motivation socially seems to be to provide hard-working models.

The social-impact theory has been advanced by Latane (1981). Latane argues that the impact of others depends on whether the target person is identifiable and on the number, importance, and proximity of the audience. If one is identifiable (can be evaluated), increases in size, importance, and proximity increase motivation. For example, in two studies Jackson and Latane (1981) show that a person who is about to perform in front of an audience is more anxious if the crowd is big and he or she is the only performer than if the crowd is small and he or she is one of a group of performers.

If one is not identifiable, Latane argues that increased size will *decrease* motivation (he labels this phenomenon social loafing). For example, Latane, Williams, and Haskins (1979) demonstrated that when people thought they could not be identified, they worked less with increases in perceived group size.

A summary of the literature dealing with the task and social context provides some important generalizations and identifies areas for future research. If we believe that many of the tasks people work on are done in groups, or unobserved, without feedback, or under conditions of change or ambiguity, then some of our traditional approaches to motivation—such as equity theory, expectancy theory, goal setting, or operant conditioning—may be hard to apply or simply inappropriate. Under these circumstances we may be able to instill high motivation through task or social mechanisms, such as enrichment, norms, evaluations apprehension, or models. The key point is that we need to do a better job *diagnosing* which set of procedures is applicable under certain sets of conditions. We return to this point later.

THE MOTIVATION–BEHAVIOR LINK

Let us assume that we have highly motivated employees who want to do well and who are ready and willing to try hard. Does this mean that performance will be excellent? Perhaps, but probably not. There are lots of circumstances in which motivation simply is not enough or is mostly irrelevant for predicting behavior.

Tradtional Explanations: Ability

An examination of Fig. 3.2 suggests that one obvious variable that may be as important or more important than motivation is ability. Simply swinging hard is not a guarantee that you will hit the ball. The literature on performance has recognized for years that ability and effort combine to produce behavior (see Campbell et al., 1970).

Even though industrial psychologists have invested lots of time and research effort in the development of ability measures, there seems to be a more basic question that has frequently been overlooked. There is very little work that tries to determine the relative contributions to behavior made by these two factors. Except for the model developed by Hackman and Morris (1975) for the group context, very little has been done in the way of developing conceptual and measurement technologies for addressing this question.

What I am suggesting is that some tasks require behavior that is almost completely under the control of ability whereas others may simply require lots of effort. Probably some small degree of both is needed no matter what the behavior, but the point is that in many cases motivation may contribute little to behavior and performance. Again, better diagnostic procedures are needed to determine those settings in which behavior is primarily the result of motivation or ability.

Social, Task, and Situational Factors

Although the study of ability contributions to behavior have been investigated frequently, the factors represented on the lower half of Fig. 3.2 have received far less attention. All of these factors (e.g., social factors, administrative technology, machine technology, and the environment) can be described as facilitating or limiting conditions that make it easy or difficult for the motivated person with appropriate abilities to carry out his or her intentions. That is, even if one wants to work hard and has the skills to do the job, there are a set of social, task, and environmental factors that may limit the extent to which the behavior is actually demonstrated.

These limiting or facilitating conditions have been widely recognized in theory. Steiner (1972), Hackman and Morris (1975), and Shiflett (1979) all point out that certain task or group-process conditions are necessary for high performance. Steiner (1972), for example, suggests that people need to be motivated, to have the resources (ability), and to have the appropriate information, tools, and coordination to do the job. It is these latter factors that concern us in the present section.

When people are working together *as a group* (that is, they are interdependent), it is often necessary for individuals' behavior to be coordinated with others' (even Dr. J cannot score without the ball). The meshing of what people are supposed to do requires coordination and cooperation.

The types of variables that have been researched empirically on cooperative or coordination strategies all emphasize one major point: The strategy by which a group solves a problem can and should be explicitly matched to the people and task at hand (Hackman & Morris, 1975). For example, Liddell and Slocum (1976), and Weed, Mitchell, and Moffitt (1976) both demonstrated that the proper mix of people on different types of tasks is important for good performance. All the literature on group interdependence has demonstrated over and over again that when people are interdependent, a cooperative problem-solving strategy works best and a reward system with low differential reward (relatively equal pay) is better than one with high differential reward (see Rosenbaum, Moore, Cotton, Cook, Hieser, Shovar, & Gray, 1980, for a recent review). At a more general level, people like Hackman and Morris (1975) and O'Brien (O'Brien & Ilgen, 1968; O'Brien & Owens, 1969) have tried to suggest theories of matching group strategies, tasks, and people. For example, Kabanoff and O'Brien (1979) demonstrated the differential effectiveness of collaboration or coordination depending on whether the task was a problem-solving, discussion, or production one. The point is clear: When people are working in groups, the strategy for solving the problem and who works with whom may be as important or more important than issues of motivation or ability. At the very least, inappropriate strategies and mixes will limit the degree to which motivation and ability will be translated into action.

The other factors illustrated in Fig. 3.2 (e.g., administrative and machine technology and the environment) are also important, but they have been researched less frequently. At a theoretical level, perhaps the most recent and articulate discussion of these variables has been presented by Peters and O'Connor (1980). These authors discuss a number of situational constraints and argue that the potential performance of good workers is frequently limited by these constraints. The types of variables with which they are concerned are things like tools, equipment, budget support, needed information, time, the work environment, help from others, and so on. In an empirical paper (Peters, O'Connor, & Rudolf, 1980), they demonstrate the importance of these variables.

We have sorted these factors into three general classes of variables. The first of these is called administrative technology, or those systems that are used administratively (i.e., by management) to ensure good performance. For example, the concept of staffing is important. The right number of people must be assigned to the various tasks (see Moos, 1976, for a discussion). Also important is the idea that job or task descriptions must be clear and unambiguous. People need to know what is expected of them. All the literature on role clarity addresses this topic (see Van Sell, Brief, & Schuler, 1981, for a review). Finally, schedules and planning are important. Even though someone works along, his or her efforts may need to be coordinated with others'. Operations systems people have recognized and researched this problem for years.

The concept of machine technology is that workers are often dependent on machines or materials to accomplish their tasks. A poor-running machine or a machine that is often inoperable can seriously limit output no matter how hard one tries. Also, materials must be available when they are needed. Except for the Peters and O'Connor (1980) paper, little recognition of these variables appears in the literature.

Finally, the job environment may help or hinder the employee. High noise levels can have a negative effect on productivity, as can clutter or disorganized work environments (Moos, 1976). There is also some recognition that spatial work arrangements can be important. For example, both Oldham and Brass (1979) and Sundstrom, Burt, and Kamp (1980) have demonstrated that privacy can be an important factor for performance. The Oldham and Brass (1979) research showed that people who move into open-space offices are often less satisfied, less motivated, and *more distracted* than they were previously.

To summarize, having the ability and the desire is not enough. Various task, social, situational, and administrative factors may constrain or modify behavior. In some settings more variance in behavior may be accounted for by these factors than by ability or effort. The point to emphasize for future research is that organizations must do a thorough task or job analysis *before* they worry about the issues of selection (i.e., selection of abilities) or motivation. In order for ability and effort to have their maximum effect on behavior, these social and situational issues must be taken into account so that machines, schedules, and the task environment facilitate rather than hinder highly motivated employees.

THE BEHAVIOR–PERFORMANCE LINK

Fig. 3.3 expands the last half of the flow diagram presented in Fig. 3.1. Here we are concerned with the contribution of behavior to performance and performance

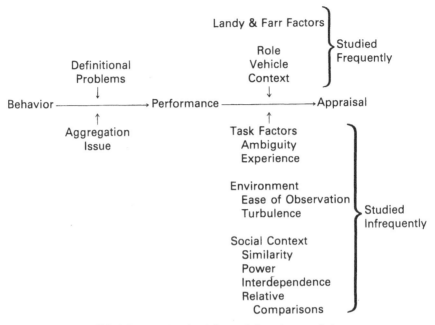

FIG. 3.3. Social and task factors influencing appraisal.

to appraisal. In both cases it is important to point out that these constructs are distinct. Behavior is usually different from performance and the actual performance demonstrated by an individual may be different from the way it is appraised. These two topics are the focus of the next two sections.

The relationship of behavior to performance is partly a definitional issue. Performance is frequently defined as an aggregate of behaviors over time, tasks, or people. It is not impossible for performance and behavior to be the same, but in most cases they are not (Mahoney, 1981). One should keep in mind, however, that motivation and ability contribute to behavior directly and only indirectly to performance.

Without going into too much detail, we should point out that the definition of performance often results in some difficult decisions or unintended consequences. For example, the more that performance is defined in behavioral terms, the most important is direct observation for valid assessment of performance. On the other hand, more global or countable criteria (e.g., output, waste) may be easier to assess but the types of behaviors that contribute to these criteria may be harder to describe. Also, when people work together in teams and are interdependent, it is hard to know the extent to which individuals contribute to a group product (e.g., Did Gene Upshaw, an offensive lineman for the Oakland Raiders, make a more or less important contribution than Jim Plunkett, the quarterback, to the Raiders' Super Bowl Victory?).

What we are saying is that the task or work setting may to some extent determine whether behavioral/nonbehavioral or individual/group criteria are used. What must be recognized is that to the extent that performance is defined as nonbehavioral or as a group product, the more difficult it is to use performance as an indication of individual behavior. The logical implication is that it is hard to directly assess the contribution of motivation and ability to behavior when behavior is not an important criterion or when the contribution of specific behaviors to performance is unknown.

THE PERFORMANCE–APPRAISAL LINK

Given that we have an agreed-upon performance criterion, the next step is to ensure that we have valid assessments of the criterion. As has been thoroughly demonstrated by Kane and Lawler (1979) and Landy and Farr (1980), there is lots of slippage in this link. Landy and Farr's review points out that roles (rater and ratee characteristics), the measurement vehicle, and the context in which the rating is done are all important factors related to validity. Many studies are available that demonstrate the effect of these first two sets of variables.

However, Landy and Farr (1980) go on to say that "It is appalling to note how little systematic research has addressed the impact of position and organizational characteristics on performance rating [p. 95]." In an attempt to discuss what factors may be important, Fig. 3.3 lists some task, environment, and social factors in the situation that may effect appraisal.

The task factors have to do with some ways that the rater may be influenced by the task itself. Kane and Lawler (1979), for example, point out that task ambiguity may be important. If there are many different ways to solve a problem and many solutions, it may be more difficult to make valid appraisals than if the task and the outcome are clear-cut. Also, if the supervisor has had little experience with the task, it may be difficult for that person to assess accurately the causes of good or poor performance. A paper by Mitchell and Kalb (1982) has demonstrated that supervisors who have had actual experience with a task are more likely to blame poor performance on external factors than are supervisors who have not had task experience. If one assumes that leaders tend to err in the direction of blaming a subordinate for poor performance (Green & Mitchell, 1979), then task experience may help to reduce that error. We would also expect that task difficulty might reduce the validity of the ratings.

Some infrequently researched environmental or situational factors mentioned by Kane and Lawler (1979) are the observability of the ratee and the turbulence of the task environment. The logical hypothesis would be that ratings are more valid when the ratee can be directly observed and when the turbulence of the environment is low.

The social factors focus on the relationship between the rater, ratee, and other group members. There is more research here and a number of factors can be identified that influence appraisals. First, a paper by Senger (1971) demonstrated that the more similar the rater and ratee, the higher the ratings. The effect has been recently demonstrated again by Wexley, Alexander, Greenwalt, and Couch (1980).

A second social factor is power. On a number of occasions Kipnis (1972, 1976) has shown that with increased power the rater is more critical and deprecating of the ratee. Similar predictions are discussed by Green and Mitchell (1979) in their review of supervisor attributions and responses to a poor performer. Essentially, the greater the power, the more the subordinate is blamed for poor performance.

A third variable is the degree of interdependence among group members. In one study we recently completed (Liden & Mitchell, 1981), we were able to demonstrate that when leaders felt the group members worked interdependently, they rated a poor performer less severely than when they believed the person worked independently. In both conditions, the actual performance was exactly the same, but the *rated* performance varied as a function of perceived interdependence. A study by Ilgen, Mitchell, and Frederickson (1981) also demonstrated that interdependence affected ratings; Kane and Lawler (1979) also discuss this variable.

A fourth and final factor has to do with the ratee's role in the group. To some extent, ratings are relative comparisons (Grey & Kipnis, 1976) and the rating or feedback made by a supervisor is often influenced by this social context (O'Reilly & Weitz, 1980). In one recent study (Mitchell & Liden, 1981) we demonstrated that the more a subordinate was a popular group member or showed group leadership skills, the less negatively he or she was rated when he or she performed poorly.

In summary, performance ratings are more than just a sum of the parts (rater plus ratee plus measure). They are influenced by social and contextual factors as well. The research in this area is comparatively sparse and needs more work in the future.

IMPLICATIONS

The purpose of this paper was to describe the ways in which social, task, and situational factors influence motivation, performance, and appraisal. We began with motivation, discussing its social causes and the facilitating or inhibiting conditions that determine whether motivation results in behavior. From there we pointed out how behavior is aggregated to represent performance and how various social or situational factors can lower the validity of appraisals.

In an attempt to discuss the implications of the paper, we follow a somewhat different sequence. Rather than following the theoretical or logical sequence of events as previously laid out, we focus on how one could or should use the information discussed. That is, we discuss the major points in the order in which they are important for practice.

The first task that one needs to tackle in any organization is the definition of performance. This process was not thoroughly discussed in this paper, nor was it meant to be. However, everything else that is said rests on the assumption that performance is clearly defined and that reliable measurement is available. We might add that the more closely performance is defined in behavioral terms, the easier things are in other phases of our analysis.

So, given that we can define and measure performance, three major points emerge. First, task, social, and situational variables will affect the validity of performance ratings. Although a debate is still going on about the effectiveness of different kinds of rater training (Bernardin & Penrce, 1980; Latham, Wexley, & Pursell, 1975), it does seem possible that exercises, films, and learning experiences could reduce the errors. We have, for example, developed a film that we have used to train raters to pay attention to external or environmental causes of performance when making ratings and evaluations of subordinates' performances (Heerwagen, 1981). More research is clearly needed on how the social and situational factors influence appraisal and how errors or biases can be removed.

A second major point is that behavior is determined by many factors. Considerable work needs to be done to develop ways to determine the relative contributions made to behavior by motivation and ability as well as the extent to which behavior is deflected or determined by administrative technology, machine technology, the environment, or the social context.

The issue here is our ability to diagnose the important things a manager should be doing to influence behavior. If motivation is not very important, a sophisticated Management By Objectives (MBO) or reinforcement program simply will not do any good. Initially, we have to determine that motivation makes a difference. If not, perhaps ability is important and selection or training would be the areas on which to concentrate. If schedules and coordination and plans and machines control most of the variance in behavior, then time needs to be spent examining these regulating systems. The point is that a manager's focus should be determined by an accurate, preliminary diagnosis of the causes of behavior.

Finally, the last point is that even when performance is defined in behavioral terms and motivation is clearly important, we need to do more diagnostic work. Most of our traditional motivational approaches assume *managerial control* (i.e., observe behavior, give feedback, administer rewards, set goals). In many cases this control does not exist. People frequently work on ambiguous tasks, in teams, alone, or at least out of the sight of a supervisor, and so on.

What we need is a better understanding of *social control*. That is, we need to do more research on how models, norms, evaluation apprenension, the task itself, and social cues affect motivation. Equally important, we have to learn how to use these tools—that is, we have to learn how to influence norms and social cues and provide models so that positive motivation occurs.

Thus, the basic conclusions are that we need better procedures for diagnosing what contributes to behavior and motivation and that throughout the diagnosis, a greater emphasis needs to be placed on social and situational factors. The work place of the future is likely to contain more and more jobs requiring interdependence and social interaction and cooperation. Our ability to implement our knowledge will depend on the extent to which we can successfully incorporate these ideas into our theories and research.

REFERENCES

Alderfer, C. P. A critique of Salancik and Pfeffer's examination of need satisfaction theories. *Administrative Science Quarterly*, 1977, *22*, 658–669.

Atkinson, J. W. *An introduction to motivation*. Princeton, N.J.: Van Nostrand, 1964.

Babb, H. W., & Kopp, D. G. Applications of behavior modifications in organization: A review and critique. *Academy of Management Review*, 1978, *3*, 281–290.

Bernardin, H. J., & Penrce, E. C. Effects of rater training: Creating new response sets and decreasing accuracy. *Journal of Applied Psychology*, 1980, *65*, 60–66.

Campbell, J. P., Dunnette, M. D., Lawler, E. E., III, & Weick, K. E., Jr. *Managerial behavior, performance, and effectiveness*. New York: McGraw-Hill, 1970.

Campbell, J. P., & Pritchard, R. D. Motivation theory in industrial and organizational psychology. In M. D. Dunnette (Ed.), *Handbook of industrial and organizational psychology*, Chicago: Rand McNally, 1976, 62–130.

Carrell, M. R., & Dittrich, J. E. Equity theory: The recent literature, methodological considerations, and new directions. *Academy of Management Review*, 1978, *3*, 202–210.

Connolly, T. Some conceptual and methodological issues in expectancy models of work performance motivation. *Academy of Management Review*, 1976, *1*, 37–47.

Cottrell, N. B. Social facilitation. In C. G. McClintock (Ed.), *Experimental social psychology*, New York: Holt, Rinehart & Winston, 1972.

Davis, T. R. V., & Luthans, F. A social learning approach to organizational behavior. *Academy of Management Review*, 1980, *5*, 281–290.

Ferris, G. R., Beehr, T. A., & Gilmore, D. C. Social facilitation: A review and alternative conceptual model. *Academy of Management Review*, 1978, *3*, 338–347.

Goodman, P. S. Social comparison process in organizations. In B. M. Staw & G. R. Salancik (Eds.), *New directions in organizational behavior*, 1977, *1*, 97–132.

Green, S. G., & Mitchell, T. R. Attributional processes of leaders in leader–member interactions. *Organizational Behavior and Human Performance*, 1979, *23*, 429–458.

Grey, J., & Kipnis, D. Untangling the performance appraisal dilemma: The influence of perceived organizational context on evaluative process. *Journal of Applied Psychology*, 1976, *61*, 329–335.

Hackman, J. R., & Lawler, E. E. Employee reactions to job characteristics. *Journal of Applied Psychology*, 1971, *55*, 259–286.

Hackman, J. R., & Morris, G. G. Group tasks, group interaction process, and group performance effectiveness. In L. Berkowitz (Ed.), *Advances in experimental social psychology* (Vol. 7). New York: Academic Press, 1975.

Hackman, J. R., & Oldham, G. R. Development of the Job Diagnostic Survey. *Journal of Applied Psychology*, 1975, *60*, 159–170.

Hackman, J. R., & Oldham, G. R. Motivation through the design of work: Test of a theory. *Organizational Behavior and Human Performance*, 1976, *16*, 250–279.

Hackman, J. R., & Oldham, G. R. *Work redesign*. Reading, Mass.: Addison-Wesley, 1980.

Heerwagen, J. *The effects of attribution and solution costs on supervisors' responses to poor performance*. Unpublished doctoral disseration, University of Washington, 1981.

Hellriegel, D., & Slocum, J. W., Jr. *Organizational behavior: Contingency views*. New York: West Publishing, 1976.

Hill, R. E., & Miller, E. L. Job change and the middle seasons of a man's life. *Academy of Management Journal*, 1981, *24*, 114–127.

Huse, E. F., & Bowditch, J. L. *Behavior in organizations: A systems approach to managing*. Reading, Mass.: Addison-Wesley, 1977.

Ilgen, D. R., Mitchell, T. R., & Frederickson, J. W. Poor performers: Supervisors and subordinates' responses. *Organizationsl Behavior and Human Performance*, 1981, *27*, 386–410.

Jackson, J. M., & Latane, B. All alone in front of all those people: Stage fright as a function of number and type of co-performers and audience. *Journal of Personality and Social Psychology*, 1981, *40*, 73–85.

Jewell, L. N., & Reitz, H. J. *Group effectiveness in organizations*. Glenview, Ill.: Scott, Foresman, 1981.

Kabanoff, B., & O'Brien, G. E. The effects of task type and cooperation upon group products and performance. *Organizational Behavior and Human Performance*, 1979, *23*, 163–181.

Kane, J. S., & Lawler, E. E. Performance appraisal effectiveness: Its assessment and determinants. In B. Staw (Ed.), *Research in organizational behavior* (Vol. 1). Greenwich, Conn.: JAI Press, 1979.

Kast, F. E., & Rosenzweig, J. E. *Organization and management: A systems approach*. New York: McGraw-Hill, 1979.

Katz, R. Time and work: Toward an integrative perspective. In B. M. Staw & L. L. Cummings (Eds.), *Research in organizational behavior* (Vol. 2). Greenwich, Conn.: JAI Press, 1980.

Kavanagh, M. Performance appraisal. In K. Rowland & G. Ferris (Eds.), *Personnel management*. Boston, Mass.: Allyn & Bacon, 1981.

Kipnis, D. Does power corrupt? *Journal of Personality and Social Psychology*, 1972, *24*, 33–41.

Kipnis, D. *The powerholders*. Chicago: University of Chicago Press, 1976.

Korman, A. K. *The psychology of motivation*. Englewood Cliffs, N.J.: Prentice-Hall, 1974.

Korman, A. K., Greenhaus, J. H., & Badin, I. J. Personnel attitudes and motivation. *Annual Review of Psychology*, 1977, *28*, 175–196.

Landy, F. J., & Farr, J. L. Performance rating. *Psychological Bulletin*, 1980, *87*, 72–107.

Latane, B. The psychology of social impact. *American Psychologist*, 1981, *36*, 343–356.

Latane, B., Williams, K., & Haskins, S. Many hands make light the work: The causes and consequences of social loafing. *Journal of Personality and Social Psychology*, 1979, *37*, 822–832.

Latham, G. P., Wexley, K. N., & Pursell, E. D. Training managers to minimize rating errors in the observation of behavior. *Journal of Applied Psychology*, 1975, *60*, 550–555.

Lawler, E. E., III. *Motivation in work organizations*. Monterey, Calif.: Brooks/Cole, 1973.

Lichtman, R. J. Goal setting and group norms as determinants of job performance in a simulated work setting. *Proceedings of the National Meetings of the Academy of Management*, Detroit, Mich.: 1980.

Liddell, W. W., & Slocum, J. W. The effects of individual–role compatibility upon group performance: An extension of Schutz's FIRO theory. *Academy of Management Journal*, 1976, *19*, 413–426.

Liden, R. G., & Mitchell, T. R. *The effects of group interdependence on supervisor performance evaluations*. Working paper, University of Washington, Seattle, 1981.

Locke, E. A. Personnel attitudes and motivation. *Annual Review of Psychology*, 1975, *26*, 457–480.

Locke, E. A. The ubiquity of the technique of goal setting in theories and approaches to employee motivation. *Academy of Management Review*, 1978, *3*, 594–601.

Luthans, F. *Organizational behavior.* New York: McGraw-Hill, 1977.

Mahoney, T. A. Compensation for work. In K. Rowland & G. Ferris (Eds.), *Personnel management,* Boston: Allyn & Bacon, 1981.

March, J. G., & Simon, H. A. *Organizations.* New York: Wiley, 1958.

Mawhinney, T. C., & Behling, O. Differences in predictions of work behavior from expectancy and operant models of individual motivation. *Proceedings of the Academy of Management,* 1973, 383–388.

Mayes, B. T. Motivation: A comparison of theories. *Academy of Management Review,* 1978, *3,* 51–58.

Mitchell, T. R. Organizational behavior. *Annual Review of Psychology,* 1979, *30,* 243–281.

Mitchell, T. R. Expectancy-value models in organizational psychology. In N. Feather (Ed.), *Expectancy, incentive and action.* Lawrence Erlbaum Associates, 1980.

Mitchell, T. R. Motivation: New directions for theory, research, and practice. *Academy of Management Review,* 1980, *7,* 80–88.

Mitchell, T. R., & Kalb, L. S. The effects of job experience on supervisor attributions for a subordinate's poor performance. *Journal of Applied Psychology,* 1982, *67,* 181–188.

Mitchell, T. R., & Liden, R. C. *The effects of social context on performance evaluations.* Working paper, University of Washington, Seattle, 1981.

Moos, R. H. *The human context.* New York: Wiley, 1976.

O'Brien, G. E., & Ilgen, D. Effects of organizational structure, leadership style, and member compatibility upon small group creativity. *Proceedings of the American Psychological Association,* 1968, *3,* 555–556.

O'Brien, G. E., & Owens, A. Effects of organizational structure upon correlations between member abilities and group productivity. *Journal of Applied Psychology,* 1969, *53,* 525–530.

Oldham, G. R., & Brass, D. J. Employee reactions to an open-plan office: A naturally occurring quasi-experiment. *Administrative Science Quarterly,* 1979, *24,* 267–284.

O'Reilly, C. A., & Caldwell, D. F. Informational influence as a determinant of perceived task characteristics and job satisfaction. *Journal of Applied Psychology,* 1979, *64,* 157–165.

O'Reilly, C., & Weitz, B. Managing marginal employees: The use of warnings and dismissals. *Administration Science Quarterly,* 1980, *25,* 467–484.

Peters, L. J., & O'Connor, E. J. Situational constraints and work outcomes: The influence of a frequently overlooked construct. *Academy of Management Review,* 1980, *5,* 391–398.

Peters, L. J., O'Connor, E. J., & Rudolf, C. J. The behavioral and affective consequences of situational variables relevant to performance settings. *Organizational Behavior and Human Performance,* 1980, *25,* 79–96.

Rakestraw, T. L., Jr., & Weiss, H. W. The interaction of social influences and task experience on goals, performance, and performance satisfaction. *Organizational Behavior and Human Performance,* 1981, *27,* 326–344.

Roberts, K. H., & Glick, W. The job characteristics approach to task design: A critical review. *Journal of Applied Psychology,* 1981, *66,* 193–217.

Rosenbaum, M. E., Moore, D. L., Cotton, J. L., Cook, M. S., Hieser, R. A., Shovar, M. N., & Gray, M. J. Group productivity and process: Pure and mixed reward structures and task interdependence. *Journal of Personality and Social Psychology,* 1980, *39,* 626–642.

Ryan, T. A. *Intentional behavior: An approach to human motivation.* New York: Ronald Press, 1970.

Salancik, G. R., & Pfeffer, J. An examination of need satisfaction models of job attitudes. *Administrative Science Quarterly,* 1977, *22,* 427–456.

Salancik, G. R., & Pfeffer, J. A social information processing approach to job attitudes and task design. *Administrative Science Quarterly,* 1978, *23,* 224–253.

Schachter, S., Ellertson, N., McBride, D., & Gregory, P. An experimental study of cohesiveness and productivity. *Human Relations,* 1951, *4,* 229–238.

Schwab, D. P., Olian-Gottlieb, J. D., & Heneman, H. G., III. Between subjects expectancy theory research: A statistical review of studies predicting effort and performance. *Psychological Bulletin*, 1979, *86*, 139–147.

Senger, J. Managers' perceptions of subordinates' competencies as a function of personal value orientations. *Academy of Management Journal*, 1971, *14*, 415–424.

Shiflett, S. Toward a general model of small group productivity. *Psychological Bulletin*, 1979, *86*, 67–79.

Staw, B. M. Motivation in organizations: Toward synthesis and redirection. In B. M. Staw & G. R. Salancik (Eds.), *New directions in organizational behavior*, Chicago, St. Clair Press 1977.

Steers, R. M., & Mowday, R. T. The motivational properties of tasks. *Academy of Management Journal*, 1975, *18*, 703–714.

Steers, R. M., & Porter, L. W. The role of task-goal attributes in employee performance. *Psychological Bulletin*, 1974, *81*, 434–452.

Steiner, I. *Group processes and performance*. New York: Academic Press, 1972.

Sundstrom, E., Burt, R. R., & Kamp, D. Privacy at work: Architectural correlates of job satisfaction and job performance. *Academy of Management Journal*, 1980, *23*, 101–117.

Turner, A. N., & Lawrence, P. R. *Industrial jobs and the worker*. Boston: Harvard University, Division of Research, Graduate School of Business Administration, 1965.

Umstot, D., Bell, C. H. Jr., & Mitchell, T. R. Effects of job enrichment and task goals on satisfaction and productivity: Implications for job design. *Journal of Applied Psychology*, 1976, *61*, 379–394.

Umstot, D. D., Mitchell, T. R., & Bell, C. H., Jr. Goal setting and job enrichment: An integrated approach to job design. *Academy of Management Review*, 1978, *3*, 867–879.

Van Sell, M., Brief, A. P., & Schuler, R. S. Role conflict and role ambiguity: Integration of the literature and directions for future research. *Human Relations*, 1981, *34*, 43–71.

Vroom, V. H. *Work and motivation*. New York: Wiley, 1964.

Weed, S. E., Mitchell, T. R., & Moffitt, W. Leadership style, subordinate personality and task type as predictors of performance and satisfaction with supervision. *Journal of Applied Psychology*, 1976, *61*, 58–66.

Weiner, B. *Theories of motivation: From mechanism to cognition*. Chicago: Rand McNally, 1972.

Weiss, H. M., & Nowicki, C. E. Social influences on task satisfaction: Model competence and observer field dependence. *Organizational Behavior and Human Performance*, 1981, *27*, 345–366.

Weiss, H. M., & Shaw, J. B. Social influences on judgements about tasks. *Organizational Behavior and Human Performance*, 1979, *24*, 126–140.

Wexley, K. N., Alexander, R. A., Greenawalt, J. P., & Couch, M. A. Attitudinal congruence and similarity as related to interpersonal evaluations in manager–subordinate dyads. *Academy of Management Journal*, 1980, *23*, 320–330.

White, S. E., & Mitchell, T. R. Job enrichment versus social cues: A comparison and competitive test. *Journal of Applied Psychology*, 1979, *64*, 1–9.

White, S., Mitchell, T. R., & Bell, C. H. Jr. Goal setting, evaluation apprehension and social cues as determinants of job performance and job satisfaction in a simulated organization. *Journal of Applied Psychology*, 1977, *62*, 665–673.

Yukl, G. A., & Latham, G. P. Interrelationships among employee participation, individual differences, goal difficulty, goal acceptance, instrumentality and performance. *Personal Psychology*, 1978, *31*, 305–324.

Zajonc, R. B. Social facilitation. *Science*, 1965, *149*, 269–274.

Comments on Mitchell

Paul S. Goodman
Mark Fichman

Our review of Mitchell's paper, *The Effects of Social, Task, and Situational Factors on Motivation, Performance, and Appraisal,* is divided into three sections. First, we give a brief representation of the concepts and theory in order to facilitate our analysis of Mitchell's work. Second, we identify and discuss the critical issues in the Mitchell paper. Last, we delineate our position concerning some of the major research issues on the relationship of social, task, and situational factors to performance.

Mitchell attempts to develop an integrative framework for describing how motivation, performance, and appraisal are linked together. He acknowledges the central problem of integrative frameworks—that of pulling together a large, highly differentiated set of research findings into a coherent system of relationships.

The premise with which Mitchell begins is a general performance sequence (Fig. 3.1 in Mitchell) that directs our attention to a cycle of performance energized by arousal. Given arousal, an ordered flow of motivation, behavior, performance appraisal, and feedback (with accompanying consequences) ensues, completing the cycle. Mitchell then elaborates on this sequence by developing his ideas on the social, task, and situational factors that affect the strength of arousal, and the moderating factors that affect the strength and direction of motivation and behavior (Fig. 3.2 in Mitchell). He then describes the way these factors influence the translation of behavior into performance, and performance into appraisal (Fig. 3.3 in Mitchell).

60

CRITICAL ISSUES.

Mitchell's central point is that the scope of analyses of the performance sequence has been too narrow. He describes a set of social, task, and situational factors that should affect different aspects of the performance cycle, but that have not been recognized in performance research. He calls our attention to factors that need to be considered in providing a more powerful analysis of the performance sequence. Several arguments flow from this larger framework. He argues that in many cases we cannot adequately understand the performance sequence without simultaneously considering both traditional approaches and social, task, and situational factors.

Conditions often exist, Mitchell claims, that are not adequately explained by traditional approaches and that can be better understood using some of the social, task, and situational factors displayed in Figs. 3.2 and 3.3 in his paper. Following this line of reasoning, Mitchell argues that this broader framework can provide researchers and practitioners with a larger choice set of constructs for both explaining and influencing the general performance sequence in organizations. We have identified six general issues with the Mitchell paper:

Purpose Versus Accomplishment

The most direct way to evaluate a paper is to determine the relationship between the author's goals and the results. Although the paper gives no succinct goal statement, the following is probably sufficient:

> We concentrate on social, task, and situational factors that influence motivation, performance, and appraisal. . . . these factors have in general been underrepresented in current theories of motivation and performance. . . . this paper aims to identify some productive avenues of research.

Unfortunately, this statement is not very precise. We see at least two alternative interpretations. If the purpose is to focus researchers' attention on the social, task, and situational factors that affect motivation and performance, the paper is clearly a success. Mitchell identifies a large list of factors that may affect motivation, performance, and appraisal processes. A researcher of motivation and performance would clearly be sensitized to the importance of these other variables after reading the paper.

However, if the purpose is to extend our theoretical understanding of the relationship between social, task, and situational factors to motivation and performance, the paper needs much more analytic work to achieve it. That is, there is a significant difference between saying a certain set of variables is important and specifying the functional relationships among those variables. The functional relationships may be specified in hypotheses or in models of performance. It might be argued that one cannot write out general hypotheses, but must generate hypotheses specific to a given type of performance—a task that would be precluded in a paper such as the one under review. We do not agree. There are probably general models of performance that can be applied, and if specific performance hypotheses are most appropriate, one should at least provide some guidance for generating those hypotheses and offer some examples.

The critical problem with the Mitchell paper is that it stays on too general a level. It tells us that social, task, and situational factors are important, but not how to incorporate them into a model of performance. We know that they are important, but we do not know how to utilize them theoretically.

Use of Concepts

The next issue we address is the development of the basic concepts of *arousal, motivation, task factors, social factors,* and *situational factors* that Mitchell uses as independent variables. Mitchell has drawn well-established and well-supported examples of task and social factors, causing few difficulties for us. We focus on *arousal, motivation,* and *situational* factors. Our interest is in how each of these three concepts is defined, and whether they are as distinct as Mitchell seems to imply.

Arousal is never clearly defined for purposes of discussion in this paper. Arousal, whether caused by needs or social facilitation, appears to be treated as a unidimensional construct. However, a number of writers have developed evidence for complex effects of arousal that should be incorporated into this framework. In his analysis of activation, Scott (1966) describes the reward properties of arousal and argues for a curvilinear functional form of the arousal–reward relationship. In his review of attention and effort, Kahneman (1973) argues persuasively that arousal may have an impact on attention and the processing of information. Work on arousal and social facilitation indicates that arousal levels can also have an impact on the response repertoire available to an individual (Zajonc, 1965). Thus, the linkage of arousal with other concepts in the framework may be more complex than Figs. 3.1 and 3.2 indicate (see later discussion, *Arrow Management*).

Mitchell defines *motivation* as "the combination of psychological processes that cause the arousal, direction, and persistence of voluntary actions that are goal directed." Mitchell's working definition and discussion are useful, but a few difficulties arise here. In his model (Fig. 3.1), arousal precedes motivation, whereas in his working definition arousal is a constituent of motivation, a distinction that should be clarified. His point about persistence (which it is rarely addressed) is well taken, although it should be noted that Atkinson and Birch (1970) have begun to model persistence by looking at the simultaneous operation of multiple motives.

The last factor to be discussed is the use of *situational factors.* It would be useful to develop some definition of the domain from which concepts are being drawn and to establish how the domain is to be distinguished. For example, should we treat administrative technology as a situational factor (e.g., schedules) or as a task factor (e.g., schedules as an input to job characteristics)? Should we treat interdependence as a task factor (e.g., influencing autonomy) or as a social factor? Again, the issue is defining domains and seeking clear distinctions.

The second question regarding situational factors is whether they are clearly distinguishable from traditional theory, or whether they are partially integrated with it. Most of the situational constraints concern the opportunity of the individual to perform his or her role. Manning, as originally defined by Barker (1965), is explicitly described in terms of variation in the opportunity to perform a role in a given setting. Most traditional motivation theories are implicitly dealing with the same issue.

The question of what paths/alternatives are available to an individual is a similar issue. If situational constraints block alternatives (i.e., opportunities to perform), those paths become less attractive, and alternative paths are chosen. In fact, one of the most serious difficulties in making equity-theory predictions about behavior in organizational settings is that too many paths are open to the person dealing with perceived inequity (Weick, 1966). Although we agree that it is critical to examine situational constraints more intensively, it seems to us that more traditional approaches have not ignored this question entirely.

To conclude, what we are seeking are more precise definitions and specifications of theoretical domains and more attention to the possible integration of task, social, and situation factors into the more traditional literature.

Use of Current Theories

In Mitchell's paper there is a review of current theories of motivation—goal setting, expectancy, operant conditioning, and equity theory—in light of the social, task, and situational factors. His major conclusion is that:

> the . . . literature dealing with task and social context provides some important generalizations and identifies areas for future research. If we believe that many of the tasks people work on are done in groups, unobserved, without feedback, or under conditions of change or ambiguity, then some of our traditional approaches to motivation—such as equity theory, expectancy theory, goal setting, or operant conditioning—may be hard to apply or simply inappropriate.

Earlier Mitchell said, ". . . for many jobs, the traditional choice models of motivation may be inappropriate or difficult to apply." The essence of Mitchell's position seems to be that current motivation models cannot deal with or have not dealt with task, social, or situational factors. We disagree. The theories Mitchell cites can deal with these three external factors, and there are empirical studies to document this point.

It is difficult to think about the theoretical work on expectancy theory without acknowledging the effects of task, social, and situational constraints. Expectancies about effort and behavior are affected by individual and task characteristics. Expectancies about behavior–reward connections are affected by the structural characteristics of the reward system. These expectancies should change as we move from individual, group, or organizational pay systems (Lawler, 1971). The concept of boundary conditions has been empirically demonstrated by Graen (1969), Dachler and Mobley (1973), and others. Goodman and Moore (1976) have shown how expectancies about a new reward system change over time as a function of the task, social, and situational factors.

Similarly, Jackson's (1965) RPM model of norms is premised on group members' expectations that rewards and punishments are contingent on certain behaviors. Work by House and his colleagues (House & Mitchell, 1974) has extended expectancy theory into the domain of leadership, explicitly addressing social and task factors and their impact on motivation. In fact, Graen's VDL model (Graen, 1976) is an explicit attempt to incorporate social factors (e.g., interdependence) into an expectancy framework. Although we agree with the theme of Mitchell's distinction, we feel it is one that has begun to be addressed and does not fall outside the domain of more traditional motivation theories.

Mitchell's discussion of the "new" research on "task" effects on performance (Hackman & Oldham, 1976) seems to imply that this work is at variance with some of the more traditional motivation theories. This position is difficult to follow, because much of the Hackman/Oldham work grew out of earlier work (Hackman & Lawler, 1971) that was based specifically on expectancy theory.

It is difficult to think about the theoretical work on equity theory without acknowledging the effects of task, social, and situational factors. The concept of social comparison is based on the existing social arrangements. Distribution rules that specify the nature of appropriate input–outcome relationships are derived from existing social norms (Goodman, 1977). Lawler's comprehensive model of pay equity is based on task, social, and situational factors. Empirical work on equity (Goodman, 1974; Goodman & Friedman, 1971) indicates that these three contextual factors are important.

Our argument can be summarized as follows: The role of task, social, and situational factors has been incorporated theoretically into current theories of motivation. Also, there are empirical studies that deal with the effects of these factors on motivation and performance. Although we would not argue that the "answer is in," we would stress again that there has been theoretical and empirical work that has focused our attention on the importance of social, task, and situational factors.

Conceptualization of Performance and Level of Aggregation

Another problem in the Mitchell paper is the conceptualization of performance. Early in the paper Mitchell says, "The behavior itself or behavior in aggregate over settings or times is defined as performance." Later he says, "The relationship of behavior to performance is partly a definitional issue. Performance is frequently defined as an aggregate of behaviors over time, tasks, or people.'' Neither of these statements provides a clear definition of performance. Is there some objective concept of performance, or is the identification of performance socially defined? Is the definition of performance a descriptive or normative phenomenon? What is the role of constituencies in defining performance? What is the relationship between level of aggregation and the definition of performance? Mitchell does argue that individual performance is more difficult to identify in interdependent groups, but that does not address the question of the relationship of performance to different levels of aggregation. In an interdependent group, there can be both individual and group performance indicators. What we need to clarify is whether the definition of performance changes as one changes the level of aggregation (individual versus group), and how to determine the appropriate level of analysis.

Arrow Management

We would like to return to the framework Mitchell has proposed and view it in a different light. Given that we accept the premises for Mitchell's argument, we want to look at a few examples through the general performance sequence to ask if his model (Figs. 3.2 and 3.3) is properly constructed for the task he has set. That is, are the variables appropriate, and are the relationships he specifies consistent with his arguments? We provide examples from the elaborated general performance sequence, rather than give an exhaustive analysis.

We have discussed earlier some of the conceptual problems with arousal. These problems have implications here, because arousal then appears at several points in the performance sequence. If arousal is driven by evaluation apprehension, then it may also appear as a moderator of the arousal–motivation linkage. A similar argument can be made based on the notion that arousal has reward properties, and thus may be sought by an individual. Additionally, if arousal influences the available behavioral repertoires (increased arousal resulting in choice of dominant response), then it may intervene or moderate the motivation–behavior linkage. In sum, arousal is an appropriate variable, but it is not clear that the appropriate relationships have been identified for it in the framework.

The concept of manning illustrates other problems in Mitchell's theoretical sequence. Barker (1965) argues that settings demand certain behaviors of people, and if the setting is undermanned, this creates a state of arousal and more complex and varied tasks for each individual to carry out. An undermanned setting thus influences behavior by creating arousal and altering the task and role characteristics of each person in the setting. Should manning be a conditioner of task characteristics and arousal and/or a moderator of the motivation–behavior linkage?

Let us consider one more variable as an example of the difficulty of specifying relationships. It is argued that ease of observation influences the performance–appraisal linkage. How conceptually distinct is this from issues of evaluation apprehension? Are they really different? That is, if ratee behaviors are not observable, are we not dealing with a potential social-loafing situation? If so, how will we specify those linkages and the implications of variation in the performance–appraisal linkage on arousal and the arousal–motivation link?

Our intention here is not to create clutter and complications, but to question which of the variables are necessary, which ones overlap conceptually, and where they should appear in the framework. A final point is to ask if the model can be pruned to increase conceptual manageability. For example, Mitchell argues (though we are not sure the data support him) that "one's attitudes and reactions to a task . . . may be more a function of what one's coworkers say about the task than the actual task properties themselves." Might it follow, then, that we can trim away tasks as moderators in favor of social cues to build a more parsimonious framework?

Another area that highlights the need for precision and clarification throughout Figs. 3.2 and 3.3 is in Mitchell's treatment of ability. His discussion does not tell us how ability is functionally related to behavior. Is there some linear relationship between ability and behavior, or is some other functional form more appropriate? The traditional literature talks about ability and motivation as multiplicatively related. Mitchell argues that the amount of each (ability and effort) that is needed for performance is probably variable. He does not tell us what form this should take and under what conditions ability matters. By constrast, Schmidt, Hunter, and Pearlman (1981) argue that it is unlikely that many of the moderating relationships (e.g., organizational climate, technology) often proposed between ability and performance (which encompass half the general performance sequence) would stand up to rigorous statistical testing. That is, the ability–performance linkage does not vary as a function of other variables (e.g., task differences) in their study. The burden of proof on Mitchell is to give a more precise formulation of the conditions under which the ability–performance relationship will be affected by outside variables, so we can verify which viewpoint is correct.

Level of Theoretical Specification

A related issue concerns the level of theoretical specification. Mitchell's basic argument about the effects of social, task, and situational factors is represented in a diagram (Figs. 3.2 and 3.3). The diagram pictures the points at which the three contextual variables affect various links among arousal, motivation, and performance.

The problem is that this level of theorizing is very general. The reader is confronted with a host of variables, yet there is no indication which variables are critical. We know little about the functional relationship among the variables. There are probably issues of simultaneity, but these are not identified.

It is a very common practice in the organizational literature to draw flow charts or diagrams in which concepts are linked by arrows. Arrow theorizing clearly has a place. It helps the writer and reader to understand the system of variables in a simplified way. The necessary next step is to develop a more precise understanding of the complex relationships among the key variables. Unfortunately, much theoretical work stops at the general level of the diagram. In many cases, arrow theorizing dominates the theoretical development.

To remedy the problem, we advocate first the development of specific models of performance through a fine-grained analysis (Weick, 1977). What is needed is clarity in definition of variables. Otherwise one person's task variable is another person's situational constraint, a condition that renders firm conclusions from research impossible. The second element needed is clear operational specifications of each variable. Third, we need to identify the underlying theoretical processes that relate the independent and dependent variables. The next step is to identify the complete model that explains performance and the functional relationships. In an earlier discussion we pointed out that stating that ability moderates the relationship between motivation and performance is not very helpful. It would be more useful to specify functional relationships (e.g., multiplicative interaction, step function) between ability, motivation, and performance.

The key advantage of this procedure is that it will result in models that can be "proved or disproved." Given the general nature of the Mitchell model, it is difficult to determine how one would disprove his conceptual work. Also, we feel this procedure will develop a more parsimonious set of variables, at least compared to the array in Mitchell's work.

ALTERNATIVE APPROACHES

Moving from a discussion of Mitchell's paper, we would like to pose some alternative approaches to understanding the relationship between social, task, and situational factors and performance. It should be clear that we agree with Mitchell that these factors are important in understanding performance. His paper has clearly refocused attention on these variables.

A Performance Definition

One must provide some conceptual definition of performance prior to assessing the impact of social, task, and situational factors. We hold that performance is a socially defined output or product. Performance can be examined at any level of analysis—individual, group, department, organization, or larger collectivity.

A theme that runs throughout Mitchell's paper is that interdependencies of tasks make it difficult to identify individual levels of performance. Unfortunately, his observation does not distinguish between *identifying performance* and *assessing the relative contribution* of individuals working in interdependent tasks. Even in an interdependent group it is possible to identify both individual and group performance.

We introduce two other elements to sharpen our concept of performance: process and structure (Goodman, Atkin, & Schoorman, 1982). Process refers to those activities that contribute to the production of the final output. Like performance, process can be measured at different levels of analysis (e.g., individual, group, organization).

Structure refers to the factors of production. These factors exist prior to and are the causes of process and performance. They can be used to explain or predict performance at different levels of analysis.

The concepts of performance, process, and structure can be illustrated from some of our work in the coal-mining industry. In this industry production or performance occurs in highly interdependent crews. Also, in most mines three crews per 24-hour period comprise a department. Departments then combine to indicate mine-level production.

Performance of a socially defined output at the individual level would refer to the number of bolts bolted, number of cuts by the continuous miner, or the number of loads traveled by the shuttle car. At the crew level, the socially defined output unit is tons of coal. Performance at the department or mine level is also the number of tons produced for some time period.

Processes refer to those activities that lead to the final product for the bolter (at the individual level this might mean selecting the right bolts, testing the roof, measuring the roof, moving the machine, and so on). At the group level, in this example, the individual performance outputs are also the processes for the group level. That is, bolting, cutting, and transporting (all processes) combine to create the output at the group level.

Structure refers to the factors of production. These antecedents cause variation in performance. Different factors are specified for different levels of analysis. At the individual level, the number of bolts bolted would be a function of factors such as the quality of the machinery, environmental or physical conditions, ability and motivation of the bolter, character of the role definition, and so on. At the crew or group level, the factors of production would include quality of equipment, environmental conditions, number of miners, ability of miners, coordination mechanism both within and outside the group, and so on. In the next section we try to provide some general categories to aid in the identification of these factors.

We propose the concepts of structure, process, and performance as a first approximation for thinking about performance. These concepts can be applied at different levels of analysis and across different types of organizations. At the group and higher levels of analysis, the structure, process, and outcome concepts can be tied to input, transformation, and outcome processes. This 3 × 3 matrix provides a more complicated view of possible performance indicators (see Goodman et al., 1982, for more details).

A Performance Model

Once the performance indicator is identified, the research should turn to a fine-grained analysis of the production (performance) process. This analysis, both deductively and inductively directed, should uncover the key variables in the production function. The next step would be to specify the performance model and then estimate its properties. The purpose of this activity is to identify, in a precise way, the impact of social, task, and situational factors on performance.

The best way to illustrate our position is to begin with the concept of a production function. The production function specifies the physical relationship between outputs and various inputs. The task, as we see it, is to identify the production functions for the relevant performance indicators. This exercise can be undertaken at different levels of analysis.

In traditional economic analysis, the critical inputs in the production function have been land, labor, and capital. Although these may be appropriate at the level of the economy, other concepts need to be entered at the level of the firm and lower levels of analysis.

At the individual, group, and firm levels four factors—*labor, technology, organizational arrangements,* and *environment*— are the primary inputs in the production function. The labor factor includes skills, abilities, size, and motivation. Technology includes the characteristics of the machinery and technological processes. The organizational-arrangement factor includes programs for coordination. Environment may refer to the firm's marketplace (external) or to the work environment (internal). The capital factor also could be included if there were different access to capital (independent of technology) for different individuals or groups. This access to capital is probably more relevant in a between-firm analysis of performance than in a within-firm analysis.

The purpose of identifying these factors of production is to provide a conceptual guide for specifying the performance model. At different levels of analysis, the specific variables selected may differ. For example, in a within-firm analysis in which technology is constant, that variable would drop out.

Now the researcher is faced with three critical tasks: First, specify a complete yet parsimonious set of variables (a correctly identified model) that predict performance. Second, be sure that the selected variables are primary not secondary predictors of performance. For example, in Mitchell's list he includes schedules and machine down time as a predictor of performance. We view down time as a direct predictor of performance and schedules as one predictor of down time. Third, determine the functional relationships between each of the independent variables and performance.

To illustrate our position, let us return to the coal example and tackle the problem of explaining crew or group performance. The number of tons produced is a function of a labor component. Some obvious components concern the number of people in the crew, skill and ability levels, and motivation levels. Technological variables include the type and quality of machinery and the type of mining practices. The organizational-arrangement component would include the role arrangements within a crew, coordination mechanisms within and between crews, and so on. Also, physical conditions are important in explaining coal production. This variable corresponds to our environment factor. For each of the variables in the performance model, we a priori identified the functional relationship with performance and then tested for alternative relationships.

In previous work (Goodman, 1979) we specified several models for coal production and estimated their properties. The data suggested that: (1) it was possible to estimate the production model for coal; (2) the estimates were fairly stable over time; (3) a reasonable portion of the variance was explained; and (4) nonmotivational factors (e.g., type of mining) were primary predictors of performance variance.

Some other issues are important in understanding the development of the performance model. First, in specifying the model of group performance, we selected variables that had a *direct* rather than an *indirect* effect on performance. For example, many companies have absentee policies that affect the rate of absenteeism. This in turn affects the number of people in the crew. We did not include this organizational arrangement (absentee policy), because its effect is indirect rather than direct. Similarly, we did not estimate factors that affect motivation that in turn affect performance. The strategy was to estimate direct effects on production. To understand variations in motivation, it is necessary to develop and estimate a second model.

In Mitchell's work the task and social factors are direct predictors of motivation and indirect predictors of performance. Of his situational variables, some are direct effects (down time), others (schedules) are indirect effects.

Third, there are a variety of statistical and methodological problems in estimating production or performance models. We were confronted with issues such as simultaneity, reliability of measures, and autocorrelation of residuals. Although many of these issues are complicated, the technology to deal with them seems available.

Fourth, our approach is not unique to a particular level of analysis. We could have developed and estimated a model of "bolting performance" at the individual level, using the human, technological, and organizational factors. Or we could have moved to higher levels of analysis, such as the department or mine. Our rule for aggregation is, given a particular performance indicator, that one can move to higher levels of analysis as long as the production functions in the aggregated units are the same. That is, it is appropriate to aggregate crew performance to department performance if the individual crew-production functions are the same. Similarly, one can move from the department-level performance to estimating mine-level performance as long as the production functions are the same. That is, we want to avoid estimating some aggregate production model that is composed of very different production models at a disaggregated level.

Performance Models and Performance Measurement

There is currently a great interest in productivity. In many discussions of this topic in organizational or managerial circles, the key issue seems to be how to measure it or change it. The measurement discussion is often dominant. We have spent the last eight to ten years developing various organizational-assessment techniques (i.e., measures) to capture a variety of organizational indicators, including productivity or performance. In retrospect it is not clear that the focus on measurement is the right way to go. There are a variety of possible and even reasonable measures available.

The critical problem is in understanding performance. Variation in a performance indicator, by itself, is not easily interpretable. We need to know what factors cause performance. Variation in performance may be caused by uncontrollable factors (e.g., environmental changes, mining conditions) as well as controllable factors (e.g., role arrangements). To assess the effectiveness of an individual, group, or organization, we need to separate out sources of variation that are due to controllable or uncontrollable factors. Similarly, if we want to change performance we need to identify the critical factors of production or performance. If we want to understand performance we need to change our focus to developing specific models of performance.

In summary, Mitchell's paper provides a useful service in refocusing our attention on social, task, and situational factors as they affect performance. Our basic criticisms of his paper are: (1) it does not acknowledge that traditional theories of motivation can and do incorporate these three external factors; (2) it does not define some of the critical concepts clearly; and (3) it does not precisely specify the relationships among social, task, and situational factors and their relationships to motivation and performance.

We have tried to suggest some alternatives in defining performance and steps in modeling performance.

REFERENCES

Atkinson, J. W., & Birch, D. *The dynamics of action.* New York: Wiley, 1970.
Barker, R. G. Explorations in ecological psychology. *American Psychologist,* 1965, *20,* 1–14.

Dachler, H. P., & Mobley, W. H. Construct validation of an instrumentality–expectancy–task–goal model of work motivation: Some theoretical boundary conditions. *Journal of Applied Psychology*, 1973, *58*, 397–418.

Goodman, P. S. An examination of referents used in the evaluation of pay. *Organizational Behavior and Human Performance*, 1974, *12*, 170–195.

Goodman, P. S. Social comparison processes in organizations. In B. M. Staw & G. R. Salancik (Eds.), *New directions in organizational behavior*. Chicago: St. Clair Press, 1977.

Goodman, P. S. *Assessing organizational change: The rushton quality of work experiment*. New York: Wiley, 1979.

Goodman, P. S., Atkin, R. S., & Schoorman, D. On the demise of organizational effectiveness studies. In M. K. Cameron and D. Whetten (Eds.), *Organizational effectiveness*. New York: Wiley, forthcoming. Full title: Organizational effectiveness: A comparison of multiple models.

Goodman, P. S., & Friedman, A. An examination of Adam's theory of inequity. *Administrative Science Quarterly*, 1971, *16*, 271–288.

Goodman, P. S., & Moore, B. Factors affecting the acquisition of beliefs about a new reward system. *Human Relations*, 1976, *29*, 571–588.

Graen, G. Instrumentality theory of work motivation: Some experimental results and suggested modifications. *Journal of Applied Psychology*, 1969, *53*, 1–25.

Graen, G. Role-making processes in organizations. In M. D. Dunnette (Ed.), *Handbook of industrial and organizational psychology*. Chicago: Rand McNally, 1976.

Hackman, J. R., & Lawler, E. E. Employee reactions to job characteristics. *Journal of Applied Psychology*, 1971, *55*, 259–286.

Hackman, J. R., & Oldham, G. R. Motivation through the design of work: Test of a theory. *Organizational Behavior and Human Performance*, 1976, *16*, 250–279.

House, R. J., & Mitchell, T. R. Path–goal theory of leadership. *Journal of Contemporary Business*, 1974, *3*, 81–97.

Jackson, J. Structural characteristics of norms. In I. D. Steiner & M. Fishbein (Eds.), *Current studies in social psychology*. New York: Holt, Rinehart, & Winston, 1965.

Kahneman, D. *Attention and effort*. Englewood Cliffs, N.J.: Prentice-Hall, 1973.

Lawler, E. E. *Pay and organizational effectiveness: A psychological view*. New York: McGraw-Hill, 1971.

Schmidt, F. L., Hunter, J. E., and Pearlman, K. Task differences as moderators of aptitude test validity in selection: A red herring. *Journal of Applied Psychology*, 1981, *66(2)*, 166–185.

Scott, W. E. Activation theory and task design. *Organizational Behavior and Human Performance*, 1966, *1*, 3–30.

Weick, K. E. The concept of equity in the perception of pay. *Administrative Science Quarterly*, 1966, *11*, 414–439.

Weick, K. E. Re-punctuating the problem. In P. S. Goodman & J. Pennings (Eds.), *New Perspectives on organizational effectiveness*. San Francisco: Jossey-Bass, 1977.

Zajonc, R. B. Social facilitation. *Science*, 1965, *149*, 269–274.

Reply to Goodman and Fichman

Terence R. Mitchell

I would like to respond to the Goodman and Fichman comments with three major observations.

First, the major citicism of my paper really boils down to the need for a more detailed analysis. There is a need for more precise functional statements, more detailed definitions and precise categorization, more specification of hypotheses and relationships, and a finer-grained theoretical analysis. In general, I agree with these comments. This greater detail was not provided due to: (1) the scope of the review; and (2) the fact that in many cases I simply did not feel that I had enough information to make the statements that Goodman and Fichman request.

However, I do believe the paper served a greater purpose than simply calling people's attention to social, task, and situational factors by providing a list of such factors. More specifically, I see the distinctions I was making as both vertical and horizontal. The vertical distinctions represented in the figures contrast the traditional research areas with the social, task, and situational factors. In some cases these distinctions are very important. For example, the traditional cognitive theories of motivation depend on managerial control of motivation (setting up goals, equal distribution of rewards, administration of rewards) whereas the task and social factors are self-maintaining mechanisms of motivation (the task properties, coworker comments, and others).

The horizontal distinctions are also important. The concepts of arousal, motivation, behavior, performance, and appraisal are frequently confused and used interchangeably. Recognition of the differences among these concepts is crucial for further advances in both theory and practice.

My second observation pertains to the criticism that argues that most of the social or task factors influencing motivation could be incorporated into existing

73

theories of motivation. I would agree that theoretically such an integration is possible. However, I believe that such an integration would be more harmful than helpful because it would mask important distinctions such that just mentioned between managerial control of motivation and self-maintaining mechanisms of motivation. Barry Staw, in a recent paper on commitment to decisions, addressed a similar argument that expectancy theory could incorporate both forward-looking and retrospective reasons for commitment. He responded (Staw, 1981), "Of course, it is even possible to collapse all the antecedents of commitment into factors influencing perceived probability and valences and finally into an SEU calculation. However, this would neither reduce the number of variables with which we must deal nor improve our understanding. It would simply constitute a semantic transformation [p. 585]." His comments reflect exactly my reaction to this point.

Finally, I would like to comment on Goodman and Fichman's section on suggestions for looking at performance. I liked this section. It demonstrated nicely some ways in which performance can be defined and some ways in which contributions to performance can be assessed. However, I might add two points: First, the distinction between structure and process is not a simple one or one that is easy to implement in measurement or assessment techniques. Second, their set of variables that contribute to performance correspond very closely to those I have described. They suggest that labor (ability, motivation), technology (machinery characteristics), and organizational arrangements (coordination, roles) contribute to performance and that these contributions will vary across tasks. These factors sound very much to me like personal factors, machine technology, and administrative technology, and their methodological procedure sounds very much like my point that we must look at how different tasks will generate different weights for contributing factors. Their theory and method for the specific problem is certainly more precise than I describe in my paper and in that regard it is very helpful. But it is certainly not a dramatic departure from the type of procedure I am advocating. It is, in fact, an excellent example of just the type of work that I think we need more of.

REFERENCES

Staw, B. M. The escalation of commitment to a course of action. *Academy of Management Review,* October 1981, 557–588.

4

Facilitating Effective Performance Appraisals: The Role of Employee Commitment and Organizational Climate

Richard M. Steers
Thomas W. Lee

These authors cite six conditions that have been found to facilitate performance-evaluation systems. They include communication, legitimacy and validity, instrumentality, job standards and expectations, participation, and managerial support. The effect of employee commitment and organizational climate on effective appraisal systems are discussed in relation to each of the six facilitory factors. Steers and Lee argue that both employee commitment and organizational climate have an impact on the effectiveness of a performance-appraisal system.

Based on the proposed relationships in their model, Steers and Lee also argue that performance appraisal may in turn affect the climate of the organization and the commitment of the individual.

Dr. Cummings provides a discussion of the reciprocal relationship between organizational trust and commitment and performance appraisal in which he describes the relationship as compensatory. He states that when trust and commitment are high, there is little need for a formal evaluation system. However, when trust and commitment are low, an effective evaluation system may clarify an employee's judgments about the degree of trust and commitment he or she should develop towards the organization.

When one reads the literature on performance-appraisal systems in organizations, it becomes readily apparent that we have learned a great deal concerning measurement techniques and very little concerning the milieu in which such measurement takes place. For example, although we have considerable information about the strengths and weaknesses of behavioral-observation scales, we know much less about the conditions within the work place that facilitate or inhibit the effective use of such scales. In order to help remedy this situation, we examine one aspect of the contextual factors influencing appraisal systems. We do this by considering the interactive relationships between employee commitment, organizational climate, and appraisal systems, and by proposing a general conceptual model highlighting such interrelationships. Simply put, we argue here that commitment and climate influence performance-appraisal systems by influencing several factors that facilitate the effective use of such systems. Hence, our emphasis here is on considering *effective* performance appraisals as an outcome variable. It should be emphasized that throughout this paper we rely heavily on argument and speculation due to the dearth of empirical evidence bearing on the topic.

We address four key issues. First, we consider briefly the primary objectives of appraisal systems from the organization's standpoint. Next, we speculate concerning certain conditions that facilitate or inhibit these outcomes. Based on this, we consider the manner in which employee commitment and organizational climate affect these facilitating conditions. Finally, we consider any reciprocal relationships, or feedback loops, that impinge on the model. In all, we hope that this paper will be considered a series of hypotheses to guide subsequent research in order to further clarify our knowledge of this important topic.

OUTCOMES OF PERFORMANCE-APPRAISAL SYSTEMS

To set the stage for this paper, we must first consider what organizations hope to accomplish with performance-appraisal systems. This issue really addresses the criterion problem. How do we know when an appraisal system is indeed effective? What are we looking for in such systems?

To answer this question, we draw upon existing industry practice and academic opinion and suggest that effective performance-appraisal systems are those systems that facilitate employee evaluation, guidance and development, and motivation. Employee *evaluation* focuses on assessing the extent to which employees contribute to organizational goals through organizationally defined tasks. Evaluation provides a basis for assessing and rewarding employee worth to the organization. Employee *guidance and development* refer to the extent to which the appraisal system is successful in highlighting opportunities for employee growth and development, perhaps through such vehicles as training or counseling programs. Finally, employee *motivation* in the current context refers to the extent to which the appraisal system helps to energize, direct, and sustain human behavior in a direction desired by management. When taken together, these criteria can be considered the three primary indicators of the extent to which a performance-appraisal system is effective.

CONDITION'S FACILITATING EFFECTIVE
APPRAISAL SYSTEMS

If appraisal systems are considered effective to the extent that they achieve these three goals, it is logical to ask what conditions in the work situation facilitate or inhibit the achievement of these three goals.

Drawing upon literature from various aspects of organizational psychology and management, we posit that at least six facilitating conditions can be identified. These include the following:

1. *Communication.* Clearly, performance-appraisal systems are more effective to the extent that they provide useful and valid information concerning employee progress on tasks (McCormick & Ilgen, 1980). Such information assists with all three outcomes of evaluation, guidance, and motivation. Hence, the more ways can be found to increase information flow between superiors and subordinates, the greater the likelihood in most cases that the desired outcomes will be enhanced.

2. *Legitimacy and validity.* It would appear that outcome variables are enhanced to the extent that employees accept the appraisal system and possess a belief in the integrity and legitimacy of the system. This legitimacy is of course related to the degree to which employees believe the appraisals are valid and reliable indicators of performance. For example, we know from the literature on employee acceptance of goals that when employees accept task goals, they are far more likely to work towards their accomplishment (Locke, Shaw, Saari, & Latham, 1981; Steers & Porter, 1974). This same phenomenon applies to appraisal systems. That is, when employees feel that the organization has a right to implement a particular appraisal system, and when they further believe that the system is valid, we would expect such a system to have a sizable impact on subsequent motivation and guidance. Moreover, under such conditions, employees may be more likely to accept the particular evaluation they receive. When system legitimacy or content validity is not clearly established, it would be far easier for employees to dismiss or discount their evaluation (e.g., attributing their evaluation more to politics than performance).

3. *Instrumentality.* The third facilitating condition focuses on the extent to which the appraisal system is considered by employees to be instrumental for the receipt of desired rewards. Simply put, we would expect employees to pay more attention to appraisals when they are associated with rewards (Vroom, 1964). For example, if appraisal systems aim to increase employee motivation, would it not be wise to ensure that desired rewards were in some way tied to the appraisal? The same holds true for employee guidance and development. Such a goal would possibly be more easily achieved if employees saw a benefit to such development.

4. *Job standards and expectations.* Another factor capable of influencing the effectiveness of a performance-appraisal system is the standards and expectations associated with the assigned job. When job standards and expectations are highly specified and clear, we would expect evaluation to be easier; both superiors and subordinates would know what was expected. Moreover, clear job standards can serve to reduce employee search behavior and could in some cases facilitate development goals by identifying discrepancies between employee skill levels and job requirements. It has often been argued, for example, that a primary advantage of goal-setting programs such as Management By Objective is their increased specificity of task requirements, which reduces employee search behavior and increases task-relevant effort (Locke et al., 1981).

5. *Participation.* It has been suggested by some that allowing employees some participation in work-related events serves to increase their ego involvement in achieving successful outcomes on those events (Dachler & Wilpert, 1978; Vroom, 1960). Empirical support for this assertion is widespread though not universal (Steers & Porter, 1974). Hence, an argument can be made that increasing employee participation in the design and implementation of an appraisal system should to at least some extent increase its effectiveness, largely through increasing employee acceptance and support of the system.

6. *Managerial support.* In addition to acceptance and legitimacy on the part of employees, an effective performance-appraisal system is apparently also enhanced when it clearly receives support from top management (Ivancevich, 1972). A major criticism leveled against many appraisal systems is that top management simply ignores them or, more often, goes through the motions but does not abide by the results. In a survey of 216 organizations, Locher and Teel (1977) found that although 71% of those surveyed claimed to use performance appraisals for purposes of compensation, only 55% used them for facilitating performance improvement and only 9% used them for identifying and training and development needs. Because these are self-report data, the actual percentages may be much lower. If employees at all levels clearly understood that the appraisal system had the active support of top management—and not just the personnel department—perhaps such systems would be taken more seriously by all.

Hence, although each of these six facilitating conditions would not be expected to improve the effectiveness of all aspects of an appraisal system at all times, we would expect that each would play an important role under certain circumstances in facilitating the more effective use of appraisals. Based on this assumption, we come now to the question of how employee commitment and organizational climate influence these six facilitating conditions.

ROLE OF EMPLOYEE COMMITMENT

The question we wish to pose in this section is how employee commitment to an organization can influence the conditions that are believed to facilitate effective performance appraisals. As such, our concern with the topic of commitment is rather narrow in scope. A more detailed consideration of commitment can be found elsewhere (Mowday, Porter, & Steers, 1982; Mowday, Steers, & Porter, 1979; Steers, 1977). For our purposes, we define employee commitment as the relative strength of an individual's identification with and involvement in a particular organization (Porter, Steers, Mowday, & Boulian, 1974). Following from both the theoretical and empirical literature on commitment (summarized in Mowday et al., 1982), we can conclude that highly committed employees would generally be characterized by the following attributes when compared to less committed employees:

1. Highly committed employees have a strong belief in and acceptance of organizational goals and values (Porter & Smith, 1970).
2. Highly committed employees often exert considerable effort on a job, often leading to increased job performance (Porter, Crampon & Smith, 1976); (Steers, 1977).
3. Highly committed employees often have levels of social involvement in organizational activities, as well as higher investments in the organization and its success (Sheldon, 1971).
4. Highly committed employees often exhibit better attendance and promptness (Angle & Perry, 1981; Mowday et al., 1979; Steers, 1977).
5. Finally, highly committed employees as a group consistently demonstrate superior levels of retention and tenure in the organization (Angle & Perry, 1981; Hom, Katerberg, & Hulin, 1979; Koch & Steers, 1978; Mowday et al., 1979; Porter et al., 1974, 1976; Steers, 1977).

Given these characteristics of highly committed employees, how should employee commitment influence the specified conditions that are believed to facilitate effective appraisal systems? To answer this, let us examine each of the facilitating conditions sequentially. To begin with, as shown in Fig. 4.1, we would suggest that communication between superiors and subordinates would be enhanced in many instances when employees are more concerned about putting forth effort on the job and trying to make things work (I,2). In addition, communication may be facilitated to the extent that employees are more socially involved and feel they have more investments in organizationally relevant outcomes (I, 3; Sheldon, 1971). Employee retention and tenure (5) may also be relevant here to the extent that increased tenure allows employees to learn more about both the formal and informal communication channels as well as the personalities involved in the communication episodes (Rogers & Rogers, 1976).

The legitimacy of the appraisal system can be enhanced to the extent that employees identify with the goals and values of the organization (I,1) and feel that the appraisal system is a useful vehicle for goal attainment (Steers, 1977). Legitimacy can also be enhanced in some cases through increased social involve-

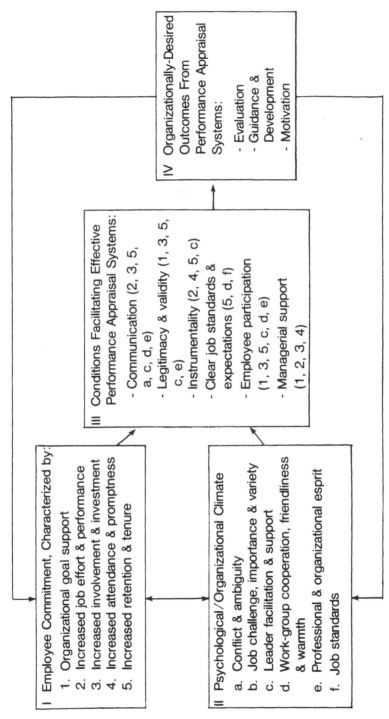

FIG. 4.1. Hypothesized relationships between employee commitment, organizational climate, and outcomes of performance-appraisal systems.

ment (I, 3) through which employees come to know the persons involved in the appraisal reviews, as well as the reasons for such reviews. Perhaps a major problem with achieving legitimacy for appraisal systems many employees' ignorance of the rationale behind such systems or the reasons for their existence. Increased social interaction between the parties to such a system may help alleviate some of this apprehension (Latham & Wexley, 1981). Finally, in some instances, increased tenure in the organization (I,5) may help a system gain legitimacy as long-term employees see the record (and consequences) of previous appraisals and conclude that it represents a useful diagnostic and guidance tool. It should be noted, however, that tenure may backfire when long-term employees see past appraisals as capricious and unfair.

The instrumentality of appraisal systems can be facilitated to some extent by increased job performance (I,2) and attendance (I,4) when such behaviors are followed by the receipt of rewards. As noted previously, increased effort towards job performance and increased attendance are characteristics of highly committed employees. Employee tenure (I,5) may also affect instrumentality to the extent that seniority influences appraisal reviews.

Job standards and expectations may be influenced to some degree by increased employee retention and tenure (I,5). That is, the longer employees remain on the job, the more likely they are to learn what is required and important and what the supervisor is "looking for" on the job.

Participation in the design and implementation of appraisals can be influenced at least in part by a combination of increased identification with organizational objectives (I,1), increased social involvement and investment (I,3), and increased tenure (I,5). That is, the more employees see the goals of the organization as important, the more likely they are to think it worthwhile to invest time and energy in making things work. Likewise, the more socially involved employees are and the longer they have been with the organization, the more likely they should be to want to become involved in the activities surrounding the appraisal system.

Finally, managerial support of the system is clearly a function of management attitudes and opinions surrounding the utility of such systems. Even so, in an indirect way, employee commitment may influence such support in cases in which management is convinced that employees are genuinely interested in helping management and the organization succeed. This may be brought about to some extent when management is convinced that the majority of the employees clearly identify with organizational goals and values (I,1) and when high social contacts exist between managers and employees (I,3). In a negative way, managerial support may also be enhanced when managers see low commitment levels characterized by poor performance (I,2) and attendance (I,4). In such cases, support for appraisal systems may be based more on a felt need for increased contact systems than on a belief in the more positive aspects of such systems.

In summary, although we clearly do not wish to suggest a direct or even overly strong relationship between employee commitment and facilitating conditions, it does appear that a good case can be made that commitment and its consequences can influence many of the conditions that are believed to lead to effective appraisal systems.

ROLE OF ORGANIZATIONAL CLIMATE

We now turn to the last major variable in our model: organizational climate. This topic has received widespread attention in recent years as researchers search for optimal working conditions both in terms of productivity and quality of working life. To date, however, no attention has been given to the role played by climate in performance-appraisal systems.

Arriving at an acceptable definition of climate is no easy matter. Jones and James (1979) have argued that it is important to distinguish between psychological climate and organizational climate. Psychological climate represents the meaning an individual attaches to the work context, whereas organizational climate represents the organization-wide aggregation of that meaning. We do not wish to enter into this definitional frey. Nor do we wish to depart from the major theme of this paper and discuss competing models of climate. Rather, we refer to psychological and organizational climate in a rather general sense and define it for our purposes as the perceived properties or characteristics found in the work environment that result from actions taken consciously or unconsciously by an organization and that presumably affect subsequent behavior (Steers, 1977). In other words, climate may be thought of as the ''personality'' of an organization as seen by its members.

Climate is clearly viewed as a multidimensional phenomenon (Schneider, 1981). Unfortunately, little agreement exists among climate researchers concerning which dimensions either exist or are most useful for purposes of organizational analysis. For our purpose here, we adopt the six dimensions developed by Jones and James (1979). Although we could use other approaches, this particular set of dimensions appears to us to have a more rigorous psychometric foundation. Even so, we should caution that in our judgment the construct validity of this and other approaches is somewhat suspect. The dimensions are not totally independent from one another and the true structural integrity of the various dimensions remains to be established. Even so, we feel this particular approach is more tenable than the more a priori dimensions identified by others. As such, it is used here for purposes of analysis.

1. *Conflict and ambiguity.* Perceived conflict in organizational goals and objectives, combined with ambiguity of organizational structure and roles, a lack of interdepartmental cooperation, and poor communication from management. Also included here are poor planning, inefficient job

design, a lack of awareness of employee needs and problems, and a lack of fairness and objectivity of the reward process.

   2. *Job challenge, importance, and variety.* Extent to which job is seen as challenging, important, and involving a variety of duties, including dealing with people. Autonomy, feedback, and high standards of quality and performance are also included here.

   3. *Leader facilitation and support.* Reflects perceived leader behavior such as the extent to which a leader is seen as helping to accomplish work goals by means of scheduling activities, planning, etc., as well as the extent to which he or she is seen as facilitating interpersonal relationships and providing personal support.

   4. *Work-group cooperation, friendliness, and warmth.* Perceived relationships among group members and their pride in the work group.

   5. *Professional and organizational esprit.* Perceived external image and desirable growth potential offered by the job and organization. Also included here are perceptions of the extent to which an open atmosphere exists in which to express one's feelings and thoughts, confidence in the leader, and consistently applied organizational policies.

   6. *Job standards.* Reflects degree to which job is seen as having rigid standards of quality and accuracy, combined with inadequate time, labor, training, and resources to complete the task. Also included here are a perceived lack of confidence and trust by supervisors and management personnel.

FIG. 4.2.   Six dimensions of psychological/organizational climate (after Jones & James, 1979).

The six dimensions suggested by the research of Jones and James (1979) are as follows: (1) conflict and ambiguity; (2) job challenge, importance, and variety; (3) leader facilitation and support; (4) work-group cooperation, friendliness, and warmth; (5) professional and organizational esprit; and (6) job standards. Definitions of each of these dimensions are provided in Fig. 4.2. Based on this, how would we expect variations in psychological/organizational climate to influence those conditions that facilitate effective appraisal conditions? In the absence of much in the way of empirical data, we can speculate as follows (these relationships are summarized in Fig. 4.1):

To begin with, we would argue that communication patterns and openness between superiors and subordinates could be greatly influenced by a climate characterized by low interpersonal conflict (II,a in Fig. 4.1). Moreover, such communication could also be improved when leader facilitation and support (II,c) and work-group cooperation, friendliness, and warmth (II,d) are both high. And finally, when a professional esprit (II,e) exists and employees feel that the atmosphere is receptive to open expression, we would again expect improved two-way communication (Porter & Roberts, 1976; Rogers & Rogers, 1976).

In order for the legitimacy of a performance-appraisal system to be increased, we argue that a climate characterized by high leader facilitation and support

(II,c) and strong professional and organizational esprit (II,e) would be helpful (House & Baetz, 1979). Under such a climate, many employees may come to feel that management and professional norms clearly support the appraisal system.

The instrumentality of the appraisal system, the third facilitating condition, may be influenced to some extent by a climate that includes leader facilitation and support (II,e). Under such a climate, employees are more likely to feel that superior performance is not only expected but that supervisors and managers will take an active role in tying performance to desired rewards (House & Baetz, 1979; Porter & Lawler, 1968).

It seems logical to conclude that a climate characterized by clear job standards (II,f)—where employees know what is expected of them—would facilitate effective performance appraisals by clarifying managerial expectations on the job (March & Simon, 1958). Job expectations could also be influenced in some instances where work groups are characterized by warmth and mutual support (II,d).

The fifth facilitating condition, employee participation in the appraisal process, may be brought about by three of the climate dimensions. These are leader facilitation and support (II,c), work-group cooperation, friendliness, and warmth (II,d), and professional/organizational esprit (II,e). That is, we would expect the atmosphere to be more conducive to employee participation when managers are clearly supportive of employees and show an interest in their views, when work groups show a genuine desire to get involved, and when the professional norms of the work place support candor and open expression of one's opinions and feelings. Without such a climate, employees may be far more reticent to make input into the process for fear of reprisal either from the manager or the work group.

Finally, managerial support, the sixth facilitating condition, may be largely unaffected by organizational climate. One could suggest that when managers sense that employees demonstrate high job standards and professional esprit, they would be more likely to support the appraisal process, but this is a tenuous argument at best. It is far more likely that the causal arrow goes in the other direction—that is, when employees feel that management strongly supports the system, changes in the climate result that facilitate increased effort and performance. In any event, it is clear that managerial support is essential in order for an appraisal system to function effectively.

Although it is difficult to generalize, we should recognize that the type of organization (private, public, military, etc.) as well as the size of the organization (small, medium, or large) can influence both the climate and its effects on facilitating conditions. For instance, military organizations or large public bureaucracies may have more specific job standards than the more loosely coupled large corporation. As a result, a climate is created in which most members know precisely what their responsibilities are. In constrast, many large corporations intentionally blur job standards to "see what an employee can *make* out of the job." Such a practice in the military would possibly incur censure rather than praise.

Similarly, consider the issue of organization size. In a newly formed and small company, work-group cooperation, friendliness, and warmth may be quite high as employees enjoy the excitement of a relatively small group of individuals tackling a new challenge. In a major established corporation, on the other hand, work roles may have become much more formalized and distant and employees may come to place more emphasis on seniority and status relationships. As a result, communication patterns and the extent or willingness of employee participation may vary accordingly. The point here, then, is that factors such as organization type or size may impinge on the model and should be recognized as potentially important variables in the study of climate and appraisal systems.

IS THE RELATIONSHIP RECIPROCAL?

Having considered on a speculative level how commitment and climate influence the appraisal process, it is logical to ask, in turn, how the appraisal process influences commitment and climate. To be more specific, if an organization emphasizes evaluation, guidance and development, and motivation as organizationally desired outcomes from the appraisal system, what effect does this have on commitment and climate?

Available studies focusing on antecedents of employee commitment to organizations suggest that commitment is influenced by at least four sets of factors: (1) personal characteristics, such as education and achievement motivation; (2) role-related characteristics, such as job scope and role conflict and ambiguity; (3) structural characteristics, such as formalization and decentralization; and (4) work experiences, such as organizational dependability, personal importance to the organization, met expectations, perceived pay equity, and positive attitudes towards the organization (Morris & Steers, 1980; Mowday et al., 1982; Steers, 1977).

Following from this, it is logical to conclude that the results of a performance-appraisal system have the potential to influence commitment at least to some degree. In particular, when employees believe that the evaluation process was carried out in a fair and equitable fashion, their commitment should be enhanced. On the contrary, when employees see their evaluations as capricious or biased, commitment to the organization should be reduced. Moreover, to the extent that the appraisal is considered by employees to facilitate their professional growth and development, the possibility increases that employees will reciprocate with a positive attitude towards the organization. Providing such guidance and development tells the employees that they are important enough for the organization to invest time and effort in them. Finally, if the appraisal system is successful in increasing employee motivation, this too may influence commitment by activating an employee's achievement motive (Steers, 1977). Hence, although it should be emphasized that we clearly would not expect a direct appraisal–commitment relationship, we would argue nonetheless that an effective appraisal process would represent a positive influence on the development of employee commitment to the organization.

Turning finally to the topic or organizational climate, we would make the same argument that a reciprocal relationship exists between appraisal system outcomes and climate. First, the extent to which the appraisal system is considered fair and equitable should have a bearing on (1) reducing conflict and ambiguity; (2) enhancing the stature of those in leadership positions; and (3) reinforcing professional esprit and job standards. Moreover, when employees see the organization as truly concerned about using appraisal systems for guidance and development, climate factors such as job challenge and importance and job standards could be influenced in a positive fashion. Finally, to the extent that the appraisal system leads to increased employee motivation, job challenge, workgroup cooperation, professional esprit, and job standards should be enhanced.

CONCLUSION

Hence, again it would appear that performance-appraisal outcomes do indeed have a reciprocal relationship with climate and commitment, although this relationship may be of modest proportion. Clearly other factors influence these relationships. Even so, we feel that based on available evidence, a sufficient case is made to establish the importance of considering employee commitment and organizational climate in the design and implementation of appraisal systems. By clearly recognizing not only the desired goals of such systems and their facilitating conditions but also how such systems are influenced by commitment and climate, we should be in a position to develop appraisal systems that prove more effective over the long run in facilitating both employee and organizational goal attainment.

In closing, we wish to voice our support for the rationale behind this conference. The topics and scope of the present conference represent a healthy sign. We feel that it is timely and appropriate that our field expand its research emphasis from focusing primarily on the reliability and validity of our measurement devices to a broader "systems approach" to performance appraisal. This is not to imply that investigating the psychometric properties of performance instruments is unimportant. On the contrary, we feel that establishing the reliability and validity of performance measures is critical for the appraisal system. We simply wish to state our belief that performance measurement and appraisal systems can be better understood if we consider the context in which these phenomena occur. In short, performance measurement should be viewed as part of a appraisal *system* and we should clearly appreciate the context within which the system is embedded. In this way, we think that one more step is taken towards improving both productivity and the quality of working life in organizational settings.

REFERENCES

Angle, H., & Perry, J. An empirical assessment of organizational commitment and organizational effectiveness. *Administrative Science Quarterly*, 1981, *26*, 1–14.

Dachler, H. P., & Wilpert, B. Conceptual dimensions and boundaries of participation in organizations: A critical evaluation. *Administrative Science Quarterly*, 1978, *23*, 1–39.

Hom, P. W., Katerberg, R., Jr., & Hulin, C. L. Comparative examination of three approaches to the prediction of turnover. *Journal of Applied Psychology*, 1979, *64*,(3), 280–290.

House, R. J., & Baetz, M. L. Leadership: Some empirical generalizations and new research directions. In B. Staw (Ed.), *Research in organizational behavior* (Vol. 1). Greenwick, Conn.: JAI Press, 1979.

Ivancevich, J. M. A longitudinal assessment of management by objectives. *Administrative Science Quarterly*, 1972, *17*, 126–138.

Jones, A. P., & James, L. R. Psychological climate: Dimensions and relations of individual and aggregated work environment perceptions. *Organizational Behavior and Human Performance*, 1979, *23*, 201–250.

Koch, J. L., & Steers, R. M. Job attachment, satisfaction, and turnover among public employees. *Journal of Vocational Behavior*, 1978, *12*, 119–128.

Latham, G. P., & Wexley, K. N. *Increasing productivity through performance appraisals*. Menlo Park, Calif.: Addison-Wesley, 1981.

Locher, A., & Teel, K. Performance appraisal: A survey of current practices. *Personnel Journal*, May 1977.

Locke, E. A., Shaw, K. N., Saari, L. M., & Latham, G. P. Goal setting and task performance: 1969–1980. *Psychological Bulletin*, 1981, *90*(1), 125–152.

March, J., & Simon, H. *Organizations*. New York: Wiley, 1958.

McCormick, E. J., & Ilgen, D. R. *Industrial psychology* (7th ed.). Englewood Cliffs, N.J.: Prentice-Hall, 1980.

Morris, J., & Steers, R. M. Structural influences on organizational commitment. *Journal of Vocational Behavior*, 1980, *17*, 50–57.

Mowday, R. T., Porter, L. W., & Steers, R. M. *Employee-organizational linkages*. New York: Academic Press, 1982.

Mowday, R. T., Steers, R. M., & Porter, L. W. The measurement of organizational commitment. *Journal of Vocational Behavior*, 1979, *14*, 224–247.

Porter, L. W., Crampon, W. J., & Smith, F. J. Organizational commitment and managerial turnover: A longitudinal study. *Organizational Behavior and Human Performance*, 1976, *15*, 87–98.

Porter, L. W., & Lawler, E. E. *Managerial attitudes and performance*. Homewood, Ill.: Dorsey Press, 1968.

Porter, L. W., & Roberts, K. A. Communication in organizations. In M. Dunnette (Ed.), *Handbook of industrial and organizational psychology*. Chicago: Rand McNally, 1976.

Porter, L. W., & Smith, F. J. *The entiology of organizational commitment*. Unpublished manuscript, University of California, Irvine, 1970.

Porter, L. W., Steers, R. M., Mowday, R. T., & Boulian, P. Organizational commitment, job satisfaction, and turnover among psychiatric technicians. *Journal of Applied Psychology,* 1974, *59,* 603–609.

Rogers, E., & Rogers, R. *Communication in organizations.* New York: Free Press, 1976.

Schneider, B. Work climates: An interactionist perspective (tech. rep.). Michigan State University, 1981.

Sheldon, M. E. Investments and involvements as mechanisms producing commitment to the organization. *Administration Science Quarterly,* 1971, *16,* 142–150.

Steers, R. M. Antecedents and outcomes of organizational commitment. *Administrative Science Quarterly,* 1977, *22,* 46–56.

Steers, R. M., & Porter, L. W. The role of task–goal attributes in employee performance. *Psychological Bulletin,* 1974, *81,* 434–451.

Vroom, V. H. The effects of attitudes on perception of organizational goals. *Human Relations,* 1960, *13,* 229–240.

Vroom, V. H. *Work and motivation.* New York: Wiley, 1964.

Performance-Evaluation Systems in the Context of Individual Trust and Commitment

L. L. Cummings

Professor Steers and Mr. Lee have encouraged me to examine the relation among constructs like organizational climate, trust, and commitment on the one hand, and performance evaluation on the other.

As we all know, the first three of these constructs are fuzzy, even muddy, Thus, first I would like to attempt to clarify what I think the meanings of some of these constructs are. In particular, I would like to focus on the conceptual distinctions among climate, trust, and commitment if these are to be applied, at the individual level, to the analysis of performance-appraisal systems.

I see climate as the most generic of the three constructs, as the most difficult to define, and, therefore, as the least valuable of the three in analyzing performance-appraisal systems. Thus, I do not use it here.

I am going to conceptualize the concept of *trust* within organizations as the withdrawal of judgement by those participating within the organization. That is, trust is the psychological state of an individual when he or she withdraws a certain amount of critical capacity in accepting the directives, dictates, suggestions, and norms of an immediate supervisor or of organizational surveillance, in general. So, trust would be indicated when individuals say:

"I Believe in *what* we're trying to achieve—I know how, let me proceed with a minimum of direct surveillance." "I do not need to be checked with or checked upon at each step of the way."

"I am, in fact, trusting of the value premises and factual premises from which you are operating; that is, I am willing, within a reasonable zone, to withdraw discrete and immediate judgment."

Commitment, on the other hand, is conceptualized as an *intention,* particularly as an intention to remain in an organizational role and to fulfill role requirements. Conceptualizing commitment as an intention is the best way to distinguish it from a number of other constructs, more behaviorally based, with which we deal in organizational behavior and Industrial-Organizational (I. O.) psychology: absenteeism and turnover, for example.

I would like to first examine the effects of trust on performance-evaluation systems. Then I focus on theorizing about the effects of commitment on performance-evaluation systems, and finally, I speak about the reverse flow—that is, the *effects* of performance-evaluation systems on trust and commitment within organizations.

EFFECTS OF TRUST ON PERFORMANCE-EVALUATION SYSTEMS

Interpersonal trust and trust between individuals and organizations, I believe, reduces the necessity for performance evaluation as a *control* mechanism. Certainly some authors and some organizations conceive of performance evaluation as primarily a monitoring system and a feedback system aimed at minimizing the deviance of actual from expected behavior. In that context, performance evaluation is primarily being thought of and operated as a *control* mechanism. The withdrawal of continuous judgment, the relaxation of unceasing critical capacity, and the willingness to accept value and factual premises on the part of a participant in an organization will reduce the necessity for performance appraisal to operate in such a role.

Trust also increases the likelihood that performance-evaluation systems will be *future* oriented and will focus on *developmental* processes. Performance-evaluation systems can be conceived of as either performance-*planning* mechanisms or as performance-*measuring* technologies. Performance-planning functions anchor perceptions of appraisers and appraisees into the *future.* That is, in fact, using performance evaluation as an expectation-generation method. Performance evaluation can also be thought of as serving a developmental purpose for individuals relating to career planning or development on the immediate and present job. I believe that as trust increases among management and employees and across organizational levels within management, the likelihood that performance evaluation will be used in a productive manner for purposes of emphasizing the future orientation of performance planning *and* for developmental purposes (as opposed to evaluative and administrative purposes in implementing reward systems), will increase. That is, as trust increases, the likelihood that performance evaluation will be used in those fashions likewise increases.

EFFECTS OF COMMITMENT ON
PERFORMANCE- EVALUATION SYSTEMS

Now let me comment about some of the theoretical relations between commitment to organizations and performance-evaluation systems. Again, I am viewing commitment as an intention to remain in a role and to fulfill role requirements in an organization.

Commitment reduces the perception of performance-evaluation systems as *directing* mechanisms operating on employee behavior. That is, as individuals increase their intentions to remain in an organization and to fulfill their role responsibilities, the relevance of performance evaluation as a directing mechanism decreases. The reasons for increased commitment are frequently unrelated to performance appraisal as a causal mechanisms (e.g., external forces such as labor market conditions, or an individual's identification with an organization's goal either intrinsically or instrumentally). This decreased relevance of performance evaluation as a directing mechanism should be particularly strong as individuals expand the time horizon of their career intentions and career planning. To put this another way, performance-evaluation systems as directing mechanisms will become much less relevant, employees and supervisors will pay much less attention to doing performance appraisals and doing them accurately. They are, in fact, less relevant or (in the case of extremely highly committed individuals) largely irrelevant mechanisms for directing day to day behavior in organizations.

Secondly, commitment reduces the need for performance evaluation as a *control* mechanism (e.g., as a mechanism for administering compensation). As commitment in organizations increases, it becomes less important to make fine-grained distinctions among performers or about a performer over time across a performance history. And it becomes less likely (and perhaps less important) that performance appraisals will be used as the primary mechanism for administering compensation. Thus, commitment reduces the need for performance evaluation as a control mechanism in an organization.

This is because as the intention to remain in an organization and to fulfill role requirements derives from sources other than the contingency between performance and pay, then the use of external mechanisms like performance appraisal to generate and sustain behavior becomes less important. In fact, it is not by accident that in many American companies that are being described as "Japanese-like" (i.e., chacterized by high commitment, long career cycles, infrequent use of external labor markets above entry-level managers, and longevity as a typical ingredient in reaching top management) a combination exists of: high employee commitment, little external search behavior by employees, *and* the very infrequent use of performance appraisals as a control *mechanism*. Performance appraisal is certainly used, but it is more likely to be used for career planning, for developmental purposes, and as an input into career mapping.

In sum, I am arguing that commitment reduces the perception of (and need for) the performance-appraisal system as a *directive* mechanism, and commitment also reduces the need for performance appraisal as a *control* mechanism.

Thus, management actions that enhance commitment can be expected to decrease the *need* for psychometrically sound performance-evaluation systems and, even when such systems are available, to decrease the frequency of their acceptance and use by line managers, place personnel staff and industrial psychologists in the ''warden's role'' (i.e., as an enforcer), thus reinforcing the most negative stereotype of these staff personnel held by significant line managers.

Trust and commitment on the one hand and psychometrically sound, tight, professional evaluation systems, on the other hand, can be considered as substitutes for one another.

EFFECTS OF PERFORMANCE-EVALUATION SYSTEMS ON TRUST AND COMMITMENT

If the substitution effects operate as here hypothesized, then effective performance-evaluation systems imply the need for less concern with trust and commitment as relevant dependent variables in organizational behavior. If behavioral direction and control are sustained via performance-evaluation systems, then trust and commitment as alternative strategies to attain such goals are less important. Trust and commitment will be considered as less relevant determinants of behavior. They will also be considered as less susceptible to managerial control when managerial attention and effort are focused on developing tight, psychometrically sound performance-appraisal technologies.

Secondly, to the extent that trust and commitment remain even minimally relevant, sound, well-developed appraisal systems will clarify the basis for an individual's judgments concerning the degree of trust and commitment that he or she should have in a supervisor or in the organization. Of course, this clarification of the basis for trust and commitment does not imply that the mean levels of trust and commitment will rise as performance-evaluation systems become more technically sound. This clarification process does imply, however, that the bases for self-selection into the organization and organizational socialization processes become clearer, sooner.

It is likely that for organizational rookies and participants of low tenure, performance-evaluation systems (and their implementation) send explicit clues about the bases for trust and commitment within an organization. The following four issues concerning the design and application of an appraisal system are particularly telling with regard to the degree and nature of trust and commitment that an individual can wisely invest in an organization:

1. Is performance appraisal focused on the methods of doing the job or on the outcomes produced in the job? It is hypothesized that focusing on outcomes will be associated with greater individual trust and commitment.

2. Are self-appraisals encouraged, merely tolerated, ignored, or discouraged? Practices that encourage and use self-appraisals in the performance-evaluation system are hypothesized to be associated with trust and commitment.

3. How many managerial levels must "sign off" on written appraisals prior to their becoming a part of an individual's personnel file and prior to their being fed back to the performer? It is hypothesized that the fewer the levels beyond the immediate supervisor who are involved, the greater the appraisee's trust and commitment.

4. Are the results of appraisals fed back to appraisees? If so, it is hypothesized that such practice will enhance appraisee trust and commitment.

In conclusion, I am convinced that performance appraisal, as a subject of professional scholarship and practice, is most likely to be taken seriously by leaders of organizations when it is emphasized as being interdependent with trust and commitment by organizations. It is much less likely to be an item of high priority when it is seen as a technocratic or measurement issue, or as the domain of the personnel staff. To me, this invites a shift towards a supplementary perspective in future research on performance appraisal. The available methods, issues, and underlying models driving most of the current research on appraisal will need to be supplemented. Appraisal as an organizational practice, as a signal about organizational values, and as a method of socialization constitute a worthy agenda for the 1980s.

II

INDIVIDUAL
CONSIDERATIONS

The most traditional approach to performance definition and measurement has depended on various aspects of differential psychology for a foundation. Thus, from this perspective one might consider individual differences in performers and evaluators. Decades ago, these differences would have been things such as tenure, organizational level, and experience. Today, the differences that are examined are much more dynamic and psychological in nature. They include subjective interpretation of the evaluator, biases, stereotypes, cognitive complexity, and similar variables. This section deals with issues concerning the individual differences that the performer and the evaluator bring to the assessment situation.

Palermo presents a broad cognitive approach to the issue of how each of us interprets our world. Borman borrows heavily from personality theory and social judgment theory to suggest some novel interpretations of the evaluation process. Mohrman and Lawler consider the implications of motivation theory for performance definition and assessment. Finally, O'Leary and Hansen consider mechanisms such as attribution processes and self-fulfilling prophecies, which are examples of evaluators' individual-difference characteristics that systematically influence their evaluations.

5 Cognition, Concepts, and an Employee's Theory of the World

David S. Palermo

Palermo proposes a theory of the mind that describes how people assign meaning to events. He suggests that individuals have theories of the world that allow them to interpret or impose meaning to ambiguous stimuli, and that this theory is fallible and subject to revision. In addition, individuals are not necessarily aware of their theories, and the theories are not always logically consistent.

Effective performance evaluation requires that we take into account how each person views him- or herself in relation his or her work, and that we consider the subordinate's perception of the performance instrument. Consistent with Mohrman and Lawler, Palermo states that the supervisor and the subordinate hold different theories of the world and that these theories change when one moves from the worker to the supervisor position. Palermo concludes that the only way to resolve the difference in theories of the world is through communication.

Dr. Higgins elaborates on some of the implications of Palermo's theoretical framework for personnel evaluation from the perspective of social cognition. In particular, Higgins discusses the possible biases involved in supervisors' evaluations of personnel and the potential problems with using questionnaires as evaluation instruments within the frameworks of the holistic and the elementistic approaches to social cognition. He also offers suggestions for improving evaluation accuracy. Higgins states that responding to questionnaires requires retrieval of information from memory and that the evaluator's response may be influenced by the type of information retrieval, the accessibility of the information, the interpretation of the information, and the impact of the formal communication in the written mode on the retrieved information.

My plan for the following discussion is to propose a conceptual framework that may help to integrate some of the concepts presented in other papers in this volume. I hope to bring together the ideas presented by Borman on implicit personality theory and personal construct theory, Lawler and Mohrman on differences in manager–subordinte definitions of performance-appraisal situations, Locke on the values of jobs being in the valuer, Shweder on surface-structure analyses and evaluation of tacit knowledge, and Schmidt on the need for theory as a prerequisite for doing performance appraisal. I want to bring these bits and pieces together within one general theoretical framework that focuses upon accounting for meaning. Once I have explicated the theory, I consider how the theory may be utilized to account for some of the pragmatic issues related to personnel performance and evaluation.

As an outsider to the field of Industrial-Organizational (I.-O.) psychology, prior to preparing this paper, I tried to get some feel for the issues and concerns of those working in the I.-O. area, with particular focus upon personnel performance, measurement and selection. As I read various papers, I was struck by a feeling of déjà vu. As a developmental psychologist who was trained in the mid 1950s at Iowa, I remember clearly the concern of my professors that developmental psychologists lacked any systematic theory. There was no lack of data collection but there seemed to be no way to hold all the data together, no conceptual glue to allow one study to be related to another. As Barker (1951), Nowlis and Nowlis (1952), and McCandless and Spiker (1956) noted at that time, developmental psychology was atheoretical and, therefore, searching but failing to find an understanding of the developmental phenomenon. Perhaps Keller, an animal researcher asked to speak to a group of developmental psychologists, put it best when he said (Keller, 1950): "... an understanding of behavior ... cannot be expected in the absence of theory. If it is not one theory, it will have to be another. There is no escaping an ultimate organization of the facts."

Although I refrain from drawing out similarities and differences between developmental and I.-O. psychology in two different eras, the points about theory that Keller was trying to make in 1950 are as important today as they were then. Theory is a prerequisite to the understanding of behavior—whether it be that of the child or that of the employee in a working situation. Theory is the conceptual framework that allows us to relate one behavior to another by providing systems of classifications and relations. More specifically, theory provides the meaning that we give to the empirical events we observe. It is, for example, your theory of what is important to job success that leads you to examine one behavior rather than another or to use one moderator variable rather than another. You have a conceptual framework that suggests that one variable, whether it be a behavioral event or a personal characteristic, is more important to job success than another. When I say more important, I mean closer to the meaning you have for what job success is.

Thus, my goal here is to provide a theory, from the perspective of a cognitive psychologist, that may provide a meaningful way to conceptualize personnel performance, measurement, and selection. The theory I propose is antithetical to that with which Keller would be comfortable. He is an empiricist in a strong behaviorist tradition. He was an operant, reinforcement theorist who focused upon the effects of reinforcement on behavior. He focused on what a cognitive psychologist would call the surface manifestations of behavior and observable stimulus control. By surface structure I mean that Keller's theory was concerned only with the directly observable. He tried to avoid the abstract. For example, if a reward did not lead to an increase in the probability of a response, then the theory led Keller to ask questions about the stimulus conditions, response variables, or alternative rewarding events. The theory of a cognitive psychologist would, in contrast, lead to questions regarding meaning. To say that reinforcement affects behavior is to assume that the reinforcing event has some meaning for the organism whose behavior is affected. When behavior is unaffected by what a researcher defines as a reward, it follows from a cognitive viewpoint that the concept of reward is not the same for the researcher and for the individual whose behavior was unaffected by the reward. For example, a pat on the back by a supervisor may be given as a reward to a worker but it might be interpreted not as a reward but as an encouragement to work harder by the employee. The stimulus event is the same in both cases, but the meaning of that event differs for the two persons. Thus, the cognitive psychologist relates behavior to the meaning of events for the individuals involved.

Cognitive Research Approach

The question of meaning, however, leads to questions that are not manifest in stimuli and responses. Consideration of meaning requires us to deal with what has come to be known as deep structure as opposed to surface structure. The notion of deep structure was introduced most recently to psychologists by Chomsky (e.g., 1957) in connection with language. By deep structure Chomsky means the underlying mental structure and processes from which the surface or observable manifestations of behavior are derived. Chomsky was arguing for what Hayek (1952, 1969) has called the primacy of the abstract. Both men, as well as Piaget, argued that the study of the abstract, not the concrete and observable, should be the focus of our work. Cognitive theorists have accepted that presupposition and, in so doing, have been attempting in recent years to develop theories about mind and not about behavior.

It should be clear, however, that in focusing upon a theory of mind and, therefore, rejecting the behavioristic paradigm, as a cognitive theorist, I am not rejecting the empirical. I am rejecting empiricism in the form proposed by the philosophy called logical empiricism. Research must continue for it is the interaction of research and theory development that leads to advances in science.

The difference between research done in a behavioristic framework and that done in a cognitive framework lies in the questions asked and the interpretations made of the data: One focuses on the abstract structure and processes of mind whereas the other focuses on the empirical relationships between directly observable environmental and behavioral events. Concern with mind requires emphasis on deep structure rather than on surface structure. It requires theories of how the mind creates and assigns meanings to stimuli rather than how the mind obtains meaning from stimuli. The behaviorist paradigm, or global conceptual framework, presupposes that meaning is out there in the environment to be picked up or learned, whereas the cognitive paradigm assumes that meaning is constructed by the person and is attributed to the environment out there. In short, cognitive psychology is paradigmatically incompatible and irreconcilable with behaviorism.

If we reject behaviorism, however, we are immediately faced with the task of constructing an alternative framework within which we can approach a characterization of the mind and a kind of research program that will sustain such a characterization. Thus, I turn to another presupposition, more specifically theoretical, that leads me directly into a theory of mind.

Ambiguity of Stimuli

The theoretical presupposition is that all stimuli are ambiguous with respect to meaning. Our environment is filled with an indefinitely large array of sensory material that we may examine and to which we may assign meanings. That world of stimuli is an ambiguous world in the sense that each of those stimuli may have an indefinite number of meanings. Exactly the same stimulus may have multiple meanings across individuals at the same point in time or across time for the same individual. In addition, different stimuli may have the same meaning to an individual at a particular point in time. For example, the meaning of ''boys'' is quite different for preadolescent and adolescent girls, and the meaning changes dramatically for any individual girl as she changes developmentally. Similarly a cigarette and an iron may have the meaning of hot at one point in time but may mean light and heavy at a different point in time.

It seems to me that the major impact that the linguist Chomsky (e.g., 1963, 1968) has had upon psychology was to focus our attention upon ambiguity. Psychologists, of course, have not been unaware of ambiguity. Every introductory text has a section on such visual curiosities as the Nekker cube, the Ames rooms, and the duck–rabbit picture in the experimental section. In clinical psychology projective techniques derive their value from their ambiguity. Chomsky noted that sentences, too, are ambiguous. Chomsky, however, went beyond the empiricist's approach of analyzing the variables that may affect the probability of seeing the multiple meanings inherent in an ambiguity. His contribution was to provide a theoretical conceptualization of ambiguity so that we can understand how a person can create two different meanings for the same stimulus at two different times. He argued, for example, that an ambiguous sentence such as "They are visiting relatives." has two meanings because there are two underlying meanings or mental structures related to the surface form of the sentence. One meaning treats the word visiting as a verb in the sentence whereas the other treats visiting as an adjective modifying relatives. Those different relations, however, are not manifest in the surface form of the sentence. They exist only in the mental structure of the person producing or comprehending the sentence. Thus, Chomsky's theoretical advance involved a distinction between the surface, exemplary, or objective stimulus level of a phenomenon and the deep-structural, abstract, or mental level of a phenomenon. Chomsky's revolutionary suggestion was that the abstract is the basis of meaning and, therefore, the level at which our theoretical conceptions should be developed.

Despite the general acceptance by cognitive psychologists of Chomsky's approach, recognition of the implications of ambiguity has not been fully realized. Ambiguity of meaning is not a curiosity that can be studied as an isolated special case found only in, for example, peculiar visual or sentential forms. The work of Bransford and his colleagues (e.g., Bransford & McCarrell, 1974), for example, has demonstrated clearly that ambiguity is the rule rather than the exception. All stimuli can be interpreted in more than one meaningful way, and, therefore, all are particulars that are ambiguous.

Given that all stimuli are ambiguous with respect to meaning, we are then faced with accounting for how we deal theoretically with that ambiguity and for the observation that we seldom note such ambiguity. If everything impinging on our sensorium has multiple meanings, why is it that we generally note only a single meaning and proceed with infrequent awareness of alternative meanings? Many persons who have faced up to this problem have suggested that the ambiguity problem is solved for us by the context. We fail to note that a sentence, for example, is ambiguous because the sentence occurs in a context that points to or determines a particular meaning among the many possible meanings. Researchers who take this position typically try to demonstrate the different meanings an event may have in different contexts (e.g., Ortony, Schallert, Reynolds, & Antos, 1978). Having demonstrated that one context leads to one meaning of an ambiguous sentence, for example, and a different context leads to another meaning, they argue that the context disambiguates the ambiguous sentence. Thus, a theory that takes into account the context will have the power to account for the meaning of any particular stimulus. The problem with this approach is that it naturally leads to an infinite regress. Because the context itself is an ambiguous stimulus, it must be disambiguated by its context, which in turn must be disambiguated by its context, and so on. One must, by definition, know the whole in order to understand the meaning of any part. There is no way, in principle, that something that is itself ambiguous can disambiguate another ambiguity.

Given this state of affairs, the meanings of stimuli must be related at some more abstract level that takes into account the whole as well as the part. Because the stimuli can have multiple meanings and because the person who interprets those stimuli is usually aware of only one meaning, it seems clear that the disambiguation must come from the person attending to the stimulus and giving meaning to that stimulus. The constraints upon meaning, by which I mean the selection of one meaning from among the many possible meanings, must come from the person and not from the stimulus. In other words, people must have some basis for making a judgment about the meanings of the stimuli about them. They must have a framework at the abstract conceptual level that makes it possible to place a meaning—that is, an unambiguous interpretation—upon the individual stimulus events in their environment. In short, they must have what I have called elsewhere (Palermo, 1981) a theory of the world that allows them to interpret that world of stimuli.

A THEORY OF THE WORLD

A theory of the world is a conceptual structure used to interpret events, objects, and relations. It is no different, in principle, from a scientific theory that is constructed to interpret events, objects, and relations within a limited domain. We use our theories to make sense of our senses: to determine the particular meanings to be placed upon our empirical experiences that could have an indeterminate number of possible meanings. Thus, the world of stimuli is presented to us for our understanding and our understanding is created through the conceptual framework I am calling a theory of the world. Furthermore, that theory allows us to construct a systematic integration of all those empirical experiences.

If we accept the hypothesis that we interpret the events in our environment within the framework of our theories of the world, there are a variety of assumptions related to and implications that follow from that position. The first basic assumption is that the world can be rendered coherent, regular, and predictable. We presuppose that the world is dependable and can be understood in a meaningful way. Although there are some aspects of the world that we admit that we do not understand, we assume that there is some regularity, organization, or structure even if we cannot comprehend it at the moment. In principle, it is understandable despite our lack of knowledge or understanding at the moment. Thus, we assume a meaningful world and we construct the best account of it that we can, recognizing that our threoies (like all theories) may be fallible and, therefore, require revision.

Given the assumption of a meaningful world, it follows, for example, that when we speak to other persons, some meaning can be given to that empirical experience. Suppose that someone comes up to you in the work situation and says, "I have been watching you work. You are a bumble bee in a garden of flowers." Although you may be sure that you are not an insect and there are no flowers around, you will not interpret what has been said as crazy. Instead, you assume a kind of contractual relation between yourself and the speaker. The contract involves a commitment to be meaningful, to make sense, to be relevant, and to tell the truth (Grice, 1975). In short, you assume that the speaker is adhering to the contract, that there is some meaning that can be imposed upon the speaker's utterance, and you, therefore, create a meaning. As others have noted (e.g., Cutting & Proffitt, 1979; Proffitt, 1976), you do the same thing in all your interactions with the environment. The point is that all empirical experiences, including language, are assumed to have meaning and, therefore, it is up to the perceiver of the messages to assign a meaning to them.

It is clear, then, that the meaning resides in the perceiver and not in the empirical experience. We assume a world of stimuli that can be known and we attempt to come to know that world. The world has structure but the knower imposes the meaning upon that structure. Borrowing from Gibson (e.g., 1977), structure refers to the physical properties of the stimuli in the world as perceived within the limits of the capabilities of the person. But, as Gibson also notes, although structure derives from physical properties in concert with a particular person, meaning comes from the person alone. The knower does not derive meaning from the world, for there is no meaning out there to be picked up or received; rather there is a knowable structure to which meaning may be given. The person, therefore, comes to know the structure primarily through the senses and creates the meaning for that structure in terms of a theory of the world.

Shifting our attention now to the meanings imposed upon the world, it is clear that the meanings we attribute to objects and events are constructed within a framework that cannot always be correct. Thus, we interpret the environment in terms of the way it ought to be according to our theories and not necessarily as it is. Thus, the worker interprets the behavior of management within the framework of the worker's theory of the world whereas management views the same behavior from the perspective of their theories. Each of us makes certain assumptions about the world and predicate other aspects of our own theories on those assumptions. We make decisions and judgments, and act according to our theories of how we expect the world to be. In general, our theories are not contradicted and, therefore, we are in a position to assume confirmation of our conceptions of the manner in which the world operates. On other occasions, however, we find that our theories are not confirmed. Failure to confirm our theories leads to consideration of additional variables and/or revision of the theories. There is, therefore, an implicit recognition that our theories are fallible and the implication that our theories are modified as we continue to use them.

Consciousness and Logical Consistency

There are two additional points that should be made about our theories of the world. First, we are not necessarily aware of our theories and, second, the theories we hold are not necessarily logically consistent. Theories are based upon a set of presuppositions and consist of interrelated sets of rules that are used to make judgments about the world and guide behaviors in that world. We seldom examine those presuppositions and rules. Consider, for example, the task of riding a bicycle. In an important sense, we need to know a great deal about gravity and other principles of physics in order to achieve success in bicycle riding. Many of us would be hard put to consciously explicate what those principles are despite our skills in riding a bicycle. Bicycle riding, however, presupposes such knowledge as a part of our theories of the world and we are consciously aware of little of that theoretical knowledge even when we try to teach another person to ride.

Whereas I do not know the physics of riding a bicycle, I do know some of the rules of language that speakers of English use, again without awareness. Take a particularly simple example such as the rules that are required to produce the proper articulation of the past tense inflection of regular verbs in English. When you inflect a verb for past tense in English, you write an "ed" on the end of the verb stem, as in the case of the verbs rub, step, and seat. When you speak those verbs in the past tense, however, you articulate the "ed" written inflection in three different ways: rubbed, stepped, and seated. There is a set of rules you follow that take into account the preceding phoneme to determine the articulation of the tense inflection. You do not know the rules and you were never taught the rules, but you never make a mistake even when you learn a new verb. In the same sense, you cannot articulate the rules for how you make judgments or decisions. That is not to say that you do not give reasons for your decisions but we know that the relation between what people say about what they do and why they do it is not a valid source of the relevant rules used. The reason people cannot give valid reasons for their behavior is that they frequently do not know their decision rules at a conscious level, just as you do not know why you articulate "ed" in a particular way. If a child is asked why he or she does something the child may quite honestly answer "I don't know." An adult, on the other hand, will often try to provide a rationale. That rationale, as I have tried to indicate, is likely to have little to do with the relevant variables.

The second point I want to note has to do with the logical consistency of one's theory of the world. There is no reason to assume that a person's theory of the world should be devoid of inconsistencies. First, it is after all a theory of the world and even our renaissance scholars cannot take into account all of science, for example, in one theory. We break up science into separate areas with separate theories that are hardly consistent with each other. Why should we expect more of an individual? Individuals develop schemata, or theories, over limited domains that may not be logically consistent with schemata that they have developed in other limited domains. An individual's overall theory of the world may provide rules that allow for inconsistencies of schemata in different domains or the schemata will be changed when inconsistencies between schemata and the total theory become apparent to the person. For example, a person may have a principle that honesty is the best policy and conceive of him- or herself as an honest person. That same individual may, however, not return money to a large department store when an error is made in his or her favor, on an inconsistent principle that the store will never miss the amount involved or some other reason that one might call a rationalization. At another level, we know that children are able to conserve mass before they can conserve weight although the same principles are involved in both. Although the child can give a perfectly valid reason why mass does not change with variations in shape, that same child may not know that weight does not change under the same conditions. The lack of a totally logical system is evidenced at all levels of human development and in all spheres of cognition. Piaget has referred to a part of what is implied here in his concept of horizontal décalage, although I believe that a lack of logical consistency is broader than implied in his presentations. The rules for conceptualizing categories and relations are often limited to narrow domains and, even when more general, have lacunae that are unexpected by someone with a somewhat different theory.

As an aside, I might note that the two points about conscious awareness and logical consistency distinguish the theories of individuals from theories in science. The latter are efforts to make our accounts of particular domains both conscious and, therefore, explicit, as in the case of the linguist's account of past-tense inflection, and logically consistent so that we do not have areas within a domain that are accounted for in a manner inconsistent with other related observations in the domain. Theories of the world held by individuals are generally tacit and often logically inconsistent.

Sources of Our Theories

Our theories of the world, like scientific theories, are fallible. And, like scientific theories, our theories are subject to revision. Consideration of fallibility and of modification in our theories leads to issues related to the origin and development of our theories. It seems clear to me that we must have theories of the world from at least the time of birth. The newborn child must have a natural implicit system of rules for classifying and responding to his or her world. Otherwise the world of the infant would be the blooming, buzzing confusion suggested by James. Furthermore, the infant's behavior with respect to the world would be in a similar random state. Neither of these conditions appears to be characteristic of the infant.

One of the most important results that has come from the upsurge of research on infants during the past 20 years is the increasing realization of the conceptual capabilities with which the child enters the world. We have now become aware that the human infant can and does categorize the world of physically different objects into classes of objects that are treated as if they were the same. We know that some bases of classification are easier for the infant than others. In short, it appears that there are natural ways of classifying or theorizing about the objects and events in the world. Furthermore, we know that the concepts the infant possesses are prototypically structured—that is, some exemplars of the concepts are better exemplars than others.

Recent research summarized by Cohen and Younger (1981) has documented the amazing capacities of infants to classify faces, abstract symbols, and even classes of objects that have overlapping features. Furthermore, this research demonstrates that infants can classify on the basis of clusters of correlated features and not just single features of objects. It would appear that the infant possesses some organizational principles that are used to interpret and respond to the world in a meaningful way insofar as the infant is concerned. The child, as the adult, has a set of rules establishing abstract concepts and organizing those concepts in relations that allow the interpretation of concrete events and responses to those events. The theory from the very beginning is a grammar of the world and the person's relations to the world. Thus, the infant enters the world predisposed to order it in particular ways.

We also know from Cohen's research that those natural, intrinsic, or biologically based theories of the world change as the child develops. Those changes are also partially determined by biological or maturational developments of the child. In addition to the natural or biologically established predispositions to abstraction and changes in abstraction, we know that the child's environment influences conceptual categorization. The child's natural predispositions to classify and relate—that is, the child's initial theory—is modified by the specific empirical experiences encountered in the child's world. When the child's theory fails, the theory must be modified. For example, the child may classify animate objects as different from inanimate objects but subsequent experience with animate objects may force the child to make distinctions within the animate category for some purposes: Some are givers of food, some bite, and some merely pass into view and out again. Initially the child may treat them all as equivalent in the sense that they are all related in an abstract class or category and are, therefore, responded to in a similar manner. When a response fails to yield an expected outcome according to the child's theory, a revision in the theory is required. This process is a continuous one throughout the individual's lifetime.

Because the empirical experiences of different individuals vary, one might expect that we would have widely different theories of the world. Clearly that is not the case. The very fact that we can communicate with each other makes it obvious that our theories of the world have many commonalities. Although communication between individuals does break down at times due to differences in theoretical world views, for the most part the commonalities in conceptual systems across individuals allow meaningful communication. The commonalities within a species are assumed to be based at one level upon the commonalities that must exist in the biological structures of the organisms involved. In the same sense that dogs can communicate with dogs, chimps with chimps, and birds with birds, humans communicate with humans because each member of a species has a biological commonality that forms, in part, the basis for the theory of the world held by that species member. The genetic characteristics of humans passed from one generation to the next, and set in motion for the individual at the time of conception, establish part of the sensory equipment, central nervous system, and other biological characteristics that underlie the common structure we will impose upon our worlds. That common biological structure establishes, in part, the manner in which we will be predisposed to classify and to relate given any empirical experience. The biological structure constrains the theories we will develop. The natural conceptual base has, of course, evolved over time as the evolution of humans has taken place.

At a second, and not entirely independent, level, the commonalities in our theories of the world are made possible by the commonalities in the culture in which societal members are immersed. The cultural commonalities, too, have evolved over time as the evolution of society has taken place. The cultural characteristics of a society are passed from one generation to the next and establish, among other things, particular languages and the rules and practices of conduct and custom that govern the conceptualization of interactions among humans in groups.

Thus, biological and cultural commonalities act to constrain our theories of the world and provide a common base that allows for similar theories in different people. Variation in theories among people are brought about by individual differences in biological structure, cultural community, and specific individual experiences. Thus, variation comes about because the same experiences have different meanings for persons with different biological structures (for example, in children of different ages); variation results because the same experiences have different meanings for persons reared in different cultures (for example, consider the differences between the meaning placed on the events of the hostage crisis by Americans and Iranians); and variation results from differences in specific individual experiences over a lifetime.

Regardless of those variables that act to constrain and those that act to diversify, we all have theories of the world from the very beginning, abstract classification systems, presumably prototypic in structure, and systems of relating abstract classes. These conceptual frameworks allow us to understand the particulars of the world. They are systems of rules for making judgments about what is and what ought to be. The empirical experiences are organized and given meaning in terms of the concepts and relations of our cognitive systems. The cognitive systems have been referred to here as theories of the world. The theory of each individual makes it possible for the individual to create a meaning for the empirical experience and, thus, avoid the inherent ambiguity of that experience.

The theoretical framework I have proposed here is not unique to me. Variations on this theme have been proposed by others. Within psychology my position differs little from the theoretical framework proposed by Lewin (e.g.,

Lewin, 1946) to account for a child's intellectual and social development, Piaget's developmental theory of intelligence (e.g., Piaget, 1971), or, more recently, Beck's theory of depression (Beck, 1976). Each of these theorists has tried to conceptualize the manner in which the individual constructs an account of the world, which in turn determines the behavioral characteristics congruent with that conceptual construction.

APPLICATIONS OF THE THEORY TO PERSONNEL WORK

Now, if you have followed my reasoning up to this point and you are willing to accept my theoretical framework for conceptualizing the cognitive characteristics of the human, you may well ask what implications an abstract theory of the world has for the theoretical and pragmatic issues with which one must be concerned as a personnel psychologist. Given the task of appraising the performance of a worker and the subsequent decisions that such appraisal entails, how does this theoretical formulation pertain? It seems to me that there are a variety of immediately obvious issues of concern. Assuming that whatever appraisal or measurement techniques we use are reliable, the primary problems revolve about validity in terms of establishing what are the best predictors, the important work criteria, the most useful placements of individuals, and the most beneficial and efficient training procedures that may create a work force in which the individual can achieve satisfaction and is motivated to work at a consistently high level.

If I am correct in stating these goals, we need to take into consideration how each person in the particular work situation conceptualizes him- or herself with respect to his or her position in the work groups, and relation to those above and below within the social structure of the minisociety that is the work force in that situation. Obviously, performance skill is a variable of considerable importance in any job but, from a cognitive perspective, one must also evaluate the individual's conception of him- or herself, the job, his or her performance and that of others, and his or her motivation within the job context.

My effort here is to provide a few examples of how the theory outlined up to this point might make contact with the pragmatic concerns of the personnel psychologist faced with the problem of researching the issues and making the necessary decisions required in the work situation.

The Meaning of an Evaluation Instrument

Consider, for example, the meaning of a personnel-evaluation instrument for two employees in a firm. Depending on their theories of the world, or the work situation in particular, one worker may view the instrument as a tool used by management to prevent the employee from advancing in the ranks of the firm.

This employee construes management as placing roadblocks in the way of the employee and the evaluation instrument is a technique to achieve that goal. This employee may see no relationship between the instrument and the nature of the job. As Landy and Trumbo (1980) have pointed out "There is often little explicit relationship between job analysis and objective indices of performance . . . [p. 113]." Another employee, in contrast, may view the evaluation instrument as a means to be used in achieving advancement. Performance on the job may be a long-range method for job advancement but doing well on the evaluation instrument is a quicker technique for getting ahead in the job context. Viewed from the perspective of a manager or plant supervisor, the same instrument may be conceived as having little to do with individuals. Such a person may view it only as a technique for achieving greater productivity for the firm. A personnel psychologist may view the same instrument as an unreliable and invalid test. Note that the stimulus has not changed in any of these cases. It is the same evaluation instrument in all cases but it has different meanings for each individual depending on the theory of the world held by each person. Given two personnel-evaluation instruments, both may be viewed in the same way by the employee but differently by the manager—for example, because one is easier to administer—and still differently by the psychologist who could consider one as valid and the other not. The stimuli have not changed—only the meanings imposed upon them by the persons involved.

Although I have been focusing upon the instrument as a whole, the same applies for each component of the instrument. If the instrument consists of test items, the question of interpretation arises with respect to each item. Not only are the words of which the items are constructed ambiguous, but the conception of the item itself as a whole may be ambiguous. In order to evaluate an evaluation instrument one needs to know how the person being evaluated construes the scale and items within the scale, and the use to which the scale will be put. What meaning is being imposed upon this environmental event by those who are taking it and those who are using it? These questions arise regardless of whether the evaluation instrument consists of an evaluation of production data, personnel data, judgmental rating scales, checklists, or combinations of these and other instruments.

Turning to a different aspect of the evaluation procedure, consider the problem faced by the supervisor who must provide an evaluation of his or her subordinates. As a rule a supervisor can probably do a reasonable job of evaluation. If you ask the supervisor, however, to justify his or her evaluations, there may be a serious breakdown in the evaluation when looked at objectively. The supervisor has an implicit or tacit knowledge of why one employee is better than another but when forced to make explicit the criteria used to make the decision, it is likely to turn out that the supervisor's objective application of those criteria will lead to misclassification of those employees. There are two problems here. First, the supervisor is not fully aware at a conscious level of what makes a good worker, although he or she is capable of making that decision on the basis of knowledge that is tacit in nature. Second, the analysis of a good worker, like any other global concept, is not subject to analysis into features or parts that add up to the whole when broken down. To take another example, we could ask how we know a car when we see one. One can list all of the features of which a car is composed: wheels, seats, engine, gasoline, fenders, and so on. The problem is that those features do not make a car if they are all laid out on the ground. It is only when the parts are put together in the proper relationships that we would concede that the item is a car. Furthermore, some features are more important than others. In the case of a person filling a job, the same analysis applies. It is further complicated by the fact that some features may be absent, and because other features are present in larger amounts or in relation to other features, a person with some criterial features absent may be evaluated more highly than someone with all the features present. Job analysis requires job synthesis in order to achieve full evaluation of what workers are achieving in their positions.

It should also be noted that the evaluation of workers may rely more heavily on tacit knowledge the higher is the job level in the industrial setting. At the level of an assembly line, one may be able to use criteria such as arriving on time, rapid performance, lack of complaints, and related so-called objective, or consciously specifiable, criteria to evaluate a worker. Even here, however, the worker's esprit de corps, for example, may be important to the total productivity of the assembly-line group. The latter is more problematic to evaluate. As you move up the employment ladder, however, evaluation relies more and more heavily on less and less objective measures and, therefore, more and more reliance is placed on tacit knowledge of the employee and the job.

Memory and Evaluation

Before leaving the supervisor's evaluation, we might consider another component of the supervisor's task. Most evaluation is based on events that have occurred in the past. Given the task of remembering from this point of view, a person must reconstruct events that are relevant to the conceptualization the person has about the information to be remembered. A supervisor, asked to justify a judgment about a person, is placed in the position of having to construct events in the past that fit with the judgment whether that is the explicit task or not. Consider, for example, the request to indicate whether person X is honest. If you respond in the affirmative you must construct a justification of that response in terms of events that support that decision. Given that the concept of honesty is an abstract concept for which the rules are only tacitly known for any individual, and that exemplars of honesty by almost any tacit set of rules are hard to come by, one is placed in the difficult position of providing a conscious rationale for a decision based on only tacitly known principles. One is forced to bring to consciousness events in the past that were initially incorporated into one's theory about the person involved and are relevant to the honesty dimension. If one has been concerned with classifying behaviors of the person in terms of the category of honesty, that may be easy, but if not, it may be difficult. Thus, it may be easy to recall—that is, reconstruct—exemplars to justify honesty if that is a category used by the supervisor in dealing with his or her personnel. If not, the supervisor is placed in the position of justifying a judgment with no explicit recall or by construction of events that seem irrelevant or are false in the sense of never having objectively occurred. What is being implied here is that the recall cue of "honesty" is a good cue for recall only insofar as honesty is a classificatory basis for identifying behavior to begin with by the person asked to search his or her schema for that person. A person asked to evaluate another person must therefore be familiar enough with the evaluation instrument in advance to know how to classify the behavior of the person to be evaluated at a later time.

What should be clear here is that we are dealing with an abstract system of rules that operate at a tacit level. It is at this level that decisions and judgments are made. The very act of requiring an objective evaluation, however, forces a conscious effort to bring to bear explicit objective criteria on the decision. The decision, however, is neither consciously made nor based upon consicously known criteria. The decision is never fully justifiable because there are always variables that are not considered consciously (or even unconsciously) because they are not relevant to the decision being made within the theoretical framework held by the person making the judgment. In the case of judgments about honesty, some persons will make better judgments—that is, more valid judgments—because the theories they hold are based on rules or principles that properly weigh the knowledge available in making the decision. In no case, however, will the decisions be perfect because the rules are principles that apply across many specific empirical circumstances that cannot all be known or taken into account. Decisions can be no more exact in their validity than predictions based upon the laws of physics can be exact in predicting the fall of a leaf from a tree. A leaf may follow a rather devious route including rising before hitting the ground, just as a person judged as honest may deviate from the principles used to guide the behaviors exhibited. Exact prediction is an elusive criterion never to be achieved.

Evaluations and Theories

Turning now to a different matter, let us consider more fully the effect of different theories of the world upon evaluations. There are two types of issues I discuss: One has to do with differences in theories held by evaluator and evaluee, and the second relates to changes in theories when one moves from worker to supervisor.

If we consider the theory of the world held by the evaluator and that held by the employee, there are good reasons to expect that there may be significant differences in each one's world views that could create a variety of problems. Consider the world from the perspective of a person at the bottom of a job scale looking up, as opposed to someone above looking down. There are likely to be differences in educational level and experience, differences in cultural background, differences in levels of aspiration, and differences in sex, among other factors, that would bring about differences in theories of the world held by persons in different positions. With that in mind, consider the differences in theories of the world that may be held by a white employee evaluated by a black supervisor, or vice versa. Not only are there predjudicial complications introduced by the exceptions to one's theory about people in general that are applied to subgroups of people but, and perhaps this is more important, there may be wide cultural differences that would affect judgments in both directions. Although there may be greater similarities between whites and blacks immersed in the culture of this country than between either blacks and other blacks or whites and other whites reared in different countries, there are certainly cultural differences between whites immersed in a white culture and blacks immersed in a black culture in this country. I mention only a few well-documented differences to illustrate. First, black and white language dialects differ (Burling, 1973). Differences in language can affect what one thinks of another person. There is good evidence that language influences evaluations and interpretations of other characteristics of individuals even when there is no objective difference between speakers (Lambert, Hodgson, Gardner, & Fillenbaum, 1960). At a more subtle level, dialect differences have been shown to relate to spelling errors (McCardle, 1980). When they err in spelling speakers of different dialects make different types of errors. The errors made by speakers of one dialect are likely to be viewed by speakers of another dialect as incomprehensible and, therefore, might be interpreted as reflecting lower intellectual levels.

There are other differences in culture, too, that revolve around the family and the values that are learned within the communities of blacks and whites (Washington & McLoyd, 1982). As with all cultural differences, these differences are rooted in past history. The point of raising the issue here is that people exhibit behaviors that derive from the rules that are appropriate to their cultures. When those same behaviors are viewed from the perspective of people raised in other cultures, the interpretation or meaning given to the same empirical experience may be markedly different. There is some evidence, incidentally, that blacks are bicultural and, therefore, likely to be able to adopt two cultural theoretical positions, whereas whites are influenced by only one culture (Washington & McLoyd, 1980). The bicultural black may, therefore, be able to perceive ambiguity of meaning more easily than the white. There is also evidence that aspects of black culture are being assimilated to white culture as well as the reverse, which has been occurring for a long time. Whites are incorporating black dialect, for example, into white dialect (Labov, 1970). It should be clear, however, that these superficial modifications in white culture to incorporate the black is no substitute for understanding black culture.

The second aspect of the differences in theories of the world I wish to note has to do with change. There are many stories and jokes about how persons change when they move from faculty positions to dean positions, worker to supervisor, noncom to officer, and so on. Such stories reflect the fact that individuals who change positions change their theories of the world. To take a simple example, the comradery that is important among workers may be manifest in behaviors viewed by a supervisor as interfering with productivity. There may be little similarity in conceptualization of the job from the point of view of worker and supervisor. The successful supervisor is likely to be one who can continue to hold the theory of the worker in mind as he or she shifts to the framework acquired and required as a supervisor. Such a person will be able to anticipate the meanings placed on events in the employment situation even when he or she places a different meaning on those events. Recognizing the ambiguity of events for persons holding different viewpoints, knowing which meanings different persons place on specific events, and being able to use that knowledge in constructive ways may be separate skills. Such skills surely are primarily tacitly known but all are likely to be important to achieve a successful transition from one position to another. It seems to me that labor–management disputes are often due to the failure to recognize and deal with differences in theories of the world held by the two sides. Even labor leaders seem to have lost contact with their own members these days, creating situations in which leaders and workers are viewing political issues from quite different perspectives.

In conclusion, let me suggest that the only way in which these issues of differences in theories of the world can be resolved is through communication. Communication will never resolve all issues but the only way you can know that my interpretation of events differs from your is if I try to communicate that to you and you try to communicate to me. Simply telling, however, will not do the job because neither of us takes all varibles into account in explaining and, therefore, no explanation can be complete (Weimer, 1979). The rhetorical exchange, however, will force, at a minimum, a consideration of an alternative view. Such consideration forces a new conceptualization that is not only the manner in which conceptual or theoretical progress is made in science but also in the worker's theory of the world regardless of the level of that worker in the employment hierarchy. One must first recognize that differences exist and then try to understand the nature of those differences by communicative exchange. As Kuhn (1970) has pointed out in relation to scientific theories, the task is not a simple one. If we are to succeed in the task of science, in general, and specifically in the evaluation of personnel performance, we must recognize that individual workers have theories of the world that differ from ours. We cannot expect to succeed in the task without some knowledge of those theories. I hope this presentation of one cognitive psychologist's theory of the world will help in that endeavor.

I have attempted here to present a cognitive psychologist's perspective on personnel performance and evaluation. This effort has focused on the need for theory to provide a conceptual framework that allows a synthesis of the performance-evaluation situation. The specific theory presented focused on the manner in which we come to place meaning upon the individual events that make up our empirical experiences. The theory takes into consideration the inherent ambiguity of all those empirical experiences and resolves those ambiguities by postulating that each individual interprets those events in terms of his or her personal theory of the world. The theory an individual uses to assign meaning to personal experiences derives from three sources: the biological structure, cultural mileau, and individual experiences of the individual. Although individual theories are under revision throughout the life span, commonalities and differences in theories across individuals may be traced to the same three sources. The last section of the paper indicated some implications that application of the theoretical framework has for pragmatic concerns in the field of personnel evaluation.

REFERENCES

Baker, R. G. Child psychology. In C. P. Stone & D. W. Taylor (Eds.), *Annual review of psychology*. Stanford, California: Annual Reviews, Inc., 1951.

Beck, A. T. *Cognitive therapy and the emotional disorders*. New York: International Universities Press, 1976.

Bransford, J. D., & McCarrell, N. S. A sketch of a cognitive approach to comprehension: Some thoughts about understanding what it means to comprehend. In W. B. Weimer & D. S. Palermo (Eds.), *Cognition and the symbolic processes*. Hillsdale, N.J.: Lawrence Erlbaum Associates, 1974.

Burling, R. *English in black and white*. New York: Holt, Rinehart, & Winston, 1973.

Chomsky, N. *Syntactic structures*. The Hague: Mouton, 1957.

Chomsky, N. *Aspects of a theory of syntax*. Cambridge, Mass.: MIT Press, 1963.

Chomsky, N. *Language and mind*. New York: Harcourt, Brace, 1968.

Cohen, L. B., & Younger, B. A. *Perceptual categorization in the infant*. Paper presented at the Eleventh Annual Jean Piaget Symposium, Philadelphia, 1981.

Cutting, J. E., & Proffitt, D. R. *Modes and mechanisms in the perception of speech and other events*. Unpublished paper, 1979.

Gibson, J. J. The theory of affordances. In R. Shaw & J. Bransford (Eds.), *Perceiving, acting, and knowing*. Hillsdale, N.J.: Lawrence Erlbaum Associates, 1977.

Grice, H. P. Logic and conversation. In P. Cole and J. L. Morgan (Eds.), *Syntax and semantics Vol. 3: Speech acts*. New York: Academic Press, 1975.

Hayek, F. A. *The sensory order. An inquiry into the foundations of theoretical psychology*. Chicago: University of Chicago Press, 1952.

Hayek, F. A. The primacy of the abstract. In A. Koestler & J. R. Smythies (Eds.), *Beyond reductionism*. New York: Macmillan, 1969.

Keller, F. S. Animals and children. *Child Development*, 1950, *21*, 7–12.

Kuhn, T. S. *The structure of scientific revolutions*. Chicago: University of Chicago Press, 1970.

Labov, W. The logic of nonstandard English. In F. Williams (Ed.), *Language and poverty*. Chicago: Markham, 1970.

Lambert, W. E., Hodgson, R. C., Gardner, R. C., & Fillenbaum, S. Evaluational reactions to spoken language. *Journal of Abnormal and Social Psychology*, 1960, *60*, 44–51.

Landy, F. J., & Trumbo, D. A. *Psychology of work behavior*. Homewood, Ill.: Dorsey, 1980.

Lewin, K. Behavior and development as a function of the total situation. In L. Carmichael (Ed.), *Manual of child psychology*. New York: Wiley, 1946.

McCandless, B. R., & Spiker, C. C. Experimental research in child psychology. *Child Development*, 1956, *27*, 78–80.

McCardle, P. *Spelling ability as a reflection of underlying phonological form in black English vernacular*. Unpublished doctoral dissertation, The Pennsylvania State University, 1980.

Nowlis, V., & Nowlis, H. H. Child psychology. E. P. Stone & D. W. Taylor (Eds.), *Annual review of psychology*. (aby: publisher,) 1952. Stanford, California: Annual Reviews, Inc. 1952.

Ortony, A., Schallert, D. L., Reynolds, R. E., & Antos, S. J. Interpreting metaphors and idioms: Some effects of context on comprehension. *Journal of Verbal Learning and Verbal Behavior*, 1978, *17*, 465–477.

Palermo, D. S. Theoretical issues in semantic development. In S. Kuczaj (Ed.), *Language development: Syntax and semantics*. Hillsdale, N.J.: Lawrence Erlbaum Associates, 1981.

Piaget, J. *Biology and knowledge*. Chicago: University of Chicago Press, 1971.

Proffitt, D. R. *Demonstrations to investigate the meaning of everyday experience*. Unpublished doctoral dissertation, The Pennsylvania State University, 1976.

Washington, E. D. & McLoyd, V. C. The external validity of research involving American minorities. *Human Development*, 1982.

Weimer, W. B. Psychotherapy and philosophy of science. In M. J. Mahoney (Ed.), *Psychotherapy process*. New York: Plenum, 1979.

Effort after Meaning in Personnel Evaluation: The "Similarity Error" and Other Possible Sources of Bias

E. Tory Higgins

The major theme of Palermo's paper is that it is not external stimuli per se that determine observers' responses or judgments, but, rather, it is the subjective, phenomenological meaning of the stimuli to the observer. People are motivated to actively create and assign meaning to stimuli—the "effort after meaning" (Bartlett, 1932)—rather than simply to be passive receptors of the meaning inherent in stimuli. As a social psychologist, I am very comfortable with Palermo's constructivistic, phenomenological orientation because this orientation has had a long history in social psychology—from Lewin, Asch, Heider, and the "New Look" in perception to current models of attribution and social cognition (e.g., Cantor & Kihlstrom, 1981; Higgins, Herman, & Zanna, 1981; Jones & Davis, 1965; Kelley, 1967; Schachter & Singer, 1962).

Indeed, Palermo's theoretical framework involves a number of assumptions that have also been made by social psychologists. First, all stimuli are ambiguous with respect to meaning. Second, the same stimulus may have multiple meanings across individuals at the same point in time or across time for the individual. Third, disambiguation must come not simply from the context in which the stimulus occurs but also, or mainly, from the person attending to the stimulus and giving meaning to the stimulus. Fourth, people assume a meaningful world and construct the best account of it they can from the theories of the world they possess for intepreting the world of stimuli. Fifth, a person's environment influences conceptual categorization. Thus, differences in current context as well as long-term differences in specific individual experiences contribute to variation across individuals in categorization and judgment.

A final assumption made by Palermo is very important but is, unfortunately, given too little emphasis in current models of social cognition: Theories of individuals involve tacit knowledge about the world, are recognized as potentially fallible, and are continually modified as they are used. That is, our interpretive theories are those "fantasies that work," and, people must be "data-driven" as well as "theory-drive." Social psychologists tend to focus almost exclusively on the *assimilation* aspect of adaptation to the environment, whereas Palermo, following the developmental tradition, gives equal weight to the *accommodation* aspect of adaptation. There may, indeed, be an increase with age in the relative importance of assimilation, but the field of social cognition has suffered from paying too little attention to the accommodation or "data-driven" aspect of person perception.

In the remainder of his paper, Palermo applies his theoretical framework to various practical concerns of the personnel psychologist making decisions in the work situation. I personally found his comments and suggestions to be very stimulating and provocative. Judgments concerning the heuristic value of these suggestions, however, are best left to I. O. practitioners. What I plan to do instead is to elaborate on some of the implications of Palermo's theoretical framework for personnel evaluation from the perspective of social congition, or, to be more accurate, from the perspective of my particular "theory" of the social-cognitive world. Given space constraints, my discussion is restricted to two issues: some possible biases involved in supervisors' evaluations of personnel and some potential problems with using questionnaires as evaluation instruments.

SUPERVISORS' EVALUATIONS

Let me first consider the situation in which a supervisor must provide an evaluation of his or her personnel. Palermo suggests that the judgment of a good worker is not subject to analysis into features that add up to the whole when broken down. This position is representative of the "holistic" approach to social judgment, which argues that social judgment is a gestalt-like process in which the elements are in dynamic interrelation to one another such that an accurate judgment cannot be made from the individual elements alone (e.g., Asch, 1946; Hamilton & Zanna, 1974; Ostrom, 1977). The alternative "elementistic" approach argues that knowledge of the importance and value of each element considered in isolation is sufficient to allow an accurate judgment of the combination of elements (e.g., Anderson, 1971; Osgood, Suci, & Tannenbaum, 1957). The "elementistic" approach is especially problematic when people make judgments of role occupants, which is the case when supervisors evaluate personnel. For example, we have found that even though "casual" and "surgeon" when presented alone are both evaluated positively, the evaluation of "casual surgeon" is decidedly negative (Higgins & Rholes, 1976). Similarly, the evaluation of "trusting detective" is less positive than the evaluation of either "trusting" or "detective." An elementistic approach is also problematic when evaluating a list of attributes. For example, the evaluation of "friendly" or "helpful" is much less positive, and may even become negative, when combined with "insincere." This is because "insincere" provides additional, and contradictory, information about the stimulus person's underlying intent, which influences one's inferences concerning the nature of the "friendly" or "helpful" behavior. It is not simply because "insincere" is negative, because the evaluation of "friendly" or "helpful" is not affected when combined with a negative attribute that provides no additional information about underlying intent, such as "unattractive" or "uncreative."[1] Thus, in evaluating a subordinate, a supervisor should not rely on a strategy that involves simply combining the independent value of each of the worker's different attributes.

Unfortunately, there is one type of "holistic" strategy that supervisors could, and probably often do, use when evaluating personnel that is itself problematic. A number of cognitive psychologists have argued that categorization of stimuli involves a judgment of the similarity between stimulus and category members (e.g., Brooks, 1978; Rosch, 1978; Tversky & Gati, 1978). One type of similarity judgment involves a consideration of the similarity between the stimulus and a particular member of the category, usually a focal, prototypic, or salient category instance (cf. Brooks, 1978; Rosch, 1978). If the stimulus and category member are judged to be sufficiently similar (a "holistic" judgment), then the observer will decide that the stimulus is also a category member. This, in turn, will lead the observer to infer that the stimulus possesses additional characteristics of category members that may not be currently observable in the stimulus—that is, the observer is willing "to go beyond the information given." For example, if you identify the toe of a shoe under a towel, you will be willing to infer that the object possess additional, but as yet hidden, attributes of shoes, such as a heel. This strategy of analogical categorization plus inference rarely leads us into trouble when making judgments of physical objects because typically our notion of the cooccurrence of attributes for a physical object is quite realistic. The same cannot be said for social objects, however.

Notions of the cooccurrence of appearance attributes and dispositional attributes may be quite unrealistic. Nevertheless, a supervisor may judge a worker to be similar to some particular individual with whom he or she is familiar, perhaps on the basis of similarity in general appearance or conversational style, and then infer that the worker also possesses the same skills or personality of this

---

[1]It should be noted that, in contrast to other holistic positions (e.g., Asch, 1946; Hamilton & Zanna, 1974), I am *not* arguing that an attribute has different "meaning" in different contexts, but only that its implications (or "sense") are different when combined with different attributes. As Paulhan has suggested, "meaning remains stable throughout the changes of sense" (see Vygotsky, 1962, p. 146).

other individual (the referent person or social analogue). That is, a "similarity error" can occur because a supervisor is willing to infer that a worker possesses one or more traits (e.g., ability) similar to a referent person simply because one salient trait of the worker (e.g., sloppiness) reminds him or her of the referent person (cf. Kahneman & Tversky, 1972; Nisbett & Ross, 1980; Sarbin, Taft & Bailey, 1960). Even if these traits do cooccur to some extent in the real world, it would not be legitimate to assume that they cooccur in the worker. Occupational counselors are guilty of this error when they advise a client concerning his or her probable success in a particular occupation on the basis of how closely the client's attributes match those of successful practitioners of the occupation. In fact, one possible cause of positive and negative "halo effects" in personnel evaluation (see Borman, this volume) may be the use of positive or negative social analogues when evaluating workers. What is needed, but, unfortunately, is not yet available, is a reality-tested model that predicts how the interrelation among particular person attributes (or types of attributes) leads to specific kinds of performance in particular contexts, just as we have physical models that predict the functional implications of particular physical attributes of objects.

More generally, the "similarity error" involves people's willingness to infer one kind of similarity between entities (e.g., between different people, traits, or behavior) because of the existence of a different kind of similarity between the entities when there is little or no cooccurrence between these two kinds of similarity.[2] In the preceding example, similarity between a current worker (the target person) and a previous worker (the social analogue) with respect to appearance may lead to the inference that the current worker will also be similar to the previous worker with respect to ability when, in fact, there is little relation between appearance and ability. Inference from social analogues is only one kind of similarity error. The similarity error may also contribute to the tendency for people to assume a stronger interrelation among traits than is, in fact, evident in the interrelation among actual trait-related behaviors—the "systematic distortion process" (see Borman, this volume; Shweder, this volume). Similarity between two traits (e.g., polite and honest) with respect to the desirability of their consequences for others may lead to the inference that the traits also reflect a similar underlying orientation towards others when, in fact, there need be little relation between the social desirability of trait-related behaviors and the social orientation underlying these behaviors. This kind of similarity error would result in people's overestimating the cooccurrence of particular traits across persons ("the system-

---

[2]Kahneman and Tversky (1972) provide some interesting examples of one kind of similarity error in their discussion of the "representative heuristic", which involves the application of relatively simple resemblance criteria to problems of categorization. (See also Nisbett & Ross, 1980.) To the extent that the judgment of category membership is biased by the use of this heuristic, inferences based upon the presumption of membership will be incorrect.

atic distortion process''), as well as overestimating the coexistence of particular traits in specific persons (positive and negative "halo effects").[3]

It may even be that general willingness to infer traits or dispositions from behavior (see Nisbett & Ross, 1980) is due in part to a similarity error. Forming a concept of a type of behavior may involve noticing a similarity in appearance and/or outcome among a set of behavioral instances. People may then infer that these behavioral instances are also similar with respect to motivation or disposition. Thus, people may assume that there is a strong tendency for an act with a particular kind of appearance or outcome to cooccur with a particular kind of motivation or disposition even though there need not be a strong relation between similarity of appearance or outcome and similarity of motivation or disposition. In fact, inferring similarity of disposition from similarity of outcome is a form of teleological reasoning. Of course, the fact that the *same* word or morphological root can often be used to designate both the type of behavior and the type of person or disposition contributes to this error (e.g., "cheating" and "a cheater").

In sum, there is a need for personnel evaluators to be sensitive to the possible role of such similarity errors in biasing their judgments of workers. Personnel evaluators need to stick to the behavioral evidence as much as possible and to control the natural temptation to "go beyond the information given" in their search for meaning.

QUESTIONNAIRES AS EVALUATION INSTRUMENTS

The second general issue I wish to discuss is the use of questionnaires as evaluation instruments. In responding to questionnaires, people typically have to provide information about themselves: information about their activities, behaviors, personal attributes, attitudes, opinions, beliefs, and so on. This requires that they retrieve various kinds of information about themselves from long-term memory. Thus, a person's response to a question can vary depending on what information is retrieved at that moment in time, as well as on his or her interpretation of that information. Salancik and Conway (1975), for example, have evidence suggesting that people's self-judgment of how religious they are may vary depending on

---

[3]Other kinds of similarity error may contribute to the "systematic distortion process". In any society, there are conventional social analogues that exemplify what traits society believes should or do co-occur. Thus, because Boy Scouts are supposed to be and are believed to be both polite and honest, people may assume that these traits co-occur in others. (My thanks to Anne Locksley for this example.) It may even simply be that because certain traits (or, more specifically, their behavioral manifestations) are similar in their features (i.e., perceptual or functional similarity) they are assumed to be similar in when and where they occur (i.e., spatio-temporal similarity or contiguity), thus leading people to expect similar traits to co-exist in others.

whether their previous proreligious acts or their previous antireligious acts are easier to retrieve, when ease of retrieval is experimentally manipulated. One must, therefore, consider the aspects of questionnaire taking that might influence the retrieval likelihood of self-information. Let us consider two factors: the communicative nature of questionnaire-taking and the impact of particular questions on the relative accessibility of different constructs.

Most psychologists' conceptions of communication reflect Shannon and Weaver's (1949) model of communication in which message information is defined in terms of uncertainty reduction and the purpose of communication is the accurate transmission and reception of information (the "information transmission" approach to communication). In the fields of speech communication, philosophy, linguistics (especially semiotics), anthropology, and sociology, however, an alternative conception of communication has been proposed (e.g., Austin, 1962; Burke, 1962; Garfinkle, 1967; Grice, 1971; Searle, 1970). This approach conceptualizes communication as a "game." For example, Wittgenstein (1953) spoke of the "language-game" in order to emphasize that the use of words occurs within a general framework of actions. Describing communication as a "game" is meant to capture the notion that communication is purposeful social interaction that occurs within a socially defined context and involves conventional rules and strategies for obtaining various goals. The rules for communication include that communicators should take the recipient's characteristics into account and that communicators should produce a message that is both appropriate to the context and circumstances and appropriate to their communicative intent or purpose. Moreover, there are a variety of communication goals in addition to accurate information transmission, such as "face" goals, "social relationship" goals, "social reality" goals, and "entertainment" goals. In fact, there is considerable evidence that communicators are often willing to sacrifice message accuracy for the sake of other communication goals (cf. Higgins, 1981). Indeed, it is quite possible that respondents to questionnaires may sacrifice accuracy of self-description for the sake of goals such as self-enhancement or pleasing the questionnaire giver.

From the perspective of the "communication game," one would predict that the description of a stimulus will vary depending on the nature of the communicative situation. In our own research, we have found that communicators will describe the same stimulus person in very different ways as a function of the attitude of their listener and the amount of information about the stimulus person that the communicator and listener hold in common (Higgins, 1981). We would expect that the same variability of description as a function of communicative situation would occur when the stimulus person is the self. Thus, self-description in a questionnaire communicative situation may be quite different than self-description in another kind of communicative situation.

Responding to a questionnaire involves formal communication in the written mode with some authority figure as the recipient. A respondent's communication goals, as well as the retrievability of different aspects of self-information, may be very different in this kind of communicative situation. There is considerable evidence, for example, that mode of communication (i.e., oral versus written) can have significant effects on stimulus description and subsequent memory for the stimulus (cf. Olson, Hildegard, & Torrance, in press). Obtaining self-descriptions in a different communicative situation could yield very different self-information. In fact, it may be that one reason for the typically low predictability of behavior from attitude and personality questionnaires (cf. Zanna, Higgins, & Herman, 1982) is that the questionnaire communicative situation is less similar to the type of situation in which the to-be-predicted behavior occurs than other kinds of communicative situations. Perhaps self-descriptions would be more predictive of subsequent performance if they were obtained in communicative situations that more closely resembled (e.g., in context, goals, formality, style of interaction, etc.) the situation in which the performance takes place.

What must be recognized is that there is no single "truth" with respect to an employee's personality, attitudes, or beliefs, but various truths that are evident in different situations (e.g., at work, at home, on vacation, at parties, etc.). Thus, when the literature suggests that questionnaire measures of personality or attitudes typically do not strongly predict the respondent's behavior across all situations, the solution, it seems to me, is not to design questionnaires that predict the respondent's behavior across a greater percentage of situations, but to design questionnaires that predict the respondent's behavior for the specific situation (or set of situations) of direct concern to the questionnaire giver.

Finally, let us briefly consider the role of construct accessibility in questionnaire responding. A number of recent studies in the cognitive and social psychological literature have demonstrated that momentary individual differences in construct accessibility (i.e., the likelihood of utilizing different aspects of stored information) can be produced experimentally through task instruction, mood induction, or prior exposure to particular verbal material. These differences in construct accessibility lead to temporary processing differences, which in turn can have long-term behavioral and cognitive consequences (cf. Higgins & King, 1981; Posner, 1978; Wyer & Srull, 1981). For example, one study varied the relative accessibility of different trait constructs for different subjects by unobtrusively exposing subjects to different trait terms (e.g., "adventurous" versus "reckless"; "persistent" versus "stubborn") as part of a supposed test of "perception" (see Higgins & King, 1981). In a subsequent "reading comprehension" task, subjects tended to use the primed or activated contructs to characterize a stimulus person, and these judgments, in turn, had an increasing effect over time on subjects' liking for the stimulus person. Another study demonstrated that priming different trait constructs *after* exposure to stimulus-person information influenced subjects' memory for the stimulus information, and this effect increased over time (see Higgins & King, 1981).

The findings of the construct accessibility literature suggest that one must be very careful in constructing questionnaires because the verbal material contained in a questionnaire (both the instructions and the items) could accidentally prime or activate particular constructs of the respondent. This, in turn, could influence the respondents' retrieval and characterization of the stored information used to answer the questions. Moreover, respondents' own responses to earlier questions could prime constructs that would influence their responses to later questions.

An additional problem is that there are also chronic or long-term individual differences in construct accessibility that could cause individual differences in how particular questionnaire items are interpreted. As Kelly (1955) has noted, "Construct systems can be considered as a kind of scanning pattern which a person continually projects upon his world. As he sweeps back and forth across his perceptual field he picks up blips of meaning [p. 145]." We have found that there is relatively little overlap in people's long-term accessible constructs, and that people are more responsive to stimulus-person information that matches their most accessible constructs (see Higgins, King, & Mavin, 1982). There is, in fact, some preliminary evidence that males and females have different accessible constructs and that these differences are associated with sex differences in responding to the "same" questionnaire items (D. N. Jackson, personal communication). Thus, ostensibly the "same" questionnaire item could be interpreted differently by respondents with different accessible constructs (which may be associated with a variety of demographic variables), and the different interpretations would lead to different responses on that item. Individual differences in construct accessibility could also lead to interrater conflict in judging the "same" behaviors of a ratee, as Borman (this volume) also points out. What this suggests is that one must take a more ideographic approach to the construction of questionnaires if one wishes the items to be the "same" for different respondents.

In summary, social stimuli are often ambiguous and can be interpreted differently by the same individual at different points in time and by different individuals at the same point in time. Phenomenologically, each alternative interpretation can provide the same "click of comprehension" and can seem equally reasonable or satisfying. The predictive validity of the alternative interpretations, however, can differ markedly. That is, our fantasies of the social world do not differ so much in whether they make sense intuitively as in whether they work. Thus, it is necessary to develop procedures and strategies of personnel evaluation that are geared to the specific goals of the evaluation. As Wittgenstein (1953) has pointed out, we must approach the issue of meaning within a framework of action. Consideration of the social-cognitive factors that can bias judgment and decision making will hopefully facilitate the construction of personnel-evaluation fantasies that work.

REFERENCES

Anderson, N. H. Two more tests against change of meaning in adjective combinations. *Journal of Verbal Learning and Verbal Behavior,* 1971, *10,* 75–85.

Asch, S. E. Forming impressions of personality. *Journal of Abnormal and Social Psychology,* 1946, *41,* 258–290.

Austin, J. L. *How to do things with words.* Oxford, Eng.: Oxford University Press, 1962.

Bartlett, F. C. *Remembering: A study in experimental and social psychology.* Cambridge, Eng.: Cambridge University Press, 1932.

Brooks, L. Nonanalytic concept formation and memory for instances. In E. Rosch & B. B. Lloyd (Eds.), *Cognition and categorization.* Hillsdale, N.J.: Lawrence Erlbaum Associates, 1978.

Burke, K. *A grammar of motives and a rhetoric of motives.* Cleveland: World Press, 1962.

Cantor, N., & Kihlstrom, J. (Eds.). *Personality, cognition, and social interaction.* Hillsdale, N.J.: Lawrence Erlbaum Associates, 1981.

Garfinkel, H. *Studies in ethnomethodology.* Englewood Cliffs, N.J.: Prentice-Hall, 1967.

Grice, H. P. Meaning. In D. D. Steinberg & L. A. Jakobovits (Eds.), *Semantics: An interdisciplinary reader in philosophy, linguistics, and psychology.* London: Cambridge University Press, 1971.

Hamilton, D. L., & Zanna, M. P. Context effects in impression formation: Changes in connotative meaning. *Journal of Personality and Social Psychology,* 1974, *29,* 649–654.

Higgins, E. T. The "communication game": Implications for social cognition and persuasion. In E. T. Higgins, C. P. Herman, & M. P. Zanna (Eds.), *Social cognition: The Ontario symposium* (Vol. 1). Hillsdale, N.J.: Lawrence Erlbaum Associates, 1981.

Higgins, E. T., Herman, C. P., & Zanna, M. P. (Eds.). *Social cognition: The Ontario symposium* (Vol. 1). Hillsdale, N.J.: Lawrence Erlbaum Associates, 1981.

Higgins, E. T., & King, G. Accessibility of social constructs: Information processing consequences of individual and contextual variability. In N. Cantor & J. F. Kihlstrom (Eds.), *Personality, cognition, and social interaction.* Hillsdale, N.J.: Lawrence Erlbaum Associates, 1981.

Higgins, E. T., King, G. A., & Mavin, G. H. Individual construct accessibility and subjective impressions and recall. *Journal of Personality and Social Psychology,* 1982, *43,* 35–47.

Higgins, E. T., & Rhoes, W. S. Impression formation and role fulfillment: A "holistic reference" approach. *Journal of Experimental Social Psychology,* 1976, *12,* 422–435.

Jackson, D. N. Personal communication, 1981.

Jones, E. E., & Davis, K. E. From acts to dispositions: The attribution process in person perception. In L. Berkowitz (Ed.) *Advances in experimental social psychology.* New York: Academic Press, 1965.

Kahneman, D., & Tversky, A. Subjective probability: A judgment of representativeness. *Cognitive Psychology,* 1972, *3,* 430–454.

Kelly, G. A. *The psychology of personal constructs.* New York: W. W. Norton, 1955.

Kelley, H. H. Attribution theory in social psychology. In D. Levine (Ed.), *Nebraska symposium on motivation,* 1967, *15,* 192–238.

Nisbett, R., & Ross, L. *Human inference: Strategies and shortcomings of social judgment.* Englewood Cliffs, N.J.: Prentice-Hall, 1980.

Olson, D., Hildegard, A., & Torrance, N. (Eds.).I*The nature and consequences of literacy.* Hillsdale, N.J.: Lawrence Erlbaum Associates, in press.

Osgood, C. E., Suci, G. J., & Tannenbaum, P. H. *The measurement of meaning.* Urbana: University of Illinois Press, 1957.

Ostrom, T. M. Between-theory and within-theory conflict in explaining context effects in impression formation. *Journal of Experimental Social Psychology,* 1977, *13,* 492–503.

Posner, M. I. *Chronometric explorations of mind.* Hillsdale, N.J.: Lawrence Erlbaum Associates, 1978.

Rosch, E. Principles of categorization. In E. Rosch & B. B. Lloyd (Eds.), *Cognition and categorization*. Hillsdale, N.J.: Lawrence Erlbaum Associates, 1978.

Salancik, G. R., & Conway, M. Attitude inferences from salient and relevant cognitive content about behavior. *Journal of Personality and Social Psychology*, 1975, *32*, 829–840.

Sarbin, T. R., Taft, R. & Bailey, D. E. *Clinical inference and cognitive theory*. New York: Holt, Rinehart, & Winston, 1960.

Schachter, S., & Singer, J. E. Cognitive, social and physiological determinants of emotional state. *Psychological Review*, 1962, *69*, 379–399.

Searle, J. R. *Speech acts: An essay in the philosophy of language*. Cambridge, Eng.: Cambridge University Press, 1970.

Shannon, C. E., & Weaver, W. *The mathematical theory of communication*. Urbana, Ill.: University of Illinois Press, 1949.

Tversky, A., & Gati, I. Studies of similarity. In E. Rosch & B. B. Lloyd (Eds.), *Cognition and categorization*. Hillsdale, N.J.: Lawrence Erlbaum Associates, 1978.

Vygotsky, L. S. *Thought and language*. Cambridge, Mass.: MIT Press, 1962.

Wittgenstein, L. *Philosophical investigations*. New York: Macmillan, 1953.

Wyer, R. S., Jr., & Srull, T. K. Category accessibility: Some theoretical and empirical issues concerning the processing of social stimulus information. In E. T. Higgins, C. P. Herman, & M. P. Zanna (Eds.), *Social cognition: The Ontario symposium* (Vol. 1) Hillsdale, N.J.: Lawrence Erlbaum Associates, 1981.

Zanna, M. P., Higgins, E. T., & Herman, C. P. (Eds.).)*Consistency in social behavior: The Ontario symposium* (Vol. 2). Hillsdale, N.J.: Lawrence Erlbaum Associates, 1982.

6

Implications of Personality Theory and Research for the Rating of Work Performance in Organizations

Walter C. Borman

Borman first discusses implicit personality theory and its implications for performance rating. One implication is that the correlations between performance dimensions, especially interpersonal aspects, are probably inflated and conform to the evaluator's theory of behavior. He suggests one method of coping with such rater distortion through an adaptation of behaviorally anchored rating scales in which behavioral examples of dimensions are recorded by raters. Borman next describes the relationship of the trait–situation controversy to work performance. In particular, he outlines Epstein's argument for behavior stability across time and situation. He reviews research suggesting that there may be more consistency in work behavior than in behavior in general, probably because a smaller variety of situations is encountered in the work setting than in daily experiences, and relatively stable abilities underlie performance in most jobs. Borman introduces personal-construct theory and suggests applications of construct systems to perceptions of work behavior. One implication of this theory for performance rating is that we should alter the individual's personal construct systems to conform to the performance areas with which the raters should be concerned in evaluating an employee's performance.

Shweder stresses the need to attend to the distinguishing features or the content of the performance situations. He says that it is incorrect to believe that personalities and minds consist of abstract underlying structures that influence any task or problem. Instead, he focuses on the importance of the content of the situation as a determinant of various behaviors.

This discussion has three major sections. The first considers implicit personality theory (IPT) and its implications for performance rating. The second explores the

nature of work performance in light of the trait–situation controversy in personality psychology. And the third section introduces personal construct theory and
speculates about applications of interpersonal construct systems to perceptions of
work behavior. The purpose of the paper is to examine each of these areas in
personality theory and research, first to help provide new ways of looking at
issues and research in performance measurement, and second to suggest potentially fruitful directions for performance-appraisal research and practice.

IMPLICIT PERSONALITY THEORY

In general, research on Implicit Personality Theory (IPT) has been concerned
with persons' perceptions of relationships between traits—that is, with how
people construe traits to covary in other persons (Schneider, 1973). In this
section on IPT, I focus on: (1) studies of the halo effect (e.g., Berman & Kenny,
1976; Koltuv, 1962; Nisbett & Wilson, 1977); (2) investigations of factor structure similarity in personality ratings with differing ratee samples (e.g., Norman,
1963; Passini & Norman, 1966); and (3) studies of the systematic-distortion
hypothesis along with the issue of IPT "validity"—that is, how closely IPTs
reflect reality in stimulus persons (e.g., D'Andrade, 1965; Lay & Jackson, 1969;
Mulaik, 1964; Shweder, 1975; Shweder & D'Andrade, 1980).

Studies of the Halo Effect

Researchers have long noticed what seems to be inflated correlations between
dimensions in ratings made of others' personalities or job performances (e.g.,
Newcomb, 1931; Thorndike, 1920)—that is, correlations higher than warranted
by actual ratee behavior. Of course, one problem with studying halo is that the
actual "true" level of the dimension intercorrelations is not typically known,
rendering impossible any precise estimate of halo (Borman, 1975; Johnson,
1963; Schwab, Heneman, & DeCotiis, 1975). As late as 1963, it could be stated
that no experimental validation of halo had been offered (Johnson, 1963). However, in recent studies in which *actual* levels of relationships have been known
(e.g., Borman, 1975; Nisbett & Wilson, 1977), halo has been found, suggesting
that individuals do distort the magnitude of relationships between dimensions of
personality and job performance.

   An example of a study focusing on halo is found in a paper by Borman
(1975). He prepared six vignettes of hypothetical first-line supervisor ratees,
using behavioral examples that had been sorted reliably into a single performance
dimension, and assigned a narrow range of effectiveness scale values by individuals knowledgeable about the job. Each vignette consisted of six such examples, one representing each of six performance dimensions. The performance
examples, then, essentially "told a story" about each supervisor. An important

feature of this approach is that the mean effectiveness scale values of the examples served as performance "true scores" for each supervisor vignette on each performance dimension, and the variance of the true scores within ratee across dimensions, then provided the target against which the halo of individual raters' evaluations could be assessed. The key result of this study for our purposes here is that the variances of the subjects' ratings were significantly lower than the actual (target) variances, even after raters were instructed in a brief training course to avoid the halo error. Thus, raters generally failed to make distinctions between performance on the dimensions compared to the true score standard. Results of this study and the few other studies allowing an assessment of halo suggest that people do seem to overestimate relationships between dimensions in evaluating others.

Factor Analysis Studies of Personality Ratings

A series of studies have shown that the factor structure of personality ratings is relatively unaffected by how well raters know ratees. Passini and Norman (1966) provide an exemplar of this finding. These researchers asked college students who were unacquainted previously (they had only been together for about 15 minutes) to rate each other on 20 scales drawn from the Cattell Personality sphere. Ratings were intercorrleated, and the 20 × 20 correlation matrix factor analyzed. The factor structure was rotated to the varimax criterion and a five-factor solution appeared to be most psychologically meaningful.

The most interesting aspect of this study is that the factor solution obtained here is remarkably similar to solutions obtained when persons rate others whom they know well or with whom they are merely acquainted (Norman, 1963; Tupes & Christal, 1958, 1961). Importantly, a similar structure emerges when subjects are asked essentially to rate the semantic similarity of these trait terms (Hakel, 1974; Norman & Goldberg, 1966). Passini and Norman (1966) conclude that

> . . . persons who have only the most superficial information about one another can draw upon their more or less comparable prior experiences and whatever easily observable cues are available to them to yield peer rating structures that are highly similar to those obtained from subjects who are intimately acquainted with one another [p. 48].

In other words, the similarities in factor structure imply that the raters are using *their own* categories to judge others—that is, their implicit personality theories. A conclusion that may be drawn from this work, then, is that rather than reflecting "real structure" in ratee behavior, the relational structure of personality ratings is largely a function of *the expectations* raters have of correlations between dimensions in ratees.

However, it is also possible to conclude that semantic structure of personality ratings *reflects reality* regarding correlations between dimensions in target ratees. It seems logical that persons in a culture develop ideas about semantic similarity of descriptors based on actual experiences observing others, and thus form "what goes with what" ideas veridical to the way characteristics of persons actually covary in human interaction. Work on the systematic-distortion hypothesis (D'Andrade, 1965; Shweder, 1975; Shweder & D'Andrade, 1980) addresses this issue more directly.

Systematic Distortion in Ratings

This research related to distortions in correlations between dimensions in the direction of *semantic relationships* between those dimensions.

D'Andrade and Shweder (D'Andrade, 1974; Shweder, 1975; Shweder & D'Andrade, 1979, 1980) have investigated this aspect of IPT. They examined data from studies in which observers made recordings of behavior immediately after viewing individual ratees, *and* observers also made memory-based ratings on dimensions meant to reflect constructs tapped by behavior. As in the research just reviewed, results show that memory-based ratings (rated behavior) yield correlation matrices quite similar in structure to *semantic similarity* relational matrices. Most important, however, is that comparisons of actual (recorded) behavior to rated behavior yield relatively little correspondence. In the studies reviewed, correlations between the elements of these two matrices are low, suggesting that correlations among memory-based ratings on different traits tell us more about the *conceptual covariance* of these traits than about the way behaviors related to these traits actually covary in human conduct. An example may help the reader to understand this important finding.

Newcomb (1929) conducted a study on introversion–extroversion with two groups of boys in a summer camp (Ns = 27 and 24). In the course of the study, counselors kept daily records of each boy's behavior related to each of 26 "dimensions." Examples of the dimensions are: "speaks with confidence of his own abilities," "engages in group misdemeanor," and "reads a half-hour or more during the day." These records yielded scores on each dimension (actual behavior scores). In addition, six observers evaluated each boy on each dimension upon completion of the camp (rated behavior scores). Finally, Shweder had 10 graduate students rate the conceptual similarity between each pair of dimensions. Analysis of the data involved correlating the corresponding elements of the three correlation matrices for each group. Results showed that relationships between the rated behavior correlation matrices and the conceptual similarity matrices were strikingly similar, and importantly, the rated behavior matrices were relatively *dis*similar in structure to the *actual* behavior matrices' structure.

This result is typical of what has been found in other studies with this kind of data. Shweder (1980) reports average correlations across seven studies as shown in Fig. 6.1.

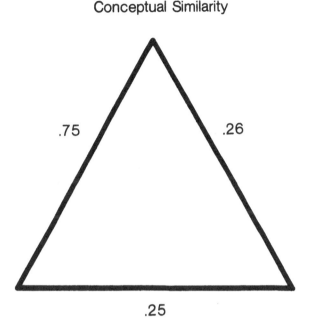

Conceptual Similarity

Rated Behavior   Actual Behavior

FIG. 6.1.   Agreement of conceptual similarity, rated behavior, and actual behavior correlations.

A somewhat different approach to assessing the "validity" of IPT is provided by Lay and Jackson's (1969) study. For each of the 21 Personality Research Form (PRF) dimensions, they identified an item that correlated highly with that item's total score and then asked subjects to rate, for each pair of such items, the probability that a respondent would answer an item true given a response of true on another item. They found that a multidimensional scaling of interitem distances generated from these data provided results similar to the structure that emerges from actual PRF self-report data. The conclusion is that the relational structure of IPT (based on the probability ratings) corresponds closely to actual personality structure (PRF responses).

A study by Stricker, Jacobs, and Kogan (1974) used a similar approach, except data were analyzed for individual subjects rather than for the group. Results suggested that, as in the Lay and Jackson study, IPT was substantially congruent with dimensions generated from personality test responses.

Of course, a different interpretation of the Lay and Jackson and Stricker et al. findings is that test responses are affected by IPT just as the conceptual similarity judgments are assumed to be, and therefore, rather than serving as a *criterion* for assessing the validity of IPT structure, self-report personality test structure may be likewise "biased" by IPT (Schneider, 1973).

On balance, research on systematic distortion suggests that our implicit personality theories may be substantially affected by semantic meaning, and by assumptions about the dimensions that belong together. Unfortunately, these assumptions may be in error. This, of course, casts doubt on the validity of our IPTs.

Halo and Systematic Distortion Considered Together

So far, I have discussed two *different* rating errors: halo and systematic distortion. It may be instructive now to examine effects on ratings of the two biases taken together. As mentioned, the term halo implies inflation of correlations among dimensions, whereas systematic distortion implies that raters make memory-based ratings, with correlations among dimensions biased in the direction of semantic similarity.

In the rated-behavior and actual-behavior correlation matrices available to the author, rating correlations are in fact higher than behavior correlations. For example, the median rating correlation in the Borgatta, Cottrell, and Mann (1958) study is .28 and for the actual behavior matrix the corresponding median correlation is .11 (using absolute values of the correlations because several of the dimension pairs are logical opposites). In the Mann (1959) data, I picked out the six dimension pairs that have the highest conceptual similarity, and the average actual behavior interdimension correlation is −.15,

In the rated-behavior and actual-behavior correlation matrices available to the author, rating correlations are in fact higher than behavior correlations. For example, the median rating correlation in the Borgetta, Cattrell, and Mann (1958) study is .28 and for the actual behavior matrix the corresponding median correlation is .11 (using absolute values of the correlations because several of the dimension pairs are logical opposites). In the Mann (1959) data, I picked out the six dimension pairs that have the highest conceptual similarity, and the average actual behavior interdimension correlation is −.15, whereas +.49 is the average correlation for the rated-behavior data. There are four dimension pairs that were rated as very *dis*similar conceptually, and for those pairs the average actual-behavior correlation is −.19; the corresponding average correlation for the rated behavior is −.32. Thus, the inflation in correlations for the behavior ratings works both ways. For conceptually similar dimensions the ratings result in inflated positive correlations and for conceptually dissimilar dimension pairs, the ratings yield inflated negative correlations.

This is even more clearly shown in a table from Shweder (1975), reproduced here as Table 6.1. There data reflect the same phenomenon; ratings (*and* conceptual similarity judgments) overestimate the relationships between behavioral dimensions both when dimension pairs are logically similar and when they are

TABLE 6.1
Conceptual Similarity Scores, Mean Rated Behavior Correlations,
and Actual Behavior Correlations[a]

Quintiles	N	Conceptual Similarity Scores (7-Point Scale)		Rated Behavior Correlations (Correlation Points)		Actual Behavior Correlations (Correlation Points)	
		M	SD	M	SD	M	SD
1	22	6.2	.29	.53	.28	.29	.21
2	22	5.2	.34	.34	.21	.18	.25
3	22	4.0	.27	−.03	.37	.08	.23
4	22	2.9	.31	−.27	.35	.02	.25
5	22	2.1	.20	−.50	.43	−.10	.22

[a]Means and standard deviations for group 2 rated behavior correlations, actual behavior correlations, and conceptual similarity scores divided into quintiles in terms of the degree of conceptual similarity for pairs of extroverted and introverted items in Newcomb's 26-item behavior list.

logical opposites. Apparently, both inflation in correlations *and* distortion towards semantic similarity occur in personality and behavior ratings, at least under the conditions studied.

"Direct" Validity of Ratings Considered

It is critical to note that what we have discussed so far refers specifically to "validity" of the *correlational structure of the ratings*—that is, correspondence between rated- and actual-behavior relational matrices. Of course, these findings have implications for validity of ratings on individual dimensions, but more direct evidence for validity comes from correlations between ratings on individual dimensions and some index of "true scores" on the corresponding dimensions. The D'Andrade and Shweder data provide one source of such validity estimates.

In a study employing a 30-minute videotape of family member interaction and offering both (1) on-line scores for "dimensions" (such as Inform, Question, Ridicule) by having raters study the tape and a transcript of that tape and also (2) raters' memory-based evaluations on these same dimensions, correlations between the ratings and "actual behavior" is in the neighborhood of .30 according to Shweder and D'Andrade (1980). In the Newcomb (1929) study, validities average .49.

It is very important to discuss these validities because they bear strongly on a point made by Shweder and D'Andrade (1980). The systematic-distortion extension of IPT does not specify that ratings are *necessarily* distorted and inaccurate, but that in the absence of relevant cues for a rater (whether there are a lack of cues *or* the cues have been attended to and forgotten), there will be nonrandom distortion in the direction of semantic, "what goes with what" relationships between dimensions.

Critiques of the Systematic-Distortion Hypothesis

As might be expected, the systematic-distortion hypothesis has been criticized especially in what Cooper (1981b) has called the "strong form" (Shweder, 1975), and the conclusions that have been drawn, again, from the "strong" systematic-distortion position, have been questioned (Block, Weiss, & Thorne, 1979; Lamiell, Foss, & Cavenee, 1980). Block, Weiss, & Thorne (1979) have provided the main attack on systematic distortion and correlational bias thinking and research. Their arguments, which are very detailed, are summarized here. Block et al. point to the nonequivalence of dimensions used in some of the studies D'Andrade and Shweder consider—that is, different definitions used by observers recording behavior for the "actual-behavior" data and raters generating the "rated-behavior" data. This could, of course, serve to reduce the validities discussed previously as well as the rated-behavior–actual-behavior matrix correlations. Block et al. also suggest correcting the rated-behavior–actual-behavior validities for unreliability, and point out that such reliabilities are not available for some of the studies.

Perhaps the most important concern voiced by Block et al. (1979) is that the "actual behavior" measures may serve as questionable criteria for ratings. The main problem has to do with the adequacy of simple counts of behaviors for reflecting a person's standing on important behavioral dimensions. The problem is very similar to industrial psychologists' quest for "true scores" of work performance against which to evaluate the accuracy of performance ratings or other measures of individuals' effectiveness. It is a tricky business to develop performance scores that on the one hand are arguably objective and nonarbitrary and at the same time reflect meaningful behavioral categories of work performance. Likewise, justifying a particular method of obtaining true scores for ratees on nontrivial dimensions of personality-related behavior presents a difficult problem.

In my judgment, the criteria used in this research provide reasonable estimates of true scores for purposes of testing the systematic distortion hypothesis. Interestingly, scores were developed in the previously described videotape study utilizing a method similar to that employed in our research on performance ratings (Borman, 1978a). Dimensions were carefully defined for the judges who had ample opportunity to review the tape along with transcripts of the verbal behavior (just as our judges viewed tapes of the performances and studied verbal transcripts). Although this approach of true-score development is open to criticism, it may come as close as is possible to generating true scores on meaningful dimensions in personality and performance.

Summary of the Impact of IPT and Systematic Distortion on Ratings

Systematic distortion in its "weaker" form (Shweder & D'Andrade, 1980) seems to be an established component of behavior ratings. In the absence of relevant information about target ratees or when sufficient time has elapsed between observation and rating to result in significant "memory decay," inter-dimension correlations of ratings are likely to be biased in the direction of semantic similarity.

Cooper (1981b) provides a review of possible reasons for halo and systematic distortion biases persisting in raters' evaluations of others. First, raters do not attend properly to their "hit rates." That is, we tend to underlearn our prediction errors from experience, and attend more to our successes in making correct perceptual judgments (Einhorn & Hogarth, 1978). Second, when we process interpersonal information, correlated features associated with a stimulus person are more likely to be attended to and remembered than uncorrelated features in the person (Tversky, 1977). And third, raters tend to adopt hypothesis-testing judgment strategies that confirm their prior beliefs about correlations between features (Snyder & Swann, 1978); essentially, we search for confirmatory evidence and then succeed at finding it. Finally, as perceivers, we tend to make initial judgments about others (usually in keeping with our prior beliefs of correlated features) and, importantly, then move to form a memory impression consisting primarily of summary information lacking in detail (Cantor & Mischel, 1979). These cognitive phenomena are likely to contribute to the kinds of biases and distortions we have discussed.

Also, Sawyer's (1966) assertions related to clinical versus statistical prediction have relevance here. He concludes that clinicians are "more likely to contribute . . . (to prediction of behavior) through *observation* than *integration* [p. 178]." In order words, the clinician (or rater) is reasonably good at observing and then recording observed behavior but poor at combining and integrating these observations to make summary evaluations to others. Thus, work on halo and systematic distortion along with certain supporting research in social cognition and clinical judgment is very suggestive of significant biases and distortions in ratings and limitations in raters' abilities to make evaluative judgments.

Implications of IPT Research for Performance Measurement

The most direct implication of IPT research for performance rating is that correlations between dimensions, especially in the interpersonal aspects of the job, are probably inflated and conform more to raters' implicit theories of work behavior than to actual behavior. Consider for a moment the raters' task in a typical organizational setting within the context of the D'Andrade–Shweder research. The rater usually attempts to remember a ratee's performance over a six-month or even year-long period. He or she may have notes and documents to help remember specific instances of performance, but often the ratings are based on memory of impressions developed over time. On the other hand, in most work settings there is considerable opportunity for the rater to gather performance information on a ratee.[1]

My guess is that a fair test of the systemtic distortion hypothesis with memory-based performance ratings made by raters on the basis of retrospective examination of performance over time will reveal that this kind of distortion does indeed occur with evaluations of performance. We have seen that performance ratings tend to yield inflated interdimension correlations, and some distortion towards semantic similarity in ratings is also likely to occur in my judgment.

Consideration of halo, systematic distortion, and possible sources of these biases by Cooper (1981b) and Feldman (1981) yield definite implications for the way in which performance information on individuals should be gathered. Research reviewed so far suggests that raters do a poor job of remembering, evaluating, and then combining and integrating behavioral information generated during interpersonal activities. One remedy for this is to take the rater out of the judgment process as much as possible.

Borman (1978a), Cooper (1981b), Feldman (1981), and Landy and Farr (1980) have discussed the performance-rating judgment process, and they provide some suggestions on where these distortions or biases are likely to occur. Borman (1978a) presented a three-step model of the rating process. The first step involves observing individual work behaviors, the second, making judgments about the effectiveness of each behavior, and the third, weighting and combining these judgments to form a single rating on a dimension. We have seen that it is during the first step in this process that the rating is least sensitive to distortion. The two subsequent steps require the kinds of judgment and integration that are most problematic.

Cooper (1981b) elaborated on Borman's depiction of the rating process with an 11-step sequential model. He also describes the kinds of random and systematic errors likely to enter into the process at each step. Only the first two steps appear unlikely to generate the types of biases we have discussed: observing ratee actions and encoding these observations into short-term memory (perhaps

---

[1]Cooper (1981a) at least partially addressed the question of systematic distortion in performance ratings by studying the D'Andrade–Shweder paradigm in the job-performance domain, but results were not in keeping with the systematic distortion hypothesis. The conceptual similarity matrix predicted the rated behavior matrix to a degree ($r = .55$), but the rated behavior–actual behavior matrix correspondence was higher ($r = .89$). As Cooper (1981a) points out, however, this was probably not an adequate test of systematic distortion in performance ratings because the rated behavior ratings were recorded immediately after viewing each ratee, perhaps before memory decay became a factor.

recording them in some way, as well). Subsequent steps in the model refer to short- and long-term memory decay, retrieval of the (decayed) information from memory, comparing remembered observations and impressions of the ratee with rater and rating-scale standards, and actually making the rating. All of these steps are problematic in the context of our discussion.

Likewise, Feldman (1981) offers a model related to the cognitive tasks a rater must perform in making performance ratings. He or she must attend to relevant information about ratees, organize and store this information for later recall, and integrate the information into a summary judgment (rating). In light of the difficulties previously documented, the integrating and summarizing operations will give the rater the most trouble.

The Landy and Farr (1980) model is much more ambitious and attempts to reflect the entire process of generating and using performance ratings in organizations. Focusing on the rating-judgment process aspect of the model, the observation/storage and retrieval/judgment steps represent cognitive operations in which the rater must engage during the rating process. Clearly, the observation operation is the only one in this sequence requiring minimal integration of performance information and is therefore likely free from serious distortion.

Suggested Performance Measurement Methods Offered in Light of IPT/Systematic Distortion Findings

What rating methods come closest to dealing successfully with these apparent limits in raters' ability to make error-free interpersonal judgments? Within the now-familiar behaviorally anchored rating scale (BARS) strategy, the original guidance provided by Smith and Kendall (1963), recently updated by Bernardin and Smith (1981), is in keeping with the view of the rating-judgment process discussed here. Raters should record behavioral examples of employee performance relevant to each dimension. If raters do a good job of sampling the work behavior related to each dimension and provide a rich enough description of each behavior including the context of the action, then other persons knowledgeable about the job can evaluate the effectiveness levels reflected in each behavior, and the means of these effectiveness judgments.

A second approach in keeping with the seeming limits of raters' evaluative capabilities is behavioral analysis or behavior assessment, applied to the performance-measurement problem by Komaki (Komaki, Collins, & Thoene, 1980) and Cone (1980). A brief description of one Komaki study characterizes this strategy. In her work with the Marine Corps, Komaki studied preventive maintenance jobs and, as part of that work, developed a behavioral observation performance-rating system. The system was designed to evaluate a unit rather than individuals in the unit, but some parts of the rating system are appropriate for measuring individuals' performance. One dimension, Action Taken, required observers to sample a number of items in need of repair and to evaluate the preventive-maintenance actions taken using a carefully prepared checklist containing the correct or desired actions. In this manner, highly reliable and objective "ratings" of performance were generated. One might question the proportion of the relevant job performance domain that we might expect to cover using such methods, but for those jobs and dimensions adequately covered, the system certainly avoids difficulties with complex judgment-process steps.

Cone (1980) has also discussed the relevance of behavior assessment for performance measurement. He describes important issues that point up the positive *and* negative features of using behavior-assessment principles in measuring performance (Cone, 1980; Foster & Cone, 1980). A critical issue is validity of measurement. This refers both to accuracy of the observations with respect to what the researcher is intending to measure *and* to ecological validity, or how well the measurement system "covers" the constructs of interest. Regarding the first type of validity, as in research in performance ratings, it has often been more convenient to study not validity or accuracy, but some other characteristics of the ratings. Thus, for example, interobserver reliability has been examined, and one of the important findings is that agreement in ratings using even carefully developed behavior-coding systems typically starts out high, but "observer drift" (e.g., Kent & Foster, 1977) reduces this interobserver agreement as raters forget details of the coding system and/or develop idiosyncratic interpretations or elaborations of the system.

Problems with ecological validity have to do with selecting the proper behaviors to assess: behaviors that are relevant to the construct of interest. Major difficulties are likely to occur if the target construct is complex. In addition, there is the issue of which behavioral property to measure (Foster & Cone, 1980). For example, frequency, latency, and duration may be important, as well as qualitative aspects of the behavior. Unfortunately, the familiar fidelity-bandwidth problem is at work here. Very narrow (and in many cases trivial) behavior categories can be measured very precisely and unambiguously, whereas more complex (and often more psychologically interesting) categories are more difficult to measure.

Thus, we have seen that behavior analysis and assessment principles applied to performance measurement are potentially in concert with this view of performance raters' cognitive limitations related to evaluating employees. Using these principles, raters might view large samples of behavior on a job, and form behavioral categories and rules for sorting behaviors into categories. They would then "score" individual job incumbents on each category by observing each one in representative samples of situations and classifying and counting behaviors according to the scoring system. Such behavioral-measurement systems have actually been placed in operation by Komaki and her colleagues (Komaki, Blood, & Holder, 1980; Komaki, Collins, & Thoene, 1980), demonstrating that for at least some components of jobs, this kind of behavioral-measurement method might be very useful.

A previously mentioned reservation regarding behavior-analysis approaches to performance measurement is the likely difficulty in adequately measuring all elements in the performance domain for, especially, complex jobs. Consider, for example, trying to develop a behavioral-measurement system to tap successfully all important performance constructs on a management job. Some parts of such a job may be amenable to the method (e.g., interpersonal effectiveness at meetings with subordinates might be indexed by noting head-nodding behavior in support of subordinate statements, proportion of time subordinates have the floor, etc.), but the coverage of other important performance areas may well be more problematic (e.g., decision making).

Proposal for an Idealized Performance-Measurement System

An adaptation of the BARS approach referred to previously seems to offer clear advantages for an idealized performance-measurement system intended to derive relatively pure performance scores for individuals on a job. The idea of such an idealized system is to derive performance scores that are not dependent on rater perceptual processes we have discussed, but that *are* based on behavioral data sufficiently rich and detailed to render a complete and fair depiction of job performance. The proposal I discuss is impractical for application to on-going performance-appraisal systems in organizations, although features of the approach can be incorporated. Instead, the intent is to gain a glimpse of the actual structure of work behavior on some job to see how closely it comes to the structure inferred from performance ratings—that is, to obtain an estimate of the degree of distortion ratings provide in our "ratings picture" of job performance.

I believe that the strategy of gathering large and representative samples of ratee-performance examples provides a potentially rich source of highly relevant raw behavior data that can be used in this idealized system. Features of behavioral examples, as formulated by Flanagan (1954) and Smith and Kendall (1963), seem well suited for providing usable raw behavioral units. Actual ratee behavior along with the context in which this behavior occurred are both represented in such examples.

The most important reason for favoring an approach employing behavioral examples for this purpose is that the entire performance domain is likely to be sampled. In our work with behavior scaling (e.g., Borman & Dunnette, 1975), we have been most impressed with the coverage of the performance domain provided by a sampling of behavioral examples generated by persons knowledgeable about the job. The inductive approach of sampling widely each ratee's behavior relevant to each area of performance in a form that includes information on the context appears to offer a potentially excellent behavioral unit for analysis, with considerable advantages over counts of specific behaviors.

Proceeding with this idealized proposal, to obtain an estimate of the actual covariance structure of performance on a job, we could first record over a period of time behavioral examples of actual performance for a number of individuals on a target job. I realize this is a tall order. It would require an extensive time/

situation sampling plan to obtain a representative sample of behavioral examples for each job incumbent. Indeed, I suspect that the only way to generate such samples of behavioral information is to videotape on-going work behavior in a natural setting so that the tapes and transcripts of the verbal behavior can be studied to extract the examples. Perhaps performance in the Center for Creative Leadership's "Looking Glass" organizational simulation should be videotaped. This simulation is designed to present a diverse sampling of management tasks,it is realistic in portraying situations managers typically face, and it provides a relatively long stream of behavior that would help generate the necessary large number of examples.

The second step in this approach is to content analyze the examples generated to form relatively specific performance dimensions. Next, it would be possible to get persons familiar with the job's performance requirements to sort each performance example into a dimension and assign an effectiveness level to the behavior. Finally, incumbents could be scored on each dimension by averaging the effectiveness levels (perhaps weighted in some way) for all of their examples on each of the dimensions. With a large enough sample of incumbents, this data matrix can yield a rough estimate of a "true" performance-covariance matrix, and this matrix might be compared to covariance matrices generated from performance ratings assigned using typical performance-appraisal methods.

If performances in the "Looking Glass" or some other simulation were videotaped, we might have subjects' viewing these performances and making ratings under varying conditions, and these ratings could then be compared to the target behavior-performance scores. It would be important in such research to follow Feldman's (1981) advice to give rater subjects other tasks besides their behavior-observation–performance-rating task to increase the realism of the setting for performance appraisal and, along with it, the generalizability of results to actual field applications. In sum, I recognize that this plan is quite cumbersome, but it is offered in the spirit of obtaining experimentally an idea of the "true" covariance structure for a job and providing reasonably realistic stimulus materials to enable study of rating distortions and accuracy in ratings.

A Different Reaction to "Negative" IPT Research Results: Studying the Performance-Rating Process

In this section of the paper, performance-measurement systems that *avoid* the rating process have been presented, these systems keeping performance scores as much as possible untainted by rater biases that have been documented in IPT and related research. A completely different approach is to actively study the rating process to learn as much as possible about it, the goal being to make use of this knowledge to change performance-appraisal practices.

Indeed, one purpose of this paper is to stimulate research on process by introducing research strategies and findings from work in personality psychology into performance appraisal. Likewise, recent papers in Industrial– Organizational psychology journals have begun to specify how the performance-rating process might be studied: (1) from an attribution perspective (Feldman, 1981; Green & Mitchell, 1979; Stone & Slusher, 1975); (2) in relation to interpersonal constructs and category systems (Borman, 1978a; Feldman, 1981; see also the third section of this paper); (3) with a focus on rater individual differences correlates of rating behavior (Borman, 1979; Schneier, 1977); and (4) within a policy-capturing framework (Zedeck & Kafry, 1977).

Another possible approach to studying the performance-rating process is to study "rating styles"—that is, different strategies for making ratings, preferences for using certain performance cues, methods of combining information to arrive at ratings, and so on. A recent study characterizes this approach and demonstrates how difficult such research may be in comparison to "product" research.

In a doctoral dissertation study, Banks (1979) devised a procedure to identify the behavioral cues used by raters. In particular, Banks' research examined: (1) interrater agreement in specific cues used to make ratings on individual dimensions; (2) within-rater consistency of certain rating-style variables; and (3) differences in outcome-rating errors (e.g., halo) made by persons classified according to folk concepts about effective rating styles.

In this study, Banks had subjects view each one of six of the 5-to-9-minute manager performances on the Borman (1978a) videotapes and rate each performer on only one of six performance dimensions, such that different dimensions were rated each time. Subjects had before them computer consoles with seven buttons corresponding to seven effectiveness levels (1 = very ineffective; 7 = very effective), and they were instructed to press one of those buttons each time they viewed behavior they thought was relevant to the performance dimension being considered. The particular button pushed (of the seven) indicated the rater's judgment of the behavior effectiveness. Also, the buttons were attached to a timing device that provided an exact record of where in the tape each button was pressed. Finally, subjects were instructed to provide a brief verbal description of the behavior they were attending to each time they pressed a button.

Results of the study showed first that different raters tend to identify different behaviors as relevant for making evaluations on a dimension. Apparently, the subjects looked for or attended to a substantially separate set of cues when searching for behavior relevant to performance on a dimension. Second, the within-subject, across-trial reliability of certain rating-style variables was high: for number of cues attended to (button presses per tape), the intraclass $r = .95$, for response latency (time to first button push), $r = .77$. Also, verbal reports were classified according to: (1) global versus specific; (2) behavioral versus evaluative; and (3) descriptive versus prescriptive (what the ratees did versus what they *should* have done), and within-rater stabilities of the proportion of global and behavioral cues were high ($r = .88$ and .85, respectively). Finally, raters were classified as effective or ineffective according to "folk concepts" of good rating styles—that is, using relatively specific (versus global) information, employing many (versus few) behavioral cues, and attending to both effective *and* ineffective performance within ratee. Raters with relatively effective styles in this regard provided ratings with lower restriction of range error. In this research, stability of some of the style variables is especially heartening, suggesting that to some extent "rating styles" in appraising others' performances are relatively consistent and thus may reflect meaningful individual differences in behavior related to the performance-rating process.

Summary

Thus, we have seen that work on IPT and related areas in personality and social psychology have important implications for research and practice in performance appraisal. We concluded that relatively serious errors, biases, and distortions are likely to occur in performance ratings as they are usually generated, and that one way to address this problem is essentially to avoid asking raters to perform memory and judgment activities on which research suggests they do poorly. Adaptations of selected performance-measurement methods were offered relative to this avoidance theme. Also, an idealized study to map the performance space in a job was presented as a possible way to obtain relatively objective, yet rich and relevant performance information on individuals in jobs.

In addition, a strategy was briefly presented to study the performance-rating process in a long-term effort to learn enough about this process to improve the accuracy of ratings in the future. We are beginning to specify research directions focusing on the rating process, and an example of research on "rating styles" showed how difficult yet potentially rewarding such research might be. Of course, it is also possible that such research will suggest that performance-rating systems *should not* rely on rater judgments. Nonetheless, research in this direction should proceed.

THE TRAIT–SITUATION CONTROVERSY IN PERSONALITY PSYCHOLOGY AND CONSISTENCY–VARIABILITY IN EMPLOYEE JOB PERFORMANCE

The trait–situation "controversy" in personality psychology relates to disagreement about whether stable, enduring traits in people largely dictate behavior, or whether situations, differing meaningfully in stimulus characteristics, determine behavior to a great extent. A third interactionist position hypothesizes that different situations elicit different behaviors in different people. That is, to understand human behavior, we must attend to both persons *and* situations.

The Positions

Trait Position.   The trait position contends that relatively stable individual differences in personality have broad meaning for the way persons conduct themselves in different situations. If we know how a person stands on certain relevant traits, we can predict how that person will act in various situations. Selected arguments for this position from Bowers (1973), Epstein (1979), Stagner (1977), and others are as follows:

1. Many of the studies that demonstrate low across-situation correlations of traits utilize very different situations, and thus variability in the stimulus characteristics is greater than what is typically encountered in everyday life (Bowers, 1973).
2. Laboratory studies usually *place* subjects in situations whereas in real life we can to some extent choose our environment, which in turn leads to stability in our behavior (Bowers, 1973; Epstein, 1979).
3. Assessment of personality has shown relatively high temporal stability in traits, and this suggests, albeit indirectly, that traits are important determiners of behavior (Bäckteman & Magnusson, 1981; Block, 1971; Olweus, 1979).
4. The unit of analysis employed in research favoring a situationist position is often focused at the individual-behavior level rather than at a level that considers behavioral tendencies that are likely to be more stable (Bowers, 1973; Epstein, 1979).
5. Traits have been reasonably successful at predicting important outcome variables, more successful than situationists have claimed (Hogan, DeSoto, & Solano, 1977; Stagner, 1977).
6. Multitrait–multimethod studies of trait measures have shown relatively high convergent validity (Block et al., 1979; Stagner, 1977).

As can be seen, some of these points contradict pro-situationist research whereas other points support the usefulness of trait concepts.

Situationist Position.   The situationist position contends that there is little stability in personality; instead, the situation and its stimulus characteristics largely dictate a person's behavior. Mischel (1968) has often been cited as the main proponent of this view, although it should be noted that his position is far from one of extreme situationism (Mischel, 1979; Mischel & Peake, 1981). The main prosituationist arguments are as follows:

1. Behavior related to a trait in one situation rarely correlates highly with other behavior related to the same trait in other settings (Mischel, 1968).
2. Scores on trait measures correlate minimally with behavior in specific situations (Mischel, 1968; Vernon, 1964).

3. ANOVA analyses involving person, situation, and person–situation interaction components often show situation (and the person–situation interaction)
accounting for considerable variance in behavior (Endler, 1966; Magnusson,
1971).
   4. Ratings of others, sometimes used to help support a trait position, reflect
more stability in ratee behavior than is actually warranted (Jones & Nisbett,
1971; Shweder, 1975).

Interactionist Position.   This position contends that consideration of only the
person or only situations is insufficient for fully understanding human conduct.
Behavior is a joint function of the person and the situation. What this means is
that the rank order of individuals on a trait may be relatively consistent, but only
within certain situational constraints. To learn more about human behavior we
therefore need to classify situations in some way *in addition to* classifying
behaviors. Trait-oriented psychologists have identified stable clusters of behaviors designated as traits, which are useful when employed in research, but not as
much has been accomplished regarding a similar classification of situations (Bem
& Funder, 1978).
   Unfortunately, the latter classification task is made even more difficult and
complex when we consider the impact of persons' *perceptions* of situations over
and above the objective situational characteristics. Perceptions related to situations are very likely to intervene to help determine a person's behavior in a
situation, and these perceptions may vary across persons even when the objective
situation is held constant. One kind of evidence offered in defense of the interactionist position is results of studies employing ANOVA designs indicating that
the person–situation interaction term accounts for more variance than either the
person or the situation terms (Bowers, 1973; Endler & Hunt, 1968, 1969).
Interpretation of data in these ANOVA studies has been questioned (Golding,
1975), although reanalysis using a generalizability approach confirms the importance of such interactions.
   Another view of the person–situation interaction, a view that is different from
the ANOVA interaction concept, is that situations and persons are interdependent—that is, relationships between person and environmental variables are reciprocal, and causation works in both directions. Person variables "cause"
environment through differing perceptions of that environment, and the environment has a causitive effect on person variables in that it affects behavior in
meaningful ways. The latter interpretation suggests that to some extent the environment (perceived) is a function of person variables and standing on person
variables is a function of the environment (Buss, 1977).
   Several writers have pointed to the importance of "getting beyond" the
simple debate of which term is most influential: person, situation, or their interaction. In the first place, one could design experiments to show *any* effect by

manipulating the variability in person or situation variables (Bowers, 1973; Epstein, 1979; Golding, 1975; Mischel, 1973). Across a relatively homogeneous set of situations, person variance is likely to be most influential; studying a homogeneous group of subjects in widely divergent situations will "demonstrate" the importance of situations. What is needed in this area is information about *how* persons and situations interact to determine behavior (cf. Endler, 1973).

The present lines drawn in the controversy appear to be these. Mischel (Mischel & Peake, in press), Fiske (Fiske, 1974), Shweder (Shweder & D'Andrade, 1980), and others devoted to what we might call a situationist–interactionist interpretation of personality believe that cross-situational consistency in behavior is not sufficient to warrant the use of broad trait measures in personality psychology. Those psychologists more of the trait persuasion—call them trait–interactionists to reflect their appreciation of "the situation," though to a lesser degree—believe that traits do serve a useful function in personality theory and research. We cannot resolve the issues here. Both sides agree that more data are needed to shed light on the issues. What we *can* do is outline a couple of the most intriguing directions research and thinking are taking in this controversy.

Developments in the Trait–Situation Controversy

Epstein (1979, 1980) has presented a seductively simple argument that largely explains away inconsistency in behavior across time and situation. He suggests that unreliability of behavioral measures used in personality research favorable to the situationist position is the main reason for low correlations between behaviors across time and situations. Epstein demonstrates his "solution" by using aggregated, reliable measures of (1) self-reports of emotions (e.g., happy–sad, kind–angry); (2) rated behavior (e.g., number of times subject initiated contact with others); and (3) objective behavior (hours of study). His findings suggest considerable stability in emotions and behavior over time, much greater stability than when single (and unreliable) indices are used. In another study he finds that self-report personality scales correlate moderately well with reliable self-kept records of emotional states and objective events. Importantly, Epstein (1979) argues that cross-situational stability has been demonstrated because reports of the behaviors and emotions were elicited in a range of situations representative of everyday life (they were recorded daily for about two weeks). In sum, Epstein acknowledges the importance of the situation, but believes that response dispositions—that is, relatively broad behavioral traits—can on the average explain much of behavior.

Mischel has commented on Epstein's research, and, predictably, has a different view of this work (Mischel & Peake, 1981). He first acknowledges that temporal stability in behavior within narrow ranges of situations is likely to exist as long as reliable measures of the behaviors are taken. The *real* issue, he believes, is the *cross-situational* consistency of behavior, and his reading of Epstein's data is that they are not impressively supportive. For example, Mischel & Peake (1981) eschew the personality-scale–self-rating data offered as support for this kind of stability and point out that correlations between personality scales and reliable objective behavior indices are low.

Further, they present their own data from multiple assessments of college students' conscientiousness. Examples of variables tapping this construct are psychology class attendance, study session attendance, and assignment punctuality. In all, 19 such variables were considered, and aggregated measures of each were intercorrelated. Results indicate that considerable reliability is present for individual measures (mean reliability of the across-time composites = .66), but that the average correlation *between* indicators is relatively low ($r = .20$, corrected for attenuation). Thus, the debate continues, but importantly, more data are being generated to help us understand better the psychological significance of consistency and lack of consistency in behavior.

A second development, intriguing in its implications for the trait–situation controversy, involves the search for *individual differences* in cross-situational consistency. Bem and Allen (1974) asked subjects to rate the consistency of their own behavior related to friendliness and conscientiousness in different situations and found that for those who reported high consistency, behavior across situation related to these traits was in fact relatively stable. Lower stability coefficients were obtained for individuals reporting low consistency. Thus, Bem and Allen (1974) concluded that we may be able "to predict some of the people some of the time"—namely, those who are more consistent in their behavior patterns related to individual traits.

The self-monitoring individual differences variable (Snyder, 1974) may be important in this regard. Theoretical considerations led Synder to develop the self-monitoring scale to identify persons tending to monitor closely situational cues in their interpersonal interactions (high on the scale) and persons who are less apt to rely on situational information for cues on how to act during interpersonal dealings (low on the scale). Accordingly, one would predict that persons high in self-monitoring should be less consistent than those low on the variable in terms of their behavior in different situations. Snyder and Monson (1975) confirmed this when those relatively high in self-monitoring showed more variability in self-reported likelihood estimates of performing different behaviors in different situations.

More recently, Schneiderman (1980) found higher correlations between across-trial variability scores derived from objective indices of behavior (e.g., time of eye contact, time talking in a situation) than from ratings, confirming that intraindividual variability–consistency has some generality. He also found evidence suggesting that variability may be somewhat content specific. In other words, we may tend to be very consistent in one domain of behavior, but more variable in other behavioral domains.

Implications of the Trait–Situation Controversy

I believe that the trait–situation controversy contains lessons for performance-appraisal research and practice. In this section *variability in performance*[2] across time and situations is considered and attempts to develop a measure of it are presented.

When we ask a rater to make a rating of an employee on a single dimension of performance, we are really asking (I believe) for an average or modal effectiveness rating of that individual on that category of performance. In other words, the rater is implicitly asked to ignore variability in performance level, and instead somehow average the observed performance over the time period for the appraisal. Yet, clearly, performance levels of individuals on dimensions vary to some extent across situations and time. Just as we have seen that "the situation" is probably an important factor in determining behavior relevant to the personality domain, different situations faced by employees on the job may affect their performance. Also, as the research reviewed suggests, there may be reliable individual differences in the consistency of performance on jobs.

The issue of variability–consistency in performance is of great practical importance for some jobs. For example, the power-plant operator job requires steady performance in the technical competence and decision-making areas of job performance. An operator's performing successfully in those parts of the job "most of the time" is not sufficient. In light of our review of behavioral-consistency issues in the personality domain, it is important to ask how variable performance is likely to be.

Two factors make it likely that work performance is more consistent than behavior in general. First, the number of different situations confronted in a job is typically much less than the total range of situations faced in everyday life. Of course, this depends to some extent on the job. A salesperson responsible for many different kinds of products appropriate for a wide variety of people will have more situations in which to perform than will a factory worker assigned to a single machine. But, in general, the "situation space" at work will form a relatively small subset of a person's total situation space.

In addition, situations faced at work tend to be repetitive, further reducing the variety of situational contexts to be expected on a job. Thus, with a relatively homogeneous set of situations in which to perform, the variability in job performance for individuals is likely to be less than variability of personality-related behavior across all situations confronted by these individuals.

A second reason for expecting reduced levels of variability in performance for individual employees is that relatively stable abilities underlie performance in most jobs. As we have seen, there is disagreement about the stability of behavior dependent on personality-related variables, but there exists much more agree-

---

[2]I refer here to variability in performance on single dimensions, *not* across dimensions.

ment on the consistency of behavior dependent on abilities, especially intelligence (e.g., Mischel, 1968; Olweus, 1979). It seems clear that performance on jobs is more dependent on abilities than on the behavior personality psychologists have typically studied, although, again, this varies with different types of jobs. That ability and aptitude tests have often been robust predictors of job performance (see especially the validity-generalization work: Schmidt & Hunter, 1977; Schmidt, Hunter, & Pearlman, 1981) supports the contention that these kinds of variables underlie much of performance effectiveness. Therefore, we might expect relatively high consistency in work performance because of this dependence on abilities. If this notion has merit, it also follows that on jobs with both technical and interpersonal components, performance on the technical part is likely to be more consistent than performance in the interpersonal aspects.

We have argued that reduced "situation space" and relatively stable abilities, which dictate performance levels to some degree, are two reasons to expect less variability in performance compared to variability and inconsistency in personality-related behavior in everyday life.

Another way to look at the variability-in-performance question is to consider the well-known model: Performance = Ability × Effort. As we have discussed, abilities are likely to be a stabilizing force in determining performance levels, but the motivation of individuals over time may be more variable and thus contribute to inconsistency in work performance. The main point to be made is that although stability in job effectiveness is likely to be considerable, there is also likely to be *some* variability in performance over time and in different situations. This kind of variability has been largely ignored, and yet information about distributions of performance will aid in describing a person's job performance more completely and may help increase our general understanding of the nature of performance on jobs.

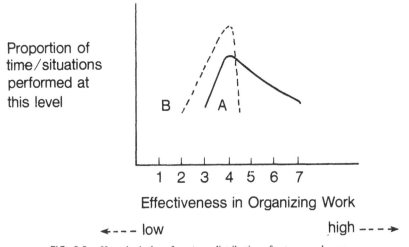

FIG. 6.2. Hypothetical performance distributions for two employees.

Consider, for example, two different performance distributions graphed in Fig. 6.2. Although these hypothetical workers have the same *modal* performance level on this dimension, B operates at close to his or her maximum performance most of the time whereas A operates at close to his or her minimum performance most of the time. Also, B is more consistent than A in performing on this dimension. Such distributions may, in addition, provide clues about the abilities and motivation of employees. A is clearly *capable* of performing at the highest level, but does not do so most of the time. B, on the other hand, is apparently limited in the level of performance possible (at least for the period rated) but works up to his or her level of capability the majority of the time. This may be stretching interpretation of such performance distributions, but the point is that *distributions* give us more information about the work performance of individual employees than do modal or average ratings.

Indexing Variability–Consistency in Work Performance

The most explicit treatment of performance variability in the performance-appraisal literature is provided by Kane (e.g., Kane & Lawler, 1978). Kane (1981) places present methods of eliciting performance information under a "Physical Measurement Model" and points out that the only parameter to be specified in this model is average performance. In his Distributional Measurement Model the standard deviation and skewness become parameters of interest. Kane views variability in effort or motivation and external constraints beyond the performers' control as two important sources of variation in job performance, sources that should be accounted for in a performance-measurement system. His Performance Distribution Assessment method does just that.

With this method the rater is asked to record for each performance factor the percent time that each level of performance *cannot be attained* because of factors beyond the ratee's control and then to note the percent time the ratee performed at or above each successive performance level. Kane (1981) provides formulas that allow computation of an average performance score, a consistency in performance score, and what he calls a negative range avoidance score, an index of how successfully the ratee avoids performing poorly. Thus, in Kane's system, variability in performance is explicitly addressed and indexed. At issue, of course, is the operational usefulness of the system. For example, can raters make reliable judgments of these percents as demanded by the method? Research is overdue to test this system in operation.

I too have been interested in variability in worker performance. I have been particularly interested in examining the interrater reliability of two simple methods of assessing performance variability–consistency. My concern is that judgments of variability in performance might be awkward for raters, foreign to the way they think about performance, and therefore difficult for them to make.

To try out these methods a study of a sample of Navy recruiters was conducted that provided peer and self-ratings of the recruiters in their same stations.

In the study, 78 recruiter ratees were evaluated such that approximately three sets of ratings were available for each ratee. Raters were asked to study each performance scale provided and rate: (1) the highest-level performance; (2) the lowest-level performance; and (3) the typical or usual-level performance observed for each ratee on each dimension. Variability scores were generated by simply computing difference scores: higest minus lowest level of performance rated on each dimension.

Interrater agreement results were in fact disappointing. Reliabilities of variability scores for individual dimensions varied from 0 to .31. When dimension-variability scores were summed to form a single consistency index for each ratee, the reliability of these composite consistency scores reached only .15. This is in contrast to interrater reliabilities of from .46 to .73 for the "typical performance" ratings on dimensions, .78 for overall "typical" performance.

A second method of obtaining variability in performance scores involved asking raters to study pairs of situations in which recruiters find themselves and to evaluate ratee performance in each situation. For example, one pair was "working with 'long-hair' prospects versus working with 'straight' prospects." Eight such situation-pair statements were administered, and differences between ratings on each of the pairs served as consistency scores. The difference scores were summed and a single overall consistency score was computed for each ratee. Interrater reliability of these composite scores was better with this method, but still quite low ($r = .30$). Possibly the use of difference scores in these methods reduces the reliability, but it is also possible that raters are simply not comfortable with making these kinds of judgments. We may be asking raters to think about performance in very unfamiliar terms. Improvements in these methods or new procedures (including Kane's) should be attempted in an effort to index *distributions* of performance effectiveness for individuals, but to date, results are not promising.

Summary

In this section we have reviewed positions taken and research conducted on the trait–situation controversy in personality psychology. A general interactionist paradigm seems best suited to learn more about both consistencies and discriminability in human behavior. It was argued that consistency in *performance* is likely to be greater than stability in social behavior because of the reduced variety of situations faced at work and the fact that relatively stable abilities are important determiners of work behavior in many jobs. However, *some* variability in performance is likely to occur on jobs, and it may be of considerable theoretical and, at times, practical interest to measure that variability. Present rating methods measure model or average performance, and ignore intraindividual variations in effectiveness. Kane's Distributional Measurement Model was described briefly as a way to address consistency in performance, but work we began suggests that raters may have difficulties in providing reliable ratings of performance variability–consistency. Future research should evaluate methods of indexing individual employees' performance distributions.

PERSONAL-CONSTRUCT THEORY

The Theory in Relation to Person Perception

George A. Kelly (1955) developed a sweeping psychological theory about humans and how they function. A full description of his theory is beyond the scope and intention of this paper, but those aspects of the theory that pertain to person perception are important for our purposes. Kelly states in his organization corollary that each person characteristically evolves, for his or her convenience in anticipating events (or other persons' activities), a construction system reflecting his or her personal way of viewing and interpreting those events. This means that individuals develop personal-construct systems, categories that they use to judge events and to make predictions about future events, *and* that they impose some of these categories on their person perceptions.[3] That is, individuals see other persons through their own "interpersonal filters," and they interpret what they see according to these target persons' perceived standing on each of their personal constructs. As Kelly (1955) puts it, ". . . man creates his own ways of seeing the world in which he lives; the world does not create them for him. He builds constructs and tries them on for size [p. 12]."

This view of personal constructs is in a sense close to the conception of implicit personality theory. Notice that like IPT, the focus is on the perceiver and the way he or she makes judgments about events and other persons. With respect to person perception, personal constructs are likely to affect the experience of observing others, to filter interpersonal information, or even to "bias" the perception of other persons. Of course, Kelly and his followers would not regard these personal constructs as *biasing* perception. But, the point is that both conceptions relate to interpersonal filters used by perceivers. Interestingly, personal-construct theory, much more than IPT research, examines individual differences in these filters and we explore this facet. Also, personal-construct research focuses on the *content* of the interpersonal dimensions as well as on their structure, and this creates additional important implications related to formation of performance judgments.

---

[3]The serious student of personal-construct theory will notice that we refer here to only one part of a person's personal-construct system—those categories that have as a *focus of convenience* events that involve interpersonal judgments. For example, we are not concerned with those constructs that might be used to judge such objects as music, art, or writing.

Role Titles

Self	Mother	Father	Brother	Sister	Spouse	Ex-flame	Best Friend	Ex-friend	Rejecting Person	Pitied Person	Threatening Person	Attractive Person	Accepted Teacher	Rejected Teacher	Boss	Successful Person	Happy Person	Ethical Person	Neighbour	Constructs
1	2	3	4	5	6	7	8	9	10	11	12	13	14	15	16	17	18	19	20	Constructs
																O	O	O		1
					O	O	O													2
O					O		O													3
	O				O	O														4

FIG. 6.3.   Sample RCRT (from Bannister & Mair, 1968).

Research on Personal Constructs

Research in personal-construct theory has been stimulated by the development of the Role Construct Repertory Test (RCRT), a protocol that in its most common form asks a subject first to record the names of persons who fit each of a number of roles (e.g., mother, father, best friend, etc.). The respondent is then asked to consider various triads of these role persons, and for each triad to identify an important way in which two of these persons are alike and yet different from the third person. Taken together, the responses constitute the subject's personal constructs. Fig. 6.3 contains a sample RCRT protocol. Two lists of constructs are then presented in Fig. 6.4 to provide a feel for the nature of personal constructs.

Research in personal-construct theory has often employed the RCRT to help subjects generate their personal constructs. This work has proceeded in several directions. Lines of research include: (1) the study of thinking among clinical groups such as thought-disordered schizophrenics (Bannister, 1963; Frith & Lillie, 1972; Widom, 1976); (2) an exploration of suicidal behavior (Kelly, 1961; Landfield, 1975); (3) the investigation of cognitive complexity (Bieri, 1961; Crockett, 1965; Metcalfe, 1974); (4) a study of the psychotherapy process (Fielding, 1975; Fransella & Joyston-Bechal, 1971); (5) an examination of interpersonal relations (Duck, 1973; Huston, 1974); (6) the study of meaningfulness of interpersonal categories and extreme response style (Cromwell & Caldwell,

College Students (Levy, 1956)

- More careful vs. more responsible
- Teamwork vs. egotist
- Understanding vs. not understanding
- More serious vs. less serious
- Sensible vs. not too sensible
- Don't give up vs. always give up

Clinicians (Borman, 1978)[*]

Responsibility: The degree to which a person is able to assess the consequences of his actions accurately, and to consider carefully the needs of persons involved with him so that he is able to act in a way that as nearly as possible makes them and himself happy and handles the situation realistically.

Commonsensical vs. Head in the Clouds: Able to operate effectively in practical situations, good tactical and strategic thinker, realistic, capable of pragmatic efforts vs. difficulty coping with practical matters, focuses on the abstract at the wrong times thereby missing the obvious, displays poor timing, cannot be relied on to make sound decisions. Unrealistic, impractical.

Egoism: Excessive love or thought of oneself. The egoist is the kind of man who uses two parking spaces with his Volkswagen. He won't heat the house because he enjoys a cold room. He eats a lot of garlic for his health though his wife can't stand the smell.

Complexity: This construct is rather hard to define precisely, but it refers in one sense to the degree of differentiation of an individual. He is complex, interesting, sophisticated, many-faceted. He knows about and has experienced many aspects of life and has integrated these experiences into his personality in a healthy way, without becoming fragmented and contradictory in personality and cognitive structure. He is the opposite of the simple, one-dimensional person who fails to arouse the interest of the people with whom he interacts.

Impulsiveness: The tendency to lack control over one's action. The impulsive man is the sort of person who jumps at your throat when teased. He will kick his car when it won't start. When contradicted, his temper will rise like boiling milk left on the stove. He might gamble a fortune on a hunch, blowing his top when luck is against him.

[*]Borman's subjects were instructed to define their constructs very carefully.

FIG. 6.4.   Samplings of personal constructs.

1962; Hamilton, 1968; Landfield, 1965; O'Donovan, 1965; and finally (7) the investigation of individual differences in personal constructs (Hamilton, 1970; Kuusinen, 1969; Sechrest, 1968).

To provide a flavor for research in personal-construct psychology, we review a study examining the effect on ratings of the meaningfulness of dimensions employed. Using the previously described Rep Grid, Isaacson (1966) asked college student subjects to provide ten personal constructs related to making judgments about other people. Isaacson then had subjects rate ten acquaintances on their own personal constructs as well as on ten Manifest Anxiety Scale items and ten Semantic Differential dimensions. Results showed that ratings on the personal constructs yielded larger variances across the target ratees than did ratings on the other dimensions. This has been a consistent finding (e.g., Adams-Webber, 1979; Bonarius, 1970); it appears that individuals prefer to use their own constructs to rate others (Bonarius, 1965; Landfield, 1965), and that they differentiate more finely between persons when employing their own dimensions. Presumably, over time an individual uses a similar set of constructs in making judgments about others, and thus grows used to and comfortable with employing these constructs to evaluate other persons.[4]

An important consideration in personal-construct research (*and* IPT research, as well) is *individual differences* in constructs and IPTs. The strategies for studying such individual differences can be divided into four categories: (1) studies of the underlying structure of IPT across all persons; (2) investigations of different "points of view" related to IPT; (3) comparisons of dimensions underlying different individuals' interpersonal categories; and (4) studies related to individual differences in constructs/IPTs using free-response methods.

Structure of IPT/Personal Constructs.   The studies reviewed in this section are not usually considered to be related to questions of individual differences in IPT. Yet, conclusions drawn in this line of research *imply* that few if any individual differences in IPT exist. The Passini and Norman (1966) study reviewed previously is an example of such a study. Conclusions from this and similar studies (e.g., Norman, 1963; Tupes & Christal, 1958, 1961) imply that there exists a "universal IPT," with individual differences nonexistent or at least unimportant. Of course, an approach that uses group data to study individual differences does not really focus on these differences and may well overlook them.

Different "Points of View".   Individual differences multidimensional scaling has been used to identify groups of subjects who differ in their patterns of perceived similarities between traits. Essentially, the multidimensional scaling analysis sorts individuals into groups according to similarities in the ways they have made judgments about how traits covary. Individuals clustered into a group are then said to have a certain "point of view," a particular way of viewing trait interrelationships—in short, a single IPT.

---

[4]This is not to say that in very different interpersonal situations (e.g., in a heated argument with two or three others versus initially meeting individuals at a party) a person uses *the same* or even very similar constructs to make judgments about others. Kelly recognized that the content of personal constructs depends to some extent on the situation the perceiver faces. To a degree, different contexts demand different sets of categories if relevant interpersonal judgments are to be made. However, personal-construct theory posits a reasonably stable core set of interpersonal dimensions an individual uses to make judgments about people within a delineated set of situations.

In this kind of study, subjects are given traits in some protocol asking them to judge the similarity of each pair of traits. The individual differences multidimensional scaling procedure then clusters subjects as previously described, and often personality and other variables are correlated with the different points of view. Using this paradigm, Pedersen (1965) found three "points of view," one of them associated with authoritarianism. Walters and Jackson (1966) identified two groups of subjects and labeled the critical dimensions that separated these groups as Interpersonal Affectivity and Harmfulness. Finally, Messick and Kogan (1966) identified a number of "points of view" for both males and females, but relationships between personality variables and dimensions separating the groups were low and difficult to define. Even though nothing definitive has been concluded from such studies, the finding of subgroups at least tends to call into question the universality of IPTs.

Dimensions Underlying Interpersonal Categories.   In studies of these dimensions, subjects are given interpersonal categories and are then asked to rate the same stimulus persons (or *roles* such as insurance salesperson, factory worker) on each of the categories. Correlations between categories are computed for each subject and factor analyses of each subject's correlation matrix are compared. The two most widely cited papers using this approach draw very different conclusions about the extent of individual differences between subjects' underlying categories. Kuusinen (1969) compared each subject's factor solution to the *group* solution (pooled across all individuals in the sample) and concluded that no meaningful individual differences were present. However, Hamilton (1970) faulted Kuusinen on his method of assessing factor congruence. He reanalyzed Kuusinen's data and supplied data on his own to reassess the magnitude of these individual differences. Applying Tucker's coefficient of congruence (Harman, 1967), a factor similarity index, and making comparisons between *individuals,* Hamilton found wide individual differences in both samples. He concluded that substantial differences are present in the underlying dimensionality of interpersonal categories for different perceivers.

Free Response Methods.   Several psychologists interested in IPT have called for more emphasis on free response in generating subjects' IPTs or personal constructs. For example, Cliff (1973) suggested that when subjects all use the same traits, the IPTs emerging from the rating task are artificially restricted and may unduly reduce many of the individual differences that might appear in a less structured task. Cronbach (1958) too has suggested more use of free-response protocols to elicit individuals' IPT. And, in his review of IPT research, Schneider (1973) concludes, ". . . so long as such (person perception) research provides perceivers with categories of explanation, it can never answer the question of which categories are 'naturally' used by perceivers [p. 307; parentheses added]."

But, perhaps the strongest proponents of free response in this domain are personal-construct theorists. Indeed, one of the central reasons for the development of the RCRT was to elicit in a clinical setting the patient's personal categories couched in his or her own terms. Kelly (1955) believed that personality assessment must take into account the person's own abstractions and generalizations about him- or herself, even when they are in rough form. Thus, a number of writers have pleaded for more use of free-response methods in describing IPTs or personal-construct systems.

Yet, only a few studies focusing on individual differences have used free-response methods. Sechrest (1968) asked nursing students to form personal constructs and found some overlap in the content of these categories but also substantial individual differences. Rosenberg, Jones, and colleagues (Jones & Rosenberg, 1974; Rosenberg & Sedlak, 1972) have used a free-response method to deduce the IPTs or underlying interpersonal dimensions of subjects. Their method requires subjects to provide words or phrases describing each of a number of persons familiar to them. Thus, both the choice of target persons and the selection of descriptors is left to the subject. Subsequently, the number of times is tallied that subjects record the same pair of descriptors (e.g., big, strong) when referring to a single target person in the protocol. Results of multidimensional scaling analyses on similarity data generated from the frequencies of descriptor cooccurrences in individual subjects' responses suggest substantial individual differences in subjects' interpersonal space (Rosenberg, 1977).

Implications for Performance Rating

Recall that a distinction was made previously regarding personal construct systems and IPT. IPT is typically concerned with the way in which dimensions covary in raters' beliefs about behavior and personalty. Personal constructs, on the other hand, have to do with both the relationships between interpersonal dimensions and the *content* of those dimensions.

Importantly, individual differences in dimension *content* appear to have additional implications for performance rating. Content in personal constructs related to viewing ratees' work behavior may to a degree affect what the rater *looks for* in observing persons at work. If one rater has as an important construct "getting along smoothly with others on the job," and a second rater does not share that construct or anything like it, the first rater may be more likely than the second to focus on work behavior related directly to that aspect of performance.

The relationships of personal constructs to perceptions of work behavior may be akin to what might be called "folk" theories of work performance. In my experience, interviews with persons about work on jobs or even casual conversation with people about their jobs sometimes reveal what appear to be deeply felt and rather idiosyncratic "theories" of job performance. Consider these statements: A sales manager says with conviction, "You know what the key to this (sales) job is? Thinking on your feet with customers." A first-line supervisor speaks, "Show me a person who comes to work on time and I'll show you a good employee," and a manager states, "You gotta be political on this (manager's) job; *that's* the way to make it." Folk theories like these held by persons responsible for performance appraisal may reflect individual's category systems that help shape judgments about how effectively employees are performing, in part because of what raters attend to in gathering performance information. If we were to use the Rep Grid to elicit personal constructs related to job performance, we might in effect be generating these kinds of folk theories.

Of course, characteristics of the work situation and of the employees themselves will in part dictate what raters observe and process when viewing work behavior. When a salesperson makes the biggest sale in the history of the region, the regional manager rater is highly likely to attend to that piece of performance information no matter what the content of his or her personal constructs might be. Also, other features of the situation that increase the salience of a particular construct will make perceivers' use of that construct more likely (Taylor & Fiske, 1978; Tversky, 1977). An example offered by Feldman (1981) is that race is more likely to be a salient construct when a ratee group has only one black person than when it contains all blacks. However, it is also plausible that perceiver differences exist in personal-construct systems related to observing work performance, and these differences may lead to differences in the work behavior attended to and subsequently in evaluations of performance. I submit that these kinds of personal-construct differences are an important potential source of inter-rater disagreement. Research is needed to: (1) determine if raters actually have and can report meaningful personal constructs related to observing work behavior; (2) evaluate the stability of these constructs in assessing work behavior in different situations and contexts; (3) examine individual differences in such constructs; and (4) assess the impact of these differences on observations of work behavior and ratings of work performance.

General Research Proposal for Investigating Performance-Related Personal-Construct Systems

Perhaps the best way to proceed in this research is to elicit constructs from individuals by asking them to list persons with whom they have worked on the target job and by presenting triads of these stimulus persons in the manner of the Kelly Rep Grid. The researcher then asks each subject to think of how two of the stimulus persons are similar in their work performance and yet different from the third for each of a number of triads, until the subject believes that he or she has provided all important constructs. Similar to what has been done in other work with the Rep Grid, "test–retest" reliability and across-situation stability of the constructs might be studied. Previous research involving interpersonal constructs suggests reasonably good stability of these constructs over time (Bieri & Blacker, 1956; Fjeld & Landfield, 1961; Hamilton, 1970; Kehoe & Reynolds, 1977).

Also, dimensionality of individual subjects' constructs can be examined by asking them to rate each stimulus person on each construct, then factoring or clustering the constructs. This method has been used in research on cognitive complexity, with some subjects' ratings yielding complex multiple-factor solutions and others more simple one- or two-factor solutions (Adams-Webber, 1979). It may be, for example, that an overall evaluative component overwhelms any differentiation between performance constructs for some or even a majority of subjects. It seems important to study individual differences in the *content* of constructs, but this is difficult because there is no good way to generate numerical indices of similarities/differences in content. A simple "trait-implication" method suggested by Borman (1978b) allows such numerical analysis.

This method provides a vehicle that allows each individual subject to define his or her own interpersonal categories according to the perceived similarity between each construct and each of a number of traits. A subject "defining" a category or construct rates the similarity in meaning between his or her category and each one of a sizable number of well-defined trait concepts. This vector of ratings then defines the category numerically. For example, consider an interpersonal construct, "affectionate." Suppose the subject with this category were given the following five traits and rating instructions:

Make ratings on a nine-point scale using the following guidelines:

9. High standing on my category implies high standing on this trait, and low standing on my category implies low standing on this trait; the two are very highly correlated.
5. High or low standing on my category implies nothing about a persons' standing on this trait; the two are uncorrelated.
1. High standing on my category implies low standing on this trait and low standing on my category implies high standing on this trait; the two are very highly correlated in a negative direction.

Make your ratings on this nine-point scale for each of your categories against each of five traits we supply here.

Category	Trait	Ratings
Affectionate	Likability	8
	Energy Level	5
	Originality	5
	Dominance	4
	Independence	3

Now consider another subject who has a category that he or she labels "Nice to me." In response to the same trait-implication task the subject might provide the following ratings:

Category	Trait	Ratings
Nice to me	Likability	8
	Energy Level	7
	Originality	7
	Dominance	6
	Independence	5

Notice what we have accomplished with this procedure. We now have numerical definitions of these categories. Further, the subjects themselves have provided the categories and *their own* definitions of the categories in the context of more widely used trait concepts, consistent with the important principle of free response. This subject-generated numerical depiction of interpersonal categories paves the way for correlational analyses to index similarity in the content of constructs.

For example, the two sets of ratings just shown are highly related ($r = .77$), and this coefficient provides a useful index of the relationship between the content of these two categories. This method might be used, then, in correlational analyses to examine similarities and differences between different subjects' work-performance constructs. The most obvious hypothesis related to the latter is that persons with similar personal constructs will tend to agree more closely in their performance ratings than persons with very dissimilar construct content.

But other questions must be investigated first to gain understanding of how individuals' performance constructs work. Do persons with a construct in common tend to "look for" the same kind of behavior in ratees? That is, do they search for performance information related to the content of their constructs? More broadly, do raters attend to, process, and remember information in line with their construct systems and fail to see and/or tend to forget ratee behavior that falls outside the domain of their category system? And, as mentioned, there are basic questions about the stability of such constructs across time and situations.

Another possibility is that raters simply lack well-defined construct systems related to judging others' *performances*. When evaluating ratee effectiveness on the job, raters may use many of the same constructs they employ in making general, personality-related evaluations of others. One interesting implication of this speculation is that raters may not think very "naturally" in performance-category terms. Performance-related rating dimensions might be awkward to use because raters are accustomed to making judgments more in the personality domain. Thus, information they have processed about ratees related to personality must be "translated" somehow to form a judgment related to performance. Personality research suggesting that we act as naive trait theorists, typically thinking about others in trait terms (e.g., Ross, 1977), lends some credence to this possibility.

The discussion so far of the impact on performance ratings of personal constructs related to work behavior has in a sense suggested a *passive* examination of these constructs and their impact. A completely different way to approach this is to try to *impose upon raters* a single, common personal-construct system that corresponds to the dimensional system they *should be* using to make performance judgments. With this strategy, considerable time and effort should be devoted to getting raters familiar with the rating dimensions and comfortable in using them within the performance-appraisal system. Raters should be made to accept the dimensional system as reflecting a useful and reasonable way to divide up the performance domain.

In addition, raters might be encouraged to organize data about individual ratees according to the dimensional system. As performance information is gathered and recorded (as in diary keeping, for example), it should be tied directly to the dimensions. In other words, raters should be strongly encouraged to look for performance data related to dimensions in the system. Over time, this might essentially *create* a common personal-construct system related to work behavior in each of the raters using the system.

This "active" notion about personal constructs and performance-appraisal dimension systems has an interesting parallel in person-construct theory approaches to dealing with clinical patients. A basic idea in treatment is to work at altering the patient's construct system to make it more useful to the person for dealing with "real-world" interpersonal situations. Here, we are talking about forming a dimensional system maximally useful from the organizations' point of view, and then attempting to alter raters' construct systems to bring them in line with the organizational system.

Summary

In sum, we have briefly reviewed person-construct theory and research, and then we explored possible effects on performance ratings of raters' construct systems related to evaluating ratee work behavior. Individual differences in such construct systems may provide one important reason for interrater disagreement in ratings. In "looking for different things" regarding ratee work performance, raters may in fact observe and process different samplings of behavior, resulting in ratings based on different performance information. Methods and strategies were offered for studying personal constructs in this domain. In addition, I introduced the notion of altering individuals' personal-construct systems to conform to dimensions with which raters *should be* concerned in evaluating job incumbents.

ACKNOWLEDGMENT

The author thanks Marvin D. Dunnette for reading and commenting on an earlier version of this chapter.

REFERENCES

Adams-Webber, J. R. *Personal construct theory.* New York: Wiley, 1979.

Bäckteman, G., & Magnusson, D. Longitudinal stability of personal characteristics. *Journal of Personality,* 1981, *49,* 148–160.

Banks, C. G. *Analyzing the rating process: A content analysis approach.* Paper presented at the meeting of the American Psychological Association, New York, August-September 1979.

Bannister, D. The genesis of schizophrenic thought disorder: A serial invalidation hypothesis. *British Journal of Psychiatry,* 1963, *109,* 680.

Bannister, D. & Mair, J. M. M. The evaluation of personal constructs. London: Academic Press, 1968.

Bem, D. J., & Allen, A. On predicting some of the people some of the time: The search for cross-situational consistencies in behavior. *Psychological Review,* 1974, *81,* 506–520.

Bem, D. J., & Funder, D. C. Predicting more of the people more of the time: Assessing the personality of situations. *Psychological Review,* 1978, *85,* 485–501.

Berman, J. S., & Kenny, D. A. Correlational bias in observer ratings. *Journal of Personality and Social Psychology,* 1976, *34,* 263–273.

Bernardin, H. J., & Smith, P. C. Clarification of some issues regarding the development and use of behaviorally anchored rating scales (BARS). *Journal of Applied Psychology,* 1981, *66,* 458–463.

Bernardin, H. J., & Walter, C. S. Effects of rater training and diary-keeping on psychometric error in ratings. *Journal of Applied Psychology,* 1977, *62,* 64–69.

Bieri, J. Complexity–simplicity variable in cognitive and preferential behavior. In D. W. Fiske & S. Maddi (Eds.), Functions of varied experience. Homewood, Ill.: Dorsey Press, 1961.

Bieri, J., & Blacker, E. The generality of cognitive complexity in the perception of people and inkblots. *Journal of Abnormal and Social Psychology,* 1956, *53,* 112–117.

Block, J. *Lives through time.* Berkeley, Calif.: Bancroft Books, 1971.

Block, J., Weiss, D. S., & Thorne, A. How relevant is a semantic similarity interpretation of personality ratings? *Journal of Personality and Social Psychology,* 1979, *37,* 1055–1074.

Bonarius, J. C. J. Research in the personal construct theory of George A. Kelly. In B. A. Maher (Ed.), *Progress in experimental personality research* (Vol. 2). New York: Academic Press, 1965.

Bonarius, J. C. J. *Personal construct psychology and extreme response style: An interaction model of meaningfulness, maladjustment, and communication.* Groningen: *University of Groningen Monograph,* 1970.

Borgatta, E. F., Cottrell, L. S., & Mann, J. H. The spectrum of individual interaction characteristics: An inter-dimensional analysis. *Psychological Reports,* 1958, *4,* 279–319.

Borman, W. C. Effects of instructions to avoid halo error on reliability and validity of performance evaluation ratings. *Journal of Applied Psychology,* 1975, *60,* 556–560.

Borman, W. C. Exploring the upper limits of reliability and validity in job performance ratings. *Journal of Applied Psychology,* 1978, *63,* 135–144. (a)

Borman, W. C. *Implicit personality theories and personal constructs: A study of individual differences.* Unpublished manuscript, 1978. (b)

Borman, W. C. Individual differences correlates of accuracy in evaluating others' performance effectiveness. *Applied Psychological Measurement,* 1979, *3,* 103–115.

Borman, W. C., & Dunnette, M. D. Behavior-based versus trait-oriented performance ratings: An empirical study. *Journal of Applied Psychology,* 1975, *60,* 561–565.

Bowers, K. S. Situationism in psychology: An analysis and a critique. *Psychological Review,* 1973, *80,* 307–336.

Buss, A. R. The trait–situation controversy and the concept of interaction. *Personality and Social Psychology Bulletin,* 1977, *3,* 196–201.

Cantor, N., & Mischel, W. Prototypes in person perception. In L. Berkowitz (Ed.), *Advances in experimental social psychology* (Vol. 12). New York: Academic Press, 1979.

Cliff, N. Scaling. *Annual Review of Psychology*, 1973, *24*, 473–506.

Cone, J. D. *The overlapping worlds of behavioral assessment and performance appraisal*. Paper presented at the First Annual Scientist-Practitioner Conference in Industrial/Organizational Psychology, Old Dominion University, Virginia Beach, Va., April 1980.

Cooper, W. H. Conceptual similarity as a source of illusory halo in job performance ratings. *Journal of Applied Psychology*, 1981, *66*, 302–307. (a)

Cooper, W. H. Ubiquitous halo. *Psychological Bulletin*, 1981, *90*, 218–244. (b)

Crockett, W. H. Cognitive complexity and impression formation. In B. A. Maher (Ed.), *Progress in experimental personality research* (Vol. 1). New York: Academic Press, 1965.

Cromwell, R. L., & Caldwell, D. F. A comparison of ratings based on personal constructs of self and others. *Journal of Clinical Psychology*, 1962, *18*, 43–46.

D'Andrade, R. G. Trait psychology and componential analysis. *American Anthropologist*, 1965, *67*, 215–228.

D'Andrade, R. G. Memory and the assessment of behavior. In T. Blalock (Ed.), *Measurement in the social sciences*. Chicago: Aldine-Atherton, 1974.

Duck, S. W. *Personal relationships and personal constructs*. New York: Wiley, 1973.

Einhorn, H. J., & Hogarth, R. M. Confidence in judgment: Persistence of the illusion of validity. *Psychological Review*, 1978, *85*, 395–416.

Endler, N. S. Estimating variance components from mean squares for random and mixed effects analysis of variance models. *Perceptual and Motor Skills*, 1966, *22*, 559–470.

Endler, N. S. The person versus the situation—a pseudo issue? A response to Alker. *Journal of Personality*, 1973, *41*, 287–303.

Endler, N. S., & Hunt, J. McV. S–R inventories of hostility and comparisons of the proportions of variance from persons, responses, and situations for hostility and anxiousness. *Journal of Personality and Social Psychology*, 1968, *9*, 309–315.

Endler, N. S., & Hunt, J. McV. Generalizability of contributions from sources of variance in the S–R inventories of anxiousness. *Journal of Personality*, 1969, *37*, 1–24.

Epstein, S. The stability of behavior: I. On predicting most of the people much of the time. *Journal of Personality and Social Psychology*, 1979, *37*, 1097–1126.

Epstein, S. The stability of behavior: II. Implications for psychological research. *American Psychologist*, 1980, *35*, 790–806.

Feldman, J. M. Beyond attribution theory: Cognitive processes in performance appraisal. *Journal of Applied Psychology*, 1981, *66*, 127–148.

Fielding, J. M. A technique for measuring outcome in psychotherapy. *British Journal of Medical Psychology*, 1975, *48*, 189–198.

Fiske, D. W. The limits for the conventional science of personality. *Journal of Personality*, 1974, *42*, 1–11.

Fjeld, S. P., & Landfield, A. E. Personal construct consistency. *Psychological Reports*, 1961, *8*, 127–129.

Flanagan, J. C. The critical incident technique. *Psychological Bulletin*, 1954, *51*, 327–358.

Foster, S. L., & Cone, J. D. Current issues in direct observation. *Behavioral Assessment*, 1980, *2*, 313–338.

Fransella, F., & Joyston-Bechal, M. P. An investigation of conceptual process and pattern change in a psychotherapy group. *British Journal of Psychiatry*, 1971, *119*, 199–206.

Frith, C. D., & Lillie, F. J. Why does the repertory grid test indicate thought disorder? *British Journal of Social and Clinical Psychology*, 1972, *11*, 73–78.

Golding, S. L. Flies in the ointment: Methodological problems in the analysis of the percentage of variance due to persons and situations. *Psychological Bulletin*, 1975, *82*, 278–288.

Green, S. G., & Mitchell, T. R. Attributional processes of leaders in leader–member interactions. *Organizational Behavior and Human Performance*, 1979, *23*, 429–458.

Hakel, M. Normative personality factors recovered from readings or personality descriptions: The beholder's eye. *Personal Psychology*, 1974, *27*, 409–421.

Hamilton, D. L. Personality attributes associated with extreme response style. *Psychological Bulletin*, 1968, *69*, 192–203.

Hamilton, D. L. The structure of personality judgements: Comments on Kuusinen's paper and further evidence. *Scandinavian Journal of Psychology*, 1970, *13*, 261–265.

Harman, H. H. *Modern factor analysis*. Chicago: University of Chicago Press, 1967.

Hogan, R., DeSoto, C. B., & Solano, C. Traits, tests and personality research. *American Psychologist*, 1977, *32*, 255–264.

Huston, T. L. *Foundations of interpersonal attraction*. New York: Academic Press, 1974.

Isaacson, G. I. *A comparative study of meaningfulness of personal and common constructs*. Unpublished doctoral thesis, University of Missouri, 1966.

Johnson, D. M. Reanalysis of experimental halo effects. *Journal of Applied Psychology*, 1963, *47*, 46–47.

Jones, E. E., & Nisbett, R. E. *The actor and observer: Divergent perceptions of the causes of behavior*. New York: General Learning Press, 1971.

Jones, R. A., & Rosenberg, S. Structural representations of naturalistic descriptions of personality. *Multivariate Behavioral Research*, 1974, *9*, 217–230.

Kane, J. S. *Improving the measurement basis of performance appraisals*. Paper presented at the American Psychological Association Convention, Los Angeles, September 7, 1981.

Kane, J. S., & Lawler, E. E., III. Methods of peer assessment. *Psychological Bulletin*, 1978, *85*, 555–586.

Kehoe, J., & Reynolds, T. J. Interactive multi-dimensional scaling of cognitive structure underlying person perception. *Applied Psychological Measurement*, 1977, *1*, 155–169.

Kelly, G. A. *The psychology of personal constructs*. New York: Norton, 1955.

Kelly, G. A. Theory and therapy in suicide: The personal construct point of view. In N. Farberow & E. Schneidman (Eds.), *The cry for help*. New York: McGraw-Hill, 1961.

Kent, R. N., & Foster, S. L. Direct observational procedures: Methodological issues in applied settings. In A. Ciminero, K. S. Calhoun, & H. E. Adams (Eds.), *Handbook of behavioral assessment*. New York: Wiley, 1977.

Koltuv, B. Some characteristics of intrajudge trait intercorrelations. *Psychological Monographs*, 1962, *76*, 552.

Komaki, J., Blood, M. R., & Holder, D. Fostering friendliness in a fast food franchise. *Journal of Organizational Behavior Management*, 1980, *2*, 151–163.

Komaki, J., Collins, R. L., & Thoene, T. J. F. Behavioral measurement in business, industry and government. *Behavioral Assessment*, 1980, *2*, 103–123.

Kuusinen, J. Affective and denotative structures of personality ratings. *Scandinavian Journal of Psychology*, 1969, *12*, 181–188.

Lamiell, J. T., Foss, M. A., & Cavenee, P. On the relationship between conceptual schemes and behavior reports: A closer look. *Journal of Personality*, 1980, *48*, 54–73.

Landfield, A. W. Meaningfulness of self, ideal and other as related to own vs. therapist's personal construct dimensions. *Psychological Reports*, 1965, *16*, 605–608.

Landfield, A. W. A personal construct approach to suicidal behavior. In P. Slater (Eds.), *The measurement of subjective variation by grid technique*. New York: Wiley, 1975.

Landy, F. J. & Farr, J. L. Performance rating. *Psychological Bulletin*, 1980, *87*, 72–107.

Lay, C. H., & Jackson, D. N. Analysis of the generality of trait-inferential relationships. *Journal of Personality and Social Psychology*, 1969, *12*, 12–21.

Levy, L. H. Personal constructs and predictive behavior. *Journal of Abnormal and Social Psychology*, 1956, *53*, 54–58.

Magnusson, D. An analysis of situational dimensions. *Perceptual and Motor Skills*, 1971, *32*, 851–867.

Mann, R. D. *The relation between personality characteristics and individual performance in small groups*. Unpublished doctoral dissertation, University of Michigan, 1959.

Messick, S. J., & Kogan, N. Personality consistencies in judgment: Dimensions of role constructs. *Multivariate Behavioral Research*, 1966, *1*, 165–175.

Metcalfe, R. J. Own versus provided constructs in a Rep test measure of cognitive complexity. *Psychological Reports*, 1974, *35*, 1305–1306.

Mischel, W. *Personality and assessment*. New York: Wiley, 1968.

Mischel, W. Towards a cognitive social learning reconceptualization of personality. *Psychological Review*, 1973, *80*, 252–283.

Mischel, W. On the interface of cognition and personality: Beyond the person–situation debate. *American Psychologist*, 1979, *34*, 740–754.

Mischel, W., & Peake, P. In search of consistency: Measure for measure. In M. P. Zanna, E. T. Higgins, & C. P. Herman (Eds.), *Consistency in social behavior: The Ontario Symposium of personality and social psychology* (Vol. 2). Hillsdale, N.J.: Lawrence Erlbaum Associates, 1981.

Mulaik, S. A. Are personality factors raters' conceptual factors? *Journal of Consulting and Clinical Psychology*, 1964, *28*, 506–511.

Newcomb, T. M. The consistency of certain extrovert–introvert behavior patterns in 51 problem boys. *Contributions to Education* (No. 382). New York: Columbia University, Teachers College, 1929.

Newcomb, T. An experiment designed to test the validity of a rating technique. *Journal of Educational Psychology*, 1931, *22*, 279–289.

Nisbett, R. E., & Wilson, T. D. The halo effect: Evidence for unconscious alteration of judgments. *Journal of Personality and Social Psychology*, 1977, *35*, 250–256.

Norman, W. T. Toward an adequate taxonomy of personality attribute: Replicated factor structure in peer nomination personality ratings. *Journal of Abnormal and Social Psychology*, 1963, *66*, 574–583.

Norman, W. T., & Goldberg, L. R. Raters, ratees, and randomness in personality structure. *Journal of Personality and Social Psychology*, 1966, *4*, 681–691.

O'Donovan, D. Rating extremity: Pathology or meaningfulness. *Psychological Review*, 1965, *72*, 358–372.

Olweus, D. Stability of aggressive reaction patterns in males: A review. *Psychological Bulletin*, 1979, *86*, 852–875.

Passini, F. T., & Norman, W. T. A universal conception of personality structure? *Journal of Personality and Social Psychology*, 1966, *4*, 44–49.

Pedersen, D. M. The measurement of individual differences in perceived personality-trait relationships and their relation to certain determinants. *Journal of Social Psychology*, 1965, *65*, 233–258.

Rosenberg, S. New approaches to the analysis of personal constructs in person perception. In *Nebraska symposium on motivation 1976*. Lincoln/London: University of Nebraska Press, 1977.

Rosenberg, S., & Sedlak, A. Structural representations of perceived personality trait relationships. In A. K. Romney, R. N. Shepard, & S. Nerlove (Eds.), *Multidimensional scaling: Theory and applications in the behavioral sciences. Vol. 2 Applications*. New York: Seminar Press, 1972.

Ross, L. The intuitive psychologist and his shortcomings: Distortions in the attribution process. In L. Berkowitz (Ed.), *Advances in experimental social psychology* (Vol. 10). New York: Academic Press, 1977.

Sawyer, J. Measurement *and* prediction, clinical *and* statistical. *Psychological Bulletin*, 1966, *66*, 178–200.

Schmidt, F. L., & Hunter, J. E. Development of a general solution to the problem of validity generalization. *Journal of Applied Psychology*, 1977, *62*, 529–540.

Schmidt, F. L., Hunter, J. E., & Pearlman, K. Task differences as moderators of aptitude test validity in selection: A red herring. *Journal of Applied Psychology*, 1981, *66*, 166–185.

Schneider, D. J. Implicit personality theory: A review. *Psychological Bulletin*, 1973, *79*, 294–309.

Schneiderman, W. A personality dimension of consistency versus variability without the use of self-reports or ratings. *Journal of Personality and Social Psychology,* 1980, *39,* 158–164.

Schneier, E. C. Operational utility and psychometric characteristics of behavioral expectations scales: A cognitive reinterpretation. *Journal of Applied Psychology,* 1977, *62,* 541–548.

Schwab, D. P., Heneman, H. G., & DeCotiis, T. A. Behaviorally anchored rating scales: A review of the literature. *Personnel Psychology,* 1975, *28,* 549–562.

Sechrest, L. B. Personal constructs and personal characteristics. *Journal of Individual Psychology,* 1968, *24,* 162–166.

Shweder, R. A. How relevant is an individual difference theory of personality? *Journal of Personality,* 1975, *43,* 455–484.

Shweder, R. A. Factors and fictions in person perception: A reply to Lamiell, Foss, and Cavenee. *Journal of Personality,* 1980, *48,* 74–81.

Shweder, R. A., & D'Andrade, R. G. Accurate reflection or systematic distortion? A reply to Block, Weiss, and Thorne. *Journal of Personality and Social Psychology,* 1979, *37,* 1075–1084.

Shweder, R. A., & D'Andrade, R. G. The systematic distortion hypothesis. In R. A. Shweder (Ed.), *Fallible judgment in behavioral research: New directions for methodology of social and behavioral science* (Vol. 4). San Francisco: Jossey-Bass, 1980.

Smith, P. C., & Kendall, L. M. Retranslation of expectations: An approach to the construction of unambiguous anchors for rating scales. *Journal of Applied Psychology,* 1963, *47,* 149–155.

Snyder, M. Self-monitoring of expressive behavior. *Journal of Personality and Social Psychology,* 1974, *30,* 526–537.

Snyder, M., & Monson, T. C. Persons, situations, and the control of social behavior. *Journal of Personality and Social Psychology,* 1975, *32,* 637–644.

Snyder, M., & Swann, W. B., Jr. Hypothesis-testing process in social interaction. *Journal of Personality and Social Psychology,* 1978, *36,* 1202–1212.

Stagner, R. On the reality of traits. *The Journal of General Psychology,* 1977, *96,* 185–207.

Stone, T. H., & Slusher, E. A. Attributional insights into performance appraisal. *JSAS Catalog of Selected Documents in Psychology,* 1975, *5,* 253.

Stricker, L. J., Jacobs, P. I., & Kogan, N. Trait interrelations in implicit personality theories and questionnaire data. *Journal of Personality and Social Psychology,* 1974, *30,* 198–207.

Taylor, S. E., & Fiske, S. T. Salience, attention, and attributions: Top of the head phenomena. In L. Berkowitz (Ed.), *Advances in experimental social psychology* (Vol. 11). New York: Academic Press, 1978.

Thorndike, E. L. A constant error in psychological ratings. *Journal of Applied Psychology,* 1920, *4,* 25–29.

Tupes, E. C., & Christal, R. E. Stability of personality trait rating factors obtained under diverse conditions. USAF WADC Technical Note, 1958, 58–61.

Tupes, E. C., & Christal, R. E. Recurrent personality factors based on trait ratings. USAF ASD Technical Report, 1961, 61–67.

Tversky, A. Features of similarity. *Psychological Review,* 1977, *84,* 327–352.

Vernon, P. E. *Personality assessment: A critical survey.* New York: Wiley, 1964.

Walters, H. A., & Jackson, D. N. Group and individual regularities in trait inference: A multidimensional scaling analysis. *Multivariate Behavioral Research,* 1966, *1,* 145–163.

Widom, C. S. Interpersonal and personal construct systems in psychopaths. *Journal of Consulting and Clinical Psychology,* 1976, *44,* 614–623.

Zedeck, S., & Kafry, D. Capturing rater policies for processing evaluation data. *Organizational Behavior and Human Performance,* 1977, *18,* 269–294.

In Defense of Surface Structure

Richard A. Shweder

Some ideas are so good they deserve to be true, but (alas) are not. One of those deserving, but misleading, ideas is the idea that mind and personality consist of abstract underlying structures (e.g., "reversible operations," "anxiety-prone-ness") that impose form on any concrete task, problem, or situation that happens to come along. The difficulty with the idea of "abstract structure" is the implication that one can be indifferent to content and still make sense of actual cognitive, affective, and interpersonal functioning. What many cognitive scientists and personality researchers have discovered is that one cannot be indifferent to whether (for example) the intellectual task is conservation of *number* or conservation of *liquid quantity* or whether the affect-eliciting stimulus is a *job interview* or a *dentist's drill* (e.g., Brainerd, 1978; Flavell, 1980; Mischel, 1968, 1973; Mischel and Peake, 1981; Moos, 1969). Whether or not a particular abstract structure (reversible operations, anxiety) gets applied depends on the task.

Allport (1960) buys in to the idea of "abstract structure." In his classic discussion of personality traits, he notes that "the stimulus is not the crucial determinant in behavior that expresses personality; the trait itself is decisive. Once formed, a trait seems to have the capacity of directing responses to stimuli into characteristic channels [p. 132]."

Piaget shares Allport's Platonic image: "Object constancy," "reversible operations," "the predicate calculus" are all abstract representations of mental capacities that are supposed to direct cognitive responses to particular tasks into characteristic and general channels of functioning.

This essay is a brief defense of content, the task, the stimulus, "surface structure." In contrast to Allport and Piaget I argue that one cannot afford to be indifferent to content or to "apparently" irrelevant details of a task or situation, especially if one's goal is performance measurement or the assessment of actual functioning. Perhaps those who study visual perception can be indifferent to content. The laws of visual perception may be the same whether you are viewing a boxing match or staring at a cow. But how people think, feel, and act is not packaged or stabilized at the abstract level of (for example) "anxiety-ridden" functioning, "dependent" functioning, or "formal operational" functioning. The person who starts biting his or her nails, sweating, and fidgeting during an interview is not typically the person who feels tense and jittery when speaking before a group. The person who is unflappable when trapped in an elevator is no less likely than a blanching elevator mate to "go to pieces" when he or she finds him- or herself unable to solve an important problem at work (Mischel, 1968, 1973; Mischel and Peake, 1981; Van Heck, 1981). Attention to detail—attention to the distinguishing and special features of particular performance sites—is where the action is.

Consider, for example, intellectual functioning. Recent work suggests that by varying the content of a task it is possible to elicit preoperational thinking from an adult (Wason, 1969; Wason & Johnson-Laird, 1972) or formal operational thinking from a four year old (Macnamara, Baker, & Olson, 1976); and that the person who functions at a formal operational level on one problem is not typically the same person who functions at a formal operational level on a second problem. Indeed, to cite one example, Roberge and Flexer (1979) discover that performance on formal operational tests for propositional logic and combinatorial thinking correlate a mere $-.07$ (for eighth graders) and $.17$ (for adults). They are joined by others in their conclusion (Roberge & Flexer, 1979) that:

> if, as Piaget and others hypothesize, formal operational thinking reflects an organized structure of second-order operations, one would expect to find a basic consistency in performance across tasks, particularly for groups of subjects who are presumably well-established in the formal operational stage. However, the minimal association between scores on the tests . . . provides little evidence of the functional interdependence among these logical operations that is claimed by proponents of the structural whole (structure d'ensemble) model of formal operations [p. 482]. (Also see Brainerd, 1978.)

Intellectual functioning is often task specific and, thus, manipulable. Wason and Johnson-Laird (1972; also Wason, 1969), for example, present subjects with a formal operation "hypothetical contradiction task." Imagine the following task: You are presented with a series of cards. You are told that each card has a number on one side and a letter on the other. You have been hired to inspect cards to make sure that a certain rule for producing cards has not been violated. That rule is: *If there is a vowel on one side of the card there must be an odd number on the other side.* Four cards are on the table before you: K, A, 7, 8.

Remember, each of these four cards has a letter on one side and a number on the other. Now, which and only which of the four cards *must* be inspected to make sure the rule is not violated? Answer this question before reading any further!

Wason and Johnson-Laird discover that fewer than 10% of college-educated adults draw the proper deduction from the rule. "If there is a vowel on one side there must be an odd number on the other side" (if *p* then *q*) implies "if there is not an odd number on one side then there must not be a vowel on the other side" (if not *q* then not *p*); hence, inspect the A and the 8! Furthermore, many subjects have difficulty recognizing the source of their error. Thus, they recognize that an "A" card with an "8" on the back is a rule violation, but they fail to mentally rotate that card. They do not recognize that an "A" card with an "8" on the back is the same as an "8" card with an "A" on the back. Hence, also inspect the "8." In other words, subjects seem to lack "reversible operations"; they function at a preoperational level. Yet, when Wason and Johnson-Laird introduce slight changes in the content (but not the abstract form) of the task, a majority of their subjects all of a sudden perform at a formal operational level. Wason and Johnson-Laird (1972) conclude that "formal operational thought is less general than Piaget supposed [p. 193]." More importantly, Wason and Johnson-Laird demonstrate that details of the content about which you think can be decisive for how you cognitively function.

A similar point is made by Van Heck (1981) with regard to affective functioning (also see Shweder, 1979, 1981). Van Heck examines the abstract personality structure known as "proneness to anxiety." Anxiety is assessed utilizing self-report, observational, and physiological measures. Van Heck also analyzes details of the performance sites in which anxiety might be observed. He discovers that his subjects perceive anxiety-provoking situations as coming in (at least) four kinds: (1) threats to interpersonal status (e.g., a job interview); (2) inanimate environmental threats (e.g., sitting on an airplane just before takeoff); (3) threats of punishment (e.g., breaking something that does not belong to you); and (4) threats of pain (e.g., the dentist's drill approaches your mouth). Van Heck discovers that those who are more anxious than others in one of these types of situations are not typically more anxious than others in the other situations. The content of the situation matters: It is the decisive determinant of who is more or less anxious.

Van Heck's observational data are quite illuminating. Subjects are observed in diverse anxiety-provoking situations (oral exams, public speaking, threatened with electrical shock, confronted with an unsolvable problem, etc). Behavior in these situations is coded for diverse response modes, all theoretically related to anxiety (restless hand movements, tense laughing, downward gaze, posture, etc.). Van Heck discovers that 0% (I repeat, 0%) of the variance of observed behavior is accounted for by stable individual differences in the (purported) abstract structure "proneness to anxiety." The way people line up on anxiety in an oral exam tells you little about how those same people line up on anxiety when they get "stuck" solving a problem. Only 1% of the variance of observed behavior is accounted for by stable situational differences. In other words, how situations line up in terms of being anxiety provoking for one person tells you little about how those same situations line up in terms of being anxiety provoking for the next person. A job interview gets on some people's nerves more than a dentist's drill, and vice versa for other people. Notably, a whopping 33% of the variance is accounted for by stable response modes; in other words, anxiety is more likely to get expressed in some ways (biting lips) than other ways (nervous laughter) and there is some tendency for this "hierarchy of response mode likelihood" to be stable across persons and situations.

Van Heck's findings are not idiosyncratic. Mischel and Peake (1981) examined the purported abstract structure "conscientiousness" among college students. Utilizing reliable, aggregated measures of such variables as "room neatness," "assignment neatness," "class attendance," and so on, and correcting their measures for attenuation, Mischel and Peake discovered average cross-situational consistency coefficients of .20. The mundane world of cognitive, affective, and interpersonal functioning does not seem to instantiate the supposed directive influence of underlying abstract structures (also see Mischel, 1968).

Why have we been so indifferent to content in the study of human performance? Perhaps one answer is that we all too readily assume that to do "science" is to search for deep structures and general processes. The "periodic table of elements" model of science has a firm grip on the brains of many social scientists. Perhaps a second answer is that occasionally the search for deep structures and general processes is successful. A third possible answer is suggested by the "systematic-distortion hypothesis" (D'Andrade, 1965, 1974; Shweder, 1975, 1977a, 1977b, 1981; Shweder & D'Andrade, 1979, 1980), with special reference to our understanding of individual differences in social behavior. Borman (this volume) provides an excellent overview of this line of research. The basic idea is that many of the most popular social-science procedures for gathering data on personality differences (summary ratings by peers or observers) stimulate the rater to report conceptually associated memory items as though they actually cooccurred.

For example, I suspect systematic-distortion processes may be at work in the summary ratings by teacher-observers reported in Moskowitz (1978). Focusing on the abstract structures "dependency" and "dominance," Moskowitz assesses the performance of children in a preschool. Over an eight-week period of time, four hours of on-line observational data are collected on each of 56 children. "Dependency" is assessed for each of five response modes or content areas: seeking help, seeking supervision, being near, touching, and seeking recognition. "Dominance" is assessed for each of five response modes or content areas: commanding, threatening, directing, displacing, and making suggestions. Classroom teachers (the children's "supervisors," so to speak) were asked to make summary ratings on the children for each response mode or content area. What is striking is that in the teachers' summary ratings the response modes or content areas seem almost mutually substitutable, each an expression of the (purported) abstract motivational structure "dependency" or "dominance." For the summary ratings of teachers the average intratrait consistency coefficient is .50 for dependency and .57 for dominance. Thus, for example, "seeking help" and "seeking supervision" are correlated .74 in the teachers' ratings. "Threatening others" and "displacing others" are correlated .94. However, in the direct observational data "seeking help" and "seeking supervision" correlate a mere .14 whereas "threatening others" and "displacing others" correlate − .03. For the on-line observational data the average intratrait consistency coefficient is .04 for dependency and .25 for dominance. Remember, this is observational data aggregated over eight weeks of observation.

Summary-rating tasks seem to direct the attention of observers to the conceptual relatedness of rating items; theoretically associated items get reported as though they went together despite observational evidence to the contrary. As D'Andrade (1965) remarked: One of the hazards of science is the ease with which we confuse "propositions about language" with "propositions about the world [p. 215]." The search for abstract personality structures has been fueled by that confusion.

When we do look at the world of individual differences in social behavior using reliable, "on-line" observational teachings, what we discover is that "generalizations decay" (Cronbach, 1975). And, they do not decay over time alone. They decay across minor changes in task, context, or response mode. If one wanted to know whether some child is going to spend time "displacing" other children one would not want to examine the child's "threat" behavior. The "wise" stay as close to the situation and response mode of interest as possible. Indeed, individual differences in many domains (e.g., anxiety) are so dynamic and unstable that individual differences destabilize as people become more familiar with the particular performance site. It is less familiar situations that elicit more consistent behavior (Van Heck, 1981).

Borman's excellent contribution to this volume speaks for itself; I have only a few remarks to make. The systematic-distortion hypothesis is sometimes cast as a problem in memory retrieval and sometimes as a problem in information integration. Borman is sensitive to the distinction. Unassisted, our everyday information-integration skills can be quite deficient. For example, imagine you know that "John has self-esteem." Which is the better inference: (1) therefore, John probably is not a leader; or (2) therefore, John probably is a leader? Most observers choose the second inference. Yet when interrogated most observers believe that approximately 50% of the people they know have self-esteem whereas only 15% are leaders. Because the observers' own base-rate estimates suggest that "most people with self-esteem are not leaders" it is the first inference just cited that should be endorsed. Integrating our inferential judgments with what we think we know is not a trivial task. More work needs to be done on the cognitive processes (memory, information integration) that produce systematic distortion.

Borman identifies factors leading to the stability of individual differences. For example, he notes that in many work settings the lack of variation in performance sites favors consistency in behavior. The point is a sound one. Note, however, that the lack of variation in a performance site may be offset by the "familiarity" effect previously noted. Individual difference rankings sometimes destabilize just because a setting remains the same. Under familiar conditions behavior spontaneously varies.

Borman also notes that individual differences in skills are more stable than individual differences in motivation or interpersonal behavior. Again, this is a nice point, although I would emphasize that not all skilled performances are merely the expressions of individual talent and training. Skilled performances vary in their dependency on props, interpersonal relationships, and interpersonal coordination. I would bet that "underdogs" are less successful in tennis or squash than in football or basketball (where "upsets" are probably more likely).

Finally, I'm less inclined than Borman to treat cognitive functioning as a special case. I.Q., or "brightness," may well be more general than most "traits" of social behavior (e.g., dependency). However, I.Q. is only one part of the story on mind. In many areas of cognitive functioning, individual differences can be quite task specific, as my brief excursion into formal operational thinking suggested. Freud is well-known for his slogan: Where there is Id let there be Ego. Perhaps less well-known is the slogan: Where there is structure let there be content!

REFERENCES

Allport, G. W. *Personality and social encounter.* Boston: Beacon Press, 1960.

Brainerd, C. J. *Piaget's theory of intelligence.* Englewood Cliffs, N.J.: Prentice-Hall, 1978.

Cronbach, L. J. Beyond the two scientific disciplines of scientific psychology. *American Psychologist,* 1975, *30,* 116–127.

D'Andrade, R. G. Trait psychology and componential analysis. *American Anthropologist,* 1965, *67,* 215–228.

D'Andrade, R. G. Memory and the assessment of behavior. In T. Blalock (Ed.), *Measurement in the social sciences.* Chicago: Aldine-Atherton, 1974.

Flavell, J. H. *Structures, stages and sequences in cognitive development.* Paper presented at 1980 Minnesota Symposium on Child Psychology. (Available from J. H. Flavell, Department of Psychology, Stanford University, Stanford, California 94305.)

Macnamara, J., Baker, E., and Olson, C. L. Four-year-olds' understanding of *pretend, forget* and *know:* Evidence for propositional operations. *Child Development,* 1976, *47,* 62–70.

Mischel, W. *Personality and assessment.* New York: Wiley, 1968.

Mischel, W. Towards a cognitive social learning reconceptualization of personality. *Psychological Review,* 1973, *80,* 252–283.

Mischel, W., and Peake, P. In search of consistency: Measure for measure. In M. P. Zanna, E. T. Higgins, and C. P. Herman (Eds.), *Consistency in social behavior: The Ontario symposium of personality and social psychology* (Vol. 2). Hillsdale, N.J.: Lawrence Erlbaum Associates, 1981.

172   SHWEDER

Moos, R. H. Sources of variance in responses to questionnaires and in behavior. *Journal of Abnormal Psychology*, 1969, *74*, 405–412.

Moskowitz, D. S. Analyzing personality constructs for internal consistency and transituational generality. Unpublished doctoral dissertation, University of Connecticut, 1978. *Dissertation Abstracts International*, 1979, *40*, 4328 (University microfilms #7914176).

Roberge, J. J., & Flexer, B. K. Further examination of formal operational reasoning abilities. *Child Development*, 1979, *50*, 478–484.

Shweder, R. A. How relevant is an individual difference theory of personality? *Journal of Personality*, 1975, *43*, 455–484.

Shweder, R. A. Illusory correlation and the M.M.P.I. controversy. *Journal of Consulting and Clinical Psychology*, 1977, *45*, 917–924. (a)

Shweder, R. A. Likeness and likelihood in everyday thought: Magical thinking in judgments about personality. *Current Anthropology*, 1977, *18*, 637–648. (b)

Shweder, R. A. Rethinking culture and personality theory Part I: A critical examination of two classical postulates. *Ethos*, 1979, *7*, 255–278.

Shweder, R. A. Fact and artifact in trait perception: The systematic distortion hypothesis. In B. A. Maher & W. B. Maher (Eds.), *Progress in experimental personality research* (Vol. 11). New York: Academic Press, 1981.

Shweder, R. A., & D'Andrade, R. G. Accurate reflection or systematic distortion? A reply to Block, Weiss and Thorne. *Journal of Personality and Social Psychology*, 1979, *37*, 1075–1084.

Shweder, R. A., & D'Andrade, R. G. The systematic distortion hypothesis. In R. A. Shweder (Ed.), *Fallible judgment in behavioral research. New directions for methodology of social and behavioral science, No. 4.* San Francisco: Jossey-Bass, 1980.

Van Heck, G. L. M. *Anxiety: The profile of a trait.* Unpublished doctoral thesis, Department of Psychology, Tilberg University, The Netherlands, 1981. (Available from G. L. M. Van Heck, Department of Psychology, Tilberg University, P.O. Box 90153, 5000 Tilberg, The Netherlands.)

Wason, P. C. Regression in reasoning? *British Journal of Psychology*, 1969, *60*, 471–480.

Wason, P. C., & Johnson-Laird, P. N. *Psychology of reasoning.* London: B. T. Batsford, 1972.

7

Motivation and Performance-Appraisal Behavior

Allan M. Mohrman, Jr.
Edward E. Lawler III

Drs. Mohrman and Lawler believe that the impact of evaluation can be best understood by examining underlying motives. In their paper, they focus upon the effect of organizational context and characteristics of the formal performance-appraisal system on the motivation of the employee to engage in private performance appraisal (judgment, attention) and public appraisal (activities involving more than one person). The organizational factors that may have a moderating effect on performance appraisal are the characteristics of the job, the structure of the organization, and the organizational climate. Using the expectancy model, Mohrman and Lawler describe the manner in which the definition of the situation is converted into motivated behavior. They conclude that an exclusive focus on performance measurement will not provide an understanding of effective performance appraisal behavior. If appraisal behavior is viewed as motivated, an individual's definition of performance appraisal that is consistent with organizational goals should improve the effectiveness of performance appraisal.

In commenting on the Mohrman–Lawler paper, Bartlett objects to the suggestion to abandon measurement solutions and presents examples of some effective measurement solutions to motivation problems in performance appraisal. In addition, he urges going beyond the Mohrman and Lawler approach to identify motivational problems in performance appraisal.

In response to Dr. Bartlett's comments, Mohrman and Lawler agree that measurement design is important, but they reemphasize that motivational issues are often ignored in performance appraisal. They also agree with Bartlett on the need to identify motivational constructs involved in performance appraisal.

This paper is concerned with what motivates the behavior involved in carrying out performance appraisals (PA) in organizations. Typically, research and theory concerned with motivation has focused on how PA affects the subsequent work behavior of the appraisee; here we focus on what motivates the PA behaviors themselves. PA behaviors are simply one subset of the total set of role behaviors organizational members perform. The particular purposes of PA create contexts that give PA behaviors unique and complex meanings that are worthy of study for what they can teach us about motivation and assessment. In addition, as we come to understand more about the results of certain PA behaviors (such as allowing participation in the process by appraisees), we also become more concerned with their quality (e.g., with bias in measurement).

THE APPROACH

We can distinguish between two classes of PA behaviors. One is private in nature and the other is public. The former includes internal acts of cognition, judgment, attention, perception, evaluation, attribution, and so on, but it also might include the making and retention of private notes and other documents. The latter consists of all activities involving more than one person. A large portion of public behavior involves the communication of appraisals among people—for example, feedback of appraisals from appraiser to appraisee, requests from appraisees for such feedback, the recording of appraisals on forms that eventually are seen and used by others.

If we regard performance appraisal to be a particular case of human information processing, then the information being collected, evaluated, and used is subject to distortion and bias (Feldman, 1981). Distortion and bias can occur in both private and public activities. Both, for instance, are subject to unconscious bias due to preconceived stereotypes, but just as we can consciously adjust our private biases by controlling our data-collection patterns (Feldman, 1981), we can bias our public communication of appraisals by withholding (or adding) data. All these are examples of behavior (Salancik & Pfeffer, 1978) that can be seen as motivated.

We go about our day-to-day activities privately appraising the behavior of others and ourselves. The motivation behind these appraisals seems to be part of our fundamental need to undertand, predict, and control our individual worlds (Kelly, 1955; Weick, 1979). Day-to-day appraisals of ourselves and others may also be a source of esteem through social comparison. They may also provide data that can be used later to obtain extrinsic rewards (arguing for a pay raise) and to fulfill mandated role behavior (e.g., doing an appraisal of a subordinate).

We also engage in public appraisal behaviors as part of our day-to-day existence. Upholding behavioral norms through social rewards and punishment are all part of the normal fabric of social life. We might engage in social appraisals to build esteem or exert control over others. Public appraisals are necessary to determine whether norms of behavior in a social unit are being transgressed or adhered to. When social units are task oriented, some appraisal of behaviors is common for even the most minimal performance and is often carried out in an informal way. Although we have distinguished between private and public behaviors, this does not mean that the motivating sources of these behaviors are individual and social, respectively. In fact, in this paper we stress the importance of the individual's definition of the situation as a key in the motivation, both public and private. These definitions in turn are influenced by social and context factors.

Informal appraisal behaviors can simultaneously satisfy individual needs and be functional in work effectiveness, but there is no guarantee that they will be. The forms and procedures that make up formal appraisal systems can be understood as social mechanisms that are created to control evaluation and decision-making processes that would ordinarily occur informally (Feldman, 1981). The hope is that the formal system will "clean up" the appraisals and make them more functional from the organizations' points of view.

A formal system does not eliminate the need for focusing on individuals. Many, if not all, of the behavioral "breakdowns" we see in formal PA systems (e.g., measurement bias, failure to comply with procedures) are best understood by focusing on the motivations of the individual participants in the appraisal process. As is shown later in Fig. 7.5, organizational contexts are critical in determining the definitions individuals develop of situations, which in turn determine motivations and behavior.

In the following sections we first discuss PA as a formal system and then the organizational context. Next we deal with the impact both of these have on motivating PA behaviors. Finally, we consider the implications of our discussion for the design of PA systems.

PERFORMANCE APPRAISAL AS A FORMAL SYSTEM

Appraisal systems usually involve three aspects: (1) a human-resource management system in which appraisal is a formal subsystem designed to accomplish a number of objectives; (2) a formal system that specifies particular methods, procedures, and instruments as vehicles for appraisal; and (3) an activating system of mechanisms by which the first two aspects are put into practice.

Human-Resource System

The potential central role of performance appraisal in a larger integrated system for human-resource management is becoming more important to organizations. As corporations review their compensation systems or their human-resource planning systems, they often come to realize the importance of having "valid" performance information. The ultimate purpose in all cases is organizational effectiveness. It is assumed that organization performance is an aggregate of individual performance. The instrumental nature of the purposes and decisions are depicted in Fig. 7.1 as eventually affecting future performance and organizational effectiveness.

According to many expectancy theories, individual behavior stems from the skills and ability, motivated effort, and role understanding of the individual. Performance-appraisal information can be used in a number of ways that can eventually affect these factors so that they are moved in a direction that will improve performance. Appraisal information can indicate whether or not previously used selection criteria were able to predict performance. Adjustment in selection criteria should affect the level of skills and abilities found. Appraisal can also identify those individuals approprite for new job placement or promotion as well as validate previously used promotion and placement criteria. When pay is based on performance pay increases can act as incentives to increase effort and performance. Various modes of feedback and performance-oriented discussions between appraisers and appraisees are undertaken in an effort to increase effort and role understanding and to improve skills and abilities. For any of the formal system objectives to be accomplished, data need to be obtained from the formal appraisal and transmitted to others.

FIG. 7.1.   Organizational uses and impacts of performance appraisal.

Whether the same performance data are appropriate for all the potential uses is a question that is not always asked in organizations. Many formal PA systems do not differentiate and implicitly or explicitly collect the same data for all uses. Although formal systems may fail to provide different measurements for different purposes, we should not assume that system users also fail to differentiate. On the contrary, the system users may well see different data as appropriate for the different purposes. Indeed, they may create informal systems that communicate such data.

Formal Performance-Appraisal System

Although the logic behind Fig. 7.1 is relatively clear, the organizational means by which the measurement and the various connections are made is problematic. Much of the design of PA systems involves specification of measures and linkages. Indeed, there seems to be an eternal search for the perfect measurement instrument. Much of the work by industrial psychologists on performance appraisal, for example, has focused on developing and "validating" different appraisal forms. The issue of motivations of the appraiser and appraisee has been almost totally ignored. The link between appraisal and salary is a good example of a relationship that evokes constant refinement and search for perfection in some organizations. Solutions range from subjective "judgment calls" about appropriate pay for a given performance level to computerized algorithms that automatically convert ratings into pay levels. Pay–performance linkages need to attend to timing issues also. It is hard, for instance, to base salary on performance when salary planning precedes appraisal.

Overall, much of PA design effort in organizations is focused on the "nitty-gritty" procedures, instruments, and techniques required to actually accomplish the PA linkages of Fig. 7.1. The more linkages an organization tries to make, the more complicated the design becomes and, as we see later, the more complex the motivational issues involved.

Activating System

Even if specification of the microelements of PA design is relatively complete, it is by no means automatic that the procedures and linkages specified will in fact come to pass. First, the people expected to carry out the system obviously need to be told what they are to do. Designers must communicate the system through orientation sessions and written policy and procedures. Knowing what one is supposed to do, however, does not guarantee that one will do it. Individuals also need the ability to perform the various behaviors required of them. Thus PA systems sometimes include formal training and skill-building components for its users. Finally, people have to be motivated to carry out the activities. Approaches to doing this include evaluating appraisers based on whether they have done appraisals and developing information systems that identify when appraisals are late.

ORGANIZATIONAL CONTEXT OF APPRAISAL

Appraisal systems do not exist in a vacuum. The organization presents a context with a number of dimensions, each of which may have a distinct moderating effect on the appraisal system. Among the key contextual dimensions are the job characteristics and functional areas of the employees being appraised, the structural nature of the organization, such as its authority relationships and its communication networks, and less easily defined aspects, such as the climate, the culture, and the nature of interpersonal relationships.

Most designers of PA systems, especially when they are members of the organization, implicitly attend to its contextual dimensions. Nevertheless when such dimensions are not explicitly and systematically taken into account, there is a real danger that they may work to destroy the potential effectiveness of a PA system. In some cases only if they are altered is it possible to do "valid" performance appraisals.

Some examples illustrate the potential nature of contextual effects. Our research, for instance, indicates that current PA practices tend to work better (in terms of affective and behavioral—outcomes—that is, people are more satisfied with events and appraisal behaviors are more positive and functional) when the job of the person being appraised has well-specified duties and priorities (Resnick & Mohrman, 1981). Nevertheless, many organizations choose to vaguely describe certain jobs in order to retain entrepreneurial behavior; thus the typical prescription of better job analysis would not be appropriate. Indeed, the whole idea may not fit the culture of the organization. Using PA in such situations can be detrimental both in the short run (when appraisal events become dissatisfying and dysfunctional) and in the long run, if pressure is exerted on the organization to move away from a functional cultural norm. In such situations one might expect very little motivation to engage in appraisal.

Other examples of poor contextual fit include individually oriented appraisal in an organization that relies on the work group as the basic unit of production, organizations with egalitarian norms that implicitly emphasize hierarchical power by having one-over-one approval of appraisals, organizations with matrix structures that undermine their own logic by using appraisals based on a single-boss hierarchy (Davis & Lawrence, 1977). The frequent assumption that an employee's hierarchical boss is the appropriate appraiser may not be well-founded if that person has no access to, direct information about, or expertise in the job performance of the appraisee. Hierarchically based systems may also have a politicizing effect on career decisions. Finally, systems that are designed to be participative do not fit in autocratically run organizations, as is discussed next.

When contextual misfits occur, PA systems can be expected to break down because of accumulated dysfunctional behaviors in such contexts. The key to understanding breakdowns lies in how these contextual conditions influence individuals' definitions of the situations and the individuals' resultant behaviors.

SYSTEMS, CONTEXT, AND RESULTANT BEHAVIOR

No matter how complete the design of the PA system, no matter how detailed the procedural and policy manuals, no matter how well-articulated the uses of forms, data, and the decision algorithms using the data, recommendations achieve nothing until implemented in individual behavior.

Definition of Situation

The determinants of each individual's behavior is that individual's "definition of the situation" (see Fig. 7.2). This is a popular term that has run as a thread through an influential portion of the literature in sociology (Ritzer, 1975). It has also had its parallels in the psychology and organizational-psychology literature. One prominent example is the value-expectancy model of motivation (Lawler, 1973) in which expectancies, instrumentalities, and values form individuals' definitions of situations and motivate particular behaviors. The model in Fig. 7.1 is in essence a potential definition of the situation provided by the formal PA system and a source of expectancies and instrumentalities held by individuals. Depending on the system and the organization, the various outcomes might be more or less present. The real existence of the elements and connections does not guarantee that they will be perceived and be part of the individual's definition, just as their absence does not guarantee that they will not be perceived.

Despite the best-laid design plans, appraisal systems have both intended *and* unintended consequences in the individual's definition of the situation. In some organizations, for example, results are typically reviewed by the supervisor of the appraiser. Often this is done after measurement but before feedback or other

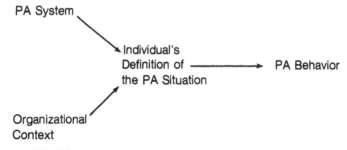

FIG. 7.2.   Determinants of Performance Appraisal Behavior.

subsequent uses of the results. It is intended as a quality monitoring of the measurement or appraisal. Our research has found that it often has an unintended consequence of creating the impression for the appraisee that the appraisal is "locked in." In situations in which the original measurement is perceived by the appraisee to have excluded pertinent data, such a review may in fact eventually result in increased dissatisfaction and turnover.

Role of Context

The organizational context influences the meaning given by the individual to the appraisal situation. Hierarchical structures, for example, foster interpretation of the supervisor review as a technique to foster control by the appraiser. In competitive climates it is difficult to convince employees that appraisal is done solely for developmental purposes. If it is connected to pay raises, we would expect to find, in contexts in which a particular job expertise is scarce in the labor market, that appraisal is used as a lever by which managers can get greater pay for subordinates who are being wooed by other corporations. In short, the context often determines the meaning and use of the appraisal.

One element of the context, the culture or climate of the organization, can influence the way behavior is evaluated and interpreted when public and private appraisals are made. For example, our research shows that in highly participative plants, evaluations tend to focus on the degree to which individuals support their work teams and engage in team behaviors, a factor that rarely comes up in traditional cultures. Culture may also affect the kinds of attributions appraisers make about the causes of performance and what level of performance is acceptable. For example, an ideal "Theory Y" organization would tend to attribute "good" results to people and "bad" results to situations, the reverse of tendencies in "Theory X" organizations (MacGregor, 1960). If culture can affect attributions, then individuals in people-oriented cultures may be more prone to look for ways that poor performance can be improved by training or by changing the situation. Organizations that are highly performance oriented may be more likely to experience failure on important standards and to attribute the failure to individuals. Individuals seeking to avoid such attribution can be driven to extreme behavior (e.g., Perry & Barney, 1981). The attribution literature has identified a number of conditions under which attributions can change or assume biased patterns (e.g., situations with high affective bonds, situations in which consequences are serious and not trivial). This suggests that one concrete way of understanding culture may be in terms of the extent to which these conditions affecting attributions are present or absent.

Definitional Effects

It is important to note that definitional dynamics are ultimately in the control of the individual and can only partially be influenced or overcome by traditional

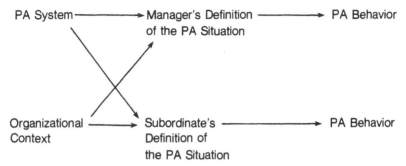

FIG. 7.3.   Determinants of interacting performance appraisal behaviors.

responses to PA problems, such as more valid measurement instruments. Characteristics of the individual such as past experience with appraisal and self-esteem may affect the definition of the situation.

Fig. 7.3 depicts a simple illustration of how two definitions of a situation can interact. In this particular case we pick the two individuals most commonly comprising the social membership of the performance-appraisal event—the manager-appraiser and the subordinate-appraisee. In the previous section, the degree of fit between the context and the appraisal system was described as partially dictated by the objective reality of the two but was ultimately a matter of definition for each individual actor. In Fig. 7.3 we see yet other points at which incongruity or misfit may potentially occur—that is, between the different definitions and behaviors of the two actors. A common example of such incongruity is the manager's perceiving feedback discussion as developmental whereas the subordinate sees it as evaluative—for instance, information about an upcoming pay raise.

We recently collected some questionnaire data that illustrate the potential differences between appraiser and appraisee (in this case manager and subordinate) definitions of the situation. We asked a stratified random sample of over 300 manager-subordinate pairs a number of questions pertaining to many aspects of the most recent PA events in which they had participated. Table 7.1 presents some illustrative results. Respondents were asked to indicate the extent to which a number of possible purposes should have been and actually were accomplished in their most recently completed appraisal. The patterns indicate some significant differences between managers and subordinates in desired purposes and perceptions of their accomplishment.

The purpose perceived to be accomplished to the greatest extent (although evidently not as highly as desired by surbordinates is "document the subordinate's performance." Managers see too much attention being devoted to this purpose. Obviously, this could create a situation with contradictory pressures to both increase and decrease "documenting" behaviors.

Although both managers and subordinates agreed that appraisal should be used to "determine appropriate pay," they disagreed on the extent to which it

TABLE 7.1
Rated Desirability and Achievement of Appraisal Objectives:
Proportion Responding at Three Levels[a]

Group	Desired			Accomplished		
	Not at All	Low to Moderate	High to Great	Not at All	Low Moderate	High Great
Document Subordinate's Performance						
Manager	0	41	58	0	11	89
Subordinate	1	13	86	4	30	67
Determine Appropriate Pay						
Manager	10	25	65	19	42	39
Subordinate	5	24	71	31	43	27
Communicate and Explain Pay Decisions						
Manager	20	32	47	30	40	30
Subordinate	8	23	68	42	41	17

[a]Cell entries are percentages.

had actually been used to do so. The PA experiences to which the data refer have apparently established a perception of pay for performance for the managers but not for workers. Managers are not convinced that appraisal should have been used to "communicate and explain pay decisions," and indeed pay was often not discussed, contrary to the desires of subordinates. Ignoring these appraisee desires can be dysfunctional. Further analyses carried out on these data indicate that when pay decisions were communicated and explained appraisal seemed to be more satisfying to both parties and more open to constructive discussion of other issues, such as needed areas of performance improvement (Prince & Lawler, 1981). Apparently in an organizational context where pay for performance is a strong cultural norm, pay is a subject that should be discussed during PA. Avoidance tends to define a situation that, ironically, increases the saliency of the pay issue, drives out open discussion of other issues, and creates dissatisfaction with PA.

Differences between manager and subordinate definitions of the situation are by no means isolated. When we performed paired T-tests between manager and subordinate responses on all the questionnaire items that could be compared we found that the two groups of responses significantly differed on 68% of the items. Differences in definitions of the situation between PA participants is neither an isolated nor insignificant occurrence.

Even in situations in which the definitions and behaviors are compatible, the result may still be dysfunctional and contrary to original PA system intentions. We can illustrate this by expanding an earlier example. In the situation described in which the manager's boss reviewed and signed off prior to the manager's feedback to the subordinate we saw the following: Not only did the subordinate see such an action as "locking in" the appraisal but the manager consciously utilized such a prefeedback review as a legitimation of his appraisal and a substantiation of his hierarchical superiority over the subordinate. It was such an important tool for him that he refused to alter this practice even though all managers were requested to do so by the plant manager. The subordinate discovered during one appraisal that completely erroneous data had been used. When this was brought to the manager's attention during feedback, the manager, rather than give up an important source of authority, acknowledged the error but felt compelled to explain it as purposeful and necessary in order to make the system operate equitably. Because the subordinate accepted the fabrication as reality, such an explanation caused considerable distortion in the subordinate's understanding of what the system was all about.

Expectancy Predictions

The manner in which the definition of the situation is converted into behavior can be modeled by a value-expectancy approach. In doing so we are not so much interested in positing the model as *the* way of explaining behavior or testing its usefulness as we are interested in using the model as a heuristic to understand the important forces motivating appraisal behavior. We think of motivation as the tendency of an individual to withhold or exert effort in behavioral directions. The expectancy model considers motivations to stem from the expectations the individual has that those efforts will result in the target behaviors, that the accomplishment of the target behaviors will result in a variety of outcomes, and that the expected outcomes will be, on the whole, valuable or satisfying to the individual (see Lawler, 1973; Vroom, 1964). A simple version of this model appears in Fig. 7.4.

Fig. 7.5 develops the expectancy concept a little further by illustrating some of the possible connections that may be perceived to exist between different behaviors and outcomes. Fig. 7.5 is not meant to describe a reality of the actual

FIG. 7.4.   Expectancy-model characterization of the actor's definition of the PA situation underlying PA motivations.

PA Behavior   Outcomes

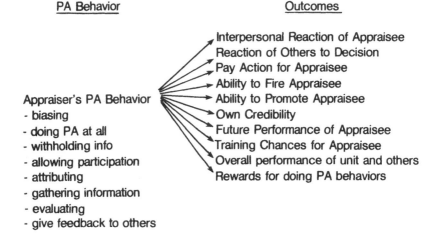

Appraiser's PA Behavior
- biasing
- doing PA at all
- withholding info
- allowing participation
- attributing
- gathering information
- evaluating
- give feedback to others

Interpersonal Reaction of Appraisee
Reaction of Others to Decision
Pay Action for Appraisee
Ability to Fire Appraisee
Ability to Promote Appraisee
Own Credibility
Future Performance of Appraisee
Training Chances for Appraisee
Overall performance of unit and others
Rewards for doing PA behaviors

Appraisee's PA Behavior
- accept feedback from
  others
- self appraisal
- defend self
- seek career guidance

Self Esteem
Interpersonal Reaction of Appraiser
Pay Action
Promotion
Validity of Information from Appraiser
Ability to Improve own Performance
Training Opportunities
Development of skills, abilities
Rewards for doing prescribed PA
behaviors
Better understanding of role

FIG. 7.5. Possible outcomes perceived to result from appraisal behavior.

outcomes; rather, it is meant to characterize a possible definition of the situation that the actor may have. As such, Fig. 7.5 can be interpreted as the determinant of the individual actors' motivations to perform PA behaviors. Fig. 7.5 in particular and Fig. 7.4 in general are possible pictures of what the actors (appraiser or appraisee) might have in mind. They also represent a model that social scientists sometimes adopt to describe or hypothesize actual relationships among the variables. Research indicates that organizational actors can, in general, be considered to carry expectancy-type pictures of the world in their heads that influence their organizational behaviors (e.g., Mitchell, 1974). To understand the actual content of the expectancy model (e.g., expectancies, valences) we need to understand how situations come to be defined by the organizational actors. More generally, we are interested in the social definition process by which expectancy models are created as well as the models themselves, for it is through social processes that we can manage the individual's definition and subsequent behavior. We need to include in the individual's definition of the situation such things as perceived ability to effect certain PA behaviors, an appropriate understanding of the PA role in which one finds oneself, the expected first- and second-level outcomes likely to occur due to certain behaviors, and the values the individual places on such outcomes. Appraisers, for example, are not going to put much effort into using a form they neither understand nor feel they have the ability to use (ability to discriminate among performance levels, for instance). Neither will they be motivated to feed back negative appraisals if they expect a nasty scene from the appraisee especially if they see no longer-term possibility for performance improvement and the organization does not reward them for it.

As indicated in Fig. 7.5 we need to explain not only the appraiser's behavior but the behavior of others in the appraisal system as well. Appraisees, for instance, may not openly participate in developmental feedback or in complete presentation of self-generated data to be used for appraisal if they feel that such openness will be used against them (a climate of distrust). Personnel administrators and higher-level managers have been known to change appraisals in order to avoid the appearance of inequities across various organizational units. Such individual behaviors can in the aggregate yield a system much different than intended by design. The emerging reality is even further compounded by the interaction of these behaviors.

The reasons why appraisal systems often fail to yield valid data about performance can be partially understood by using the expectancy approach. Looking first at the accuracy of private appraisals, Fig. 7.6 shows the types of expectancies that an organization must create to positively influence the accuracy of PA evaluations.

The figure suggests that if an organization wants an appraiser to base the appraisal on a certain reference standard on a specific behavior, it must not only identify the standards and make information on them available, but it must also motivate the appraisee to use them. Rewarding appraisers who keep records or who develop agreements with subordinates about performance can motivate them to use good decision processes in forming their own judgments.

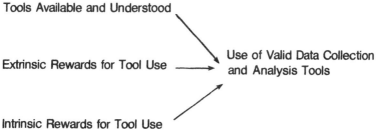

FIG. 7.6. Conditions leading to use of PA tools.

The extrinsic rewards in the situation can range from pay increases for the appraiser to a requirement that a certain form be filled out in order for the appraisee to receive a pay increase, which, in turn, would help the appraiser gain esteem, or acceptance from the appraisee. The intrinsic rewards may stem from having been involved in developing the tool and as a result feeling a commitment to using it or feeling it is a better tool.

The analysis supports one further interesting point: Better forms and better measurement systems are likely to be effective only if the organization motivates individuals to use them. Even if forms are used they must have a controlling effect on the private appraisal. Private biases are only controlled to the extent the form programs the lenses through which the appraiser perceives performance, and are uncontrolled to the extent that the form allows uncontrolled perceptions to be fitted into the categories of the appraisal. Further, they are only likely to solve the organization's "validity problem" if appraisers are in turn motivated to report the private appraisals accurately.

An accurate private appraisal of an individual's performance by an appraiser by no means guarantees that an accurate appraisal will enter the formal system. The appraiser must be motivated to provide an accurate report or at the least must not be motivated to give an inaccurate report. Fig. 7.7 suggests some expectations on the part of the appraiser that might lead to the reporting of inaccurate data. It shows some of the kinds of negative consequences that individual appraisers might perceive would result from accurate appraisals. They include losing control over the reward system and an interpersonally uncomfortable confrontation with the appraisee. Sometimes appraisers try to have the best of all worlds by having multiple public appraisals: one for the appraisee (favorable), one for the organization's reward system (targeted to a desired pay action), and one for determining who gets a particular job assignment (accurate if the appraiser is held responsible for the resulting performance). This behavior is often motivated by just the kinds of motivation shown in Fig. 7.7.

This analysis leads to some interesting thoughts about what conditions are most likely to lead to accurate public reporting of private appraisals. Briefly, it suggests this is likely when individuals are rewarded for doing it and of course not punished for doing it. It is hard to reward accuracy extrinsically because it is difficult to measure. About all that can be done is to look for convergent validity, to require good backup data for appraisals, or to rely on intrinsic motivations towards accuracy perhaps through establishment of value consensus. When appraisals are used by others for multiple purposes individuals are particularly likely to be motivated to distort their appraisals in order to avoid "misuse" of their appraisals.

Ultimately it seems that the best way to get accurate reporting is to do nothing with the data, because any use is likely to result in problems for the appraiser. Of course if nothing is done there is little sense in making the data public. Perhaps the most sensible conclusion is that the use of appraisals should be carefully

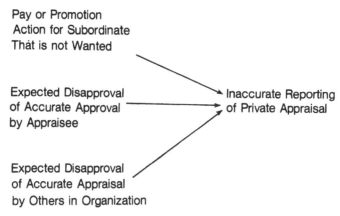

FIG. 7.7. Expectations fostering inaccuracies in performance appraisal.

thought out and that targeted uses be made of specific appraisal judgments (e.g., only for pay) so that the tendency to misrepresent is limited and potentially controllable. Finally, organizations should be careful to avoid thinking that by automatically converting ratings to such things as pay actions they have solved the problem of managers' making bad pay decisions. Most likely what they have done is assure that pay decisions will be based on bad data, because appraisers will give data that support the pay action they want to achieve.

In order to illustrate further the usefulness of the expectancy approach to thinking about performance-appraisal behavior, we can apply it to two traditional issues in appraisal: the failure of superiors to conduct appraisal and the tendency of appraisers to rate subordinates unrealistically high. Looking first at the issue of superiors' conducting appraisals we can make some rather specific predictions about when superiors are likely to go "public" with their appraisals. This is likely to happen only when the perceived consequences of doing so outweigh the advantages of not doing so. For many individuals, going public with an appraisal is not so socially or intrinsically rewarding that it will be done in the absence of some organizational rewards for doing so. Thus, one prediction is that in order to get compliance with a policy requiring that people be appraised, organizations must measure whether appraisers actually carry out the behavior and then link rewards/punishments to these measures. Training may also produce compliance with the policy if it helps to reduce doubt that the appraisal can be constructively carried out—that is, if it reduces the perceived negative consequences of the behavior. Finally, if carrying out an appraisal is instrumental for the accomplishment of some other activity the individual wants to accomplish (e.g., get a pay raise for a subordinate) it is more likely to be carried out, although perhaps not without a bias dictated by the ultimate purpose.

A common complaint in organizations is that appraisers rate "all appraisees" highly. In terms of the outcomes that are typically associated with giving high and low ratings, it is hardly surprising that managers behave this way in many organizations. Indeed, specific organization policies tend to motivate this (e.g., policies linking pay to performance results). The solution to this problem is not to be found in a better appraisal form but in a reward system that encourages appraisers to engage in appropriate rating behaviors. For example, peer-group norms can be developed that say that it is unfair for a manager to rate all his subordinates highly because it makes life difficult for other appraisers. (Of course this raises the design issue of how to create and maintain such group norms.) Alternately, appraisers who without justification rate everyone highly can, in turn, be rated as poor performers because they fail to carry out an important part of their job: appraising the performance of others. In the absence of these steps it is hardly surprising that appraisers tend to rate highly; it often brings raises for subordinates, social rewards from subordinates, and the avoidance of confronting the appraisee about his or her poor performance.

In summary, we are arguing that in order to understand the rating behavior of an appraiser we need to focus on the perceived consequences of giving particular ratings. This means looking at how rating data will be used, who will see it, what the anticipated reaction from the appraisee will be, and what connections there are between the appraisal results and such other systems as the pay system, the human-resource planning system, and so on.

IMPLICATIONS

The major thesis of this paper has been that performance-appraisal behavior can be and indeed should be viewed as motivated behavior. Numerous examples in this paper illustrate that when this view is taken it can be made more understandable and tractable. This is not to argue that performance-measurement methods are unimportant, but rather that an exclusive focus on them is unlikely to produce effective performance-appraisal behavior.

The view strongly suggests that the improvement is ultimately a matter of creating a shared social definition of performance appraisal that is consistent with the original intent. Doing so depends initially on convincing actors that such a definition is viable. In the long run, it also depends on the subsequent reality created by the behaviors stemming from this social definition, which must be perceived as reinforcing and not contradicting the original design. This point suggests a number of conclusions about what type of knowledge and practice is needed to improve outcomes:

1. The amount of improvement that is likely to be gained by better measurement instruments is small.
2. Many contexts may need to be changed before valid appraisal can be done in them.

3. Much more knowledge about how systems are seen or defined by actors is needed if we are to design effective systems.

4. Organizations need to look at the uses they will make of PA results and determine if they encourage the production of valid data that is likely to be valued for that purpose.

These conclusions in turn suggest a final point: Organizations are made up of connected subsystems; therefore research and practice that consider subsystems by themselves are likely to be misleading and simplistic at best. Perhaps the future will see performance-appraisal research and practice that consider the connection among context, social definition, motivation, and appraisal behavior.

ACKNOWLEDGMENTS

Support for the preparation of this paper was provided through the Office of Naval Research Organizational Effectiveness Program (Code 452) under Contract Number N00014–81–K–0048; NR 170–928.

REFERENCES

Davis, S. M., & Lawrence, P. R. *Matrix, Reading,* Mass.: Addison-Wesley, 1977.

Feldman, J. M. Beyond attribution theory: Cognitive processes in performance appraisal. *Journal of Applied Psychology,* 1981, *66*(2), 127–148.

Kelly, G. A. *The psychology of personal constructs,* (Vol. 1). New York: Norton, 1955.

Lawler, E. E. III. *Motivation in work organizations,* Monterey, Calif.: Brooks/Cole, 1973.

MacGregor, D. *The human side of enterprise,* New York: McGraw-Hill, 1960.

Mitchell, T. R. Expectancy models of job satisfaction, occupational preference and effort: A theoretical, methodological and empirical appraisal. *Psychological Bulletin,* 1974, *82,* 1053–1077.

Perry, L. T., & Barney, J. B. Performance lies are hazardous to organizational health. *Organizational Dynamics* Winter, 1981, 68–80.

Prince, J. B., & Lawler, E. E. III. *The impact of discussing salary action in the performance appraisal meeting* (Tech. Rep.). Los Angeles: Center for Effective Organizations, University of Southern California, 1981.

Resnick, S., & Mohrman, A., Jr. *An appraisal of performance appraisal: Summary results of a large scale study.* (Tech. Rep.). Los Angeles: Center for Effective Organizations, University of Southern California, 1981.

Ritzer, G. Sociology: A multiple paradigm science. *The American Sociologist,* 1975, *10,* 156–167.

Salancik, G. R., & Pfeffer, J. A social information processing approach to job attitudes and task design. *Administrative Science Quarterly,* 1978, *23,* 224–253.

Vroom, V. H. *Work and motivation.* New York: Wiley, 1964.

Weick, K. E. *The social psychology of organizing.* Reading, Mass.: Addison-Wesley, 1979.

Would You Know a Properly Motivated Performance Appraisal If You Saw One?

C. J. Bartlett

The paper on motivation and performance-appraisal (PA) behavior by Mohrman and Lawler is based on the basic premise that all behavior is motivated. Because performance-appraisal behavior is obviously behavior it must be motivated. Following from this they also conclude that most appraisal problems are motivational in nature. Examples of motivational problem fall into two general categories: the context within an organization and individual biases. Context problems include culture and climate in the organization and expected outcomes resulting from appraisal. Individual biases include the traditional ones of leniency and halo.

Because of these motivational problems the authors conclude that better measurement is not likely to bring about much improvement in performance appraisals. Although appraisal problems are not only a function of inadequate measurement, the authors appeared to entirely discount measurement by presenting a formal design that is a typical example of poor measurement. Even the best measurement methodology developed over the past 50 years may not solve all of the motivational problems, but abandonment of that measurement-oriented research entirely does not seem wise either.

In taking a measurement perspective it is a responsibility to take into account the motivation of the actors involved in the process. There are at least some measurement-oriented solutions to these problems. In the Mohrman & Lawler introduction of the influence of context they report, ''Our research . . . indicates that current PA practices tend to work better (in terms of affective and behavioral outcomes) when the job of the person being appraised has well-specified duties and priorities.'' How do job duties get well-specified and prioritized? Proper measurement demands a job analysis with carefully delineated tasks that have been psychometrically scaled for importance, frequency, and difficulty. These tasks are then typically translated into behavioral examples of job performance, which are then evaluated for priorities. The backbone of PA measurement is adequate operational definition of performance. There is little hope if the nature of job performance is not specified and prioritized.

Another point made by Mohrman and Lawler is that bias is an example of a motivational problem and is not a measurement issue. Control of bias in rating has long been recognized as a measurement issue. Thirty years ago Wherry culminated several years of research on rating, where control of bias was the central issue, with a psychometric theory of rating. The theory has since been restated in two sources (Wherry, in press; Wherry and Bartlett, 1982). According to that theory, careful attention to measurement issues will help to control for both bias in the observation of behavior as well as bias in the recall of the observations by the rater. First the job must be defined in terms of objectively observable behaviors on the basis of a thorough job analysis. Raters should be trained in the observation of those behaviors of the ratee. Multiple raters making multiple observations can help to ensure different perspectives, which may result in the reduction of bias and random error. At the time of observation, maintaining a record, such as keeping a diary, can help to ensure better recall of those observations. Improved rating formats that specify the behaviors performed by the ratee can further reduce the bias of recall. Examples of such formats include the behaviorally anchored and behavior checklist rating scales. The forced-choice rating systems require the rater to make decisions based on behavioral observations and makes a direct attack on the control of bias by controlling the effect of invalid performance. Because context can affect bias of both observation and recall, definition of the various contexts in which behaviors occur provides a further control of bias. Finally the use of multiple methods and multiple raters can result in a cancallation of competing biases of raters as well as contexts. Such a procedure has also been suggested by Lawler (1967).

Although careful measurement methodology in the design and implementation of a PA system can alleviate some of the problems of context and bias that result from a poorly designed system, problems do manifest themselves once an appraisal system has been put into operation. I would like to look at some examples of these problems that I have encountered, which may have motivational issues underlying them.

One problem that has received little attention in the research literature is the issue of the difference between ratings that are collected for research purposes only (e.g., selection-test validation or other research) and ratings that are collected for administrative decision making (e.g., promotion). Ratings used for real purposes show greater leniency, but when this is a fairly consistent phenomenon it does not present a great problem in making comparative judgments. However, we have found at least two situations in which ratings collected for research purposes have shown on correlation with ratings collected for real purposes. This *zero* correlation occurred even though the ratings for both situations had demonstrated reliability. It is clear that the ratings under research only and real conditions are not measuring the same thing. It is not clear exactly what they are measuring, however.

Appraisal for research purposes differs from appraisal for administrative purposes, and both of these undoubtedly differ from appraisal that is used for feedback or counseling purposes. I believe it would be useful to look at specific situations or contexts in which inconsistent appraisal behavior has been found and attempt to examine motivational issues that may be a function of those situations. For example, an examination of these three different rating contexts—research only, real, and feedback—might show different outcomes. Ratings for research purposes only have few important consequences for either the ratee or the rater. The ratee may not even be aware that the ratings have been conducted and the rater knows that ratings of poor employees will not have negative consequences for that individual. On the other hand, ratings used as part of the promotion process usually have possible negative consequences for employees. Only a small proportion of the ratees are promoted; thus negative feedback and confrontation with the unpromoted have a high negative valence. The expected outcomes when ratings are used for supervisory feedback and counseling are not clear, but are a function of relationships between rater and ratee, organizational use, training opportunities, and so on.

Another interesting perspective for examining motivational issues is to examine the reasons why appraisal is not accepted by the actors in the process. Rigorously designed multiple methods often give different answers. Rather than building confidence in the system, these conflicting results lead to doubt regarding the efficacy of the entire system. Which appraisal is the true measure of performance? Errors are intolerable when personnel decisions affecting individuals are at stake. Even when two methods are in close agreement, a few large discrepancies are inevitable, yet those few will be known system wide. Why are they inevitable? Consider the example in which two systems are highly correlated (e.g., $r_{12} = .80$). Assuming a standard deviation of 10, the standard error of estimate in predicting one from the other will equal 6. That could lead to a 12-point discrepancy in the two systems in 5% of the cases—clearly, enough to provide examples to undermine confidence in the system. On the other hand, the use of only a single method for multiple purposes is unlikely to be accepted either. When a rating system that controls for bias (e.g., forced choice) may be useful for evaluation, such systems are not understood by the rater or ratee and are useless for providing feedback. Systems that are straightforward, but do not control for bias, may be useful for feedback, but when used administratively the ratings are so badly distorted they are useless for any purpose.

In order to meaningfully discuss motivational issues it is necessary to go beyond the Mohrman and Lawler paper. The specific examples this discussion has provided demonstrate what some of the problems, which may be motivational in nature, are. However, that is not enough to help us understand why they occur or how to improve PA systems and their use. In order to conduct the research necessary to understand or manage motivation in PA behavior, it is necessary to develop and identify the motivational constructs involved. How can motivation be managed or studied unless we know what it is? I had hoped that Mohrman and Lawler would address this question. An example of research that has attempted to define the motivational constructs leading to the utilization of evaluation-research findings is provided by Weiss (1978). Weiss found that managers were likely to utilize evaluation-research findings on the basis of their belief in the technical quality of the research, the political acceptability of the findings, and the feasibility of putting the program into use. Wagner (1981) translated these constructs into appraisal-system terms and used a measure of them to predict rater error. She found that rater *acceptability* of the system was likely to lead to fewer errors of inconsistency across time and rating method; however, the expected relationships with the traditional rating errors of halo and leniency were not found.

In addition to a need for better definition of the motivational constructs in order to study or understand the relationship between motivation and appraisal, a better understanding of rating is necessary. What is rating accuracy? Are leniency and halo really rating errors? A recent study by Bernardin and Pence (1980) demonstrated that although training of raters can result in reduced halo and leniency, the trained raters also rated less accurately. If we are to understand what factors (including motivation) affect the quality of appraisal, we must be able to recognize the difference between high- and low-quality ratings.

If we are to understand and improve the appraisal process in terms of motivational problems, it is necessary to: (1) utilize the best methodology to design the formal appraisal system; (2) provide a model that will help to identify the important motivational constructs; and (3) define the constructs that will identify the *quality* of the outcomes of the appraisal. Finally, given the current state of the art, ''Would you know a properly motivated performance appraisal if you saw one?''

ACKNOWLEDGMENT

I would like to acknowledge David Schoorman for his helpful comments and critical review of both the Mohrman and Lawler paper and this discussion. However, any shortcomings of this discussion are the author's responsibility.

REFERENCES

Bernardin, H. J., & Pence, E. C. Effects of rater training: Creating new response sets and decreasing accuracy. *Journal of Applied Psychology*, 1980, *65*, 60–66.

Lawler, E. E. The multitrait–multirater approach to measuring managerial performance. *Journal of Applied Psychology*, 1967, *51*, 369–381.

Wagner, M. J. *Constraints affecting the utilization of performance appraisal systems.* Unpublished master's thesis, University of Maryland, 1981.

Weiss, C. H. Usefulness of social research for decision making in mental health. (doctoral dissertation, Columbis University, 1977). *Dissertation Abstracts International*, 1978, *38*, 5730–573a.

Wherry, R. J. A theory of rating. In F. J. Landy & J. L. Farr, *Performance theory and measurement*, New York: Academic Press, in press.

Wherry, R. J., & Bartlett, C. J. (Ed.) The control of bias in ratings: A theory of rating. *Personnel Psychology*, 1982, *35*, 521–555.

Reply to Bartlett

Edward E. Lawler, III
Allan M. Mohrman, Jr.

We find Bartlett's comments both supportive and puzzling. We do not understand why Bartlett said we present "a formal design that is a typical example of poor measurement." First of all, we did not present a formal design at all and we agree that measurement design is important. Indeed, the question of what is the most important, design or motivation, is the wrong issue. Good data require both good measurement and proper motivation. The latter is often forgotten and played down; hence, the strong emphasis in our paper on motivation.

Bartlett says that it is necessary to go beyond the paper in order to identify the motivational constructs involved in PA. He notes: "How can motivation be managed or studied unless we know what it is?" We agree with him that we need constructs. In our view we presented some useful ones in the paper. Thus, we are somewhat confused by Bartlett's comments that adequate constructs are not presented. Our view is that they are, and that they need to be used more in appraisal research. Finally, we showed that if they are used, they can help explain behavior, which, after all, is the major issue in understanding and improving performance appraisal.

Finally, we are impressed with the findings that Bartlett reports about appraisal for research versus appraisal for administrative decisions. They seem to us to support our view that appraisers report different data when they perceive that the outcomes of reporting them are different. That is, different outcomes and uses motivate the production of different data. This seems to provide strong support for the overall thrust of our paper.

8 Performance Evaluation: A Social-Psychological Perspective

Virginia E. O'Leary

Ranald D. Hansen

Drs. O'Leary and Hansen discuss the implications of self-fulfilling prophecies and perceptions of causes research for performance evaluation. When expectations that one individual holds for another individual prompt confirming behavior, the evaluator's "prophecy" has been fulfilled. O'Leary and Hansen discuss the negative effects of this process on such interactions as those involving persons with handicaps or mental illnesses, or those between unattractive and attractive persons.

The authors also review research on perception of cause (based primarily in attribution theory). According to attribution theory, individuals may succeed on a task because of their ability, effort (hard work), or good luck, or because of the difficulty of the task. Perceivers tend to view men's success as caused by ability and women's success as caused by effort or luck. In addition, attributional research indicates that rewards are differentially distributed based on whether the perceived cause of performance was primarily effort or ability. The authors state that biased expectations based on group membership clearly influence perceptions and behaviors towards targets, and possibly result in the targets' confirmations of the expectations. O'Leary and Hansen conclude that appropriate interventions to counteract these errors can be designed by understanding these processes in the performance situation.

Dr. Ilgen describes three areas of disagreement with O'Leary and Hansen. First, Dr. Ilgen believes that the literature on gender differences is conceptually sterile and that both the size and effect of sex differences are not compelling. Dr. Ilgen's second concern is O'Leary and Hansen's implied direction for future research. He does not agree that useful information about the evaluation process will continue to be provided by the sex-role difference and sex-effects literature. Last, Ilgen argues that more information about the evaluation process can be obtained by investigating the accuracy of evaluation rather than investigating the effects of sex difference and sex-role stereotypes.

During the last decade social psychologists have followed the developments in cognitive psychology and have adapted a number of these to deal with questions that are (or may be) germane to Industrial-Organizational psychologists interested in the process of performance evaluation. Specifically, social-psychological studies of stereotypes, impression formation, implicit personality theory, attributional processes, schema formation, sampling errors, and decision making as they relate to the current study of cognitive processes have entered the mainstream of social-psychological research.

An early conceptual contribution is reflected in a movement away from a motivationally based view of stereotypes, as represented in the work of Katz and Braly (1933) and Adorno, Frenkel-Brunswick, Levinson, and Sanford (1950), and towards a view of stereotyping as a process of information categorization reflected in the work of Allport (1954/1958). More recently, the work of Weiner (1974, 1979) on the attribution of success and failure, the work of Kelley (1967, 1972a) on general attribution processes, and that of Jones and his colleagues (Jones & McGillis, 1976) on the differential cause of an observer's and actor's behavior have extended the social-psychological research framework with implications for performance evaluations.

Contemporary research suggests that the abstract representations or schemas that an individual has for a group (based on race, sex, nationality, or in-group–out-group membership) not only guide our search for new information and direct our attention to specific behaviors but also affect our memory for events and our distribution of rewards—two outcomes central to the performance-evaluation process (Hamilton, 1979).

Among the areas of on-going social-psychological research and theory that may be expected to have an impact on performance evaluation are: stereotyping and implicit personality theory (Ashmore, 1981; Ashmore & Del Boca, 1979; Brewer, 1979; Hamilton, 1981; McCaulay, Stitt, & Segal, 1980; Pryor & Ostrom, 1981; Taylor, 1981); behavioral decision theory (Carroll & Payne, 1976; Einhorn, Kleinmunpz, & Kleinmunpz, 1979; Slovic & Lichtenstein, 1971); scripts and schema (Markus, 1977; Shank & Abelson, 1977); Self-fulfilling prophecies (Jones, 1977; Snyder, Tanke, & Berscheid, 1977; Word, Zanna, & Cooper, 1974); perceptions of cause (Hansen, 1980; Hansen & O'Leary, in press; Jones & McGillis, 1976; Kelley, 1967, 1972; Weiner, 1974, 1979). The focus of this chapter is limited to a discussion of self-fulfilling prophecies and perceived cause on the grounds that I.-O. psychologists may be less familiar with these areas of social-psychological research than the others.

Recently, Landy and Farr (1980) proposed a process model of performance rating in which it is assumed that there are certain rater and ratee characteristics that are brought to the rating task and that have main and interactive effects on the rating process. From a social-psychological perspective, the impact of these main effects and interactions on performance evaluations can best be understood as specific instances of the more general phenomena of social perception, attribution, and social interaction (Yarkin, 1981).

SELF-FULFILLING PROPHECIES

The concept of self-fulfilling prophecy was introduced into the social-psychological literature in the late 1940s. According to Merton (1948) "the self-fulfilling prophecy is, in the beginning, a false definition of the situation evoking a new behavior which makes the originally false conception come true [p. 423]." Thus, the self-fulfilling prophecy involves a process by which expectancies held by a perceiver about a target actually influence the target's behavior in ways that confirm the perceiver's expectancy.

Considerable research on the self-fulfilling prophecy has been conducted in both laboratory (e.g., Meichenbaum, Bowers, & Ross, 1969) and applied settings (e.g., Rosenthal & Jacobson, 1968). Based on the results of this research it can be concluded that one person's expectation of another's behavior may serve as a self-fulfilling prophecy. Darley and Fazio (1980) outlined a sequence of events presumed to characterize such interaction, including:

1. Perceiver developing a set of expectancies about the target person.
2. Perceiver then acting towards the target person in a fashion consistent with his or her expectations of the target.
3. Target interpreting the meaning of perceiver's action.
4. From the interpretation the target person responding to perceiver's action, and
5. Perceiver interpreting the target's action.

Perhaps the best-known study in this area was conducted by Rosenthal and Jacobson in 1968 and published under the title "Pygmalion in the Classroom." In that investigation it was shown that children from whom the teacher was led to expect greater intellectual growth demonstrated such growth relative to other students in the class. In the language of attribution, such results suggest that the perceptions of others affect self-perception resulting in a self-fulfilling prophecy with positive consequences.

However, as the studies of stigma suggest (Goffman, 1963), the consequences of self-fulfilling prophecies are not always positive. For example, the results of studies by Kleck, Ino, and Hastorf (1966) and Kleck (1968) indicate that physical stigma (an obvious physical handicap such as a leg amputation) has an inhibitory effect on both the verbal and nonverbal behaviors exhibited by individuals interacting with "handicapped persons." Similar effects have been found in studies manipulating mental illness as stigma variables. In such studies, subjects in the "mentally ill" conditions actually perform better than those in the normal condition. However, measures of the duration of verbal interaction during both the performance trials and rest periods have revealed shorter interactions between stigmatized others and naive subjects, suggesting that a person's behavior in social interactions is influenced by how he or she believes others have perceived him or her. It is not unreasonable to suggest that ratee characteristics such as sex, race, and physical handicap may function as "stigma variables," particularly when those characteristics connote lower status, stereotypically defined.

In a series of studies examining the influence of social stereotypes on social interaction, Snyder and his colleagues (Snyder & Swann, 1978; Synder et al., 1977) have obtained evidence for the existence of a behavioral confirmation process in which the perceiver's expectations about the behavior of a target may actually result in actions confirming the perceiver's expectations. In one study (Snyder et al., 1977), male "perceivers" were required to interact on the telephone with female "targets" whom they were led to believe were physically attractive or unattractive. Men who anticipated interaction with attractive women perceived them as sociable, poised, and humorous. Men who anticipated interaction with unattractive women perceived them as awkward, serious, and socially inept. Further, the actual behavior of men who believed their partners to be attractive was judged by raters as more socially warm and outgoing. Evidence of the hypothesized behavioral confirmation process was also obtained. Females in the "attractive condition" were judged by raters to exhibit greater animation, greater enjoyment of the conversation, and greater liking for their male partners.

The person-perception literature provides ample documentation of the existence of a physical-attractiveness stereotype that has been termed "What is beautiful is good" (Berscheid & Walster, 1974; Brigham, 1980; Dion, Berscheid, and Walster, 1972). Although ratings of male and female stimulus persons are generally in the same direction on the attractive–unattractive dimension, the physical-attractiveness stereotype appears stronger for females than males (e.g., Bar-Tel & Saxe, 1976; Miller, 1970; Morse, Gruzen, & Reis, 1976).

Studies of physical attractiveness conducted in a task (as opposed to a social) context do not often obtain main effects, although frequently attractiveness interacts with the sex of the stimulus person in influencing perceptions (e.g., Wallston & O'Leary, 1981). Indeed, some studies actually find that unattractive women are viewed as more qualified for traditionally masculine positions than attractive ones (e.g., Cash, Gillen, & Burns, 1977; Dipboye, Arvey, & Terpstra, 1977), a phenomenon described as "beauty is beastly" by Heilman and Saruwatari (1979).

Illustrative of the operation of the self-fulfilling prophecy in laboratory situations are a series of studies by Zanna and his colleagues (Word et al., 1974;

Zanna & Pack, 1975). To test the hypothesis that whites who interacted with blacks would display nonverbal behaviors corresponding to negative evaluations (e.g., greater distance, less eye contact) relative to whites who interacted with whites, Word et al. (1974) asked white subject-interviewers to participate in a discussion with both black and white confederate applicants in a study allegedly designed to assess the process by which decisions between two identical job applicants are made. Results based on raters' evaluations of the actual interactions between interviewers and interviewees indicated that fewer positive behaviors were directed towards black than towards white applicants.

In a second experiment, the results of immediacy cues (i.e., the extent to which communication behaviors enhance closeness to and nonverbal interaction with another) on subsequent interactions were examined. In the immediate condition the interviewee sat close to the interviewers, whereas in the nonimmediate condition the interviewer sat far from the interviewee. Subjects in the nonimmediate condition were judged significantly less adequate for the job than those in the immediate condition. Further, behavioral reciprocity was evidenced by the fact that subjects in the nonimmediate condition exhibited fewer positive responses towards the interviewer. Word and his colleagues (1974) interpret these findings to suggest that "nonverbal, immediate cues mediate, in part, the performance of an applicant in a job-interview situation [p. 119]." To the extent that characteristics of the ratee, such as age, sex, or race, determine immediacy cues, we may reasonably anticipate differences in the performance of these ratees in interaction situations.

Clearly, self-presentation should be considered when exploring the linkages between social perception and social interaction. Recently, von Baeyer, Sherk, and Zanna (1981) found that female subjects presented themselves (physically and verbally) to a male job interviewer in a fashion consistent with his presumed sex-role orientation. Additional research is required to explore the generalizability of these findings to other groups.

However, perceiver's expectations regarding the target do appear to influence not only the perceiver's behavior towards that target but the target's behavior towards the perceiver as well. To the extent that the perceiver's category-based expectancies are biased (either positively or negatively) we may anticipate parallel biases in the interaction sequence. In the evaluation situation "in-group" members who are male, white, able-bodied, young, and attractive may be advantaged whereas "out-group" members who are female, of color, handicapped, old, and unattractive may be disadvantaged.

PERCEPTIONS OF CAUSE

One area of social-psychological research of potential value in further understanding the process of performance rating focuses on people's naive causal explanations for why other people behave as they do. Grounded mainly in attribution research, this approach argues that understanding and predicting how people will react to events around them is enhanced by knowing what their causal explanations for these events are (Green & Mitchell, 1979). Much of the research examining the effects of ratee characteristics, such as sex, on causal attributions has been conducted within the framework of Weiner's two-dimensional taxonomy for the perceived determinants of achievement behavior (Weiner, 1974, 1979; Weiner, Frieze, Kukla, Reed, Rest, & Rosenbaum, 1971).

However, recently, several researchers have begun to study the effects of ratee variables on causal attributions using models offered by Jones and Kelley (Jones & Davis, 1965; Jones & McGillis, 1976; Kelley, 1967, 1972a; Orvis, Cunningham, & Kelley, 1975) and a model proposed by Hansen (1980). Both attributional perspectives offer mechanisms whereby perceivers might arrive at different causal explanations for the perceived determinants of achievement behavior (Weiner, 1974, 1979; Weiner et al., 1971).

According to Weiner's formulation a person may succeed on a task because of her or his ability, because he or she tried hard, had good luck, and/or was engaged in a task that was easy. Failure, on the other hand, may result from low ability, lack of effort, bad luck, and/or a difficult task. These four causal elements vary along two dimensions: the source controlling the outcome of a given performance (internal versus external) and the stability of the factor influencing performance outcome over time (stable versus unstable). The studies of perceived sex differences in causal attributions for performance using this taxonomy suggest that the explanations offered for the success or failure of women and men differ markedly (Cash et al., 1977; Deaux & Emswiller, 1974; Deaux & Taynor, 1973; Etaugh & Brown, 1975; Feather & Simon, 1975; Feldman-Summers & Kiesler, 1974; Haccoun & Stacy, 1980; Yarkin, Towne, & Wallston, in press). A man's successful performance on a task is generally attributed to his skill, whereas a woman's identical performance is attributed to luck or effort. Men's failure on a task is attributed to (bad) luck, women's to (low) ability. Two of the most frequently cited studies exploring the effects of sex on causal attributions for success and failure were conducted by Deaux and Emswiller (1974) and Feldman-Summers and Kiesler (1974). In the first, male and female subjects evaluated a man or a woman on a male- or female-oriented task. Performance by a male on a masculine task was attributed to his skill, whereas an equivalent performance by a female on the same task was attributed to her luck. Contrary to predictions, the reverse was not obtained for performance on a feminine task. Feldman-Summers and Kiesler (1974) asked male and female subjects to attribute cause for the identical performance of women and men on logical and mathematical problems and as physicians specializing in either pediatrics or surgery. Subjects of both sexes attributed greater motivation to women than men regardless of their success (or failure).

The tendency of perceivers to view men's success as caused by ability and women's success by effort or luck has been replicated in a number of studies

WEINER'S 2 x 2 TAXONOMY FOR PERCEIVED DETERMINANTS OF ACHIEVEMENT

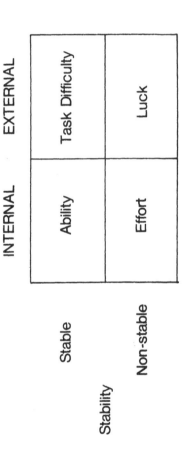

FIG. 8.1. Weiner's 2 × 2 taxonomy for perceived determinants of achievement (from Weiner et al., 1971).

(Deaux & Emswiller, 1974; Feather & Simon, 1975; Haccoun & Stacy, 1980; Yarkin et al. 1981). This tendency is most consistent and pronounced when the task is one at which males are expected to excel.

Given the existence of stereotype-based biases favoring men in male-dominated, achievement-related settings (cf. Mednick, Tangri, & Hoffman, 1975; O'Leary, 1977), it may not be unreasonable to anticipate less-positive reactions to stimulus persons (predominately female) whose behavior is perceived as caused by factors outside their control (external) and/or those that are unstable.

One explanation offered for this evaluation bias (Lockheed & Hall, 1976; Unger, 1976) is related to the effect of sex as a status characteristic. Because the male sex is more highly valued, men's behavior is frequently valued more, even when compared to equally effective behavior performed by women. Although competent persons are generally rated more favorably than incompetent ones, when women and men are asked to rate male and female stimulus persons along the competency dimension, they typically agree that men are more competent than women (cf. Deaux, 1972; Dipboye et al., 1977; Dipboye, Fromkin, & Wiback, 1975). The landmark study evidencing the competency bias favoring men was conducted by Goldberg (1968), and the finding has been replicated in studies requiring both women and men to evaluate the artistic merit of paintings (Pheterson, Kiesler, & Goldberg, 1971), the qualifications of student applicants for a study abroad program (Deaux & Taynor, 1973), and the qualifications of applicants for employment (Haefner, 1977; Henemann, 1977; Rosen & Jerdee, 1974, 1978; Zickmund, Hitt, & Pickens, 1978). Although this finding is considered to be well established, it has not always been replicated (cf. Wallston & O'Leary, 1981).

Several attempts have been made to establish the conditions under which a woman's achievement may be regarded as meritorious as a man's. The results indicate that women are as likely to be evaluated as being as competent as men when their performance is judged exceptional, either on the basis of explicit criteria (Abramson, Goldberg, Greenberg, & Abramson, 1977; Jacobson & Effertz, 1974) or by some authoritative source (Deaux & Taynor, 1973; Pheterson et al., 1971).

Another situation in which women may be viewed as competent is suggested by Abramson and his colleagues, who found that when women were depicted as achieving unexpected success (in traditionally male occupations) their achievement was magnified. Jacobson and Effertz (1974) also obtained results illustrating the "talking platypus phenomenon" (Abramson et al., 1977): "It means little what the platypus says, the wonder is it can say anything at all [p. 123]." However, other researchers (Cash et al., 1977; Nilson, 1976) have found that unexpected success in sex-atypical occupations results in lower (not higher) competence ratings. Findings such as these have lead Nieva and Gutek (1980) to suggest that the promale bias so frequently obtained does not reflect reactions to sex per se but to sex-role incongruence.

Differences in the perceived cause of success (when it is acknowledged) may be expected to produce different reactions to that success. For example, most organizational rewards are designed to recognize personal accomplishments. To be judged deserving of a reward, it is necessary to be perceived as having played a role in the (successful) outcome.

Unfortunately, as recent history suggests, the kind of role one is assumed to have played may vary as a function of sex. The case of Mary Cunningham, former Vice-President for Strategic Planning of Bendix Corporation, provides a particularly dramatic example of the effects of sex on causal attributions. Mary Cunningham left her job at Bendix Corporation in 1980 amid a flurry of speculations regarding whether she and her mentor, Chief Executive Officer William Agee, had been involved in an affair. It has been suggested by more than one observer that in this case the media—as well as those most directly involved in the situation—exposed hidden uneasiness about the rise of women executives. In an interview Ms. Cunningham observed that the controversy over her rapid rise at the Bendix Corporation would never have occurred had she been a man. She aptly pointed out that when her mentor, William Agee, became Chief Financial Officer of the Boise Cascade Corporation at 31 and Chairman of Bendix at 38, he was hailed as a genuis. Cunningham accrued no such accolades when she moved from a position as Agee's Executive Assistant to Vice-President for Strategic Planning within a 15-month period. Instead, gossip and innuendos so riddled the company's offices in Southfield, Michigan, that Agee took the unusual step of gathering 600 employees to tell them that Cunningham's promotion was based solely on merit. Instead of settling the gossip, however, Agee's action backfired, drawing national attention to what had been up to that point, an internal matter.

It is possible to analyze Cunningham's story within the causal-attribution framework, which suggests that people simply do not perceive the cause of women's successful performance as due to the same factors as identical success achieved by men. Perceivers' inferences about the prior probabilities associated with women's and men's behavior form the basis for understanding the different attributions made for women's and men's achievements. In a series of experiments conducted by Hansen and O'Leary (in press), perceivers' naive expectations regarding the cause of a behavior were found to differ as a function of the sex of the performer. Perceivers of both sexes explained women's behavior with personal attributions (dispositions) and men's behavior with attributions to environmental stimuli (entities). The behavior of performers acting in ways believed to have low prior probabilities for people of their sex was more likely to be attributed to dispositions than to entities. Thus, the strongest personal attributions were made for a woman performing a male-linked behavior and the strongest environmental attributions were made for a man performing the same behavior.

In another study, the impact of behavioral expectancies based on category membership were demonstrated. When presented with causal quandries such as

"12 different women (men) completed 12 different tasks or played 12 different games (accomplishments)" and asked to solve for variance, perceivers of both sexes ascribed the variance in women's behavior less to the environmental stimuli in the presence of which the behaviors were performed (entities) and more to differences among the women (dispositions). The reverse was true for perceivers of men. However, even in this first series of studies, the hypothesized sex-determined attributional phenomenon (entity versus disposition) was strongest for perceivers of both sexes who exhibited overreliance on *environmental* factors when asked to explain the cause of a man's behavior than when asked to explain the identical behavior performed by a woman.

In order to explore the effects of beliefs about prior probabilities for behavior based on the performer's membership in a sex category on causal attributions and desires for information, another study was conducted using a behavioral outcome independent of any expectation based on sex: consumer product rating. Subjects viewed a video of six people (either women or men) rating six different brands of the same product (disposable diapers or shaving creams). They were asked to indicate the extent to which the differences among people's ratings were due to "differences among the products" or "differences among raters." There was a tendency to explain variance in men's behavior more in terms of differences among the products (entities) to which they were responding rather than differences among the men (persons) and to explain women's behavior in terms of differences among women. These results suggest that perceivers of both sexes rely more heavily on environmental factors when asked to explain the cause of the behavior of a man than when asked to explain an identical behavior performed by a woman.

To date, there has been only one attempt to explore the relationship between the causal explanations for the performance of women and men described by Weiner's taxonomy and category-based expectations regarding performance outcomes and behaviors (O'Leary & Hansen, 1981). In that study, success was attributed more to ability than to effort, but less to task difficulty, than was failure for both men and women. Contrary to predictions, men's outcomes were no more likely to be perceived as caused by ability than were those of women, but men's outcomes were perceived as caused by effort, which is diagnostic of, rather than compensatory for, ability.

The implications of these findings for performance evaluation are that the perceived cause of an employee's level of performance may have a dramatic impact on personnel actions. For example, Heilman and Guzzo (1978) asked men and women Masters of Business Administration students to make recommendations regarding the appropriateness of various personnel actions taken on equally successful employees. Four different causes—skill, effort, task ease, and luck—were offered to account for these successes. The results demonstrated the impact of causal ascriptions for performance on evaluations of the performers. Rewards were thought appropriate and were judged preferable to "no action" for those performers who were instrumental in causing their own success. These data are particularly relevant to understanding how and why the work achievement of women and men are differentially rewarded. Women, far more often than men, are seen as incidental in bringing about their own successes. Of even greater theoretical interest is the finding that personal explanations for success did not reap equivalent reward.

Success seen as deriving from ability or skill garnered different rewards than did success seen to result from effort. Skill-produced success had a more favorable impact on performance evaluation than did effort-produced success. Only when success was ascribed to skill was a promotion seen as the most preferred personnel action and a promotion as well as a pay raise recommended. Evidently, being viewed as hardworking does not have as favorable organizational consequences as being viewed as capable. These findings imply that women are assumed to be successful primarily because of effort and are apt to be bypassed when the most meaningful organizational rewards (promotions) are distributed.

In contrast to Heilman and Guzzo's view is an attributional model offered by Green and Mitchell (1979) to describe and understand leader behavior. Within their framework, causal attributions to effort are viewed as primary determinants of performance evaluation, rewards, and punishments (Weiner & Kukla, 1970). From their perspective, when success is accompanied by effort, the performance of a person will be evaluated most positively.

If effort is a critical determinant of reward and men receive greater rewards for identical performance than do women, one would logically expect men's success to be attributed more to the exertion of effort than women's. However, the opposite obtains. Why does hard work seem to produce a deficit in performance evaluations? Which causal attributions—effort (Green & Mitchell, 1979) or ability (Heilman & Guzzo, 1978)—mediate organizational rewards? The answer may lie in a more detailed analysis of causal perceptions related to effort.

THE MEANING OF EFFORT

Certainly, both effort and ability are perceived as facilitating higher performance (Anderson & Butzin, 1974). In a recent investigation perceivers were provided with information about the level of effort a person expended (low, below average, above average, high) and their level of ability (low, below average, above average, high) on a cognitive task and were asked to predict the person's performance level on a 17-point scale labeled at 0 for "very low" and at 16 for "very high." Significant main effects due to both effort and ability levels are obtained. Increases in either effort or ability levels produced high predictions of performance outcome.

The implications of these perceived relationships between ability and effort levels in producing a given level of performance are straightforward. The per-

Effects of Ability and Effort Levels on
Predicted Performance Levels

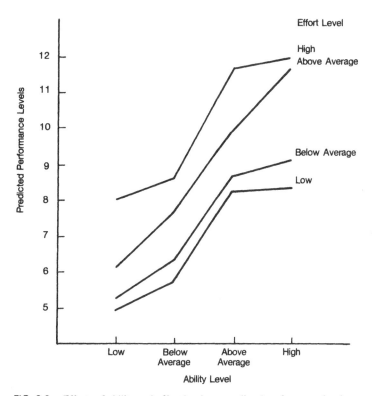

FIG. 8.2.   Effects of ability and effort levels on predicted performance levels.

ceiver knowing only performance outcome should infer higher levels of effort and ability as performance increases. Higher performance outcomes should be perceived as diagnostic of higher effort and higher ability. Lower performance should be diagnostic of both lower effort and lower ability. To test these hypotheses, two experiments were conducted. In one, perceivers were provided with descriptions of performance outcomes for either men or for women and were asked to predict level of ability for each person. In the second experiment, perceivers were given the same materials and were asked to predict the level of effort. Inferred effort and ability levels increased with performance levels. However, the pattern was influenced by the performer's sex.

At each performance level, women were judged as having expended more effort than their male counterparts to obtain the same outcome. The pattern of ability inferences was different, however. At low levels of performance, women were judged as having more ability than men who had achieved the same performance level. At high levels of performance this trend was reversed. The relative parallelism of inferences about effort suggests that performance outcome was perceived as equally diagnostic of women's and men's effort levels. However, the significant interaction obtained on inferences about ability suggests that performance outcomes were seen as more diagnostic of men's ability levels.

It is important here to distinguish between inferring levels of ability and/or effort from performance outcome and attributing performance outcome to ability and/or effort (Hansen & Stonner, 1978). Performance outcome is diagnostic of an internal facilitative force (i.e., ability or effort) to the extent that performance is attributed to that force. Thus, the greater impact of performance level on inferences of men's than of women's ability levels suggests that men's performance was more likely to be attributed to their ability. The equal impact of performance levels on inferences of men's and women's effort levels implies that men's performance was attributed no less than women's to their effort level. This

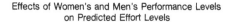

Effects of Women's and Men's Performance Levels
on Predicted Effort Levels

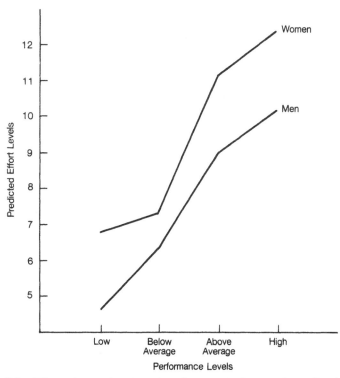

FIG. 8.3.   Effects of women's and men's performance levels on predicted effort levels.

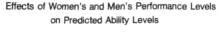

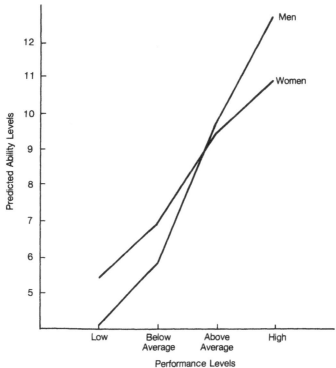

FIG. 8.4.   Effects of women's and men's performance levels on predicted ability levels.

interpretation of these data logically relates to the findings that: (1) promotion
was seen as the most reasonable organizational reward for success attributed to
ability; and (2) men are more likely than women to be promoted although their
performance may be equal.

Thus far the relationship of effort level to performance level has been described as a positive linear function. However, attribution theorists (e.g., Anderson, 1974) have proposed that effort level, although positively related to performance level, is negatively related to perceived ability level. From this
perspective, performance level is inferred to increase with increased effort. If
two people are seen achieving the same performance level although they exert
different levels of effort, an additional contributing factor should be perceived as
being negatively related to effort. That force may well be ability. Thus, a woman
may be judged less able than a man partly because her perceived higher effort
level is viewed as compensating for her lower ability level. The proposition that
greater effort is perceived as a priori evidence for that person's lower ability

(given that performance outcomes are equal) assumes that effort is (inversely) related to ability level.

It appears that effort must be located at a different attributional level than ability. Ability is a more "embedded" inference (Heider, 1958). An experiment was conducted to test the hypotheses that effort was perceived as related both to ability level and to motivational level. Subjects, not knowing performance outcomes, were asked to describe the relationship of effort to motivation level and to ability level. They judged that *both* increased ability and increased motivation could be inferred from increased effort. Thus, increasing effort may not be taken as diagnostic only of ability but may also be perceived as diagnostic of motivational level. Here again, it is hypothesized that sex of performer influences the inference process.

It is thus proposed that motivation of men is likely to be seen as intended to produce environmental effects. If so, men are more likely to be seen as motivated by external facilitative forces, whereas women are more likely to be seen as motivated by internal facilitative forces. The contention that the exertion of effort by men is subject to manipulation through the differential application of external rewards is supported by achievement theorists who have recently postulated the existence of a number of sex-related achievement orientations (Spence & Helmreich, 1978; Veroff, 1977; Veroff, McClelland, & Ruhland, 1975). For example, unlike men, women are motivated to strive for success without the benefit of help or the threat of surveillance (autonomous achievement motivation). This variety of achievement motivation reflects the process orientation (Depner, 1975; Kipnis, 1974; Veroff, 1977). Women are also concerned with another process mode: responsibility achievement (i.e., "Trying hard, doing

TABLE 8.1

Varieties of Achievement Motivation (With the Cognitive Inquiries
Each Implies to Define Standards of Excellence for Successful
Accomplishment)[a]

From where does the person derive the standard of excellence?	In considering accomplishments does the person evaluate the process or the impact?	
	Process Emphasis	*Impact Emphasis*
Self	Autonomous achievement (Did I do it alone and by my choice?)	Power achievement (Did *I* have an impact?)
Social Reference	Responsibility achievement (Did I try as hard as I was supposed to?)	Competitive achievement (Did I do it as well as or better than others, or the best?)
Impersonal Task	Competence achievement (Did I do that sort of thing?)	Task achievement (Did I solve that particular task?)

[a]Veroff, 1977.

Representation of An Attribution Model Indicating the
Major Inferential Relationships Described

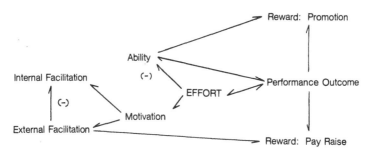

FIG. 8.5. Representation of an attribution model indicating the major inferential relationships described.

their best''). In contrast to men, whose primary achievement concerns center on whether the game is won or lost, women are more concerned with how it is played (Kidd & Woodman, 1975; Veroff, 1977; Zander, Fuller, & Armstrong, 1972). They are more interested in building competence than in having an impact with their competence (competence achievement motivation) (Veroff, 1969, 1977). Men define success in terms of achievement outcome or impact—besting others publicly (assertive competence) (Veroff, 1969, 1977). The importance of the presence of others for men's performance is dramatically illustrated by the fact that under relaxed conditions men's achievement motive scores are lower than women's, yet when men are exposed to arousal instructions stressing mastery and competence, their motive scores increase, whereas women's do not. These findings suggest that men *are* more sensitive to environmental demands than women.

The attributional implications of this tendency can be most easily discussed within the framework of intrinsic motivation (c.f. Deci, 1975). The bulk of the evidence has shown that internal and external facilitative forces are additive in determining effort (Arnold, 1976; Calder & Staw, 1975; Deci, 1975). Observers viewing people operating under different reinforcement contingencies who are exerting similar effort infer less intrinsic motivation as external facilitation increases. More importantly, as women are perceived as exerting higher effort than men, a woman under the same reinforcement contingency as a man should be viewed as being more internally motivated. Indeed, given the usual state of affairs of a man's being provided more reward than a woman, the inference of a man's lower level of intrinsic motivation is supported (Kelley, 1972b); he is exerting less effort for more money.

The implications of this attributional divergence for the allocation of organizational rewards appear obvious. For the supervisor interested in maximizing efforts with the least cost, the allocation of external awards should appear more efficacious when applied to men's than women's efforts. The provision of rewards (i.e., promotions and pay raises) to men should be perceived as inducing a greater increment in their effort level than the same reward applied to women. Indeed, evidence obtained in research on intrinsic motivation suggests that the provision of reward to women may result in a decline in effort expended as a function of lowered intrinsic motivation. As Lawler (1973) has noted, the traditional organizational solution to low productivity (low effort) has been to increase extrinsic motivation. This approach has led to the undesirable escalation of salary and promotion. He has argued that increasing intrinsic motivation (e.g., by making the job more interesting) would be a more cost-effective approach. Ironically, our analysis implies a readily available mechanism for accomplishing this goal: hiring women. Whether or not such an analysis can be extended to other low status groups remains an empirical question. However, Yarkin, et al. (in press) have recently obtained evidence that white males' success was attributed more to ability and less to motivation and luck than that of white females, black males, and black females. The extension of these attributional effects to race corroborates Deaux's (1976) suggestion that "sex is merely one example of a more pervasive characteristic of the attribution process, whereby stereotypes and expectations influence the attribution which is selected [p. 314]." The attention devoted here to exploring the effects of sex on perceivers' causal attributions for performance has been predicted on the assumption that such an extension is warranted.

IMPLICATIONS FOR PERFORMANCE-EVALUATION RESEARCH

At the beginning of this discussion of performance evaluation from a social-psychological perspective, five areas of contemporary social-psychological theory and research with potential for elucidating bias in the performance-evaluation process were identified. The focus of self-fulfilling prophecies and perceptions of cause was intended to be illustrative of research exploring the relationships among social-perception variables, attribution, and social interaction in order to better understand sources of self-perpetuating attributional efforts that may affect the evaluation process.

Clearly, biased expectations based on category membership affect perceptions of, and behavior towards, persons representative of those categories, and can result in behavioral confirmation of the erroneous expectations. Differential attributions resulting in different behavioral outcomes based on ratee characteristics such as sex and race have also been demonstrated. Finally, an attributional model has been suggested to help explain why differential reward allocation based on sex is a social reality. Until the cognitive and perceptual processes that yield different evaluations for identical performances are clearly understood, we may anticipate little change in the inequities of performance evaluations that affect out-group members.

Research or methods to enrich raters' cognitive scripts and/or schemas is indicated. The fact that members of various out-groups (e.g., women, minorities, those with physical handicaps) comprise relatively unique populations and are therefore less likely to be represented in complex cognitive schemata undoubtedly contributes to the sequence of attributional errors frequently made when evaluating members of these groups. Research focusing on increasing our understanding of the attributional processes relevant to performance evaluation may ultimately lead to the design of interventions necessary to counteract errors.

REFERENCES

Abramson, P. R., Goldberg, P. A., Greenberg, J. H., Greenberg, J., & Abramson, L. M. The talking platypus phenomenon: Competency ratings as a function of sex and professional status. *Psychology of Women Quarterly,* 1977, 2(2), 114–124.

Adorno, T. W., Frenkel-Brunswick, E., Levinson, D., & Sanford, N. *The authoritarian personality.* New York: Harper, 1950.

Allport, G. W. *The nature of prejudice.* Garden City, N.Y.: Doubleday Anchor, 1958. (Originally published, 1954.)

Anderson, N. H., & Butzin, C. A. Performance = motivation × ability: An integration-theoretical analysis. *Journal of Personality and Social Psychology,* 1974, 30(5), 598–604.

Arnold, H. J. Effects of performance feedback and extrinsic reward upon high intrinsic motivation. *Organizational Behavior and Human Performance,* 1976, 17(2), 275–288.

Ashmore, R. D. Sex stereotypes and implicit personality theory. In D. L. Hamilton (Ed.), *Cognitive process in stereotyping and intergroup behavior.* Hillsdale, N.J.: Lawrence Erlbaum Associates, 1981.

Ashmore, R. D., & Del Boca, F. K. Sex stereotype and implicit personality theory. Toward a cognitive social psychological conceptualization. *Sex Roles,* 1979, 5, 219–248.

Bar-Tal, D., & Saxe, L. Physical attractiveness and its relationship to sex role stereotyping. *Sex Roles,* 1976, 2, 123–133.

Bersheid, E., & Walster, E. Physical attractiveness. In L. Berkowitz (Ed.), *Advances in experimental social psychology* (Vol. 7). New York: Academic Press, 1974.

Brewer, M. B. In-group bias in the minimal intergroup situation: A cognitive-motivational analysis? *Psychological Bulletin,* 1979, 86, 307–324.

Brigham, J. C. Limiting conditions of the "physical attractiveness stereotype." *Journal of Research in Personality,* 1980, 14, 365–375.

Calder, B. J., & Staw, B. M. Self-perception of intrinsic and extrinsic motivation. *Journal of Personality and Social Psychology,* 1975, 31(4), 599–605.

Carroll, J., & Payne, J. *Cognitive and social behavior,* Hillsdale, N.J.: Lawrence Erlbaum Associates, 1976.

Cash, T. F., Gillen, B., & Burns, D. S. Sexism and "beautyism" in personnel and consultant decision-making. *Journal of Applied Psychology,* 1977, 62, 301–310.

Darley, J. M., & Fazio, R. H. Expectancy confirmation processes arising in the social interaction sequence. *American Psychologist*, 1980, *35*, 867–881.

Deaux, K. To err in humanizing: But sex makes a difference. *Representative Research in Psychology*, 1972, *3*, 20–28.

Deaux, K. Sex and the attribution process. In J. H. Harvey, W. J. Ickes, & R. F. Kidd (Eds.), *New directions in attribution research* (Vol. 1). New York: Wiley, 1976.

Deaux, K., & Emswiller, T. Explanations of successful performance on sex-linked tasks: What is skill for the male is luck for the female. *Journal of Personality and Social Psychology*, 1974, *29*, 80–85.

Deaux, K., & Taynor, J. Evaluation of male and female ability: Bias works two ways. *Psychological Reports*, 1973, *32*, 261–262.

Deci, E. L. *Intrinsic motivation*. New York: Plenum, 1975.

Depner, C. E. *An analysis of motivational factors which contribute to sex differences in the expression of achievement motivation*. Unpublished manuscript, University of Michigan, 1975.

Dion, K., Berscheid, E., & Walster, E. What is beautiful is good. *Journal of Personality and Social Psychology*, 1972, *24*, 285–290.

Dipboye, R. L., Arvey, R. D., & Terpstra, D. E. Sex and physical attractiveness of raters and applicants as determinants of resume evaluations. *Journal of Applied Psychology*, 1977, *62*, 228–294.

Dipboye, R. L., Fromkin, H. L., & Wiback, K. Relative importance of applicant sex, attractiveness and scholastic standing in evaluations of job applicant resumes. *Journal of Applied Psychology*, 1975, *60*, 39–43.

Einhorn, H., Kleinmunpz, D., & Kleinmunpz, B. Linear regression and process training models of judgement. *Psychology Review*, 1979, *86*, 465–485.

Etaugh, C., & Brown, B. Perceiving the causes of success and failure of male and female performers. *Developmental Psychology*, 1975, *11*, 103.

Feather, N. T., & Simon, J. C. Reactions to male and female success and failure in sex-linked occupations: Impressions of personality, causal attributions, and perceived likelihood differential consequences. *Journal of Personality and Social Psychology*, 1975, *31*, 20–31.

Feldman-Summers, S., & Kiesler, S. B. Those who are number two try harder: The effect of sex on attributions of causality. *Journal of Personality and Social Psychology*, 1974, *30*, 846–855.

Goffman, E. *Stigma: Notes on the management of spoiled identity*. Englewood Cliffs, N.J.: Prentice-Hall, 1963.

Goldberg, P. A. Are women prejudiced against women? *Transaction*, 1968, *5*, 28–30.

Green, S. G., & Mitchell, T. R. Attributional processes of leaders in leader–member interactions. *Organizational Behavior and Human Performance*, 1979, *23*, 439–458.

Haccoun, D. M., & Stacy, S. Perceptions of male and female success or failure in relation to spouse encouragement and sex-association of occupation. *Sex Roles*, 1980, *6*(6), 819–831.

Haefner, J. E. Sources of discrimination among employees: A survey investigation. *Journal of Applied Psychology*, 1977, *62*, 265–270.

Hamilton, D. L. A cognitive-attributional analysis of stereotyping. In L. Berkowitz (Ed.), *Advances in experimental social psychology* (Vol. 12). 1979.

Hamilton, D. L. *Cognitive processes in stereotyping and intergroup behavior*. Hillsdale, N.J.: Lawrence Erlbaum Associates, 1981.

Hansen, R. D. Common sense attribution. *Journal of Personality and Social Psychology*, 1980, *39*(6), 996–1009.

Hansen, R. D., & O'Leary, V. E. Actresses and actors: The effects of sex on causal attributions. *Basic and Applied Social Psychology*, in press.

Hansen, R. D., & Stonner, D. M. Attributes and attributions: Inferring stimulus' properties, actors' dispositions, and cause. *Journal of Personality and Social Psychology*, 1978, *36*, 657–667.

Heider, F. *The psychology of interpersonal relations*. New York: Wiley, 1958.

Heilman, M. E., & Guzzo, R. A. The perceived cause of work success as a mediator of sex discrimination in organizations. *Organizational Behavior and Human Performance,* 1978, *21*(3), 346–357.

Heilman, M. E., & Saruwatari, L. R. When beauty is beastly: The effect of appearance and sex on evaluations of job applicants for managerial and non-managerial jobs. *Organizational Behavior and Human Performance,* 1979, *23,* 360–372.

Henemann, H. G. Impact of test information and applicant sex on applicant evaluations in a selection simulation. *Journal of Applied Psychology,* 1977, *62,* 524–526.

Jacobson, M. B., & Effertz, J. Sex roles and leadership: Perception of the leaders and the led. *Organizational Behavior and Human Performance,* 1974, *12,* 383–396.

Jones, E. E., & Davis, K. E. From acts to dispositions: The attribution process in person perception. In L. Berkowitz (Ed.), *Advances in experimental social psychology* (Vol. 2). New York: Academic Press, 1965.

Jones, E. E., & McGillis, D. Correspondent inferences and the attribution cube: A comparative reappraisal. In J. H. Harvey, W. J. Ickes, & R. F. Kidd (Eds.), *New directions in attribution research* (Vol. 1). Hillsdale, N.J.: Lawrence Erlbaum Associates, 1976.

Jones, R. A. *Self-fulfilling prophecies: Social, psychological, and psychological effects of expectancies.* Hillsdale, N.J.: Lawrence Erlbaum Associates, 1977.

Katz, D., & Braly, K. Racial stereotypes of one hundred college students. *Journal of Abnormal and Social Psychology,* 1933, *28,* 2980–290.

Kelley, H. H. Attribution theory in social psychology. In D. Levine (Ed.), *Nebraska symposium on motivation.* Lincoln: University of Nebraska Press, 1967.

Kelley, H. H. Attribution in social interaction. In E. E. Jones, D. E. Kanouse, H. H. Kelley, R. E. Nisbett, S. Valins, & B. Weiner (Eds.), *Attribution: Perceiving the causes of behavior.* Morristown, N.J.: General Learning Press, 1972. (a)

Kelley, H. H. *Causal schemata and the attribution process.* Morristown, N.J.: General Learning Press, 1972. (b)

Kidd, T. R., & Woodman, W. F. Sex and orientations toward winning in sport. *Research Quarterly,* 1975, *46*(4), 476–483.

Kipnis, D. M. Inner direction, other direction and achievement motivation. *Human Development,* 1974, *17*(5), 321–343.

Kleck, R. Physical stigma and nonverbal cues emitted in face-to-face interactions. *Human Relations,* 1968, *23,* 19–29.

Kleck, R., Ino, H., & Hastorf, A. H. The effects of physical space upon face-to-face interaction. *Human Relations,* 1966, *19,* 425–436.

Landy, F. J., & Farr, J. L. Performance rating. *Psychological Bulletin,* 1980, *87*(1), 72–107.

Lawler, E. E., III. *Motivation in work organizations.* Monterey, Calif.: Brooks/Cole, 1973.

Lockheed, M. E., & Hall, K. P. Conceptualizing sex as a status characteristic: Applications to leadership training strategies. *The Journal of Social Issues,* 1976, *32,* 111–124.

Markus, H. Self-schemata and processing information about the self. *Journal of Personality and Social Psychology,* 1977, *35,* 63–78.

McCauley, C., Stitt, C. L., & Segal, M. Stereotyping: From prejudice to prediction. *Psychological Bulletin,* 1980, *87,* 195–208.

Mednick, M. T. S., Tangri, S. S., & Hoffman, L. W. *Women and achievement.* Washington, D.C.: Hemisphere, 1975.

Meichenbaum, D. H., Bowers, K. S., & Ross, R. R. A behavioral analysis of teacher expectancy effect. *Journal of Personality and Social Psychology,* 1969, *13* 306–316.

Merton, R. K. The self-fulfilling prophecy. *Antioch Review,* 1948, *8,* 193–210.

Miller, A. G. Role of physical attractiveness in impression formation. *Psychonomic Science,* 1970, *19,* 241–243.

Morse, S. E., Gruzen, J., & Reis, H. The "eye of the beholder": A neglected variable in the study of physical attractiveness. *Journal of Personality,* 1976, *44,* 209–225.

Nieva, V., & Gutek, B. Sex effects on evaluation. *Academy of Management Review,* 1980, *5*(2), 267–276.

Nilson, L. B. The occupational and sex-related components of social standing. *Sociology and Social Research,* 1976, *60,* 328–336.

O'Leary, V. E. *Toward understanding women.* Monterey, Calif.: Brooks/Cole, 1977.

O'Leary, V. E., & Hansen, R. D. *Sex affects causal accounting for achievement.* Unpublished manuscript, American Psychological Association, 1981.

Orvis, D., Cunningham, J. D., & Kelley, H. H. A closer examination of causal inference: The role of consensus, distinctiveness, and consistency information. *Journal of Personality and Social Psychology,* 1975, *32,* 605–616.

Pheterson, G. I., Kiesler, S. B., & Goldberg, P. A. Evaluation of the performance of women as a function of their sex, achievement, and personal history. *Journal of Personality and Social Psychology,* 1971, *19,* 114–118.

Pryor, J. B., & Ostrom, T. M. The cognitive organization of social information: A converging operations approach. *Journal of Personality and Social Psychology.* 1981, *41,* 628–641.

Rosen, B., & Jerdee, T. H. Effects of applicant's sex and difficulty of job on evaluations of candidates for managerial positions. *Journal of Applied Psychology,* 1974, *59,* 511–512.

Rosenthal & Jacobson, '68.

Shank, R. C., & Abelson, R. *Scripts, plans, goals, and understanding.* Hillsdale, N.J.: Lawrence Erlbaum Associates, 1977.

Rosen, B. & Jerdee, T. Perceived sex differences in managerially relevant characteristics. *Sex Roles,* 1978, *4,* 837–844.

Rosenthal, R., & Jacobson, L. *Pygmalion in the classroom: Teacher expectations and pupils' intellectual development.* New York: Holt, Rinehart, and Winston, 1968.

Slovic, P. & Lichtenstein, S. Comparison of Baylsian and regression approaches to the study of information processing in judgement. *Organizational Behavior and Human Performance,* 1971, *6,* 649–744.

Snyder, M. & Swann, W. B., Jr. Hypothesis-testing process in social interaction. *Journal of Personality and Social Psychology,* 1978, *11,* 1202–1212.

Snyder, M., Tanke, E. D. & Berscheid, E. Social perception and interpersonal behavior on the self-fulfilling nature of social stereotypes. Journal of *Personality and Social Psychology,* 1977, *35,* 656–666.

Spence, J. T. & Helmreich, R. *Masculinity and femininity: Their psychological dimensions, correlates and antecedents.* Austin, Texas: University of Texas Press, 1978.

Taylor, S. E. A categorization approach to stereotyping. In D. L. Hamilton (Ed.). *Cognitive processes in stereotyping and intergroup behavior.* Hillsdale, N.J.: Erlbaum, 1981.

Unger, R. K. Male is greater than female: The socialization of status inequality. *The Counseling Psychologist,* 1976, *6*(2), 2–9.

Veroff, J. Social comparison and the development of achievement motivation. In C. P. Smith (Ed.), *Achievement-related motives in children.* New York: Russell Sage Foundation, 1969.

Veroff, J. Process vs. impact on men's and women's achievement motivation. *Psychology of Women Quarterly,* 1977, *1*(3), 283–293.

Veroff, J., McClelland, L., & Ruhland, D. Varieties of achievement motivation. In M. T. S. Mednick, S. S. Tangri, & L. W. Hoffman (Eds.), *Women and achievement.* New York: Wiley, 1975.

von Baeyer, C. L., Sherk, D. L., & Zanna, M. P. Impression management in the job interview: When the female applicant meets the male (chauvinist) interviewer. *Personality and Social Psychology Bulletin,* 1981, *1,* 45–51.

Wallston, B. S., & O'Leary, V. E. Sex makes a difference: Differential perceptions of women and men. In L. Wheeler (Ed.), *Review of personality and social psychology: 2.* Beverly Hills: Sage, 1981.

Weiner, B. *Achievement motivation and attribution theory.* Morristown, N.J.: General Learning Press, 1974.

Weiner, B. A theory of motivation for some classroom experience. *Journal of Educational Psychology,* 1979, *71,* 3–25.

Weiner, B., Frieze, I., Kukla, A., Reed, L., Rest, S., & Rosenbaum, R. M. Perceiving the causes of success and failure. In E. E. Jones, D. E. Kanouse, R. E. Nisbett, S. Valins, & B. Weiner (Eds.), *Attribution: Perceiving the causes of behavior.* Morristown, N.J.: General Learning Press, 1971.

Weiner, B., & Kukla, A. An attributional analysis of achievement motivation. *Journal of Personality and Social Psychology,* 1970, *15,* 1–20.

Word, C. O., Zanna, M. P., & Cooper, J. The nonverbal mediation of self-fulfilling prophecies in interracial interaction. *Journal of Experimental Social Psychology,* 1974, *10,* 109–201.

Yarkin, K. L. *Evolution of research on the relationship between attribution and social interaction.* Unpublished manuscript, Vanderbilt University, Nashville, Tennessee, 1981.

Yarkin, K. L., Towne, J. P., & Wallston, B.S. Attributions of causality based on sex and stimulus persons: Blacks and women must try harder. *Personality and Social Psychology Bulletin,* in press.

Zander, A., Fuller, R., & Armstrong, W. Attributed pride or shame in a group and self. *Journal of Personality and Social Psychology,* 1972, *23*(3), 346–352.

Zanna, M. P., & Pack, S. J. On the self-fulfilling nature of apparent sex differences in behavior. *Journal of Experimental Social Psychology,* 1975, *11,* 583–591.

Zickmund, W. C., Hitt, M. A., & Pickens, B. A. Influence of sex and scholastic performance on reactions to job applicant resumes. *Journal of Applied Psychology,* 1978, *63,* 252–255.

Gender Issues in Performance Appraisal: A Discussion of O'Leary and Hansen

Daniel R. Ilgen

O'Leary and Hansen suggest that (1) more attention must be paid to superior–subordinate interactions if we are to understand the performance-appraisal process and that (2) the social-psychological literature offers several suggestions for understanding these interactions. I wholeheartedly agree. In particular, cognitive social-psychological research offers several suggestions for helping us understand performance-appraisal judgments.

Although I agree with the general assumptions of the preceding presentation, I disagree with the orientation and implied focus of O'Leary and Hansen's approach to understanding supervisor–subordinate interactions with respect to interpersonal judgments. Our opinions appear to diverge with respect to three issues. First, O'Leary and Hansen imply that more direct support for performance-appraisal concerns is available in the social-psychological literature than I feel is there. My reading of that literature leads me to conclude that it is a rich source of excellent ideas that may lead to a better understanding of the performance-appraisal process. However, both the size of the effects and the nature of the experimental paradigm would lead me to urge that we exercise more caution in applying this literature to our problem than was implied from O'Leary and Hansen's paper. I speak to this issue more later.

My second concern is with the implied directions for future research. Given the nature of the research being conducted by the authors and reported here by them, I inferred that they believe that research within the paradigm of the basic research model for sex-difference and sex-role effects will continue to provide useful information for understanding performance appraisal. Although I believe that the research by Hansen and O'Leary is well done and interesting and contributes to the sex-difference and sex-role literature of social psychology, I also

believe that the utility of this work for advancing our understanding of performance appraisal is more limited than they imply.

Finally, it is apparent that O'Leary and Hansen had a not-so-hidden agenda—
to argue that sex-difference and sex-role effects in the evaluation process operate
to limit the opportunities of women in work settings. Over 50% of their presentation dealt explicitly with descriptions of sex effects. Therefore, in the remainder
of my discussion, I address myself to how these effects relate to performance
appraisal. In particular, I begin with general assumptions that I believe are totally
in agreement with those of O'Leary and Hansen with regard to the need for
unbiased evaluations of all employees. I then continue from these assumptions
and suggest that to accomplish our objectives, more rapid progress will be made
by starting with issues directly relevant to performance appraisal and working out
perhaps to sex-difference and sex-role research rather than by working from the
latter to performance appraisal as is implied by O'Leary and Hansen.

ASSUMPTIONS

Figure 8C.1 lists the underlying assumptions related to the role of performance
appraisals in effective utilization of women in the work force. The assumptions
are classified into three major sets: those dealing with women in the work force,
performance appraisal, and specific issues related to the effectiveness and use of
performance-appraisal information in the typical case of a supervisor's responding to a subordinate. None of these should come as any surprise to you. I present
them only because it is apparent from much of the literature that (1) the ultimate
objective of our efforts as stated in I. A. 1. in Fig. 8C.1 is often lost in the
rhetoric of emotional appeals with regard to some observed sex differences and
(2) some of the objectives are often ignored or not really understood in terms
of their impact. Finally, I present the specific assumptions (under II.) more as the
assumptions I feel are necessary for the effective use of performance appraisal
with respect to this issue. The assumptions are not ones that have been made
explicit by a large number of others looking at sex differences or sex-role effects.
Note that these two assumptions do not mention explicitly any gender issues.
This is no accident, as becomes clear later.

LIMITATIONS OF RESEARCH

In my opinion, there are at least three major weaknesses in the current literature
on sex differences and sex-role effects with respect to staffing in general and
performance appraisal in particular. First, much of the literature is conceptually
sterile. In many ways this may be because the assessment of sex effects is too

I. General
   A. Women in the Work Force
      1. Effective staff utilization, in the long run, depends on the unrestricted matching of individual capabilities with job requirements.
      2. Both individual capabilities and job requirements can be changed, within limits.
      3. In the past, women's skills and abilities have been underutilized.
   B. Performance Appraisal
      1. Effective staff utilization depends on the availability of evaluative information about the behavior of individuals in work roles.
      2. This information is usually based on judgments from individuals other than the individual role performer who have had sufficient opportunity to observe the individual in question.
      3. Well-designed performance-appraisal systems are among the best sources available for such information in most organizations.
      4. Research on performance-appraisal systems and processes ultimately should influence the design and implementation of such systems and/or the use of information from such systems.

II. Specific
   A. Performance-appraisal data must be accurate.
   B. Information gained from performance-appraisal systems must be used effectively for making decisions regarding the individuals evaluated.

FIG. 8C.1.   Underlying assumptions with respect to the gender issues in performance appraisal.

easy to do. I would venture to guess that there is hardly anyone in this room who has not collected data on sex effects and written something about them. Rarely do we gather data on any topic, especially field-research data, when we do not throw in an item on gender regardless of whether or not we expect any gender effects. I am not questioning the legitimacy of this practice and will continue to do this myself. However, such a practice does increase the probability of cluttering the literature with a lot of data that are likely to have little or no conceptual base. It also means that there is a high likelihood of a lot of Type-1 error in the literature on this topic. Few can resist reporting and describing the ''meaning'' of some statistically significant sex effect in their data even though when they laid out the research they had no idea what to expect with regard to this effect.

The second weakness of the literature is that the paradigm for much of the research is of little value for generalizing to work organizations. This paradigm, often termed the "paper people paradigm," involves presenting laboratory subjects with descriptions of individuals who possess certain characteristics. Subjects then describe their reactions to these stimulus persons on some questionnaire measure. Although I have no problem accepting the legitimacy of laboratory data for understanding behavior in organizations, I do feel that it is necessary that such research capture the essence of the constructs under investigation. With respect to the effects of gender on evaluations, the data are quite clear that our reactions to other individuals are very dependent on the frequency with which we observe and interact with the persons in question over an extended period of time. Because I have assumed that the use of performance-appraisal systems in organizations demands extended interaction between appraisers and appraisees (see Fig. 8C.1, assumption I.B.2) and because a large majority of the literature on gender effects lacks this time dimension, I have little or no confidence in the external validity of much of this literature for the problem that concerns us here. Although there have been several appeals by O'Leary (Wallston & O'Leary, 1981) and others (e.g., Nieva & Gutek, 1980) questioning the generalizations that can be made from these data, the use of the paradigm is still widespread.[1]

Finally, the fact the topic itself is such a value-laden one has tended to weaken the value of the literature on the topic. There are at least two effects of the value orientation. The first of these is to overinterpret the real-world implications of statistically significant effects that account for very little variance. This, of course, happens in all research. However, I think that it is worse in a literature in which there is a "right way" for the results. I must confess to being guilty of this practice myself. In a study that Jim Terborg and I did several years ago (Terborg & Ilgen, 1975), we reported a simple main effect in which we found that women were placed on routine jobs more frequently than on challenging ones. Our hypothesized interaction between gender and job challenge was not significant, but our main effect was. We were careful in the discussion to point out the limitations of the finding due to the absence of the interaction, but later references to this article have failed to pass along these cautions. Frequently the finding is misquoted as indicating that women were more frequently assigned to routine jobs than were men. In retrospect I would have been more cautious reporting something as consistent with a stereotypic belief as this.

The second effect of value-laden research is to create a restricted psychological set in the researcher that often makes it difficult to perceive alternatives that may violate preconceived ideas. This, of course, is a problem in all research (or,

---

[1] For an excellent discussion of the effects on scientific progress of active research themes that have high popular interest and a relatively standard paradigm, see D. Cartwright (1973).

I should say, in all researchers); it is more severe with research on topics related to social values. The early work on sex and sex-role stereotypes that found that stereotypes of managers and of males were more similar than those of managers and of females is a case in point. Once observed, we were much too willing to decry its existence, to continue to replicate it and to recommend that women simply try to change to fit the manager stereotype through assertiveness training or some other means. More complex but more realistic reactions to the discrepancy between manager and female stereotypes, such as suggesting changes in managerial roles and in women's and men's behaviors in them, were slow in coming. I suggest this occurred primarily because of the limited perspective created by the value-laden characteristics of the problem at hand. Again, I have no solution to this problem; it is endemic to any topic with potentially high social ramifications. I am simply suggesting that this has contributed to limiting the usefulness of the research literature particularly as it relates to applying existing research findings to staffing issues.

A PROBLEM-FOCUSED VIEW

Recall that our real concern here is the effective use of performance-appraisal information at the superior–subordinate level, particularly as it relates to appraising women employees. Our past actions have been to look to the sex differences and the sex-role literature for help with this problem by ''grafting'' that literature onto the appraisal problem. I am proposing that we start from the other direction. We should first lay out explicitly the appraisal issues. Next we should ask what we know about these issues, and then, last of all, we should look at the possible sex effects with respect to the issues identified. I conclude my discussion by taking this approach, and in the process, I hope to demonstrate that often we may best serve our objective of effectively utilizing women in the work force by totally ignoring issues of gender and concentrating instead on some rather basic issues of performance assessment and supervision.

Fig. 8C.2 identifies the major concerns with respect to the utilization of performance-appraisal information at the supervisory level. Sections I and II are the obvious givens: Performance-related behaviors take place that we assume can be objectively mapped into evaluations and labeled actual performance. These behaviors provide the basis for an evaluative judgment on the part of the appraiser (in this case, the supervisor). They are labeled Perceived Performance or Performance Appraisal. The latter serves as the input into supervisory decisions with respect to subordinates.

On the left side of Fig. 8C.2, I am suggesting that the most salient decisions based upon appraisal information are those that deal with the distribution of rewards and sanctions. The rewards themselves can be further divided into those that are relatively temporary and those that have a long-term impact on the

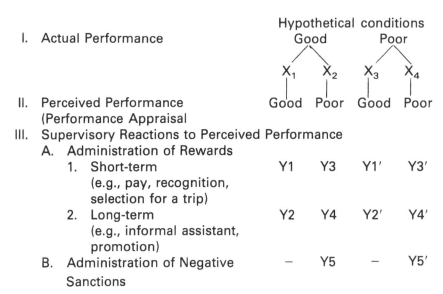

FIG. 8C.2.   Process points in performance-appraisal development and utilization at the supervisory level.

employees' careers. Finally, negative sanctions can be administered when important behaviors are seen as being below an acceptable standard and in need of correction.

On the right-hand side of Fig. 8C.2 are represented possible conditions resulting from the combination of the classes of conditions just described. First, of the four conditions resulting from the match of actual performance with perceived performance, two represent an accurate match and two a mismatch, although all are part of a continuum of accuracy that I have simplified by using only two levels of performance for illustrative purposes. The four conditions created (X_1 to X_4) offer no surprises. However, the inclusion of X_3—the condition in which those who perform poorly but are perceived as performing well—is rarely considered. This is particularly true in research on gender effects. By starting from a performance-appraisal perspective, we are more likely to recognize such omissions.

Taking the supervisors' perceptions of subordinates' performance as givens, the bottom right-hand portion of Fig. 8C.2 indicates possible reactions to the performance evaluations. Note that the first and third columns are nearly identical, as are the second and fourth. This simply reflects the fact that the supervisor is reacting on the basis of his or her perceptions independent of what may be the actual performance of the subordinate. Also note that it is assumed that negative sanctions are only considered if performance is perceived to be poor.

If we accept this construal of the major process points in the use of performance appraisals at the supervisor–subordinate interface, then to understand how to use appraisals effectively at this level, we should ask what are the major factors that influence decisions and judgments related to appraisal accuracy and reward/sanction allocation. Let me just briefly consider some of these issues.

To guide our discussion of these factors, I refer to Fig. 8C.3. This figure lists, on the far left, those characteristics of the appraisal process that I have argued are the most relevant with respect to superior–subordinate relationships and performance appraisal. On the right are three columns of factors that I am suggesting are salient with respect to influencing those issues described on the left. Finally, factors listed on the right in any given row are assumed to impact on the far-left issue through those factors listed to the left of the item in that row. This becomes more clear as we work through the elements in the figure.

It is suggested in Fig. 8C.3 that the general (or overall) issue of appraisal accuracy is most directly affected by four conditions. By far the most important of these is the first—the objectivity of the actual performance. The more objective the performance standards are, the less likely it is that factors other than task performance will influence judgments about performance. In fact, recent reviews of sex and sex-role effects on performance ratings by Wallston and O'Leary (1981) and by Nieva and Gutek (1980) both point out that it is doubtful that any gender effects on appraisals occur if the performance standards are objective. Unfortunately, only a limited number of jobs can be described by extremely objective and verifiable dimensions.

The second factor, Appraiser's Knowledge of Performance Dimensions, is in some ways related to the first. Presumably, as the dimensions of the job become more objective, the supervisor should be able to be more knowledgeable about the job. However, even with somewhat subjective job dimensions, the more knowledge the supervisor has about the job, the more valid he or she should be as a rater of performance on that job.

The third factor deals with the supervisor's opportunity to observe the subordinate's job. In most cases, this is seen as a function of the nature of the job setting, but when observations are not prescribed for the supervisor, he or she samples behaviors of the subordinate and, in this way, defines the set of observations. Extrapolating from the Hansen and O'Leary (in press) data, we might hypothesize that the sampling strategies of supervisors are a function of the attributions they make about the causes of the subordinates' performance and also that these attributions are influenced in part by the subordinates' sex. Specifically, if the performance of women is considered to be primarily a function of individual characteristics, I would hypothesize that supervisors would sample performance behaviors more frequently from women than from men.[2]

The final effect on appraisal accuracy deals with the performance expectations supervisor holds for the subordinate before actually observing performance. The data from a variety of settings show that evaluations often are biased in the direction of prior expectations. It is here that the prophecy effects discussed by

[2]I wish to thank Kay Deaux for suggesting this effect.

Performance-Appraisal Issues	Influencing Factors	
	Direct	Indirect
I. Performance Accuracy		
A. Overall (Conditions X_1–X_4)	1. Objectivity of Performance	
	2. Appraiser's Knowledge of Performance Dimensions	
	3. Observational Opportunities	
	a. Job Design	
	b. Appraiser Controlled	Attributions Sex Effects
	4. Appraiser Expectations for Appraisee performance	1. Past Experience
		2. *Sex-Role Expectations*
B. Specific Errors		
1. Underestimation of Performance (X_2)	Appraiser Expectations for Appraisee Performance.	1. Past Experience
2. Overestimation of Performance (X_3)	1. Appraiser/Appraisee Similarity	*Sex Effects*
	2. Appraiser Expectations for Appraisee Performance	1. Past Experience
		2. *Sex-Role Effects*
II. Reward/Sanction Distribution		
A. Overall (All Y_1 – Y_5 Conditions)	1. Reward/Sanction Availability	
	2. Attributions (Internal–External)	1. Actor/Observer Bias
		2. *Sex Effects*
B. Short-Term Rewards	1. Reward Availability	
	2. Attributions (Internal Unstable ≥ Internal Stable).	1. Condition Effects[a]
		2. *Sex Effects*
		3. *Sex-Role Effects*
C. Long-Term Rewards	1. Reward availability	
	2. Attributions (Internal Stable ≥ Internal Unstable)	1. Condition Effects[a]
		2. *Sex Effects*
		3. *Sex-Role Effects*
	3. *Sex (Stereotype) Effects*	
D. Sanctions	1. Sanction Availability	1. *Sex Effects*
	2. Status Differences	2. *Sex-Role Effects*
	3. Consequence Effects	

[a]By Condition Effects I mean the conditions of distinctiveness, consensus, and consistency that Kelly (1967) described as leading to attributions.

FIG. 8C.3.   Factors influencing rating accuracy and reward/sanction distributions between supervisors and subordinates.

O'Leary and Hansen (this volume) impact on appraisals. Fig. 8C.3 goes on to suggest that these expectations are a function of the supervisor's past experience with the subordinate. Likewise, the supervisor could receive such information from sources other than direct experience. I am subsuming this condition under past experience. As O'Leary and Hansen have pointed out, the literature on sex roles indicates that when the sex of the actors is congruent with sex role, individuals tend to be judged more competent than when they are mismatched, although the negative effects of mismatching appear to be more severe for females than for males (O'Leary & Hansen, this volume; Wallston & O'Leary, 1981).

Turning to the two specific types of errors in appraisal accuracy introduced in Fig. 8C.2 and repeated in Fig. 8C.3, appraiser expectations as previously described contribute to each type of error. Likewise, the expectations are seen as a function of past experience and sex-role effects. With respect to sex-role effects, the literature indicates that the direction of the effects differs as a function of the two conditions. In general, when sex-role effects are observed, good performance of females in male-oriented roles tends to be underestimated and poor performance in these roles overestimated in comparison to males. The latter effect has been labeled the "talking platypus" effect by Abramson, Goldberg, Greenberg, and Abramson(1977) who say that it matters not what the platypus says; the amazing thing is that it says anything at all.

One additional influence on overestimated performance is suggested. An extensive literature on Byrne's (1971) attraction paradigm shows that people rate others like themselves more favorably. This effect has been demonstrated with performance ratings (e.g., Hamner, Kim, Baird, & Bigoness, 1974). Although most frequently observed among ratings of performers of different races, there is also some evidence that there are differences between sexes such that like-sex performers are rated more favorably (Wallston & O'Leary, 1981).

The remainder of Fig. 8.3 deals with those factors that influence the distribution of rewards and sanctions after the supervisor has reached some evaluation of the subordinate. An overview of the influencing factors listed in the second and third columns of the figure shows that many of the explanatory concepts are similar for different rewards and/or sanctions. Therefore, rather than repeat each one for each reward, I discuss a factor only if it has not already been described.

Look at the second column under reward/sanction distribution, and note that, in every case, the availability of rewards or sanctions is mentioned. This simply deals with the obvious fact that if the supervisor does not have specific rewards or sanctions available for use, the distribution of them is curtailed. Rewards/sanctions may be unavailable because the organization cannot provide them, such as in the case of limited economic resources when the size of merit raises is severely restricted, or the supervisor may not be allowed to use a reward or sanction due to existing norms. An example of the latter is a teacher who cannot spank a child who misbehaves.

More interesting from a psychological standpoint is the effect of performance attributions on the distributions of rewards. An extensive literature exists on this topic as we have heard from O'Leary and Hansen's presentation. At the overall level, I would hypothesize that the supervisor would make rewards and sanctions contingent upon performance to the extent that performance is due to factors controlled by the role performer. In the terminology of attribution theory, this means that rewards and sanctions should be contingent on performance only when performance is attributed to internal causes. Internal causes of performance can be further subdivided into stable factors, primarily ability, and unstable factors (i.e., effort). It is assumed that this distinction will lead to differential effects on the distribution of rewards. Specifically, if performance is seen as due primarily to effort, then supervisors should want to reward the performance but not to make long-term commitments that depend on the stability of the observed behavior. On the other hand, promotions and involvement of the subordinate in meeting group goals should occur more frequently if past performance is seen as due to ability rather than to effort.

Although the preceding explanation makes intuitive sense, there is not much data to support the reward-distribution effect in organizational settings. There is, however, evidence for sex difference and sex-role effects on attributions although this evidence is almost exclusively based upon laboratory findings. Some of the stronger and more interesting data are those of Hansen and O'Leary (in press) that have just been described.

In addition to gender effects on attributions, two other phenomena have been observed. The first of these is the actor–observer bias. This bias is the tendency for those observing the performance of others to attribute performance to internal factors whereas the performer is more likely to attribute it to external causes when the performance is substandard. The other source of attributions is described by Kelly (1967) as based on the observations of behaviors and actors over occasions and time. Three dimensions on which variance is observed by the appraiser are seen as leading to attributional beliefs: distinctiveness or the extent to which the behavior is similar to or distinct from other behaviors of the actor; consensus, or the extent to which other individuals in similar settings display the same behavior; and consistency or the extent to which the actor has displayed the same or similar behaviors over several occasions. By applying a "naive analysis of variance" to these data, it is hypothesized that the individual then makes attributions about the performance that has been observed. Note that the conditions that lead to judgments about distinctiveness, consensus, and consistency do not depend on the sex of the performer although the sex may influence judgments about one or more of these dimensions. Research on sex and sex-role effects suggests that gender cues short circuit (that is, bypass) judgments about Kelly's three dimensions.

Completing our discussion of Fig. 8C.3, we see that the use of negative sanctions is influenced by two factors not related to rewards. The first of these is status differences between the superior and the subordinate. The work of Kipnis (1972) shows that as the status differential between individuals increases, the higher-status person tends to undervalue the lower-status person. The more the latter is undervalued, the more the higher-status person should feel willing to administer negative sanctions to that individual. To the extent that this occurs, this is important for women because there is evidence that both sex and sex-role incompatability influence status perceptions and that this influence tends to be a negative one for women (See Wallston & O'Leary, 1981, for a review of some of these effects.).

The final entry in Fig. 8C.3, column two, lists the interesting finding of Wood (1980) that supervisor' evaluations of subordinates are strongly influenced by the consequences of the subordinates' behavior even though the actors (subordinates) had no control over the consequences. For example, the behavior of a nurse who lets the side rail down on the bed of a sick patient is evaluated more negatively and considered to be more deserving of punishment if the patient subsequently falls out of bed and breaks a hip than if the patient does not fall out of bed. These consequence effects are listed in the figure as directly affecting the use of sanctions; no other factors are listed as leading to the consequence effects.

CONCLUSIONS

Recall our most important original assumptions: (1) women are underutilized in the work force; and (2) performance appraisals must be accurate and must lead to the effective use of rewards and sanctions if they are going to contribute to effective utilization of women in the work force. Given these assumptions, it is clear to me from Fig. 8C.3 that conducting more research on sex differences and sex-role effects is not going to contribute much to accomplishing our goals. Seldom do sex differences or sex-role effects impact directly upon the issues most salient for effective performance-appraisal utilization at the superior–subordinate level. Furthermore, when sex-difference and sex-role effects are seen as the most immediate factors influencing the process in question—as in the case of appraiser accuracy—the literature indicates that if other influences were changed, sex-difference and sex-role effects would disappear.

From a less theoretical and more empirical perspective, the utility of sex-difference and sex-role data was questioned because of their almost exclusive reliance upon the laboratory methodologies using paper people. Performance appraisal is an on-going process involving actors and observers who usually know each other quite well and usually will be working together for some time in the future. This degree of familiarity and time perspective is critical for the understanding of performance appraisal. Jack Feldman and I have discussed this at length in our chapter on performance appraisal (Ilgen & Feldman, in press). Unfortunately, sex and sex-role research often lacks this time perspective.

By now my conclusion is obvious. I too feel that we must work to ensure that performance-appraisal systems be used to improve the extent to which women are more effectively utilized in the work force. However, to accomplish this end, I feel we must pay less attention to issues of sex differences and sex-role effects and more attention to those factors that impact on effective use of performance-appraisal systems. It seems to me that such a shift in focus has a much greater chance of advancing the cause of women in the work force than does the course we are on now.

ACKNOWLEDGMENTS

Work on this paper was supported, in part, by Grant MDA 903–78–G–05 (Daniel R. Ilgen, Principal Investigator) from the Army Research Institute for the Behavioral and Social Sciences. Although the support of the agency is greatly appreciated, the ideas expressed herein are those of the author and not to be considered the position of the agency of the U.S. Army.

REFERENCES

Abramson, P. R., Goldberg, P. A., Greenberg, J. H., & Abramson, L. M. The talking platypus phenomenon: Competency ratings as a function of sex and professional status. *Psychology of Women Quarterly*, 1977, *2*, 114–124.

Byrne, D. E. The attraction paradigm. New York: Academic Press, 1971.

Cartwright, D. Determination of scientific progress: The case of research on the risky shift. *American Psychologist*, 1973, *28*, 222–231.

Hamner, W. C., Kim, J. S., Baird, L., & Bigoness, W. J. Race and sex as determinants of ratings by potential employers in a simulated work sampling task. *Journal of Applied Psychology*, 1974, *59*, 705–711.

Hansen, R. D., & O'Leary, V. E. Actresses and actors: The effects of sex on causal attributions. *Basic and Applied Social Psychology*, in press.

Ilgen, D. R., & Feldman, J. M. Performance appraisal: A process approach. In L. L. Cummings & B. M. Staw (Eds.), *Research in Organizational Behavior* (Vol. 3), in press.

Kelly, H. H. Attribution theory in social psychology. In D. Levine (Ed.), *Nebraska symposium on motivation*. Lincoln: University of Nebraska Press, 1967.

Kipnis, D. Does power corrupt? *Journal of Personality and Social Psychology*, 1972, *24*, 33–41.

Nieva, V., & Gutek, B. Sex effects on evaluation. *Academy of Management Review*, 1980, *6*, 267–276.

Terborg, J. R., & Ilgen, D. R. A theoretical approach to sex discrimination in traditionally masculine occupations. *Organizational Behavior and Human Performance*, 1975, *13*, 352–376.

Wallston, B. S., & O'Leary, V. E. Sex makes a difference: Differential perceptions of women and men. In L. Wheeler (Ed.), *Review of personality and social psychology* (Vol. 2). Beverly Hills: Sage, 1981.

Wood, R. E. *The effects of accounts and the consequences of behavior on the attributions of leaders about the causes of subordinate poor performance.* Unpublished doctoral dissertation, University of Washington, 1980.

III METHODOLOGICAL AND MEASUREMENT CONSIDERATIONS

The past 30 years are littered with redundant and often trivial studies of rating formats and procedures. We would prefer to call this rating technology rather than methodology. Methodology is more commonly thought of as a concern for the methods by which an area is examined. In that sense, the papers in this section deal with nontraditional approaches to the examination of efforts to assess performance. We are more concerned with the manner by which the research might be carried out than we are with the manner in which the evaluation of performance is carried out.

Vineberg and Joyner describe advances in military performance assessment provided by the vehicle of "hands-on testing." This enables them to distinguish between knowledge and execution aspects of performance. Hunter provides metaanalysis of data that firmly support this distinction. Hunter is further able to suggest some causal paths for understanding the intricate relationships among various components of performance. Campbell suggests some strengths and weaknesses of attempts to understand complex performance through modeling.

9 Performance Measurement in the Military Services

Robert Vineberg
John N. Joyner

The Vineberg and Joyner paper about performance measurement in the military highlights characteristics of the military that distinguish it from industry and discusses specific instruments used in the services. One distinguishing characteristic of the military is that the ultimate criterion measure is success in combat. Because this measure can rarely be obtained, readiness for combat must be substituted as a criterion. It is frequently necessary to simulate target performance, yet there is little opportunity for checking the target performance with actual performance.

In discussing the performance measures used in the military, Vineberg and Joyner focused their attention on overall suitability and technical performance. Indicators of overall suitability include supervisory ratings, rate of advancement in grade, incidence of misconduct, and type of discharge.

Technical performance is evaluated using written tests and hands-on testing (when it is appropriate for the job). The Skill Qualification Test (SQT) is the primary evaluation instrument used in the Army and is composed of three sections, a Hands-On component, a Job-Site component, and a Skills component.

The advantage of the hands-on evaluation, according to the authors, is that in comparison to written tests it tends to avoid the introduction of artificial cues which are not encountered on the job. However, they stress the need for procedures which test job-special proficiencies.

Curran reiterates the unique evaluation problems encountered in the military and elaborates on the evaluation techniques used. Two evolving techniques are computerized testing and simulation. One form of computerized testing that Curran discusses is adaptive testing, which involves using an interactive computer to select a sequence of test items. Curran also comments on the development of simulation techniques that have evolved to such a degree that they may be used simultaneously to train and to evaluate military personnel.

Evaluation of performance in the military may be concerned with the individual, collections of individuals in groups or teams, or complex systems in which the human component is but one part among many. This paper focuses on the first of these, the individual. The evaluation of individual performance is certainly the most frequent form of human-performance measurement in the military services, and the methods used are sufficiently well developed to provide a basis for discussing practices and problems.

Typical instances of individual measurement include assessing a person's qualifications for entry into service, evaluating his or her earliest career performance—training performance—and later evaluating the quality and quantity of work on the job. In addition, we have another measure at the end of every tour of duty: whether the individual, if eligible, has elected to remain in the military. In recent years high rates of turnover and unscheduled loss of personnel have caused the military services to monitor reenlistment and attrition rates closely. Finally, at all points of an individual's military career, measures are obtained of overall adjustment to the requirements of military life in terms of physical condition, motivation, adaptability, military behavior and appearance, and the like.

There are a variety of purposes for measuring performance at these several points and across these various dimensions: to diagnose training achievement; to qualify persons for assignment, proficiency pay, promotion, and reenlistment; to estimate the combat readiness of organizations on the basis of the proficiency of their members; to provide information for the prediction of future performance; and for a variety of research purposes including the validation of selection and training procedures.

For the purpose of this discussion, we have elected to omit from consideration the evaluation of performance on aptitude tests at the time of a person's entry into the service. Nor have we considered performance prior to service as reflected in biographical information gathered at the time of entry. When these kinds of predictor information are excluded, the remaining instances of individual evaluation fall into two categories: evaluation of technical performance itself and evaluation of what can broadly be considered overall suitability to military service. The former category is, of course, subsumed in the latter, but in practice the services make distinct efforts to measure technical performance separately.

MILITARY PERFORMANCE VERSUS INDUSTRIAL PERFORMANCE

Before we consider the methods and some of the issues of these two kinds of evaluation, it is well to consider a few characteristics that set the evaluation of military performance somewhat apart from its industrial counterparts. A major difference between these domains is a general absence in the military of criteria that most persons would agree are sufficient to define system performance, from which the requirements for individual performance can be derived. Industry has system-performance criteria in the form of production figures and profit and loss statements, but the military services do not. The criterion of system performance in the military is success in combat. In the absence of regular success in battle, we must define system performance as readiness for combat, and look directly to the states or conditions of its presumed constituents: hardware, personnel, and procedures. Even ignoring the question of the relationship to system output, individual performance capabilities are not easy to assess, for at least two major reasons.

First, evaluating the technical abilities of individuals requires information about their performance during job-related activities. However, time samples taken of individual activity in combat jobs confirmed what is perhaps a frequent impression, that for a variety of reasons the percentage of time spent in technical job activity is often quite low (Bialek, Zapf, & McGuire, 1977). Thus it is often true that much of an individual's activity in a military setting is not the performance of ultimate interest. Two consequences follow:

1. It is often necessary, for purposes of evaluation, to simulate the target performance.
2. Decisions made in defining the requirements of the target performance to be simulated cannot readily be checked or validated against actual performance.

Although questions may arise in an industrial or business setting, for example, in deciding how to weight various requirements of jobs in a composite criterion of performance, these questions can at least be considered in reference to actual performance. In the military the absence or infrequency of such a referent for much of the target behavior changes the issue. The question is not how should separate requirements be weighted in a criterion, but rather what are the requirements and how should they be simulated to reflect job demands?

The difficulty of answering these questions is exemplified by training for electronic maintenance jobs. Some have argued that trainees should be given considerable instruction in theory and fundamentals, which presumably will permit them to deal independently with a range of novel equipment malfunctions. Others have argued the opposite: Exposure to theoretical information should be quite limited, because it is not essential for the most typical duties and because in practice incumbents are likely to refer problems to a higher maintenance echelon. This issue is difficult to resolve in the absence of information about what job holders actually do or can be expected to do when faced with a novel situation.

A second difference between military and civilian situations is that many indicators of performance available in industrial or business settings are lacking in the military. The necessity to keep records of performance for pay purposes, for example, is obviated in the military by the contractual nature of the term of service. Indicators such as time cards and sales records are not used in the military for purposes of compensation and hence are not available. As a consequence, evaluators' judgments are of necessity less well supported by objective information. The need in industry to satisfy a customer or create a product is another built-in source of performance information. In contrast to feedback available to the peacetime military, the feedback that businesses receive from customers appears very immediate, specific, and real.

In summary, two factors combine to make performance evaluation in the military somewhat less reliable than in the civilian sector:

1. The frequent absence of the performance of interest and a consequent need for simulation.

2. The frequent absence of natural or incidental indicators of performance to support or confirm information obtained through deliberate performance appraisal.

As is shortly seen, it is particularly in the evaluation of technical performance that these factors give rise to problems. Before going on to technical performance, however, we briefly examine the evaluation of overall suitability.

EVALUATION OF OVERALL SUITABILITY

Evaluation of the factors that constitute overall suitability is provided most frequently by supervisor ratings of performance. Such ratings, in fact, with the probable exception of achievement testing during training, are the most frequent type of individual performance assessment in the military. Ratings of overall job performance and of a variety of general performance characteristics are entered in a person's record either annually or semiannually. These ratings contribute to composites used for such purposes as determining eligibility to compete for promotion, assigning promotion weights, and determining eligibility for reenlistment. The Navy's Performance Evaluation Report, for example, consists of 10-point scales designated Professional Performance, Military Behavior, Leadership Ability, Military Appearance, and Adaptability. As one might expect, such scales tend to be highly correlated and are also not greatly sensitive to differences across individuals.

Supervisor ratings are also used to validate predictors of performance. Of 112 studies published in the last 30 years that used evaluation of persons in jobs as the criterion, 78% used measures of suitability exclusively, of which 48% used ratings as the only criterion. In contrast, only 18% reported using a test of proficiency, and in only 13% did the test of proficiency involve a hands-on performance test (Vineberg & Joyner, 1982).

Indices of overall suitability other than ratings include rate of advancement in grade, incidence of misconduct (e.g., court martial, nonjudicial punishment, misdemeanors, conviction by civil court, recidivism), and type of discharge. These measures have been used in the Navy and Marine Corps as criteria in the construction of probability tables for estimating the likelihood of satisfactory military service among persons with different personal and background characteristics. These so-called "odds for effectiveness" tables are used by recruiters in screening service applicants. As predictors of various composites of these criteria, the variables of education, mental ability, and age have had multiple validities ranging from about .24 to .39 (Lockman, 1974).

EVALUATION OF TECHNICAL PERFORMANCE

When it comes to technical performance, the relatively low percentage of technical activity to other activity, noted earlier, would suggest that ratings of technical competence may inevitably be contaminated by other aspects of performance. Further, ratings are particularly unsuited for the specificity of measurement implicit in the evaluation of technical performance. (In the few instances in which task-specific ratings have been used, they have not clearly differentiated aspects of performance.) For these reasons, we do not consider that supervisor ratings used by the services can properly be considered technical performance ratings.

Technical Performance of Trainees

Most assessment of technical performance consists of the evaluation of trainees in schools. For most jobs, achievement testing in schools is accomplished mainly through multiple-choice tests of the recall of information. Hands-on testing is more frequently used in certain jobs in which it is obviously appropriate, such as rifleman, pilots, air traffic controllers, and so on, and to a much lesser extent in other instances.

The obvious reasons to evaluate technical proficiency in schools, of course, is to measure trainees' progress and to diagnose their deficiencies. But this information is then also put to use for a different purpose: the validation of selection and classification tests. Although at first glance it may appear that these tests should be validated against criterion information from the job, there are several reasons for validating against training performance.

In the first place, training performance is of interest in its own right. Failure to complete initial training satisfactorily is an immediate bar to retention in the service. Exceptional performance is sometimes prerequisite to further, specialized training or special duty. It is in the interest of the services to be able to predict training performance as accurately as possible.

Further, performance in training is often a desirable surrogate for job performance. Although it does not represent a direct criterion of job performance, it does indicate a person's ability to acquire the information and skill deemed necessary for such performance. If the purpose of evaluation is to provide an estimate of a person's ability to perform a job and that performance is dependent on learning that takes place initially during training as well as later in the job situation, then a case can be made for basing the estimate of job proficiency on a direct measure of the ability to learn, as reflected by school performance. Christal (1981), for example, has discussed the importance of learning rate in acquiring and maintaining skill as a factor to be considered in evaluating an individual's potential. Taking the view that neither the school nor the job situation provides for adequate control of learning opportunities, Christal has urged using the variable of learning rate in laboratory experiments to improve selection tests.

A second reason for using training performance as a surrogate criterion is that several practical and methodological factors limit the usefulness of information about proficiency that is collected on the job. The most immediately apparent is that job situations in the military do not lend themselves to controlled, standardized measurement. Billets within an occupational specialty differ widely in their requirements and hence in opportunities for skill development. Individuals arrive at the job at various levels of proficiency, and those judged to be less effective may be assigned different duties or assigned to a job in name only. Particularly if hands-on tests are used to assess proficiency, and unit personnel administer them, there is considerable opportunity for leniency and other forms of bias.

Technical Performance Of Incumbents

When performance is measured in the job situation, problems are encountered immediately in any attempt to measure technical performance directly. Summary ratings—admittedly the most feasible and economical measures to administer—suffer the well-known deficiencies of bias and halo. We have already mentioned how the low proportion of technical activity in the military setting provides added opportunity for the contamination of ratings. Finally, ratings require a degree of familiarity by raters with the work of persons they evaluate that is often not present or possible (Wiley, 1975; Wilson, Mackie, & Buckner, 1954).

The practical difficulties of directly observing and scoring job performance without resorting to summary ratings are, if anything, greater still. Even though in many jobs technical performance makes up only a portion of daily activity, it is difficult to obtain an adequate sampling of job requirements when observing an individual's particular activities. It is also difficult to standardize scoring, short of specifying the particular tasks the incumbent will perform as well as the procedures he or she should follow or the characteristics to be found in his or her product—all of which would tend to turn the observation procedure into a work-sample test.

In short, the difficulties of assessing technical performance directly are such that it is generally appropriate and necessary to assess technical performance by means of tests of proficiency. The remainder of this discussion focuses on some of the practices and issues involved in proficiency testing of job incumbents in the various services.

PROFICIENCY TESTING PROGRAMS

The Air Force

In the Air Force, measurement of job proficiency occurs largely through the use of two paper-and-pencil tests: Specialty Knowledge Tests, which concern job-specific information, and Promotion Fitness Examinations, which concern general military information. Both tests serve along with other factors as inputs to the Weighted Airman Promotion System (WAPS), which is used to determine a person's ranking among those eligible for promotion. Hands-on testing is used, of course, to qualify pilots. It may also occur in on-the-job training for technical skills because it is Air Force policy to include hands-on testing in its on-the-job training program. However, such testing is in practice largely a matter of local option.

The Navy

In the Navy, the major test of job proficiency is the Navy-wide examination for advancement in rank, or rate. This is a 150-item paper-and-pencil test of job information that is part of the Navy Enlisted Advancement System. In a minority of jobs, or ratings, this test is supplemented by a performance test of special aspects of the job, such as the typing test for Yeoman or Personnelman, a code speed test for Radioman, and a flag and flashing light test for Signalman. There are also a variety of other requirements, including the Personnel Advancement Requirements (PARS) and the Personnel Qualification Standards (PQS), neither of which is a test. Each is a checklist of job-related and equipment-related requirements on which a supervisor must certify an incumbent.

The Army

The only service that attempts to provide standardized hands-on testing of proficiency on a service-wide basis is the Army, with its Skill Qualification Tests (SQT). An SQT covers approximately 25 to 30 tasks, estimated to be about 25% of those in a typical job. The test consists of three components.

The Hands-On component is a performance test administered by a testing team at a centralized test site. The Job-Site component also involves a performance test, but differs from the Hands-On component in two ways. First, it is administered by the incumbent's immediate supervisor (who, being a member of the incumbent's own unit, may exhibit leniency or other forms of bias in scoring) in the job situation. Second, tests administered at various job sites will not have standardized conditions, because models of equipment, procedures, and other conditions can vary from unit to unit. The third component of the SQT, called the Skills component, is a multiple-choice, group-administered written test. A fourth component of the SQT that is sometimes used is a written test intended to substitute for those tasks ordinarily included in the Hands-On component in situations in which the facilities and equipment necessary for a hands-on test are not available—for example, when a soldier on recruiting duty in a city far from a military installation is to take an SQT for his primary Military Occupational Specialty of Armor Crewman. This is referred to as the Alternate Hands-On component.

When assembled in an SQT, each of the major components—Hands-On, Job-Site, and Skills—contains about a third of the total number of tasks to be evaluated. The Job-Site component is intended to cover about a fixed 35% of the tasks. The proportion of the Hands-On component to the Skills component depends on the nature of the occupational speciality and the skill level. SQTs for jobs in the Combat Arms such as Infantry, Artillery, and Armor tend to have a higher proportion of Hands-On items than Combat Support and Combat Service Support jobs. This has been attributed to the greater availability of equipment in the Combat Arms for use in administering performance tests. SQTs for the lower skill levels and pay grades also tend to have more Hands-On items because of the relatively small number of administrative tasks in these jobs.

SQTs are now administered annually in about 900 of the approximately 1100 occupational specialities in the Army. In the remaining 200, which represent extremely low-density positions for which it is not reasonable to construct separate SQTs, common-task rather than MOS-specific SQTs are administered.

How are the SQTs working? Not a great deal of information is available, but one unofficial Army source has indicated that the pass rate for items from the Hands-On component is about 80% and up; for the Job-Site component, about 100%; and for the Skills, or written, component, about 40% to 50%. Thus the written component is probably providing most of the discrimination; the Hands-On component, very little; and the Job-Site component, none at all. It should be mentioned, however, that the SQT was originally intended primarily as a way to "drive" training rather than a means of measuring individual differences in proficiency. Items on the SQT, particularly those of the Hands-On and Job-Site components, are described beforehand to persons who are to be tested and are intended to be used in rehearsing for the test. Indeed, for the Job-Site component, supervisors are specifically directed to administer the test only after an incumbent has received sufficient practice to demonstrate mastery.

In summary, each of the services uses paper-and-pencil tests of job information to evaluate technical proficiency in addition to summary ratings by supervisors, which evaluate a mix of technical and nontechnical aspects of performance. The Army, as part of its SQT program, also uses several types of hands-on tests to evaluate technical performance and with the advent of this program ceased to use performance ratings in the lower enlisted pay grades.

PAPER-AND-PENCIL TESTS VERSUS
HANDS-ON TESTS

Although the other services have not implemented hands-on testing to the same extent as the Army, there is unquestionably a strong degree of interest in this format and awareness that at least for some tasks the most reliable way to ensure the relevance of a test is to make it a hands-on test. A recent directive from the Department of Defense requested the services to initiate projects to demonstrate the feasibility of validating standards for enlistment and assignment against job performance rather than against training performance. It also requested the services to undertake long-term projects to validate standards against improved (meaning hands-on) measures of job performance (Memorandum, Assistant Secretary of Defense, Manpower, Reserve Affairs & Logistics, 1980).

Yet, to all appearances, there is a certain degree of misunderstanding in the military about the proper distinction to be made between paper-and-pencil and hands-on measures. Many apparently hold the view that knowledge measured by paper-and-pencil tests is of little value in estimating performance. At the extreme, an impression is created that hands-on tests measure performance as though performance were some particular, unique form of behavior somehow unrelated to the knowledge on which it depends. That performance on a given hands-on test may in fact demonstrate little more than knowledge is sometimes lost sight of. Because hands-on testing is receiving more and more attention, a few observations are appropriate about what it achieves compared to paper-and-pencil testing.

Hands-on tests, of course, have the potential for considerable fidelity, but they also have their drawbacks. Because they are costly and time-consuming to construct and administer (generally hands-on tests cannot be administered simultaneously to groups of persons unless performance lends itself to product scoring rather than process scoring), the number of tasks they can be used to evaluate in any particular situation is limited. Equally important is that, because an observer/ scorer intervenes between the behavior of a person being tested and the record of that behavior, variation in administration and scoring procedures can often be expected. This is particularly so when hands-on tests are used by military personnel. Pickering and Anderson (1976), for example, have noted that when job experts or instructors in the military are administering hands-on tests to incumbents, they typically fail to maintain standardized procedures. They are likely to coach and give feedback, as they do when conducting training.

Paper-and-pencil tests of knowledge, of course, have the potential advantages of efficiency over hands-on tests. Besides being relatively inexpensive to construct and administer, they can be used to test the recall of information without requiring the acting out of a lengthy sequence of behavior. By careful selection, tests of information can maximize the amount of crucial information that can be represented in a test.

Yet the adequacy of knowledge tests for estimating performance has been questioned. Criticism in the military has focused on the verbal demands of paper-and-pencil tests, which may not be requirements of the job itself, and on the susceptibility of such tests to irrelevant information. As often constructed, they tend to call for theoretical, terminological, and general information whether or not it is actually required in performance. To this extent they have been found to measure little of what is gained with job experience (Judy, 1960). Although guidance provided to military users (e.g., *Interservice Procedures for Instructional Systems Development*) about what should go into a test typically prescribes the inclusion only of content relevant to task performance, in practice this guidance is rarely followed rigorously (Vineberg & Joyner, 1980). Despite official policy to the contrary, we found that task-analysis information is rarely used in test construction. And although methods have been developed for alerting the test developer to discrepancies between test demands and performance requirements (Ellis, Wulfeck, & Fredericks, 1979), these require checking each test item individually for consistency with performance requirements. Because this process is inherently tedious, there is little reason to believe that such procedures will be utilized any more readily than the instructional systems-development procedures already officially adopted.

We feel that a characteristic of hands-on tests that has special practical consequence is that hands-on tests tend automatically to represent elements of knowledge and behavior that are difficult to make explicit and that are therefore often not measured when paper-and-pencil tests are used to evaluate proficiency. They do this without the need for the test developer to apprehend and represent every cue or response that may be pertinent to work behavior.

By contrast, a paper-and-pencil test can never represent all the information inherent in the performance of even the simplest task (e.g., open hatch by grasping handle, turning handle clockwise, pulling outward). Constructing a paper-and-pencil test involves deciding what behavior to represent and what to omit. Hence the paper-and-pencil test inevitably represents less than a hands-on test with the same task boundaries, involves both explicit and implicit selection of information to be represented, and presents opportunities for error in the attempt to identify the critical aspects of performance.

In particular, paper-and-pencil tests often fail to call for information about the cues and responses that elicit and constitute job behavior. To a certain extent this deficiency can be attributed to a failure to analyze task behavior adequately enough to identify critical cues. Yet, even if the test is developed from a rigorous task analysis, paper-and-pencil tests are inherently limited in this respect. It is naturally not possible to include the stimulus feature of most work situations in a written test (e.g., whether or not paint is of a proper viscosity for application cannot be easily described verbally). It is even more likely that changes in response requirements or functions will be called for. Objective paper-and-pencil tests almost always call for the respondent to select the correct response from a few alternatives that have been provided, whereas a requirement in the work situation is often to generate the correct response. Thus, even though the test developer may consider the display of knowledge an adequate index of a respondent's ability to perform in a job, a judgment will be necessary as to whether the particular way in which the knowledge is measured on a paper-and-pencil test is an adequate representation of the requirements of the criterion situation.

Further, paper-and-pencil tests often unavoidably supply cues not available to the job performer, in the course of providing the respondent with enough information to define the question. Hands-on tests require less introducing of special cues, both because they generally permit free response and because the cues that signal the initiation of successive phases of task performance are generally present in the situation and do not have to be made explicit.

The introduction of special cues is a source of unreliability of another sort as well. Tests that require artificial cues may not elicit the same behavior as would ordinarily be exhibited in a job. This problem has been encountered in so-called symbolic substitution tasks.

The Tab Test, developed to test diagnostic skills, is a case in point (Cornell, Damrin, Saupe, & Crowder, 1954; Glaser, Damrin, & Gardner, 1952). When it is used in the simulation of electronic troubleshooting, for example, test point readings and other information are obtained by lifting tabs, erasing opaque coverings, and so on. None of the effort or skill that would ordinarily be involved in setting up and reading test equipment is required. Steineman (1966) demonstrated that (presumably as a consequence) the behaviors exhibited in actually troubleshooting a superheterodyne receiver are quite different from those exhibited in a Tab Test simulation. Correlations between performance on the actual equipment and performance on the simulation ranged from $-.50$ to $+.14$. Similarly, Crowder, Morrison, and Demaree (1954) reported correlations of .12 and .16 between two forms of a Tab Test and performance on a test using actual equipment.

These sorts of differences between the requirements of performance tests and knowledge tests undoubtedly contribute to the fact that correlations between these types of tests have generally been low, ranging only up to about .30 (Engel & Rehder, 1970; Crowder et al, 1954; Mackie et al, 1978; Shirkey, 1965, 1966; Urrey et al, 1965; Yellen, 1966). Only occasionally have sizable correlations between the two methods of testing been found, usually occurring when job behavior has been intentionally represented in the knowledge test. Using this approach Vineberg and Taylor (1972) obtained correlations between knowledge tests and performance tests in four Army jobs of .58, .59, .68, and .78. Osborn and Ford (1977) derived performance tests and different types of knowledge tests from a common analysis of performance and obtained correlations between the two types of measures of .83, .80, .84, and .58.

In summary, the performance requirements represented in paper-and-pencil tests of information can differ from the performance requirements in hands-on tests if: (1) they call for information not relevant to performance; (2) the paper-and-pencil tests fail to represent information or intellectual processes relevant to performance; (3) the artificialities of their cues or conditions spuriously facilitate the recall and display of information; or (4) these or other shortcomings otherwise lead to a modification of job behavior in the test situation.

TEST FORMAT, INFERENCE, AND TYPE OF BEHAVIOR

The differences just mentioned between types of measures imply differences in the suitability of different measures for representing different job demands. Compared to the attention currently being given to performance testing itself, little attention has been paid to the relationship between task demands and the types of measures used to evaluate proficiency. Although many classification schemes have been developed for analyzing jobs and designing instruction, less work has been directed to classifying performance for test development. The question remaining is how to assign tasks or classes of tasks to the most appropriate type of measure.

Guion (1979) has suggested how degree of inference may generally be related to the different types of job-sample evidence from which job performance is estimated. Arranged on an ascending staircase of increasing removal from the job, the different types of evidence are probationary periods on the job, simulations, abstracted work samples, job knowledge, prerequisite cognitive skills, and essential attitudes. Guion suggests that there is a kind of qualitative break at the point between abstracted work samples and tests of job knowledge. Probationary activity, simulations, and abstracted work samples can be considered to provide evidence with different degrees of remoteness from job content but to represent nevertheless a "direct sample of performance on the actual job." Knowledge, cognitive skills, and attitudes, on the other hand, provide evidence requiring "more an inference than a sample."

In considering the appropriateness of different types of measures to different types of performance, we are concerned with how the degree of inference involved in estimating job performance from test performance may be a function of the type of job performance being predicted, and we find Guion's arrangement pertinent. Clearly, if one ignores differences in the nature of task demands, one may make larger inferential leaps than intended or warranted. With the results of Tab Test simulations in mind, for example, we would tend to place as much confidence in knowledge tests for assessing procedural task performance as we would in abstracted work samples for troubleshooting performance—this in spite of placing more confidence in abstracted samples generally. Again, on the basis of simulations of job performance, we would probably not be as willing to draw conclusions about job performance that requires social skills as we would about job performance that requires troubleshooting skill. The need to represent social skill may push us one step further down the staircase, so to speak, so that we would not be willing to infer such performance from any form of abstracted work samples but perhaps only from a sample of probationary activity.

One available scheme that specifies different test formats for measuring the recall of information than for measuring the application of information is the Navy Personnel Research and Development Center's Instructional Quality Inventory (IQI) cited earlier (Ellis et al., 1979). The test developer using the IQI classifies each training objective to be tested according to content type and the way in which the content is used. The five types of content are facts, concepts, procedures, rules, and principles. The three ways in which content can be used are to remember it, to use it when it has been provided to the performer ("use-aided"), and to use it when it must be recalled by the performer ("use-un-aided"). Corresponding to each cell of this classification scheme is a set of prescribed test formats. The cell for "using a rule unaided," for example, lists performance, true/false, multiple choice, short answer, and fill in as acceptable types of items.

It seems to us that more work of this type is called for. The IQI, intended for application in the quality control of achievement-test items in training, is probably not suitable to the full range of job performance. We find it useful to consider whether behavior to be tested can be classified as belonging in one of these four categories: (1) motor and/or perceptual skill; (2) application of procedures; (3) application of rules and principles; (4) problem solving, troubleshooting, decision making. Although practical considerations may always influence the ultimate selection of test format, these kinds of performance seem important in establishing what types of measures are appropriate.

If training or job behavior to be tested involves either motor or perceptual skill, such behavior should probably be evaluated by means of a hands-on performance test requiring either the performance of complete units of activity or the display of the elements of skill that have been abstracted from the complete activity. Although most performance involves some type of perceptual and motor activity, for many tasks it can be elicited merely by telling or showing the performer what to do, and it can thereby be classified as nonskilled.

The application of a procedure appears to us to be the kind of behavior that is most amenable to all types of testing. We view this category as performance that may require the recall of a sequence of steps but does not depend primarily on perceptual, motor, or cognitive skill.

Testing behavior that requires the application of rules and principles is different in at least one important respect from testing the application of a procedure. Because rules can be applied in a variety of situations (principles explain a variety of events), their applicability to a situation must be recognized. The use of a procedure, on the other hand, is generally implicit in the situation and only requires knowledge of the procedure itself.

This difference has important implications for the manner in which tasks involving the application of rules or principles should be tested. The test of rule application must be constructed to provide opportunities to reveal awareness of the relevance of the rule to the task or situation at hand as well as merely knowledge of the rule itself. Although it is possible to construct paper-and-pencil tests that do not suggest the potential relevance of a particular rule to a performer, these will ordinarily involve considerable artificiality. It is more desirable to construct tests involving some variety of simulation or abstracted work sample.

Like the application of rules and principles, problem solving, troubleshooting and decision making occur in a variety of situations. They are thus distinguished from the application of procedures in the ways just mentioned. In addition, they share characteristics that impose particular requirements for their testing. The relevant facts, response options, and solution criteria in such tasks are often not explicit in the situation but must be generated and then selected by the performer. The troubleshooter needs to devise an overall strategy and draw inferences from the results of the particular checks he or she electes to perform. The decision maker must often both establish limits to the search for the anticipated consequences of alternate courses of actions and generate a basis for making a choice.

When, as in such tasks, a variety of actions are possible and alternative responses can be justified, features of the test situation can easily influence the actions taken, and differences between job behavior and test behavior can easily arise as a function of the particular characteristics of the test. An example is the case of the previously mentioned Tab Test, in which the lack of effort required to obtain simulated meter readings on the test encourages the performer to collect more information than he or she would be likely to on the job. This concern is of less importance in procedural tasks where the circumscribed options in both test and job situations limit the differences in behavior that can arise between these situations. When the effects of test format on test behavior are not known, the most conservative course of action is to consider as questionable the use of work samples that involve abstraction and to favor simulations instead.

A particular problem that arises when one sets out to assign appropriate test formats to different kinds of behavior concerns the size of the work unit selected for testing. If an entire task is to be tested as a unit, the problem arises that many tasks are comprised of a variety of different kinds of behavior. The test format suitable for valid measurement of one element of task behavior may then not be appropriate for another. It follows that the format selected must be suitable to the component of behavior requiring the least inference from the test to the job. This often means that a simulation, rather than a format of greater abstraction, will be required.

In its SQT program, for example, the Army has elected to make the entire task the unit of training and testing, presumably to reduce errors inherent in identifying the critical features of performance. In addition, and again presumably to keep the tests relevant to job performance, the Army initially attempted to make the SQT a totally hands-on evaluation. The prohibitive expense of constructing and administering hands-on tests on such a large scale has subsequently become evident, and the SQT now uses the four components described earlier. Although the Army's reasons for adopting the whole-task approach are understandable from the point of view of test relevance, the practical problems inherent in following this course are such that an alternative to the whole-task approach seems clearly needed. To test proficiency in job situations, the military needs procedures that will permit the identification and reliable assessment of important job behavior at some less global level than the job task. It appears to us that the following procedures need to be developed for assessing technical proficiency in military jobs:

1. Rules for classifying the different behaviors in tasks.
2. Rules for assigning behaviors to their most appropriate test format.
3. Rules that indicate when unacceptable artificialities in the test would result from independently representing the different components of performance within a task.

It is, of course, easier to identify the need for such rules than to develop them. If past experience in building classification schemes is any evidence, it does not seem likely that a direct attempt to provide such a construction will succeed. It is more likely to develop slowly with the accumulation of information about the extent to which performance in different test formats is a function of the type of behavior being tested.

If recent developments become a trend, and the military services engage in more and more hands-on testing, a large amount of data will be generated, based on dozens of jobs, hundreds of tasks, and thousands of observations. Examination and analysis of data of this magnitude may suggest useful schemes for classifying performance demands and requirements that neither rational analysis nor small-scale studies have suggested thus far. Data from a program like the

Army's SQT, using both hands-on and paper-and-pencil testing, offer the particular advantage of enabling test formats to be compared in many different performance situations.

SUMMARY

The performance of individuals in the military services is evaluated throughout a person's military career for a variety of purposes, including diagnosing training achievement, determining qualification for assignment, promotion, and reenlistment, and estimating combat readiness. Conditions for the evaluation of individual performance in the military differ from those in industrial settings: System criteria from which the requirements of individual military performance can be derived are usually not available, performance of criterion duties of greatest interest is usually infrequent in peacetime, and many natural or incidental indicators of job performance are absent. For purposes of evaluation, target performance must often be designed and simulated without the possibility of being checked against actual performance.

Most evaluation of the overall suitability of individuals is accomplished by means of supervisor ratings in job settings. Evaluation of technical performance is generally accomplished by proficiency testing in both school and job settings. Most proficiency testing is conducted in school prior to actual performance in a job; this situation seems justified in that training is usually a requirement to be met prior to entry into a job, performance in training provides evidence both of skill and knowledge deemed necessary for job performance and of a candidate's capacity for learning in the job, and the characteristics of military jobs generally make them a poor location for controlled, standardized measurement.

Most proficiency testing in the military is accomplished with paper-and-pencil tests of knowledge and information. An exception is the Army's Skill Qualification Tests (SQT). These are administered annually in most occupational specialties and consist of three major components: Hands-On (a performance test), Job Site (a somewhat less standardized performance test), and Skills (a multiple-choice, paper-and-pencil test).

There is currently evidence of increasing interest in the use of hands-on tests. Although such tests are more costly to construct and administer than are paper-and-pencil tests, they have the potential for considerable fidelity and tend automatically to include all of the elements required in task performance. Their relevance is less dependent on the expertise of task analysts and test developers. Paper-and-pencil tests are less expensive to construct but may impose requirements for verbal abilities and information not relevant to performance, fail to represent stimulus-and-response requirements relevant to performance, introduce artificial cues to performance, and otherwise induce modifications of criterion behavior.

The suitability of different test formats depends on the behavioral requirements of criterion performance. Little attention, however, has been given to the
relationship between the types of measures used to evaluate proficiency and the
stimulus conditions and behavioral demands of performance. Classes of behavior
that appear to have different implications for the type of test format appropriate
for proficiency testing are motor and/or perceptual skill, application of procedures, application of rules and principles, and problem solving/troubleshoot-
ing/decision making. To select appropriate test formats between test and criterion
performance, rules are needed for (1) classifying the different behaviors to be
tested, (2) assigning those behaviors to their most appropriate test format, and (3)
indicating when unacceptable artificialities in a test would result from independently representing task components. Recent trends in the increased use of
hands-on tests in the military may provide data leading to the development of
such rules.

REFERENCES

Bialek, H. M., Zapf, D. W., & McGuire, W. J. *Personnel turbulence and time utilization in an
infantry division* (HumRRO FR–WD–CA 77–11). Alexandria, Va.: Human Resources Research
Organization, June 1977.

Branson, R. K., Rayner, G. T., Cox, J. L., Furman, J. P., King, F. J., & Hannum, W. H. *Interservice
procedure for instructional systems development* (5 vols.) (TRADOCPam 350-30). Ft. Monroe,
VA: U.S.

Christal, R. *The need for laboratory research to improve the state-of-the-art in ability testing.* Paper
presented at the First Annual Conference on Personnel and Training Factors in Systems Effectiveness, San Diego, spring 1981.

Cornell, F. G., Damrin, D. E., Saupe, J. L., & Crowder, N. A. *Proficiency of Q-24 radar
mechanics: III. The Tab Test—A group test of trouble-shooting proficiency*
(AFPTRC–TR–54–52). Lackland Air Force Base, Texas: Air Force Personnel and Training
Research Center, November 1954.

Crowder, N. A., Morrison, E. J., & Demaree, R. G. *Proficiency of Q-24 radar mechanics: VI.
Analysis of intercorrelations of measures* (AFPTRC–TR–54–127). Lackland Air Force Base,
Texas: Air Force Personnel and Training Research Center, December 1954.

Ellis, J. A., Wulfeck, W. H., II, & Fredericks, P. S. *The Instructional Quality Inventory II. User's
manual* (Special Report 79–24). San Diego: Navy Personnel Research and Development Center,
August 1979.

Glaser, R., Damrin, D. E., & Gardner, F. M. *The Tab item: A technique for the measurement of
proficiency in diagnostic problem-solving tasks* (Unpublished report). University of Illinois,
College of Education, June 1952.

Guion, R. M. *Principles of work sample testing: II. Evaluation of personnel testing programs*
(ARIBSS TR–79–A9). Bowling Green, Ohio: Bowling Green State University, April 1979.

Judy, C. J. *A regression analysis of one set of airman proficiency test scores* (WADD TN–60–139).
Lackland Air Force Base, Texas: Wright Air Development Division, Air Research and Development Command, June 1960.

Lockman, R. F. *Enlisted selection strategies* (CNS 1039). Arlington, Va.: Center for Naval Analyses, September 1974.

Pickering, E. J., & Anderson, A. V. *Measurement of job-performance capabilities* (NPRDC TR
77–6). San Diego: Navy Personnel Research and Development Center, December 1976.

Steinemann, J. H. *Comparison of performance on analogous simulated and actual troubleshooting tasks* (PRA Research Memo SRM 67-1). San Diego, CA: Naval Personnel Research Activity, July 1966.

Vineberg, R., & Joyner, J. N. *Instructional System Development (ISD)* in the armed services: Methodology and application (HumRRO–TR–80–1). Alexandria, Va.: Human Resources Research Organization, January 1980.

Vineberg, Robert & Joyner, John N. *Prediction of job performance: Review of military studies* (NPRDC TR 82-37). San Diego, CA: Navy Personnel Research and Development Center, March 1982.

Wiley, L. N. *Familiarity with subordinates' jobs: Immediate versus secondary supervisors* (AFHRL–TR–75–7). Lackland Air Force Base, Texas: Occupational and Manpower Research Division, Air Force Human Resources Laboratory, June 1975.

Wilson, C. L., Mackie, R. R., & Buckner, D. N. *Research on the development of shipboard performance measures: Part III. The use of performance check lists in the measurement of shipboard performance of enlisted Navy personnel.* Los Angeles: Management and Marketing Research Corporation, February 1954.

Assistant Secretary of Defense (Manpower, Reserve Affairs & Logistics). *Plan for validating enlistment standards against job performance* (Memorandum). July 1980.

Comments on Vineberg and Joyner

Charles R. Curran, USAF

Vineberg and Joyner present a clear discussion of the problems encountered in evaluating both technical and managerial performance in a military environment. The problems, of course, do not differ in kind from those experienced in industry but rather in the degree to which they affect the selection of appropriate performance criteria and the adoption of methodological strategies to evaluate personnel. The present discussion therefore supplements Vineberg and Joyner's review of military performance evaluation with an example in which the criterion of interest was combat success. I also provide a brief overview of some trends in technical performance evaluation, and an explanation of three relatively unique aspects of the military personnel setting affecting performance evaluation. In addition, several features of the evaluation of performance in any organizational setting are identified as needing future research attention.

Combat success has rarely been used as a performance measure. However, the Air Force Human Resources Laboratory was involved in a project that used combat success in Vietnam as the criterion of F-4 aircrew performance (the F-4 is a two-seat high-performance fighter aircraft). The effort was called Project Combat Team (Ratliff, Shore, Chiorini, & Curran, 1969; Shore, Curran, Ratliff, & Chiorini, 1970). Half of the two-man crews tested consisted of pilots in both the front and back seats of the aircraft. The other half of the test crews consisted of a pilot in the front seat and a navigator in the back seat. Combat success in similar missions over North Viet Nam was the criterion against which the performance of the two kinds of crews, pilot/pilot and pilot/navigator, was compared. The study looked at the frequency with which in-flight tasks were performed, how much time was spent performing those tasks, critical incident rates, and mission success. Results showed that a navigator performed essentially the same second-

251

seat combat tasks as pilots regardless of the kind of mission flown and did so about as well as pilots. As a result, a number of pilots were eventually released for other assignments and savings of $400 million in training cost avoidance were projected over a 5-year period.

The results of Project Combat Team illustrate the kinds of useful performance information that can be obtained in an actual combat environment on those occasions when conditions make the collection of such data feasible. More important, perhaps, is that Project Combat Team is a prime example of the kind of work that can be done by behavioral scientists in an operational setting to solve critical problems of both applied and theoretical interest. More is said on this point later.

Combat readiness (usually referred to as job proficiency) is the practical criterion used by the services over the years. Vineberg and Joyner's description of the Army's Skill Qualification Tests illustrates what can be done on a large-scale basis to evaluate military job proficiency given the current state-of-the art in administering hands-on tests. The three-tiered approach of SQTs is a clear recognition of current limitations stemming from development and administration costs and the current lack of on-site sophisticated automated testing alternatives. It is important, however, for scientists, military trainers, and personnel managers to remember that combat readiness as a criterion carries with it problems of fidelity vis-a-vis actual combat. Although certainly superior to traditional paper-and-pencil testing, job-performance evaluation strategies such as SQTs lack the overburden of stress induced by personal danger, time compression, multiplexing of critical tasks, unanticipated problems, and so on, that are part of a combat environment. Compensating for the differences between combat and noncombat performance is a constant problem for military planners.

There is on-going research under military sponsorship that will undoubtedly change the nature of direct work-performance evaluation in ways that will improve the validity of evaluations of combat readiness by shortening the inferential leap from the evaluation environment to actual job performance. Two evolving technologies that will play a large role in this revolution are computerized testing and simulation.

One form of computerized testing that will be adopted by the military in the next 5 years is adaptive testing (Wiskoff, 1981). Adaptive testing involves using an interactive computer to select a sequence of test items. A correct answer leads to a test item of greater difficulty whereas an incorrect answer leads to an easier item. Test questions are chosen from a large bank of multiple-choice questions. A tailored set of questions is thus given to each respondent based on how each question is answered. We anticipate that adaptive testing will reduce testing time, increase measurement precision, reduce susceptibility to test compromise, and reduce the cost of reproducing large quantities of hard copy test materials.

The Navy's Personnel Research and Development Laboratory in San Diego has been designated the lead military laboratory for managing the research, development, and evaluation requirements of the Services' first use of adaptive testing. The Air Force Human Resources Laboratory has been given responsibility for the development of the test item bank and the Army is responsible for procurement or lease of the eventual delivery system. Initial utilization will be as a replacement for the current Armed Services Vocational Aptitude Battery, which is a paper-and-pencil test used for recruit selection and classification. Use as a replacement for the Armed Services Vocational Aptitude Battery was specifically selected as the first application of adaptive testing because the large size of the annual testing load justifies the cost.

Subsequent applications of adaptive testing or other sophisticated computerized testing strategies will be limited only by cost, need, and the increasing availability of inexpensive computers and peripherals. Although it may be several years away, adaptive testing could become part of a totally integrated system of automated instruction and evaluation for resident training, on-the-job training, and periodic work-performance assessment.

Simulation is another aspect of evaluation strategy on the edge of revolutionary expansion. We have come a long way from the days of the first Link trainers and yet we have barely tapped the possibilities of simulation. For example, in the near future complex simulators will be used to train and simultaneously evaluate aircrew combat performance. That is a giant step from flight simulators limited to basic pilotage tasks such as takeoff, landing, and instrument flying. On a much less grandiose but no less important level, simulators will eventually be widely used to teach and evaluate a full range of repair and troubleshooting strategies both in resident training and on the job. The complexity of many weapon system components, such as aircraft avionics, make it difficult as well as dangerous to use operational systems for training and performance evaluation, as is the common practice today (Ciccinelli, 1979).

Widespread use of simulation in training and job-performance evaluation will also depend in part on high-power, compact computers. The rapidly expanding power of and continued decline in the cost of these computers may lead to an intimate marriage of instructional and performance-evaluation techniques such that both the technical and temporal distinctions now made between these two processes will become severely diminished in importance. The future in skill-performance testing sounds a lot like a trip into the space age, and that's exactly what it is!

The situation is not as bright, however, in the realm of supervisory ratings of performance. For jobs or assignments with a high proportion of administrative and management tasks (for the sake of clarity, comments are restricted to the evaluation of officers), supervisory performance ratings continue to be the primary evaluation technique. Unfortunately, as Landy and Farr (1980) show in their recent review of performance-rating techniques, little technical progress has been made in the last 20 years towards improving the validity and reliability of supervisory performance rating.

Two examples illustrate the hard realities with which managers of operational supervisory evaluation systems must live. Douglas McGregor (1960) wrote, ". . . it is probably safe to say that we can discriminate between the outstandingly good, the satisfactory and the unsatisfactory performers. When, however, we attempt to use the results of appraisals to make discriminations much finer than this, we are quite probably deluding ourselves." Even under laboratory conditions, Borman (1978) reported that, given what appear to be human limitations associated with making performance evaluations, results seem inadequate for most of the administrative uses of performance evaluations in real life.

In addition, military organizations, as they are organized for maximum combat effectiveness, may be particularly unsuitable environments for optimal performance evaluation by supervisors. The reasons are worth reviewing:

1. First, unlike industry, military assignment and promotion systems are relatively independent activities. Promotion does not carry with it assignment to a specific duty position. This difference does not have much impact on traditional performance evaluation at the end of a given reporting period because this is essentially an historical process. It is more difficult, however, to use this information to predict success in an unknown future job and such assessments of potential are an important part of officer-evaluation systems. As a result, evaluation of potential involves a subjective judgment about an officer's capabilities for assuming increased responsibilities, not for assuming a specific job.

2. Second, selections for promotion to a higher grade in the military are determined by central selection boards. Line-of-sight knowledge, a major contributor to promotion decisions in industry, is thus not a player in the selection process. Central promotion-board members do not know more about an individual than can be read in the information documented in his or her personnel file, largely in supervisory performance and potential evaluations.

3. Third, the timing of promotion consideration within the military is also relatively fixed when compared to the way in which the process works within industry. This situation is primarily a consequence of recruiting into the bottom of the grade structure. That is, unlike the lateral mobility that exists within and between civilian organizations, most officers enter the military as second lieutenants soon after college. They are therefore considered for promotion at certain intervals along with contemporaries who entered active duty at about the same time they did. As a result, when individuals are not selected along with their contemporaries, they are considered for promotion the next year with almost the same information in their personnel records, although with a different-year group of eligible officers. The practical outcome is significantly reduced promotion chances for individuals not promoted "on time" with their contemporaries.

All of these characteristics of officer personnel management subject military supervisors to considerable environmental pressures to give subordinates superior ratings because promotion largely depends on the quality of an officer's annual evaluations. The result, of course, is rating inflation.

Various techniques have been tried both in the military and in industrial organizations to reduce inflationary pressures, but as Thompson and Dalton (1970) observed, the control procedures generate their own set of problems that can be as severe as the problems they were intended to cure. The Army has recently installed a new officer-evaluation system that attempts to control inflation to some degree but it is too soon to evaluate its success. To date, however, previous organizational attempts to control the distribution of performance ratings have produced mixed results.

Finally, the published performance literature has historically dwelt on factors that affect the validity and reliability of performance ratings such as the technical aspects of various ratings strategies (e.g., behaviorally anchored rating scales, graphic rating scales, forced-choice ratings, etc.), roles, perceptions, characteristics of raters and ratees, and the interaction pattern between these individuals.

There is another side to this coin, however, that deserves greater research attention than it has received in the past—namely, the impact of an evaluation system itself on the behavior of raters and ratees and on the organization. Landy and Farr (1980) briefly touch on this issue in terms of the feedback loop between current ratings and future ratings. However, as managers of operational performance-evaluation systems can attest, there are many feedback loops and they can affect a wide variety of practices and relationships. There are concrete actions that raters and ratees may elect to take. For example, ratees may modify the emphasis they give to various elements in their jobs in order to optimize the performance that is likely to lead to high ratings (the result may not be in the best long-term interests of the organization). Supervisors may slant ratings to help a subordinate get promoted or manipulate ratings in ways designed to distribute merit salary increases on some basis other than performance. By engaging in such practices, raters and ratees are essentially "gaming" their performance ratings. When gaming occurs, the objectives of raters and ratees are in direct conflict with an organization's need for valid, reliable performance ratings.

There are other feedback loops that extend beyond the performance-evaluation process. Morale can decline significantly as ratees begin to see over time exactly how ratings generated for a new evaluation system are likely to affect them personally in ways beyond their control or beyond their supervisor's control. The working relationships between supervisors and their subordinates can also deteriorate, especially if the new system puts the supervisor in a situation in which dual roles as supervisor and implementor of organization policy are in conflict. In organizations in which a new appraisal system may encourage destructive competition between coworkers, teamwork can be significantly degraded. Even the lateral work relationships between supervisors can be altered towards or away from cooperation. An evaluation system can also change employee's perceptions of the credibility and supportiveness of an organization's personnel policies and objectives. Finally, the experience an organization's employees have with one evaluation system at least initially affects the way a subsequent evaluation system is received in terms of credibility and acceptability. These are all very real issues in an operational environment. Greater research in these areas could help organizations avoid the unforeseen and unfortunate consequences that can attend implementation of a new performance-evaluation system. Doing so, however, will require investigators to leave their laboratories and conduct more research in actual organizational environments.

In sum, remarkable changes are on the horizon for the integration of military training and technical job-performance evaluation through computerized task simulation and evaluation strategies. But, there is great need in both the public and private work sectors for new and perhaps nontraditional techniques to improve or supplant current procedures for the evaluation of managers and supervisors.

REFERENCES

Borman, W. C. Exploring upper limits of reliability and validity of performance ratings. *Journal of Applied Psychology,* 1978, *63,* 135–144.

Ciccinelli, L. F. Avionics maintenance training: Relative effectiveness of 6883 simulator and actual equipment (AFHRL–TR–79–13). Brooks AFB, Texas: Air Force Human Resources Laboratory, Air Force Systems Command, 1979.

Landy, F. J. & Farr, J. L. Performance rating. *Psychological Bulletin,* 1980, *87,* 72–107.

McGregor, D. *The human side of enterprise.* New York: McGraw-Hill, 1960.

Ratliff, F. R., Shore, C. W., Chiorini, J. R., & Curran, C. R. *Inflight performances differences of pilot and navigator F-4 second-seat crewmembers: A limited Southeast Asia combat evaluation* (AFHRL TR–69–104). Brooks AFB, Texas: Air Force Human Resources Laboratory, Air Force System Command, 1969.

Shore, C. W., Curran, C. R., Ratliff, F. R., & Chiorini, J. R. *Proficiency differences of pilot and navigator F-4 second-seat crewmembers: A Southeast Asia evaluation* (AFHRL TR–70–9). Brooks AFB, Texas: Air Force Human Resources Laboratory, Air Force Systems Command, 1970.

Thompson, P. H., & Dalton, G. W. Performance appraisal: Managers beware. *Harvard Business Review,* 1970, *48,* 149–157.

Wiskoff, M. F. Computerized adaptive testing. In *The first annual conference on personnel training factors in systems effectiveness* (NSIA PT 81–1) (Eds Monroe, B., & Farrell, F.) Washington, D.C.: National Security Industrial Association, 1981.

10

A Causal Analysis of Cognitive Ability, Job Knowledge, Job Performance, and Supervisor Ratings

John E. Hunter

Through a meta-analysis of 14 studies, Dr. Hunter investigates the relationships among three variables: ability, job knowledge and performance. Performance is measured in two ways, work sample tests and supervisory ratings. Two causal models are presented which depict the possible relationships among the three variables. The first model suggests a direct impact of ability on performance, on job knowledge, and on supervisor ratings. This implies that there is an indirect relationship impact of job knowledge on supervisory ratings. The alternative model suggests that job knowledge is directly related to supervisory ratings. The results of the path analysis provide support for the latter model.

Dr. Guion states that Hunter's findings provide evidence for the validity of ratings. However, the model is incomplete. He suggests that the model should be enlarged to include such exogenous variables as rater characteristics, ratee characteristics, and context factors.

This paper presents a metaanalysis of 14 empirical studies that assessed the correlations between three variables relevant to performance appraisal: ability, job knowledge, and performance itself. Performance is represented by two kinds of measurement: job-sample tests and supervisor ratings.

Ability should be related to performance in two ways. First, to the extent that the job calls for reasoning, planning, or memory, speed and smoothness of performance will depend on cognitive ability. Second, ability determines the extent to which the person masters the knowledge required for efficient and excellent performance. Ability is especially important if the job requires adjustment to novel circumstances or change in behavior due to changing job requirements. The greater the extent to which the job can be laid out in manuals or training programs, the greater the extent to which ability will be relevant only indirectly through its relation to job knowledge.

Knowledge can be divided into two forms: knowledge of the technical information about objects and concepts required to do the job and knowledge of processes and judgmental criteria required for efficient or correct action on the job. Lack of knowledge reduces job performance in various ways: People must either look up the information or take time away from supervisors or coworkers when asking them for help, or they make errors stemming from incomplete or erroneous information.

Job performance itself has been measured in two ways. First, some authors have constructed simulations of the job in which performance can be directly observed and measured. That is, some researchers measure performance using a job-sample test. Other researchers assess performance by having workers rated by those supervisors who know them well enough. In most cases, the only supervisor who can rate the worker is the immediate supervisor. This was true of all the studies located for this report.

There is a causal model implicit in the previous discussion. According to this model, the work-sample test should be a measure of performance. Thus there should be a causal arrow from ability to the work-sample test representing a direct impact of ability on performance, and arrows from ability to job knowledge and from job knowledge to the work-sample test representing the indirect impact of ability on knowledge and knowledge on performance. If supervisor ratings are determined entirely by job performance, then the model should have an arrow running from the work-sample test to supervisor ratings. If this model is tested using path analysis, then there are two correlations against which the model can be tested: the correlation between ability and supervisor ratings and the correlation between job knowledge and supervisor ratings. If these correlations are correctly predicted by the path model, then the partial correlation between ability and supervisor ratings is zero if either job knowledge or work-sample score is controlled; and the partial correlation between job knowledge and supervisor rating is zero if the work-sample test is controlled.

There is an alternate model for supervisor ratings. Suppose that supervisors rarely observe routine correct performance. A supervisor is called in under two circumstances: The worker has made an error or there is to be a change in job duties. If the worker has done something wrong, then the supervisor asks the worker to explain what he or she did and then tells him or her what he or she did wrong. The supervisor thus gets a much better picture of the worker's job knowledge than of the actual job performance. On the other hand, if the worker is to change procedures, it will be the supervisor who carries out the training. During this training the supervisor will get a good picture of the ease with which the worker flexibly handles two kinds of jobs or jobs under two different sets of instructions. But it is well known that interference from new instructions tends to be greatest if the old knowledge is only partially mastered. Again the supervisor is likely to form an image of the strength of the worker on the basis of job knowledge rather than performance per se. If this alternate model is correct, then there will also be a causal arrow from job knowledge to supervisor ratings. This model can be tested against only one correlation: the correlation between ability and supervisor ratings. If the model fits, then the partial correlation between ability and supervisor ratings is zero if job knowledge is controlled.

ERROR OF MEASUREMENT

If error of measurement is not eliminated from independent variables, then partial correlations and beta weights are biased. Thus a path model can only be correctly tested if error of measurement is controlled. In this study, this is done by correcting correlations for attenuation.

Most studies report reliability coefficients if a test is used in the study. Thus the study usually reports the reliability of ability, job knowledge, or the work-sample test. These reliabilities were recorded or sometimes computed from other tables when possible.

Supervisor ratings are subject to two kinds of error. First, there is error in the assessment of the impression of the single rater: for example, a coefficient alpha on the correlations between separate ratings made by the same supervisor. Second, there is halo: the tendency for each rater to form an idiosyncratic impression of the worker that is present in all the ratings made by that rater. If the single impressions are measured perfectly, then this source of error is separately measured by the interrater correlation. If the interrater correlation is given for imperfect ratings, then it simultaneously measures both sources of error.

In the studies reported here, there was no second rater. Thus interrater correlations were not given. However, a metaanalysis of supervisor rating studies was conducted by King, Hunter, and Schmidt (1980), who found that the interrater correlation for perfect measures is virtually constant across studies. That correlation is .60. This, then, represents the upper bound on the reliability of supervisor ratings in the present study. If impression-reliability information was given, then the supervisor rating reliability was correspondingly reduced (four studies); otherwise, the overestimate of .60 was used. However, in most of the studies in which impression reliability was not given, the rating was the sum of independent ratings and was thus not likely to be less than .30 to .90.

RESULTS

Table 10.1 presents the basic data extracted or computed from all studies located that presented correlations for at least three of the four variables in the design. The studies are presented in three sets: (1) the nonmilitary studies with data on all four variables; (2) the military studies, which all had correlations for all four variables; and (3) the nonmilitary studies with data on only three variables. The

TABLE 10.1
Raw Findings from 14 Empirical Studies[a]

Authors	Occupation	Sample Size	Reliability				Uncorrected Correlations					
			r_{AA}	r_{KK}	r_{WW}	r_{SS}	r_{AK}	r_{AW}	r_{AS}	r_{KW}	r_{KS}	r_{WS}
Campbell et al. (1973)	Cartographer	443	85	88	49	60	65	48	33	52	40	23
Corts et al. (1977)	Customs Inspector	186	93	67	80	34	53	50	3	49	4	18
O'Leary and Trattner (1977)	Tax Investigator	292	93	64	78	60	54	49	23	41	19	30
Trattner et al. (1977)	Claims Examiner	233	93	81	72	60	55	36	29	34	44	29
Vineberg and Taylor (1972)	Armor Crewman	368		81		60	54	36	6	50	21	13
Vineberg and Taylor (1972)	Armor Repairman	360		76		60	44	32	15	49	20	19
Vineberg and Taylor (1972)	Supply Specialist	380		92		60	36	39	10	64	30	25
Vineberg and Taylor (1972)	Cook	366		84		60	47	35	15	49	27	19
Campbell et al. (1973)	Medical Technican	456	77	85		60	39		28		39	
Drauden (1978)	Social Worker	78	46	56		55	33		29		25	
Campbell et al. (1973)	Investment Management	384	88		95	60		51	29			27
Boyles et al. (19)	Clerical Worker	59	79		68	40		69	40			38
Schoon (1979)	Medical Laboratory Worker	160		91	95	34				72	5	32
van Rijn and Payne (1980)	Firefighter	210	93	78	76	34	62	50		62		

[a]N = sample size, A = ability, K = knowledge, W = work-sample test, S = supervisor ratings.

military studies did not report reliability estimates for either the ability test or the work-sample measure. The values used were average reliabilities from other research: .80 for ability and .84 for work-sample performance.

Table 10.2 presents the basic correlational data free of the effects of error of measurement. Because performance appraisal is done on incumbent populations, no correction for restriction in range was made. The results for each correlation tend to be very similar across studies. This reflects the fact that these studies have a much higher average sample size than most validation sutides: a total of 3975 across 14 studies, or an average of 284 in comparison to the average of 68 for validation studies in general (Lent, Aurbach, & Levin, 1971).

Table 10.3 presents the data for nonmilitary studies. Correlations were averaged separately for the complete and incomplete studies. If there were large variations in path model parameters in individual studies, then the average correlations across incomplete studies could be inconsistent. Table 10.3 presents the average correlations for each set of studies and the multiple regression results needed for path analyses. The path coefficients are shown in Fig. 10.1. The path model shown is that for the alternative model in which supervisor ratings depend on job knowledge as well as on job performance. The model assuming that supervisors use only performance fails the data dramatically; the average correlation between ratings and job knowledge is higher than the correlation between

TABLE 10.2
Basic Correlations from 14 Empirical Studies[a]

Authors	Occupation	Sample Size	r_{AK}	r_{AW}	r_{AS}	r_{KW}	r_{KS}	r_{WS}
Campbell et al. (1973)	Cartographer	443	75	74	46	79	55	42
Corts et al. (1977)	Customs Inspector	186	67	58	5	67	8	35
O'Leary and Trattner (1977)	Tax Investigator	292	70	58	31	58	31	44
Trattner et al. (1977)	Claims Examiner	233	63	44	39	45	63	44
Vineberg and Taylor (1972)	Armor Crewman	368	66	44	9	60	30	18
Vineberg and Taylor (1972)	Armor Repairman	360	54	39	22	59	28	27
Vineberg and Taylor (1972)	Supply Specialist	380	44	48	14	77	43	35
Vineberg and Taylor (1972)	Cook	366	58	43	22	59	38	27
Campbell et al. (1973)	Medical Technician	456	50		41	55		
Drauden (1978)	Social Worker	78	65		58	45		
Campbell et al. (1973)	Investment Management	384		56	32			36
Boyles et al. (19)	Clerical Worker	59		86	71			66
Schoon (1979)	Medical Laboratory Worker	160				77	9	56
van Rijn and Payne (1980)	Firefighter	210	73	59		81		

[a]N = sample size, A = ability, K = job knowledge, W = work-sample test, S = supervisor rating.

TABLE 10.3
Correlations for the Nonmilitary Studies[a]

		Complete Studies (N = 1154)				Incomplete Studies (N = 636)			
		A	*K*	*W*	*S*	*A*	*K*	*W*	*S*
Cognitive ability	A	100	70	61	34	100	58	60	41
Job knowledge	K	70	100	65	43	58	100	79	50
Work sample	W	61	65	100	42	60	79	100	42
Supervisor rating	S	34	43	42	100	41	50	42	100

[a]N = sample size, A = ability, K = job knowledge, W = work-sample test, S = supervisor rating.

Multiple regression of work-sample performance on job knowledge and cognitive ability:
$$R = .68 \qquad\qquad R = .81$$
$$\beta_K = .44 \ \beta_A = .30 \qquad \beta_K = .67 \ \beta_A = .21$$
Multiple regression of supervisor rating on job knowledge and work-sample performance:
$$R = .47 \qquad\qquad R = .50$$
$$\beta_K = .27 \ \beta_W = .24 \qquad \beta_K = .45 \ \beta_W = .07$$

ratings and the work-sample measure in both data sets (i.e., $r_{KS} = .43$ versus $r_{WS} = .42$ in the complete studies; $r_{KS} = .50$ versus $r_{WS} = .42$ in the incomplete studies). The model predicts a correlation of .33 between ability and supervisor ratings in the complete data, where the actual correlation is .34: an error of .01. The predicted correlation in the incomplete studies is .30, where the actual correlation is .41: an error of .11. For a sample size of 635, this difference

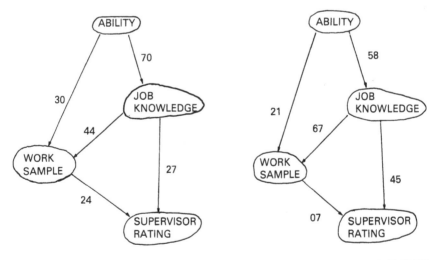

NONMILITARY COMPLETE STUDIES   NONMILITARY INCOMPLETE STUDIES

FIG. 10.1. The path models that fit the nonmilitary data with complete and incomplete studies analyzed separately.

TABLE 10.4
A Comparison of Military and Nonmilitary Correlations[a]

		Nonmilitary Studies N = 1790				Military Studies N = 1474			
		A	K	W	S	A	K	W	S
Cognitive ability	A	100	66	61	36	100	55	44	17
Job knowledge	K	66	100	70	45	55	100	63	35
Work sample	W	61	70	100	42	44	63	100	27
Supervisor rating	S	36	45	42	100	17	35	27	100

[a]N = sample size, A = ability, K = job knowledge, W = work-sample test, S = supervisor ratings.

$$R = .73 \qquad\qquad R = .64$$
$$\beta_K = .53 \; \beta_A = .26 \qquad \beta_K = .56 \; \beta_A = .13$$

Multiple regression of supervisor rating on job knowledge and work-sample performance:

$$R = .48 \qquad\qquad R = .36$$
$$\beta_K = .31 \; \beta_A = .21 \qquad \beta_K = .30 \; \beta_A = .10$$

of .11 is barely significant at the .05 level. The average error of .06 across the two sets of studies is not significant.

Because there is little difference between the results for complete and incomplete studies, all correlations across nonmilitary studies were averaged. These averages are presented in Table 10.4 along with the results for the military studies. Table 10.4 also presents the multiple regression results required for the path analysis. The resulting parameter estimates are shown in Fig. 10.2. Again

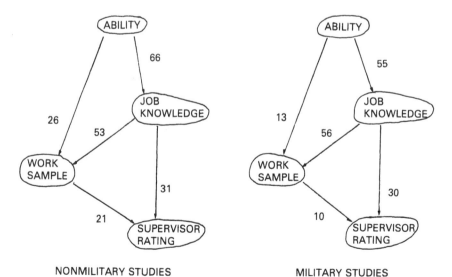

NONMILITARY STUDIES   MILITARY STUDIES

FIG. 10.2. The causal models that fit the military and nonmilitary studies separately.

TABLE 10.5
Correlations Across All Studies[a]

		All Studies $N = 3264$			
		A	K	W	S
Cognitive ability	A	100	61	53	27
Job knowledge	K	61	100	67	40
Work sample	W	53	67	100	35
Supervisor ratings	S	27	40	35	100

[a]N = sample size, A = ability, K = job knowledge, W = work-sample test, S = supervisor rating.

Multiple regression of work-sample performance on job knowledge and cognitive ability:

$$R = .68$$
$$\beta_K = .55 \quad \beta_A = .19$$

Multiple regression of supervisor ratings on job knowledge and work-sample performance:

$$R = .42$$
$$\beta_K = .30 \quad \beta_A = .15$$

the assumption that supervisors rely only on performance was disconfirmed in both data sets; the correlation for job knowledge was higher in both cases (for nonmilitary studies $r_{KS} = .45$ versus $r_{WS} = .42$ and for military studies $r_{KS} = .35$ versus $r_{WS} = .27$). The model predicts a correlation of .33 between ability and supervisor ratings in the nonmilitary data and the actual correlation is .34: an error of .01. For military data, the predicted correlation is .21 and the

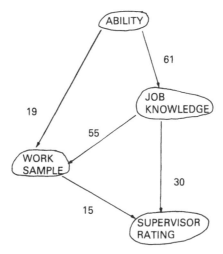

FIG. 10.3. The causal model that fits the average correlations across all studies, $N = 3264$.

actual correlation is .17: an error of −.04. Neither error is statistically significant.

Table 10.5 presents the average correlations across all 14 studies with a total sample size of 3264. Table 10.5 also contains the multiple regression results needed for the path analysis. The parameters for the path model are shown in Fig. 10.3. Again the only model presented is that that assumes that supervisors are sensitive to job knowledge as well as to job performance. Both the beta weight and the zero order correlation are larger than predicted by the performance-only model. In fact, the beta weight for job knowledge is not only greater than 0, but it is also greater than the beta weight for performance. The correlation between ability and supervisor ratings predicted by the model is .26 and the actual correlation is .27: an error of .01, which is far from large enough to be statistically significant even with a sample size of 3264.

DISCUSSION

The model shown in Fig. 10.3 shows virtually perfect fit to the average correlations across 14 studies with a total sample size of 3264. The high correlation of .53 between ability and performance derives in part from a direct causal impact of .19 and from an indirect effect of $(.61) (.55) = .34$ representing the effect of ability on job knowledge. The correlation of .67 between job knowledge and job performance is largely a direct causal impact of job knowledge on job performance—that is, though there is a small "spurious" influence due to the common impact of ability on both $(.61) (.19) = .07$. The causal analysis shows job knowledge to be twice as important as job performance in the determination of supervisor ratings.

The multiple correlation for the prediction of supervisor ratings is only .42. Because all correlations were corrected for both intrarater and interrater error of measurement, factors such as halo and leniency differences cannot be cited as explanations for this. That is, the supervisor rating that was used in this model is the average rating across the population of supervisors. These data show that factors other than job performance and job knowledge account for a very large part of the variation in ratings.

The data in the 14 empirical studies reviewed here confirm the routine assumptions of psychologists in the employment area over the last 50 years. There is a high correlation between cognitive ability and job performance that is in part the result of the direct impact of ability differences on performance but that is even more the result of indirect causal impact due to the high correlation between ability and job knowledge and the high relevance of job knowledge to job performance. There is a moderately high correlation between supervisor ratings and job performance, but this is in large part due to the extent to which supervisors are sensitive to differences in job knowledge.

REFERENCES

Boyles, W. R., Palmer, C. I., & Veres, J. G. *Empirical validation of a content validated test.* Montgomery: Center for government and public affairs, Auburn University.

Campbell, J. T., Crooks, L. A., Mahoney, M. H., & Rock, D. A. *An investigation of sources of bias in the prediction of job performance: A six year study.* Princeton, N.J.: Educational Testing Service, 1973.

Corts, D. B., Muldrow, T. W., & Outerbridge, A. M. *Research base for the written test portion of the Professional and Administrative Career Examination (PACE): Prediction of job performance for customs inspectors.* Washington, D.C.: Personnel Research and Development Center, U.S. Office of Personnel Management, 1977.

Drauden, G. *Multijurisdictional empirical validation of an entry level social worker test battery in Minnesota.* Minneapolis: Hennepin County Personnel Department, 1978.

King, L. M., Hunter, J. E., & Schmidt, F. L. Halo in a multidimensional forced choice performance evaluation scale. *Journal of Applied Psychology,* 1980, *65,* 507–516.

Lent, R. H., Aurbach, H. A., & Levin, L. S. Predictors, criteria, and significant results. *Personnel Psychology,* 1971, *24,* 519–533.

O'Leary, B. S. & Trattner, M. H. *Research base for the written portion of the Professional and Administrative Career Examination (PACE): Prediction of job performance for internal revenue officers.* Washington, D.C.: Personnel Research and Development Center, U.S. Office of Personnel Management, 1977.

Schoon, C. G. *Correlation of performance on clinical laboratory proficiency examinations with performance in clinical laboratory practice.* New York: *Professional Examination Service,* 1979.

Trattner, M. H., Corts, D. B., van Rijn, P. P., & Outerbridge, A. M. *Research base for the written test portion of the Professional and Administrative Career Examination (PACE): Prediction of job performance for claims authorizers in the social insurance claims examining occupation.* Washington, D.C.: Personnel Research and Development Center, U.S. Office of Personnel Management, 1977.

van Rijn, P., & Payne, S. S. *Criterion related validity research base for the D.C. firefighter selection test.* Washington, D.C.: Personnel Research and Development Center, U.S. Office of Personnel Management, 1980.

Vineberg, R., & Taylor, E. N. Performance in four army jobs by men at different aptitude (AFQT) levels: 3. The relationship of AFQT and job experience to job performance. Alexandria, Va.: Human Resources Research Organization (HUMRRO), 1972.

Comments on Hunter

Robert M. Guion

Professor Hunter's paper differs markedly from most in this symposium. The fact that he presented data is only a symptom of the difference. The real difference is that he has examined performance ratings as criteria in research; generally, the other presentations have concentrated on performance evaluation as a management tool for effecting change (although occasionally acknowledging differences between ratings collected for administrative purposes and those collected for research purposes). For administrative use, it may be sufficient to identify the very good and the very poor performers, with no distinctions within the vast group between. Research use, however, needs information about gradations in the level of performance effectiveness throughout the continuum ranging from ineffective to highly effective performance.

The analyses reported by Professor Hunter have interesting research implications, both in their findings and in what they did not find. Criticism of details of the analyses, such as the method of estimating reliability, might be entertaining, but they would be fruitless. Much more valuable is a concentration on the "big picture" drawn by the overall causal-path diagram. One important implication, at least for me personally, is that performance ratings are not as invalid as they have seemed.

My optimism concerning research on ratings has been low. In fact, my attitude towards performance ratings is becoming much like my attitude towards employment interviews: They have a fine public-relations value, but they are little better than a table of random numbers for making decisions about people. However, Hunter has shown that ratings of performance are valid, at least to a degree, because they are in fact based on demonstrated ability to do the job and on on-the-job knowledge that makes performance effective or ineffective. Methodological bickering would not change that conclusion.

267

KNOWLEDGE VERSUS PERFORMANCE

The finding is not exciting. It simply says that there is evidence, across 14 studies, that performance ratings are "influenced" both by the ability to perform, as indicated by work-sample performance, and by the knowledge that is prerequisite to effectiveness in performance. Of the two causal influences, job knowledge proves to have a heavier influence on performance ratings than do the performance measures. This reminds me of the old saw about the response made when the county agent asked the farmer why he had not attended some instructional meetings: "I ain't farmin' now half as well as I know how to."

Few people farm or do other chores as well as they could. No research that I have read in the last 30 years has even hinted that people might habitually reach their potential for achievement, or that performance might typically be found at an upper asymptote. This, in itself, may explain Hunter's finding.

The nature of the measure of "performance" in the Hunter analyses might also provide an explanation. Work samples are what psychometricians call "maximum performance tests," in contrast to the alternative term, "typical performance tests." A standardized work sample is clearly identified as a test of how well an incumbent *can* perform a task under standardized, idealized circumstances; it is not a test of how well he or she actually *does* it. Necessarily, work-sample performance more closely approximates an examinee's potential level of performance than the level of typical, day-to-day, unstandardized, and perhaps unobserved performance. One suspects that most supervisory ratings are more influenced by typical than by maximum level of performance; at least, many rating procedures specifically ask the rater to consider typical performance, although occasionally a rater will be asked to indicate how well a person can do when doing his or her best.

Hunter's reasoning behind the joint-influence model is probably on target: that a supervisor simply may not have many occasions to observe routine performance, and that direct contact of the supervisor with the employee to be rated is usually some sort of discussion. Moreover, Hunter argues, discussion is more likely to inform the supervisor about the level of the employee's knowledge of the job demands than about the employee's typical level of performance. In my own work, I have sought supervisory ratings in occupations as diverse as police officers, foreign-service officers, clerical workers, managers, college professors, and engineers; in no case have I found a situation other than that described by Professor Hunter. Indeed, I have come to the conclusion that asking supervisors even to describe (let alone evaluate) the typical work behavior of their subordinates is a terribly unreasonable request. It may be possible to get descriptions of the dramatic instances of behavior at the extremely high or the extremely low range of a performance scale, but I doubt that it is possible to describe behavior that is typical.

If Hunter is correct in his reasoning behind this model, it might perhaps be much more useful to ask raters simply to describe how well employees understand the facts and principles and procedures of effective performance and try to predict or change such knowledge. Perhaps, indeed, we should abandon the pretense about "objective," "true," or "hard" criteria of proficiency in performance.

One implication of the basic finding reported by Professor Hunter—that ratings are influenced more by what employees have learned *about* their jobs than by how well they can, under standard conditions, *do* their jobs—should be mentioned. This finding may very well explain why Hunter and his associates (e.g., Pearlman, Schmidt, & Hunter, 1980; Schmidt, Gast-Rosenberg, & Hunter, 1980) have found that trainability and proficiency criteria have been about equally well predicted in their validity generalization research. Most proficiency criteria are ratings; if ratings reflect trainability better than proficiency, then proficiency ratings are simply a special class of trainability ratings. Stated differently, the classification of criteria into the two categories has probably been generally unsuccessful.

ENLARGING THE MODEL

Although Hunter has found some validity for ratings, he has not found much. The main message of the analysis is sobering. Hunter concluded that ". . . factors other than job performance and job knowledge account for a very large part of the variation in rating." If we want to understand ratings, we must identify some of those other factors. Therefore, I urge researchers to work towards more comprehensive path models—towards providing statistics that can some day be placed into a larger metaanalysis—than the data from which Hunter worked in these analyses.

One might wonder whether the model should be enlarged by including more than one dimension of performance ratings. I have usually called for measures of components of performance until such time as it is shown that isolating component aspects of performance makes no particular difference. One inference that can be drawn from the validity generalization research, however, is that the findings support the concept of a general factor in performance evaluation. That is, if performance on one highly specific job can be predicted to roughly the same degree as performance on some other job, then the details of the performance requirements are probably not terribly important. For this reason, I am content in these comments to settle for overall performance as the dependent variable of the analysis. Perhaps, as data emerge, it will seem useful to analyze overall performance into smaller components. If so, it might make more sense to do analyses (one for each component) than to treat different components as different "boxes" in an enlarged path model.

To enlarge the model, we need to consider various exogenous variables that might have causal arrows drawn to performance ratings—either directly or through impact on performance or job knowledge.

Characteristics of Ratees

A first category of exogenous variables for an enlarged path model would consist of ratee characteristics beyond performance capability and job knowledge. I suggest a few here. From the point of view of organizational objectives, these are trivial characteristics; from the point of view of variance accounted for, they may be quite nontrivial indeed.

Appearance.   My hypothesis here is that people who are, in a very broad sense, more attractive than others are also more likely to receive good ratings. The hypothesized effect is on the ratings alone, not on performance or knowledge. It is well established that appearance, at least in the sense of "facial attractiveness," influences perceptions of other characteristics of people (Huston & Levinger, 1978), including perceptions of task performance (D. Landy & Sigall, 1974). I would go beyond the typical research judging the attractiveness of people by their photographs. For example, I suspect that tall men, if neither very skinny nor very fat, are generally considered more attractive than short ones (Koulack & Tuthill, 1972). Clean, well-groomed people are probably considered more attractive than sloppy, bizarre, or quaint ones. Men with deep, resonant voices are probably more attractive than those with squeaky voices. These traits do not apply only to men; with some notable exceptions, small, petite sopranos in frilly dresses seem less likely to be taken seriously during performance evaluation than their larger peers with contralto voices. I know of no research on the voice effect, but observation suggests that a choir director would be hard pressed to find a soprano section among a random sampling of women who have reached executive positions in most business organizations.

Police officers lack pretense on the appearance issue. When developing lists of dimensions for rating the "performance" of police officers, they almost always list appearance as an important dimension. One such discussion went to lengths I considered absurd, and I asked a sergeant whether he would give a low rating to an officer who had saved a life by pulling an accident victim from a car—but had torn his uniform doing so. The answer, without equivocation, was affirmative. I suspect that the sergeant is unusual only in the clarity with which he identifies his bias.

Annoyance Syndrome.   Just as elementary school teachers are thought to refer for special education those children who present behavior problems in class, so also may supervisors tend to give poor ratings to employees who bother them. Perhaps the causal model should require a box for the supervisor's tolerance for being bothered, but one suspects that an annoyance syndrome could be identified and that an index number for measuring it could be developed. Components entering the index would include such problem-producing behavior as not showing up for work, coming late, instigating coworkers to complain or to make special demands, insistence on "going by the book" when unusual circumstances require unusual pacing, or refusal to accept overtime (or, conversely, excessively persistent demands to get it).

I am not sure that bipolarity could be assumed. I am not sure, that is, that promptness, dependability, or cooperation would have as much positive influence on ratings as the annoyance syndrome would have in the negative direction. Maybe this is a variable with which a nonlinear model would be required. This is a detail, to worry about when one is doing the research; the hypothesis is simply that it takes a magnificently self-disciplined supervisor to recognize truly high performance in an obnoxious employee.

Again, the hypothesized effect is mainly on the ratings themselves, although causal arrows with performance and job knowledge could be tried in either direction or as reciprocal relationships.

Frequency of Communication with a Supervisor.   Some employees tend to avoid the supervisor; others report faithfully and often. This, too, might have a nonlinear relationship to ratings; the too-frequent communication might be an entry for the annoyance syndrome. This caveat aside, however, it is reasonable to hypothesize that: (1) the employee who communicates regularly with the boss has nothing to hide or fear; (2) such an employee gets better known than other employees; and (3) better-known employees who are in fact reasonably competent will receive disproportionately better ratings. The causal arrow is hypothesized to effect the performance ratings directly, with no indirect influences.

Interpersonal Skill.   A supervisor's evaluation of an individual employee may be influenced in part by the evaluations of that employee by his or her peers. Their evaluations may be influenced in part by the employee's performance, but they might also be influenced in part by the employee's charm. Perhaps this is a function of attractiveness (and therefore redundant), but some otherwise unattractive people can be quite charming. It seems reasonable to hypothesize that at least some unique variance could be attributed to that amorphous construct we have come to call interpersonal skill.

Characteristics of Raters

A similar category of exogenous variables would consist of characteristics of the raters themselves. A substantial list of rater characteristics could be derived from the review by F. Landy and Farr (1980). For the most part, my examples are not on their list, but it should certainly provide a number of potential causal variables. In particular, there is good reason to include several demographic variables. Following is my condensed list.

Bigotry.   There are obvious kinds of bigotry involving unreasonable racial or sex prejudice, but I would go beyond these. For example, many jobs require something of an art to be performed well. Insofar as there is an artistic element, there will be differences of opinion about how the job should be done. Some people are so prejudiced against those who do the job in the wrong way (that is, differently from their own preferences) that they cannot dispassionately evaluate the outcomes. I once worked with a supervisor who could not acknowledge that the star salesman in his store was above average. The reason was that this man who sold more merchandise than any other salesperson in the organization had an initial approach to customers that was more like Uriah Heep than like Harold Hill; the supervisor felt that the Harold Hill approach was far superior. The sales record indicated that the obsequious Uriah Heep approach had done quite well, for at least this one salesman.

The enlarged model could include any from a long list of attitudes or values. For any such attitude, the research might consider the whole range of a continuum. I have chosen deliberately, however, to use the term "bigotry" to emphasize extremely negative attitudes because I remain unconvinced that the "robustness of the linear model" is sufficient for the dramatic impact I hypothesize. The hypothesis admittedly is not well developed; essentially, it starts from the idea that there is for each person a threshold—a stimulus limen, if you will—that must be reached before there is any effect. That threshold depends, perhaps, on the intensity of the supervisor's attitude. If the supervisor is a conservative, but within moderate levels, then an employee's behavior must exemplify the most flaming sort of liberalism before it influences ratings of performance. If the supervisor's attitudes of conservatism are extreme, however, a much milder degree of liberalism could set off a "bigotry reaction."

Cognitive Complexity.   Cognitive complexity was specifically identified by F. Landy and Farr (1980) as a promising variable in the study of rater characteristics. If nothing else, the level of cognitive complexity describing a rater should influence the amount of variance to be accounted for in a set of ratings. The term implies an ability to make distinctions. The person with greater level of cognitive complexity should be able to make finer distinctions, at all portions of the range, and therefore provide a greater range of variables. It might also be suspected, however, that cognitively complex raters may also be able to make the distinctions between performance levels and job-knowledge levels more effectively than the less cognitively complex rater such that the supervisor's cognitive skill would have an indirect effect—and a valid effect—on the ratings.

Perhaps other cognitive traits should be considered in the list of potential exogenous variables. General intelligence might be one. Cognitive consistency—more habit, perhaps, than ability—might be another.

Leadership Roles.   In this box we can postulate the usual variables: initiating structure or consideration. What I have particularly in mind, however, is the degree to which the rater perceives his or her role to be an evaluative one. A current research problem may illustrate the situation. One of my students is doing a dissertation on a topic related to managerial stress. Some organizations in which there has been interest in the research have been unwilling to participate in that portion of it requiring performance evaluations. One respondent—a long-time friend—said frankly, "We can't get performance evaluations for internal administrative purposes; I certainly can't ask for them for your research." A related attitude was expressed by a police field-training officer who said, "Our job is to make them good officers; if I give a low rating, it's an admission that I have failed." In contrast, some supervisors clearly believe that it is their job to evaluate the performance of their subordinates. Surely such differences in role perceptions must influence the rating process and, perhaps, account for some of the variance in ratings.

Context Variables

A third category of variables consists of context or situational variables. In this category, before listing some suggestions, I want explicitly to rule out one; I do *not* believe it is fruitful to do causal research on rating-scale formats! There are some situational variables, however, that seem eminently worth investigation in these causal models.

Level of Peer Performance.   This seems to require very little elaboration; if a person with a given level of performance is rated in the context of a group of poor performers, his or her rating will be higher than if it were rated in the context of excellent peer performance. The context effect on human judgment seems to be well enough established to support the inclusion of such a variable in the model. The causal effect is probably a direct effect on ratings, but there may be some indirect influences on performance, too. Interestingly, a reasonable hypothesis is that the direction of the effect on performance is not necessarily the same as the direction of the effect on the ratings.

Quality of Equipment and Material.   One of the studies in Hunter's analysis involved a group of medical technicians (Campbell, Crooks, Mahoney, & Rock, 1973). No work-sample data were reported for this group. What may not be well known is that attempts were indeed made to develop such a work sample (Pike, 1969). Among the many obstacles, however, equipment, reagents, and other resources varied so much from one site to another that no reliable work-sample scores could be obtained—even when the investigators began taking some equipment and material with them as standards. Clearly, the quality of such resources influences performance; a knowledge of that quality may also influence ratings of performance.

Incentives.   This is, again, a simple-minded concept: When there is an incentive system, records will be kept that may not be available (or may not be consulted, if available) in situations without such systems. Perhaps the broader concept should be the availability of records. For some raters, such records may account for virtually all of the variance; other raters may consult such records and also consider various extenuating or facilitating circumstances.

RESEARCH ON INDIVIDUAL RATERS

This last comment brings me to what may be the major difference between Professor Hunter's and my approaches. He has been interested in metaanalysis, combining not only data across all raters within a study but across all raters in all studies. He seeks generalizations that cut across all manner of situations and all manner of raters. I am more interested in the individual rater. To what extent is the individual rater consistent? That is, for any given rater, can it be assumed that the variables that account for variance in ratings over people and circumstances will be the same from one rating task to another? Will errors of rating be predictable errors? Will the most heavily weighted variables be sensible in terms of organizational or task objectives?

Such questions concerning the rating process for individual raters call for a special case of policy-capturing research. The identification of patterns of the judgment policies of individual raters seems to be the most important kind of research on rating now needed. There are several possible approaches to policy-capturing research. One is the lens-model regression approach, exemplified by Zedeck and Kafry (1977). Another is the use of multidimensional scaling, now being done by a colleague at South Florida (Ironson, 1981). Another, I think, may be path analyses such as those described here—but at the level of the individual rater.

This, I think, is the major extension to be developed from Professor Hunter's paper. The causal model includes, but goes beyond, ordinary regression analysis. With it, it should become possible to have a clear understanding of the *major* influences on ratings made by a given rater.

How? I do not have a clear paradigm to offer. I know that I do not recommend the "paper-people" paradigm. There is no more reason to use it for raters than for interviewers, and Gorman, Clover, and Doherty (1978) have demonstrated its lack of external validity for the latter purpose.

What would be necessary would be a longitudinal study keeping records of evaluations, ratee characteristics, any changes in rater characteristics, and changes in circumstances over time. It might be necessary to watch for cyclical effects, either in context variables or performance. Such research is probably not practical for the solution of day-to-day operating problems in performance evaluations, but it may have very practical long-range implications if completely carried out in representative samples of raters. With a thorough understanding of the events and attributes that have a causal influence on the ratings made by a few raters, researchers might develop enough insight into the rating process to develop broad programs of rater training—programs that would be more fruitful than training in classical rating errors.

The basic import of Hunter's findings is that there is much to be learned about the factors that influence performance ratings. The basic import of my discussion of them is that we should get on with the task of learning it.

REFERENCES

Campbell, J. T., Crooks, L. A., Mahoney, M. H., & Rock, D. A. *An investigation of sources of bias in the prediction of job performance: A six-year study* (Final Project Report PR–73–37). Princeton, N.J.: Educational Testing Service, September 1973.

Gorman, C. D., Clover, W. H., & Doherty, M. E. Can we learn anything about interviewing real people from "interviews" of paper people? Two studies of the external validity of a paradigm. *Organizational Behavior and Human Performance*, 1978, *22*, 165–192.

Huston, T. L., & Levinger, G. Interpersonal attraction and relationships. *Annual Review of Psychology*, 1978, *29*, 115–156.

Ironson, G. H. Personal communication, August 1981.

Koulack, D., & Tuthill, J. A. Height perception: A function of social distance. *Canadian Journal of Behavioral Science*, 1972, *4*, 50–53.

Landy, D., & Sigall, H. Beauty is talent: Task evaluation as a function of the performer's physical attractiveness. *Journal of Personality and Social Psychology*, 1974, *29*, 299–304.

Landy, F. J., & Farr, J. L. Performance rating. *Psychological Bulletin*, 1980, *87*, 72–107.

Pearlman, K., Schmidt, F. L., & Hunter, J. E. Validity generalization results for tests used to predict job proficiency and training success in clerical occupations. *Journal of Applied Psychology*, 1980, *65*, 373–406.

Pike, L. W. *Prediction of job performance for negro and white medical technicians: Development of the instrumentation* (PR–69–4). Princeton, N.J.: Educational Testing Service, April 1969.

Schmidt, F. L., Gast-Rosenberg, I., & Hunter, J. E. Validity generalization results for computer programmers. *Journal of Applied Psychology*, 1980, *65*, 643–661.

Zedeck, S., & Kafry, D. Capturing rater policies for processing evaluation data. *Organizational Behavior and Human Performance*, 1977, *18*, 269–294.

11

Some Possible Implications of "Modeling" for the Conceptualization of Measurement

John P. Campbell

Dr. Campbell describes a number of alternatives for performance modeling, including psychomotor performance models, decision-making and problem-solving models, and multivariate models (latent variable and causal modeling). The alternatives to modeling performance vary along three lines: (1) the specificity and complexity of the variables in the model; (2) the focus of the model (on performance outcomes or performance process); and (3) whether it is a model of ratee performance or rater judgment. Campbell suggests that trying to improve training may be fruitless if the assumptions of the human-factors modelers are adopted. It should be more profitable to assume that they are as skilled and as motivated as they can be and to focus attention on redesigning other aspects of the system. A second direction of research suggested by Campbell is a move from the conventional paradigm of examining intercorrelations among objective indicators of performance (and calling them performance factors) to the investigation of the underlying structure of performance through causal modeling of multivariate latent variables.

Dr. Naylor discusses three major problems using the simple expression that describes a performance variable (Y) in relation to other variables (X_1, X_2). First, a definition of performance must be established prior to modeling. The second problem is determining what X variables should be selected to describe performance. Third, Naylor urges that a purpose of the model be considered. That is, is it designed to predict performance, understand performance, or evaluate the performance? Naylor states that more improvements in the predictive models will be through process-oriented models.

My assigned task was to survey in some fashion the uses of models in psychology and to speculate whether these previous applications of modeling have useful implications for the conceptualization and measurement of job performance. Dealing with this topic, which was so easily agreed to in the distant past, quickly became an exercise in grabbing at straws, poking at windmills, or otherwise hoping for the best. Even finding an appropriate metaphor was difficult.

In lieu of any eye-catching conceptual, methodological, or metaphorical break-throughs, the current paper tries to do the following:

1. Outline a number of different ways that "modeling" and "performance" can be thought about and juxtaposed. The list is illustrative only, and is not meant to be a complete taxonomy in any sense. The object is to illustrate the futility of the *general* question, "Can performance be modeled?"

2. Offer some reasons why people are, or might be, interested in modeling performance.

3. Briefly discuss a variety of specific areas in which performance, or things related to performance, are modeled in some fashion.

4. Speculate about some of the implications of these previous modeling activities for the conceptualization and measurement of complex job performance.

A SERMONETTE

Before considering the topic itself, you must be inflicted with a bit of ax grinding. Some people, perhaps most, may already believe this, but for those who do not, consider the following argument. Much of the research effort in psychology in general, in organizational behavior in particular, and in job-performance measurement especially, has indulged in seeking what I want to call general answers to general questions. That is, a very general question is posed as if a general answer actually existed, if only it could be found. Questions about general laws of the mind (e.g., $_sE_R = {_sH_R} \times D$), general principles of learning, general statements of how people are "motivated," and whether ability or motivation is more important in determining performance fall in the category. Closer to home are the historical quests for *the* criterion and the search for *the* appropriate measure of organizational effectiveness (Campbell, 1979).

The last two examples seemed to incorporate in their history the implicit assumption that there is some measure of individual or organizational effectiveness that is better than all the others and that we must find it. Two things follow from such an assumption. First, there is a lost of guilt associated with not having found something approximating the best measure. Second, a number of less-than-fruitful kinds of research are generated. For example, for both individual and organizational performance, a frequent study has involved the collection of a number of potential performance measures and their subsequent factor analysis based on a sample of people or a sample of organizations. No general truths have emerged from these studies, and none will.

By implication the same is true, I think, of the question, "How should performance be modeled?" We should not dwell on it too long in this form. Specific kinds of models may be useful for specific reasons but performance as a singular entity cannot be modeled. To say it another way, we should not expect too much from one model or from one theory.

Lest you think we are "different" than other fields, or that yours truly is beating a straw person, Jenkins (1981) has made much the same argument for cognitive psychology, as has McGuire (1979) for social psychology.

WHAT IS "MODELING?"

Within its stricter meanings the term modeling usually refers to the simulation or representation of some system (e.g., a human being) such that the model will react to stimuli or inputs in such a way that it can be used to predict the responses or outputs of the real system. Thus there are football-field–sized models of the Mississippi river system that predict the effects of snow melt in Minnesota, computerized business games that reflect how sales and profits react to changes in pricing and R & D investment, and multiple regression equations that "capture" how individual decision makers will react to a specified array of information. Most such models are either physical or algorithmic, most of the models relevant for this conference fall in the latter category. However, it is not inconceivable that someone will build a physical human model to use in testing whether changes in machine design will facilitate or inhibit the performance of the individual within the system. Some robots already come rather close.

Within its broader meanings, the term *model* is often used in much the same way as the word *theory,* or as a verbal representation of how something works. Thus, for example, theories of person perception can be used to model how performance information is used by judges to make ratings of performance. Theories of problem solving and decision making also fall in this category.

There are a number of general purposes that modeling might serve. Models can be used to *predict* outcomes or behavior. They also may incorporate some broader goal of facilitating the *understanding* of behavior. That is, the emphasis may be on understanding the process rather than on predicting the outcome. Also, models might be used to facilitate equipment or software design. Finally, they could be used as heuristic devices to suggest the most relevant future research in a particular area.

The purpose of the current chapter corresponds to none of the preceding. The purpose here is to examine selected previous work on modeling to see if it provides any guide for how job performance should be conceptualized and measured.

WHAT "PERFORMANCE" IS TO BE MODELED?

A central question for everyone at this conference is what is performance? It has been a central question at many similar conferences through the years. One implication of looking at the literature on modeling is that there are many "performances" and we should be mindful of the variety of things that might be modeled and how disparate some of them are.

For a number of investigators (e.g., Bilodeau & Bilodeau, 1969), the performance to be modeled is a very precisely measured result of a carefully specified psychomotor activity, such as time on target for two-handed tracking behavior. For others it is a reasonably well specified *choice* that must be made in a decision-making situation (e.g., Huber, 1980). For still others, it is the *process* that scientists or engineers use when trying to solve a specific technical problem (e.g., Johnson, 1980). An even more disparate focus would be the attempt to model the cognitive processes of the observer (rater) of someone else's performance as the observer responds to the request to "rate the performance of employee A."

Two things seem noteworthy about these examples. First, the performances to be modeled are qualitatively different and not easily related to one another. Nevertheless they are all legitimate domains of inquiry as regards the performance of people in jobs. Second, nobody has tried to model job performance as total job performance. We must deal with performance modeling in bits and pieces, and perhaps wisely so.

However, it also seems reasonable to assume that the central focus of this conference is on complex job performance. Consequently, for example, there should be considerable interest in the implications of human-factors models of specific psychomotor performance (e.g., two-hand tracking) for the investigation of complex job performance (e.g., the *job* performance of an airline pilot or an electronics maintenance specialist). However, the reverse is not true. We are not at the moment interested in how problems and issues associated with measuring complex job performance can be used to illuminate research on specific psychomotor behaviors, such as two-handed tracking. To say it another way, the current task is *not* to give advice to people studying psychomotor performance, decision making, problem solving, information processing, and the like. Rather, it is to consider what they do in terms of how it might help the study of performance, as "total" job performance. The remainder of this paper talks as if a number of the problems attendant to performance assessment did not exist. That is, it is obvious that the purposes for which performance appraisal is to be used, the political context in which it is done, and the motivational contingencies operating in a specific situation have a pervasive effect on what happens. Hold those issues at arm's length for a bit. They have been thoroughly discussed in previous papers. The following discussion is based on the assumption that the performance measures under consideration are to be used for research purposes.

SOME PERFORMANCE-MODELING POSSIBILITIES

This list of alternatives for performance modeling uses a very liberal definition of modeling. It includes modeling as theorizing as well as modeling as physical or mathematical representation. There are no necessary relationships among the various examples. They do not form some hierarchical taxonomy. They are simply some possibilities. The examples vary from things as specific as models of tracking performance using a pursuit rotor, to things as complex as computer models for playing chess, to models of problem solving in engineering, to models describing the bases of a specific medical diagnosis. Simple or complex though they are, most of these variables are major components of certain kinds of jobs; in that context, they should hold our interest.

The examples also vary in terms of whether the model represents the outcomes of performance (e.g., a statistical distribution of "errors" or reaction times) on the processes of performance (e.g., the heuristics used by chess masters).

Finally, it is important to make a distinction between models of ratee performance and models of rater judgment. After dwelling on problems of halo, leniency, and central tendency for so long, we are only beginning to appreciate the complexities involved in the perception and evaluation of one individual's performance by another.

1. What phenomena or characteristics of the individual are the subject of the modeling effort?
2. What form does the model take—that is, what does it look like?
3. What are the hoped for, expected, or actual payoffs from the model? That is, why use such a model? Has it done anything for us?

The last section of the paper considers how ideas generated by these modeling efforts might be further pursued in the study of performance in organizations.

HUMAN FACTORS

Perhaps the richest history of modeling in our field is in the domain of psychomotor performance, both from the point of view of basic research in learning and performance measurement and from the perspective of more applied work in human factors and engineering psychology (Alluisi & Morgan, 1976).

I have been away from human factors and engineering for over 20 years, but a brief reexamination suggests that the work in human factors virtually always conceives of an individual as an *operator* in a person/machine system. A person without a machine system to operate is of little concern. Given the focus on the individual as operator, the concentration is on modeling the functions of the operator or the errors committed by the operator.

As regards the former, there are perhaps three principal functions that are the subject of modeling: the operator as a processor of information, the operator as a decision maker, and the operator as a control mechanism (e.g., Sheridan & Ferrell, 1974).

The Operator as a Processor of Information

Think of an operator in a person/machine system before he or she decides on a course of action, or makes a move. In this state the operator is receiving information, filtering it, coding it, storing it, performing transformations upon it, retrieving it, and perhaps emitting it, such that the output is in a different form than the input (e.g., Howard Cosell looks at the action on the field and describes it verbally). The possible functions of the operator (e.g., as described by Fitts & Posner, 1967) are to *reduce* the amount of information, or to *augment* it, or to *transform* it, or to leave it the same, and then *transmit* it. Modeling by human-factors specialists usually involves the tranformation/transmitting process and the usual aim is to maximize the efficiency of the human operator in terms of the amount of information that can be transmitted per unit time.

As noted by Palermo at this conference there has been much recent work by experimental psychologists studying cognitive behavior that has tried to model cognitive processing dealing with attention, pattern recognition, coding, storing in memory, retrieving, and the like. Human-factors models add to this a consideration of the information transmitting and/or receiving capabilities of the machine system and how they are matched with the characteristics and capabilities of the human operator. Information theory a la Weiner and Shannon (Shannon & Weaver, 1963; Weiner, 1961) is perhaps the most important formal component of such system models.

Given the information-sending characteristics and/or the information-receiving requirements of the system, modeling attempts to generate the questions we need to ask about the individual and the equipment so as to allow the system to work at some specified level of efficiency.

If the information requirements of the machine system are beyond the capacities of the operator, then the system must be redesigned. If the information requirements of the machine system are below the capabilities of the operator, then there is room to upgrade the equipment. For all such design problems the research literature in cognition is the primary source for describing the information-processing capabilities of individuals.

The Operator as a Decision Maker

Going beyond a consideration of processing and transmitting information is the consideration of the operator as a decision maker. The aim here is to model choice behavior. For the human-factors specialist there is lots of choice behavior to be modeled and most of the decision models with which we are familiar have been used. For example, there are instances in which the risks are known and the various outcomes can be assessed. The classic utility model then applies. The subjective expected-utility model and particularly the signal-detection model also find wide usage. Currently there is considerable argument as to whether signal detection is an appropriate model for vigilance tasks (Long & Waag, 1981).

Another frequent problem here is modeling the determinants of reaction time in choice situations. For many person/machine systems, an accurate picture of decision latency is crucial.

The Operator as a Manual Control Mechanism

After information has been generated, processed, and transmitted, and after the information has been used to make a choice in a decision-making framework, the person/machine system must actually act and then take further action on the basis of the consequences of the first action. The dynamics of the human operator as part of the action/consequence/feedback/further-action cycle are frequently conceptualized as a servomechanism—the household thermostat is the classic example—and modeled by appealing to the engineering of control systems. Control-systems engineering is a major domain of research and practice in engineering and there is a large literature dealing with taxonomies of control problems, the type and number of parameters that are necessary to make the model "fit," the form of the functions describing the relationships among variables, and the necessity of "noise" or error components. The usual aim is to represent the control system as a system of differential equations. Thus certain portions of these models look familiar because a frequent objective is to minimize the "noise" factor at a certain point via the least-square criterion. What makes these models more than a set of equations designed to produce optimal regression weights are the feedback loops that close the system and that require continuing actions on the part of the operator to keep the state of the system (e.g., oil pressure) and/or the output (e.g., speed) within certain specified limits.

Mechanical servomechanisms have certain components and perform certain functions, depending on their complexity and sophistication. For example, both a household thermostat and the equipment that can land a plane automatically in bad weather qualify as control systems. One is just more complicated. The way they handle information and specify action is represented mathematically. The attempt is to model the human operator in an analogous fashion. The operator must observe, process information, decide on a course of action, take action, observe the consequences, process the feedback, decide on next action, and so on. Parameters such as delay, gain, lag, damping, and so on, are important components in the model. For example, when trying to model a bicycle operator, there are two control loops: (1) the movement of the handlebars around the vertical axis and; (2) the movement of the bike frame and lower body around the horizontal axis. There is a *delay* in perceiving the movement of the bike away from the criterion standard. The processing of this information must, however, show some *gain* (i.e., be faster than the movement of the bike away from the criterion). Once information is processed and a course of action decided upon, there is a *lag* associatied with the execution of the corrective movement. Finally, the oscillations about the axis must be *damped* such that they become smaller and smaller until brought into the acceptable range. If these and other parameters can be modeled successfully, then the performance of the operator (rider), given a bicycle of a certain size and a particular forward speed, can be predicted.

Notice that for this, as well as for other human-factors problems, performance outputs must be defined very carefully and measured reliably. It must be possible to specify clearly the performance standard, or criterion, against which deviations or errors can be judged. If such criterion measures cannot be found, then the operator cannot be modeled. There is a moral here someplace.

Also, besides achieving compatibility between the information requirements and transmission capabilities of the operator and the system, the characteristics of the feedback loops must be matched with requirements or characteristics of the operator's response. For example, if the response has a considerable delay, feedback should not be too early. The objective is to provide information at the optimal time for response correction (Jagacinski, 1977).

Models of the Dependent Variable

The performance (i.e., criterion) model incorporated by the conventional wisdom in industrial and organizational psychology might be portrayed as a normally distributed continuous variable that reflects the degree of individual contribution towards the organization's goals. For some purposes in a number of situations, this may be a very reasonable model (e.g., when determining which manager to promote to vice-president).

In contrast, the performance of an operator in a person/machine system is often portrayed by human-factors specialists as a distribution of errors, or deviations from a standard. Now, if errors are a rare event in a particular situation, then the normal distribution no longer applies and, for example, a poisson distribution may be a more descriptive statistical model. Besides their relative frequency, a crucial consideration is how an error is defined and how the errors made by an individual are indexed. In some situations errors may be discrete events (e.g., the ball touches the ground or it does not) and the error index is simply the frequency of these events. In most situations it gets more complicated. Consider the task of driving a car down the center of a traffic lane. Good performance is defined as minimizing the deviations from the line down the center. However, deviations of several inches (e.g., up to 12) may matter not at all. It might be stipulated that deviations of 12 inches or less are not counted as errors (i.e., receive a zero weight). At the other extreme, deviations of 5 feet or more are never the result of normal operator error and thus should not be counted in the index of operator performance. Within the 12-inch to 60-inch range, the objective is to enhance performance so as to minimize errors. But what should the error index be? Sum of the absolute deviations? Sum of the squared deviations? Sum of the fourth power of the deviations? Considerations like these have led to conceptualizations such as the "target-tube" standard (Johannsen & Rouse, 1979), which implies that only deviations outside the tube should be counted as errors.

In any event, there has been much work in human factors devoted to the modeling of errors and perhaps some of this thinking would be useful for conceptualizing job performance. For example, suppose more attention were paid to identifying specific, important errors that should be avoided. Our measurement, selection, and training efforts might then be different.

Uhlaner and Drucker (1980) have argued that a tentative beginning has been made in this direction in the development of the Skills Qualification Test (SQT) in the military. The method attempts to provide descriptions of satisfactory performance on specific tasks. Failure to meet the standard could be viewed as an error. So far the SQT has been used more for diagnostic (i.e., identifying training needs) than for assessment purposes and not much research on the technique has been done. However, further research is on the horizon and it will be interesting to see the outcome.

In a sense, the entire domain of criterion-referenced measurement is oriented towards an error model of performance. To define specific levels of "mastery" in terms of the actual tasks or knowledge that must be demonstrated is to define a standard from which deviations can be noted. Because criterion-referenced measurement now carries with it a certain amount of theorizing about what reliability and validity mean and how a score should be defined (e.g., Linn, 1980), perhaps it would bear closer examination as an appropriate performance model for certain situations.

Implications of Human-Factors Modeling

Given this cursory look at human factors, perhaps we should pause and ask why it is at all useful to consider such topics. Are not the variables ecompassed by such carefully constructed models of person/machine systems several steps removed from the complex and messy notion of job performance with which we are concerned? Maybe yes and perhaps no. Consider the following points.

First, certain assumptions are made about the human operator that seem contradictory to our particular conventional wisdom. For example:

1. The operator is assumed to be reasonably competent and reasonably motivated. Thus emphasis on selection and motivation, which most of us hold so dear, is downplayed. It is the system that must adapt.

2. Similarly, training the operator to perform better is not really a consideration. The capabilities and limitations of the operator are taken as givens. Again,
achieving the system's objectives must be accomplished by machine design, not
by changing the human operator.

3. Performance must be defined very precisely such that deviation from the
standard can be measured and deviations can be attributed to machine limitations, operator limitations, or random error. Systematic biases not under control
of the operator or the machine must be excluded from performance.

Second, given at least these assumptions, suggestions such as the following
ing seem worthwhile:

1. We have to spend more time *stipulating* what the definition of performance shall be. Performance measures should not be developed by reviewing an
existing job situation, or by identifying possible criterion measures, or by sub-
jecting them to tests of relevance, reliability, and bias. People who know the job
and have the responsibility for managing it should stipulate what performance
should be. That is, the meaning of performance is not something to be "discovered"; it should be imposed.

2. If one individual is to judge the performance of another, there is no use
fighting against the limitations of human perception, information processing, and
memory. Forget about training raters. Rather, the system should be designed to
augment the capabilities of the human operator (i.e., performance rater). That is,
can the performance to be observed be systematically sampled and observed by
some means other than the operator? Can memory, storage, and retrieval be
taken over by some other subsystem? At the appropriate time, can a representative sample of the complete performance record be displayed for the judge or
rater? Techniques such as management by objectives and the detailed vita of the
academic are examples of such augmentations. However, they are still relatively
crude. How can we do better?

3. Thinking of the individual as part of a control system leads to certain other
kinds of implications. Much human-factors work is devoted to shortening the
time interval between the execution of the action and the feedback concerning its
consequences. For example, a missile is fired at a moving target but it will take
some time to reach the target and the operator will not know for a few seconds
whether the aiming response was accurate. Should he fire again? Additional
machine technology can be used to predict the accuracy of the shot and provide
more rapid feedback, within some margin of error. Can similar augmentation be
provided for more complex job tasks? The development of management-information systems is one example of such augmentation. What else might we do?

In general, if we want to apply human-factors modeling in larger contexts we
must think about how to get managements to define performance more com-

pletely, how to match the system characteristics to the operator characteristics, and how to further augment the system to enhance performance.

MODELING DECISION MAKING AND PROBLEM SOLVING

Decision making and problem solving are important components of many jobs. If the terms are interpreted broadly, then there is indeed a very large literature devoted to modeling problem-solving and decision-making behavior. Perhaps they are the best examples we have of substantive task components that can be modeled in such a way that the same model is useful and has a similar meaning across a wide variety of jobs.

Most of us are already aware of the major categories of such research and the major types of models that have resulted. Consequently, I would like to jump almost immediately into the current issues and consider the modeling of decision-making and problem-solving behavior, in that order.

Modeling Decision Making

Viewing decision making as choice behavior, we can make the usual distinctions between normative and descriptive models. Within the normative category, models can be distinguished by the way in which they define an optimal or a good decision (e.g., Min/Max, max/min, utility maximization, etc). Descriptive models can be divided into those that try to model the process (e.g., Subjective Expected Utility) and those that try to model the outcome (e.g., policy capturing).

To a considerable extent the history of modeling in these domains has been concerned with comparing what people do with what is defined to be optimal. For example, how do the probabilistic judgments of individuals compare to Bayes theorem? As a result of these research efforts, a number of human biases have been described. A partial list is as follows:

1. Tversky and Kahneman (1971) have shown us that all kinds of decision makers (including experts) commit the so-called *representativeness error* and believe that even small samples are highly representative of their respective populations.

2. Similarly, people overestimate the *reliability* of data (in the measurement sense) and often act as if measurement error does not exist. For example, forecasts of future events, based on fallible data, do not regress to the mean like they should.

3. Tversky and Kahneman (1973) also document the *availability bias* in which events that are more easily recalled (because of a higher associative

strength perhaps) are judged more likely, in contradiction to their actual likelihood.

4. People seem to possess stereotypes or "anchor judgments" for a wide variety of decision situations and additional information changes their anchor or stereotype only with great difficulty.

5. One specific variety of the preceding is the *conservation bias*. That is, it has often been shown that decision makers do not revise their judgments enough, on the basis of new information, as compared with the optimal revision rendered by Bayes theorem.

6. People tend to be *overconfident* about their judgments in the sense that their confidence judgments do not correlate with the extent of available information or with the accuracy or optimality of the judgment.

7. The *hindsight* error (Fischhoff, 1975) is a special case of overconfidence and refers to the overestimates people make of the accuracy with which they could have made a past decision, if only they had been asked to do so.

8. We should also not forget March and Simon's (1958) classic characterization of the human decision maker as a suboptimizer with limited proclivities for search behavior and strong preferences for the most easily quantifiable outcomes.

9. Related to the March and Simon notions are some of the results from policy-capturing studies that use some variant of Brunswick's lens model to determine what kinds of information actually have the greatest weight in decision making. In general, people seem to use far less information than is available. Further, the way in which information is combined is well described by the linear regression model. The configural combinations typically are not nearly so descriptive.

A comparison between descriptive and optimal models leads to a relatively direct conclusion that human beings are lousy decision makers badly in need of help. This conclusion had generated a great deal of work in *decision aids* such as the following:

1. The multiattribute utility modeling procedure (Huber, 1980) forces decision makers to be explicit about the outcomes that are relevant and about their relative utilities. The model then portrays the kind of decision that would be generated by an optimal combination of the elicited information (Edwards, 1962).

2. A number of firms market computer software that permits an explicit and rapid use of Bayes theorem to revise probabilities.

3. The Kepner–Tregoe training system (1965) certainly speaks to improving decision making via an exhaustive and detailed analysis of the various alternatives.

4. Modeling the actual decision-making behavior of the individuals to be aided via computerized policy-capturing techniques permits giving feedback as

to what was actually done and may reveal specific ways in which the decision-making behaviors of individuals could be enhanced.

So far, none of these decision aids has proven wildly successful (Einhorn & Hogarth, 1981; Slovic, Fischhoff, & Lichtenstein, 1977). However, a number of the people working in the area of behavioral decision models have begun to experience a more fundamental worry. That is, can we be so sanguine about our definition of optimal decision-making behavior and our condemnation of the ways in which individuals actually make decisions (Einhorn & Hogarth, 1981)? Perhaps what we formerly regarded as biases and shortcomings are really adaptive mechanisms that should be explored.

For example, although an individual decision rule may indeed be suboptimal if employed on a large number of occasions, in the context of a discrete event it may be the "optimal" thing to do. Bayes theorem, or regression models, assume that the system will remain stable over the long term. If it does not, then the formerly optimal is no longer optimal. Also an individual may know that feedback will be forthcoming and there will be a chance to correct the decision. Thus individuals know they can function as control systems and a nonoptimal decision that can be altered on the basis of feedback may protect against the small probability of a large loss early in the process. Finally, perhaps overconfidence is functional because it promotes action. People realize that checks and balances in the system will stop them from making really serious errors.

One major conclusion that seems to follow from the preceding is that we know very little about the processes by which people actually conceptualize and resolve choice situations. Difficult though it is, and Nisbett and Wilson (1977) notwithstanding, we need more descriptive research that focuses on the decision process. Perhaps we could better model decision behavior if we did not spend quite so much time in the laboratory comparing subjects' overt choices to standards of optimality derived from the conventional wisdom of normative decision making.

Problem Solving

Attempts to model various aspects of complex problem-solving behavior have, in contrast to research in behavioral decision making, made rich use of descriptive research and protocol analysis (Simon, 1979). Beginning in the 1950s, a frequent paradigm has been to generate written protocols of individuals working through prescribed problems and to use these protocols to aid in the construction of a computer program that models the cognitive processes of the problem solver. A considerable amount has been learned about the problem-solving process and work on this kind of modeling goes on at a fairly good pace (Simon, 1979).

What are the implications of this research for problem solving as a part of complex job performance? There is at least one major implication: When highly proficient and less proficient performances are compared, in terms of what is revealed by their protocols, there are significant and recognizable differences in the way problems are defined and structured, in the amount of information stored in memory, and in the processes by which solutions are searched for. One specific distinguishing feature is in the use of efficient heuristics by highly competent problem solvers and the inability of the novice to use simplifying heuristics to aid in defining the problem and searching for possible solutions (Newell & Simon, 1972).

Heuristics and scripts (Schank & Abelson, 1977) are also used by human-factors researchers to model such things as automobile driving. For example, Bekey and others (Bekey, Burnham, & Sev, 1977) talk about the "look-ahead" heuristic and the "finite-state" heuristic as a means for matching your speed to the flow of traffic. One involves focusing on the second and third car beyond the one you are following and the other requires a judgment as to the relative speed of your car versus the one directly ahead. Some heuristics are more effective than others and all are more effective than attempting to react continuously to the *distance* between your car and the one directly ahead.

It seems very possible that the investigation of job performance would benefit if the differences between good and bad performance were studied in terms of these controlling heuristics. What makes an effective manager different in this regard? What makes an effective electronics technician different from a less effective one? To the extent that a job has a significant problem-solving component, it can be studied via this approach.

A cognitive psychologist on my own campus is currently engaged in studying problem-solving performance in a variety of professions via this framework (Johnson, 1981). The general technique is to go to the people in the profession (e.g., engineering, internal medicine, law) and get them to help in developing prototypic case problems that can be expected to elicit job-relevant problem-solving behavior. After some pretesting to check the construct validity of the problem, a new sample of professionals is asked to work on the problem and to verbalize their thought processes as accurately as they can. The protocols are then content analyzed so as to describe the heuristics that were used. For example, one interesting finding is that very difficult problems in medical diagnoses are not solved consistently until the physician quits thinking in terms of: "Given a particular disease or condition, what are the symptoms?" and switches to "Given a symptom, with what disease(s) is it consistent?" This transformation seems not to occur until considerable professional experience has been acquired. The almost universal response of the knowledgeable, but inexperienced, types when told the answer (i.e., the diagnosis) was, "Oh, I knew that." Unfortunately, their heuristics did not let them assess their store of information in a useful way.

An Aside

I now offer my favorite heuristics for the problem-solving behavior of applied psychologists:

1. Before collecting any data, express in writing, very precisely, the ways in which the information will be used and what will be said or done as the result of the data coming out one way or the other.

2. If you find yourself beginning a study because you have mastered a technique and want to try it out, stop immediately and do something else.

3. If you discover yourself constructing a questionnaire to measure a self-perception of some kind, stop at once. Use a different method.

4. Use multivariate analyses only as a last resort.

5. If you are stuck on a problem, ask someone in a related area for advice. Do not spend all your time talking to people who occupy the same niche you do.

In part, these statements are based on personal bias, and I am sure you can add statements of your own. They are also consistent with some protocol data we have collected from a sample of established researchers (Campbell, Daft, & Hulin, 1981). Perhaps even the performance of applied psychologists could be improved by taking advantage of this kind of modeling and a more systematic study of our own heuristics.

MULTIVARIATE MODELS: LATENT VARIABLES AND CAUSAL MODELING

One domain of modeling that does deal with total performance is multivariate analysis as it pertains to the structural analysis of performance "scores." Historically, the factor-analytic model based on classical measurement theory has prevailed, and a total performance score can be viewed as made up of: (1) a score on the general factor plus error; or (2) the sum of scores on a set of group factors plus error; or (3) some combination of the two that forms a hierarchical solution. Regardless of which specific variant is used, the totality of performance is modeled as the sum of the scores on a set (sometimes equal to one) of latent variables (factors, constructs, etc.) that can be reflected only imperfectly by observable data. It follows from this kind of modeling that the latent structure of performance should be investigated and factor analysis has been the usual means by which this is done.

Recently, a new look has been given to the investigation of latent structure via the increased use of causal modeling and confirmatory analysis (Bentler, 1980; James, Mulaik, & Brett, 1981). For a given a set of imperfect observable indicators of performance (i.e., criterion measures), a specific latent structure is hypothesized as the explanation for the pattern of intercorrelations among the indicators). Both the latent variables and a specific set of causal orderings among them are hypothesized, which rules out performance models based on a simple sum of components. Some components may stand in causal relationships to one another. For example, proficiency on "motivating subordinates" may be caused by "proficiency at setting goals and planning work" because the lack of clear direction and guidance is the biggest deterrent to employee motivation (or so the theory might go). Further, certain features of the latent structure, such as the hypothesized number of latent variables, can be subjected to a statistical test for goodness of fit.

Now, we all realize that multivariate causal models and confirmatory analysis are quite demanding of data and cannot be applied willy-nilly. However, independent of the *test* of the goodness fit for the hypothesized latent structure, I believe this kind of performance modeling can have great benefit at the front end. It does us little good any more to proceed in an exploratory mode and factor a convenient list of available criteria or ratings in an attempt to "discover" basic performance factors. We need to sit down and *theorize* about the structure of performance. What are the elements in the structure, how are they interrelated, how are they ordered, how invariant should the structure be across jobs, and so on?

The preceding statement invites consideration who does the theorizing the source of theory about the structure of performance. To pose two alternatives, is it the investigators or the people in the organization (e.g., the management) who propose the theory? It is probably both. Certainly one of the primary reasons for the development of behaviorally anchored rating scales was to permit (force?) the relevant people in the organization to define the content of performance via the critical incident method. It is interesting that performance factors are defined operationally as observables, with the assumption that each scale will be virtually a direct isomorphic reflection of a latent variable. Thus the categories that hold up through retranslation are meant to reflect reasonably fundamental dimensions of performance. If there are nine such scales, then a subsequent factor analysis should show nine factors. Unfortunately, the construct validation of performance factors of any kind never seems to go beyond this. If fewer than nine factors appear, we quickly jump to questions of halo and leniency, and don't explore the latent structure any further.

Applying causal/confirmatory analysis leads to other benefits besides the initial theorizing. For example, an application to some of the existing data on performance measures may indicate that only one latent variable is needed to account for all these intercorrelation matrices. If, for example, we consider the measured criteria as the dimensions produced by the BARS procedure in a series of studies, there are at least three possible explanations for such a finding: (1) the management was fibbing when it said (via the scale development) that there are nine performance factors that are important; (2) the management may indeed perceive nine important performance factors but when asked to rate an individual on all nine, it can respond to only one; or (3) the people who described the incidents and developed the factors may believe there are nine factors, but in reality job holders operate along only one. One could design studies to investigate these or other alternative explanations and the use or the causal/confirmatory model would, I think, lead to even more interesting research questions about performance in the attempt to disentangle the alternative explanations.

COGNITIVE MODELS OF THE RATER

Research in cognition, personality, and social psychology has dealt increasingly with models of the individual as an observer and judge. Such models are extremely relevant for the study of performance rating. To grasp the enormity of such research, simply think of all the different kinds of performance judgments that are made every day in the United States and the economic, personal, and political consequences of these judgments. Now consider the portrayal of the process via models of person perception, information processing, attribution processes, and decision-making or probabilistic judgment. These models, as they portray the performance-rating process, were discussed at some length in other papers at this conference (e.g., Borman, this volume). Interested readers are also referred to Feldman (1981) for an introduction.

The composite picuture of the performance-rating process derived from these various sources seems dismal indeed. Consider the following abbreviated recitation:

1. It is probably the case that most raters have no clear idea of what aspects of "performance" to observe on a day-to-day (or period-to-period) basis. Performance is not articulated very well in most organizations. As a result, stereotypes, or other implicit theories within the rater, operate to direct the attention of the rater towards selected apects of an individual's performance.

2. The subordinate's performance is probably seldom sampled systematically or very extensively. Sampling error must surely operate with a vengeance.

3. The perception of the rater involves assignment of the individual to cognitive categories (e.g., "man," "good looking," "educated," etc.). The surplus meanings attached to these stereotypic categories (e.g., good-looking people are smarter) may color the way information about the ratee is coded for storage in memory.

4. Given the assignment of the potential ratee to a series of cognitive categories, the information acquired is then further encoded and "chunked" for storage in memory.

5. Selective decay occurs while information about the ratee is stored in long-term memory.

6. At some point a judgment is required and information must be retrieved. Retrieval is subject to a host of recency/primary effects and other associative biases.

7. The available information must be integrated and transformed to match the requirements of the rating task.

With so much opportunity for sampling, perceptual recall, and transformation errors, it is a wonder that performance ratings have any "validity" at all. However, the reasons for mentioning them here is not to become more discouraged. It is to reinforce the notion that the human judge has limitations, and to suggest that the rating task should perhaps try to accommodate to these limitations rather than to fight against them or make them worse. In a sense the rater can be viewed as the "operator" in a system and, as per much of the work in human factors, besides considering better selection and training of raters, we would again consider ways to match the system characteristics to their capabilities.

IMPLICATIONS FOR THE STUDY OF JOB PERFORMANCE

On the basis of this brief consideration of some modeling activities, what might be some suggestions for future directions? The following are offered.

Maybe we ought to give up on the whole notion of trying to find new and better ways to train raters. What if we adopted the assumption and strategies of the human-factors modelers and started from the premise that experienced people in an organization who understand the organization's goals and understand the basics of the appraisal task are about as skilled as they are going to get. Also, they are about as motivated as they are going to be. The leverage, then, is to be found in the redesign of other parts of the system. The system that provides performance information must better compensate for the information-processing limitations, perceptual biases, and memory limitations of the human perceiver and judge. The recent and expanding research on rating as a cognitive process and the renewed attempts to use theory and research from experimental cognitive and social psychology are all to the good. However, before using this sort of research to talk about training raters to reduce their biases, improve their sampling of observations, and so on, we should ask if there are also some engineering-type solutions to be pursued. For example, is there some way to virtually force raters to observe behavior more systematically and to produce fuller accounts of performance at shorter intervals and to store the information someplace besides in memory? Behavior-expectation scaling was intended to be a step in this direction, but it is by no means a comprehensive procedure for systematically collecting and storing information about job performance. Perhaps something like the following would be useful in some situations.

First, the major dimensions of performance would be defined and agreed upon. For example, I think the attempts to develop behavior-expectation scales for police officers have accomplished this for the job of entry-level police officer. There is considerable agreement across studies and across populations of judges (e.g., rank and file versus police management) as to what the major factors are (Campbell, 1976). Similarly, there is considerable consensus concerning the major performance areas within which academics in large research-oriented universities are to be judged.

A second step might be to provide a procedure whereby the incumbent periodically summarizes what he or she has done in each area. At the same time the supervisor summarizes the major errors or deviations that were observed. Both incumbent and supervisor are given the opportunity to file a rebuttal to the other's description. A third party then transforms all information to a standard form and it is computer stored. The reporting periods are determined at random but vary across a range appropriate for each particular job. Because the information is computer stored, it can be accessed in different ways depending on the purposes of a particular appraisal. For example, if the purpose is to make a promotion decision, the relevant information for all candidates can be retrieved as a single array. If a research study needs a criterion measure, then multiple judges could be used to read all the information for each person and to rate or rank all of them at the same time using a common data base.

In some situations such a procedure would die of its own weight but in others it might be quite feasible. Certainly there must be other procedures that could also augment the limitations of the rater. For example, the Delphi procedure could be used to provide feedback to raters (whether the data are supervisory, peer, or self-ratings). That is, a panel of raters would first provide individual assessments of a particular ratee. The assessments of each individual judge (rater) would then be made available to all judges, and everyone would be asked to make the assessment again. This would provide considerable feedback about what aspects of performance were missed that others documented, discrepancies from the modal response, consistency across raters, and so on. Supervisory, peer, and even self-ratings could be included in the same Delphi panel, or separate Delphi panels could be used. These and other variations could serve to build in a feedback or control system that would damp out many of the errors or deficiencies of individual operators (i.e., raters).

Now, all of this is not to ignore the importance of the rater's motivation and the contingencies under which he or she must operate. Almost any system can be sabotaged if the proper reinforcers for doing so are present. The motivational considerations should not be slighted, but neither should the engineering or technical considerations.

A second general redirection might result if we questioned our usual paradigm of searching for performance by looking at the surface covariations among a series of ratings or other available indicators. Examples of this "conventional" paradigm would be intercorrelating a number of "objective" indicators, doing a principle-components analysis, and thereafter talking about factors of performance. Similarly, a frequent strategy is to intercorrelate ratings of nine to twelve dimensions, find the one, two, or three factors that explain the correlations, and then speak of these as performance factors.

I have mentioned at least two possible alternatives to this view:

1. We could further pursue the underlying structure of performance via the causal modeling of multivariate latent variables. I am not particularly optimistic that if we apply these models to existing data we will learn very much from the actual statistical tests of whether a particular model fits the data. In many cases in

which a model is applied, the data do not seem to be up to it (e.g., too much unreliability, too much artifactual correlation, too little correspondence between the theory being tested and the measures themselves, etc.). However, the payoffs might come from: (1) the demands such models make for an a priori theory of what explains how the measured variables are intercorrelated in terms of latent variables and; (2) the further investigation of the latent variables as constructs in a construct-validity frame-work. We have never really applied construct valida-tion explicitly to the study of complex job performance, but it deserves to be a research program in its own right.

For example, suppose we proposed two competing explanations of manage-ment performance. To simplify things, consider only two latent variables, the skill with which managers build sound interpersonal relationships among their subordinates and between themselves and their subordinates, and the skill with which they identify goals and set priorities. One explanation says that sound interpersonal relationships must be developed before goal specification can be successful. The second view says that subordinates must have a clear idea of what they are supposed to do and an understanding of what the organization is about before they can seriously attend to interpersonal relationships.

I chose this example to illustrate that using a questionnaire measure of consid-eration and initiating structure in a survey, and submitting the data to a path analysis, is not the way to proceed. We should think of a variety of ways these two latent variables could manifest themselves and we should use a number of studies to explore the process by which one phenomenon might facilitate an-other. Only by an active and multifaceted program of construct validation can we begin to approximate the meaning of the latent variables and discern their causal orderings, if any. A specific path-analytic model may indeed never be tested.

2. A second alternative is to borrow again from the human-factors side of the business and really expand our efforts to develop strategies for *stipulating* what performance should be. The basic assumption is that the definition of what performance should be is necessarily an expert judgment. Consequently, such judgments must be articulated in such a way that they constitute a detailed description of what performance means in a particular situation and how good from bad performance is to be distinguished. At this point the models to apply are scaling models and it is the consistency, completeness, and so on, with which such judgments are made and scaled that are of interest. Scale development in behavioral-expectation scaling is a step in this direction, but it does not go very far. Alternative methods and multiple groups of judges are not used, judges are not really faced with the task of developing a complete definition of perfor-mance, and so on. In general, a lot more of the judgments of the relevant parties (e.g., management) must be investigated before we can arrive at a more usable definition of performance. For example, managers could be asked to describe very complete scenarios of how good, bad, and mediocre performers deal with major tasks or problems. Consistency across such expert judges could be check-ed. In a kind of retranslation step, additional judges could rate the scenario in

terms of the level of performance they think is represented and they could further describe any extenuating circumstances under which a particular script would represent a more effective or ineffective thing to do.

In essence, the suggestion here is to have managers participate in a very thorough criterion-referenced test-development procedure (Linn, 1980) such that a fairly complete description of what good performers would do is provided.

Perhaps it would be wise to go even further and do a comprehensive analysis of "errors" as in human-factors research. That is, a taxonomy of errors could be developed for a particular position, say personnel administrator, and then descriptive data could be collected on job incumbents over a relatively long period of time to refine the taxonomy and select the better methods of error observation. Although this does take a rather attenuated view of performance (i.e., it focuses on the negative rather than the positive), it also provides an easier measurement task and should generate a good deal of leverage with which to improve performance. After all, performance then becomes analogous to tracking behavior and the object is to damp out the deviations from the standard.

The preceding recommendations are not meant to be a complete list by any means. Nor are they necessarily internally consistent or well integrated. But this is symptomatic of things as they should be. Performance modeling should not attempt to be a singular and well-integrated strategy. A number of strategies should be pursued by researchers with different theoretical and value orientations. Some people hate multivariate models, others worship them. Some people want to discover the meaning of performance, others want to impose it. Some people believe subjective ratings are no damn good, others believe objective measures are just subjective measures at least one step removed, and so on. For the foreseeable future, at least, there is much to be gained from this diversity. It should be nurtured.

REFERENCES

Alluisi, E., & Morgan, B. Engineering psychology and human performance. In L. Porter & M. Rosenzweig (Eds.), *Annual review of psychology* (Vol. 27). Palo Alto: Annual Reviews, 1976.

Bekey, G., Burnham, G., & Sev, J. Control theoretic models of human drivers in car following. *Human Factors*, 1977, *19*, 399–413.

Bentler, P. M. Multivariate analysis with latent variables: Causal modeling. In L. Porter & M. Rosenzweig (Eds.), *Annual review of psychology* (Vol. 31). Palo Alto: Annual Reviews, 1980.

Bilodeau, E. A., & Bilodeau, I. (Eds.). *Principles of skill acquisition.* New York: Academic Press, 1969.

Campbell, J. P. *The assessment and prediction of police performance: A review and critique.* Report to the Metropolitan Council, St. Paul, Minnesota, 1976.

Campbell, J. P. On the nature of organizational effectiveness. In P. Goodman & H. Pennings (Eds.), *New perspectives in organizational effectiveness.* San Francisco: Jossey-Bass, 1979.

Campbell, J., Daft, R., & Hulin, C. *Problem finding and problem formulation in organizational research.* Paper presented at the APA Division 14 Conference on Innovations in Methodology, Greensboro, N.C., March 1981.

Edwards, W. Dynamic decision theory and probabilistic information processing (PIP). *Human Factors,* 1962, *4,* 59–73.

Einhorn, H., & Hogarth, R. M. Behavioral decision theory. In L. Porter & M. Rosenzweig (Eds.), *Annual review of psychology* (Vol. 32). Palo Alto: Annual Reviews, 1981.

Feldman, J. Beyond attribution theory: Cognitive processes in performance appraisal. *Journal of Applied Psychology,* 1981, *66,* 127–148.

Fischhoff, B. Hindsight—forsight. The effect of outcome knowledge on judgment under uncertainty. *Journal of Experimental Psychology: Human Perception and Performance,* 1975, *1,* 288–299.

Fitts, P., & Posner, M. *Human performance.* Belmont, Calif.: Brooks/Cole, 1967.

Huber, G. P. *Managerial decision making.* Chicago: Scott, Foresman, 1980.

Jagacinski, R. A qualitative look at feedback control theory as a style of describing behavior. *Human Factors,* 1977, *19,* 331–347.

James, L., Mulaik, S., & Brett, J. *The logic of causal analysis: Conditions for modeling and testing causal hypotheses with naturally occurring events.* Workshop presented at the APA Division 14 Conference on Innovations in Methodology, Greensboro, N.C., March 1981.

Jenkins, J. J. Can we have a fruitful cognitive psychology. In H. E. Howe, Jr. & J. H. Flowers (eds.) *Nebraska symposium on motivation.* Lincoln: University of Nebraska Press, 1981.

Johannsen, G., & Rouse, W. B. Mathematical concepts for modeling human behavior in complex man–machine systems. *Human Factors,* 1979, *21,* 733–747.

Johnson, P. *The assessment of professional competence.* Paper presented at the Minnesota Proseminar, Minneapolis, May 1980.

Johnson, P. M. The assessment of professional competence. Paper given at the Minnesota Industrial/ Organization Psychology Proseminar. University of Minnesota, Mpls., June, 1981.

Kepner, C., & Tregoe, B. *The rational manager.* New York: McGraw-Hill, 1965.

Linn, R. Issues of validity for criterion referenced measures. *Applied Psychological Measurement,* 1980, *4,* 547–562.

Long, G., & Waag, W. Limitations on the practical applicability of C and B measures. *Human Factors,* 1981, *23,* 285–290.

March, J., & Simon, H. A. *Organizations.* New York: Wiley, 1958.

McGuire, W. J. *Toward social psychology's second century.* Paper presented at the American Psychological Association Convention, New York, September 1979.

Newell, A., & Simon, H. *Human problem solving.* Englewood Cliffs, N.J.: Prentice-Hall, 1972.

Nisbett, R., & Wilson, T. Telling more than we can know: Verbal reports of mental processes. *Psychological Review,* 1977, *84,* 231–259.

Schank, R. C., & Abelson, R. Scripts, plans, goals, and understanding. Hillsdale, N.J.: Lawrence Erlbaum Associates, 1977.

Shannon, C. E., & Weaver, W. *The mathematical theory of communications.* Urbana: University of Illinois Press, 1963.

Sheridan, T. B., & Ferrell, W. R. *Man–machine systems: Information, control, and decision models of human performance.* Cambridge, Mass.: MIT Press, 1974.

Simon, H. A. Information processing models of cognition. In L. Porter & M. Rosenzweig (Eds.), *Annual review of psychology* (Vol. 30). Palo Alto: Annual Review, 1979.

Slovic, P., Fischhoff, B., & Lichtenstein, S. Behavioral decision theory. In L. Porter, & M. Rosenzweig Eds.), *Annual review of psychology* (Vol. 28). Palo Alto: Annual Reviews 1977.

Tversky, A., & Kahneman, D. The belief in the law of small numbers. *Psychological Bulletin,* 1971, *76,* 105–110.

Tversky, A., & Kahneman, D. Availability: A heuristics for judging frequency and probability. *Cognitive Psychology,* 1973, *5,* 207–232.

Uhlaner, J., & Drucker, A. Military research on performance criteria: A change in emphasis. *Human Factors,* 1980, *22,* 131–139.

Weiner, N. *Cybernetics* (2nd ed.). New York: Wiley, 1961.

Modeling Performance

James C. Naylor

When I first learned that John Campbell had agreed to discuss performance modeling, I admired him for his courage but doubted his sanity. After seeing the results of his efforts I congratulate him for being able to make possible an utterly impossible task. Trying to impose sense and order on the performance-modeling literature is a bit like trying to walk across a muddy field on a pair of stilts. You can see where you want to go but it is unlikely that you will get there.

What is so very treacherous about the topic of performance modeling is that at first blush it seems so deceptively simple. Essentially, all we are trying to do in modeling performance is to take some performance variable, Y, and express its relationship to certain other variables $(X_1, X_2, \ldots X_K)$. Thus we can express our goal in very straightforward terms as an interest in the general statement

$$Y = f\{X\}$$

where Y = performance variable
$\{X\}$ = variables that may influence Y
f = form of the influence relationship.

As Campbell has so aptly pointed out, however, the difficulties hidden by this simple statement begin to be immediately apparent as soon as one begins asking a number of necessary questions.

WHAT Y ARE WE TRYING TO MODEL?

When we talk about performance, just what, exactly, do we mean? This question is particularly difficult to cope with when we are dealing with the complex behavior that is typical in most work environments.

299

It is certainly not easy to find appropriate Y measures in many types of jobs. This issue is actually the age-old criterion problem to which Campbell referred. He suggests that the Y problem is not best solved by using some form of job or task analysis but rather by asking the people who are accountable for the activities of the job incumbents whose performance is to be measured and modeled. I particularly liked his comments on this issue because I think that many of us, including myself, often let ourselves lose sight of this very important issue.

It may be a challenging academic and scientific probelm to isolate and identify the basic behavioral dimensions of a task. It may be even more challenging to develop a way of combining these measures into some exciting composite. But, in most jobs, performance is a construct in the eye of the beholder, usually a superior, and may actually bear little resemblance to the aforementioned composite derived from task analysis. I agree wholeheartedly that performance—the Y variable—should be imposed rather than discovered! One only has to look at the endless search for fundamental performance dimensions such as that carried out by Fleishman (1954) to grasp the futility of that approach to determining Y.

WHAT X'S ARE WE TO CHOOSE TO MODEL?

Traditionally the dominant population from which our X's have been selected has been the population of environmental and task characteristics. This has been particularly true in attempts to model performance in certain basic psychological-process areas, such as perception, motor skills, information processing, decision making, and choice behavior. Campbell correctly pointed out that modeling efforts in these areas have been much less inclined to sample X's directly from the individual-difference (ID) domain or even from those variables that influence IDs, such as training.

I believe, that the explanation for this somewhat one-sided approach to the selection of X's is to be found in the f term of our original model. When we say that Y is a function of X, we usually have an implicit understanding that causality pertains—that Y is influenced by X, rather than just being associated with or covarying with X. Because nearly all ID variables are not subject to manipulation but only to observation, it is really not appropriate to use them in a functional statement implying causality, which is what the research on basic performance processes is all about.

Certainly in those instances in which true functionality is not the intent of the model, we see many ID X's included: The massive and confusing literature involving factor-analytic models of behavior is an all-too-depressing illustration of this type of performance modeling.

Can I offer any underlying principles concerning the selection of X's? Perhaps, but to do so we first need to move to the final element of our simple model.

WHAT KIND OF A FUNCTION DO WE WANT?

Much of Campbell's paper deals with this most complex of questions. It is in our consideration of f that we must face the issue of why we want to model in the first place, because that question and its answer will dictate how we seek an anwer to f. It seems to me that one can define three different kinds of objectives that might be served by modeling Y. Perhaps there are others, but these three seemed to encompass all the modeling efforts with which I am familiar.

DO WE WANT TO SIMPLY PREDICT Y?

In cases in which prediction itself is the dominant intention of the modeler, the desired function has two primary characteristics. First, it should fit the data as well as possible in the sense of explaining the maximum amount of Y variation. Second, it should be parsimonious in the sense of using the least number of parameters it needs to accomplish the first objective.

Pure prediction models have been with us since primitive humans first learned to use the associations between observed events as predictive aids. In I/O psychology the entire field of selection and placement research has epitomized the use of the purely predictive model.

The outstanding characteristic of the purely predictive model is its pragmatism. One need not worry whether the f represents any meaningful underlying process. Its sole purpose is to "capture" the process as totally as possible. An example from my own modeling work, which is a perfect illustration of predictive modeling, is the work we did in the 1960s and 1970s on policy capturing (e.g., Naylor & Carroll, 1969). In study upon study, we examined our ability to capture the judgment performance of people using different types of Y's and different sets of X's. These studies and those like them in other fields (such as modeling complex tracking performance) clearly demonstrated the power of the simple linear model to capture performance variance. Further, they certainly provided insights into what things (X's) influence performance. But what is important to remember is that they told us little or nothing about the psychological process *underlying* performance. The truth is that we probably gained more *psychological* insight into how people make judgments from talking to our subjects after the research was over than we did from our beautiful equations. Campbell has discussed this point, mentioning our need to go beyond the model to examine the process.

Do We Want to Understand Y?

Here our focus becomes the nature of f. We want f to represent the psychological process by which the X variables influence, determine, or even create Y. Thus the nature of the objective usually means that f is imposed by the observer, rather than being derived directly from the data. I think several examples from early psychophysics can serve to illustrate this type of modeling. Consider Weber's historic law $\Delta S/S = K$. This function, empirically derived, was actually not a performance model of any type because performance is not represented in the functional statement. However, when Fechner took Weber's law and postulated equal sense distances such that Just Noticeable Differences were psychologically equivalent experiences wherever they occurred on the response continuum, he gave us his famous $R = K \log S$, a functional statement between behavior and a stimulus variable. This *was* an attempt to understand the basic psychological process. Similarly, when Thurstone asked the psychological question of how one makes comparative judgments among stimuli, he postulated stimulus–response excitation distributions that permitted him to derive his historic Law of Comparative Judgment:

$$\bar{R}_1 - \bar{R}_j = Z \sqrt{s_1^2 + s_2^2 - 2r_{12}s_1 s_2}.$$

This too is a classic example of a model of a particular kind of performance derived in an attempt to understand a process that is based upon certain a priori assumptions about the process itself.

Campbell dealt briefly with this type of modeling in his paper. He referred to it as seeking general answers to general questions. I am not certain from his comments whether he approves of models for this purpose or not.

Models for understanding are very difficult to deal with because they can never be proved or disproved. Rarely in psychology or in any science are we able to totally validate a model, and the more complex the type of behavior are we trying to understand, the more impossible it becomes to validate. Although we can often test one model against another, such tests are obviously relative and not absolute. Generally we use such models because they are the closest we are ever going to get to systematically describing psychological processes and they also make us feel more comfortable about our ability to understand behavior and performance. Perhaps this latter reason is sufficient justification by itself.

Do We Want an Evaluative Model?

The third major objective of performance models is that of evaluation. Here the model's purpose is to provide a standard of performance against which the individual's behavior may be compared. They are normative models intended to represent what people should do as opposed to what they actually do. They are models of optimality. They are prescriptive rather than descriptive.

Examples of evaluative models are numerous. In judgment research we have such examples as Bayes' theorem, decision trees, linear programming, and dynamic programming. The linear model representing the ecological side of the

Brunswik lens model is an ideal example of an evaluative model. On a more macro level, we have prescriptive performance models in such forms as the Managerial Grid and the Vroom-Yetton Leadership Model.

The dominant chracteristic of optimal models is that they require a concept of a true correct behavior. You cannot construct a model for an optimal Y unless you have some clear way of specifying what Y is optimal. Sometimes it is easy to do this and sometimes it is not easy at all. For example, if I am interested in troubleshooting performance on some type of equipment I can easily specify optimality—it is identification of the trouble. Further, I can build an optimal troubleshooting decision-tree model against which I compare actual performance.

In the case of more complex behavior the notion of optimality is often quite frustrating. Consider the behavior of teacher performance. We have been trying to solve the issue of what is good or optimal teacher behavior for over 50 years with little or no real success. Until we get a satisfactory definition of optimality we are kept from constructing any models that use it as a criterion and are thus left unable to construct any meaningful models for good teaching.

The real difficulty with optimal models is that they always require a value judgment. Someone, either an individual or "society," has to provide the answer to the question of what is good and what is bad performance. In complex work environments this is often very difficult to accomplish, as we all know.

With this brief taxonomy of models in mind, let me now turn to the question of what we can reasonably expect in terms of future developments of models of each type. These expectations will probably be as disappointing to you as they are to me.

In the case of both predictive and evaluative models, the future does not appear particularly exciting. All we can look forward to are: (1) further attempts to define and measure both Y observed (actual performance) and Y optimal; (2) the use of different sets of X's; and (3) occasional new developments in f that take us a bit beyond the basic descriptive and optimal models we now process. Catastrophe theory is a recent such development that comes to mind because it provided us with a mathematical model for discontinuous step-function processes that were not previously available.

In the case of process-understanding models the future is a bit more exciting. The recent network theory models of performance on simple reaction-time tasks used by Schweickert (1978) appear to be a major step into a new family of analytical models of cognitive processes. Tversky and Kahneman's (1981) prospect theory is another example more directly applicable to judgment and choice behavior.

A few final comments of a more or less random nature. It is my personal belief that future improvements in predictive models will most likely come from our ability to make substantive advances in process-type models. To do so, however, is exceptionally difficult. Thus research on process models has shown us that individuals only use a small part of the information available when they make judgments, but this amount varies greatly from person to person. They have also shown us that people only attend to, or see as important, certain kinds of stimuli, but that what is attended to varies substantially from person to person and from situation to situation. Process-model research has shown us that we typically process information in a sequential manner and that the specific sequence is very important to the resulting judgment. Unfortunately the sequence will vary from person to person and with the type of judgment called for. I could go on and on. So far we have been frustrated in our efforts to use this kind of knowledge in our predictive models for obvious reasons of complexity—the predictive model becomes so complex and expensive it just is not worth it when so often the simple linear additive model predicts so well.

A second feeling I have is that it may indeed be fruitful to spend more time asking people what they do as a precourse to modeling. I am pleased that in his paper Campbell has the same view. Bob Guion, in his paper, argued that subjects cannot tell us what they are doing, referring to the results obtained in policy-capturing research. These data consistently showed that a subject's stated order of variable use (or importance) usually failed to correspond to the actual magnitude ordering of the raw-score regression weights in their captured policy. It is important to realize, however, that this argument assumes that the regression equation truly represents what people were doing (the basic process) rather than simply being a best-fit predictive equation. In actual fact, when we have asked subjects in human-inference studies what they were doing, we often got highly complex arithmetic rules from our S's, such as $Y = \sqrt{(X_1)(X_2)}$, or $Y = Y_{t-1} \pm (Y_{t-1} - Y_{t-2})$, or even more complex rules. Even though the linear model $Y = b_1 X_1 + b_2 X_2$ ended up fitting their predictions quite well, the fact was, I am convinced, that: (1) the subjects were quite capable of telling me what they were doing and (2) it was not what we were modeling. I have never been accused of being a phenomonologist, but I do see merit in asking people to tell me what they are doing. It is up to us to then determine the usefulness of the information thus obtained. Some years ago on my sabbatical in Sweden, I was struck by the degree to which cognitive psychologists were employing the TAT, or Think Aloud Technique, in studying problem solving. Perhaps we should be more willing to use this tool in our research on process in models of performance.

In conclusion, I believe we should use models when they serve our needs, and ignore them when they do not.

REFERENCES

Fleishman, E. A. Dimensional analysis of psychomotor abilities. *Journal of Experimental Psychology*, 1954, *48*, 437–454.

Naylor, J. C., & Carroll, R. M. A test of the progression–regression hypothesis in a cognitive inference task. *Organizational Behavior and Human Performance*, 1969, *4*, 337–352.

Schweickert, R. A critical path generalization of the additive factor method: Analysis of a Stroop task. *Journal of Mathematical Psychology*, 1978, *18*, 105–139.

Tversky, A., & Kahneman, D. The forming of decisions and the psychology of choice. *Science*, 1981, *211*, 453–458.

IV
SOCIOPOLITICAL
CONSIDERATIONS

The definition and assessment of performance does not occur in a cultural vacuum. The value systems of managers, psychologists, and workers all play a role in the choosing of variables for examination and in the consideration of "feasible" administrative strategies. This section deals with some of these broader social, political, and philosophical considerations.

Locke considers the meaning of performance and reward in a capitalist, socialist, and mixed economy. Goldman presents a Marxist view of the role that performance evaluation and definition play in modern industrial environments.

12

Performance Appraisal Under Capitalism, Socialism, and the Mixed Economy

Edwin A. Locke

Dr. Locke contrasts the characteristics of three economic systems—capitalism, socialism, and the mixed economy—and lists the implications of each system for the performance evaluation process.

Under capitalism performance appraisal is based on the price system and profit system. Locke states that because capitalism is based on a merit system and rewards ability as valued on the market, the employer's errors in evaluation are self-correcting or at least self-limiting. The organization with poor evaluations will not do well financially.

Socialism, according to Locke, eliminates the economic foundation on which objective performance evaluation is based. Prices and wages are set arbitrarily under socialism and do not reflect voluntary transactions between the buyer and seller. The implications for performance appraisal are: There are no means of determining whether wages are too high or too low; there are no means or incentives for judging the effectiveness of the performance appraisal system; there is no protection for the worker (no market for fair wages and no alternative employers).

In a mixed economy, there is an unstable mixture of the advantages of capitalism and the disadvantages of socialism. In the private sector, evaluation is still based on merit (profit), though the workings of the market are limited by regulations; in the public sector performance evaluation is based on seniority and exam scores and is affected by politics.

De. Lerner raises two issues with Dr. Locke. She argues against Locke's implication that capitalism is based on utopian ideas concerning human rights. She also objects to Locke's vew that political systems are reducible to economic ones. She discusses the implications for performance evaluation, stating that evaluation is difficult in any modern society and impossible where utopian assumptions dominate (socialism). She describes egalitarianism as the most common utopian basis and discusses how it has been incorporated into selection and placement procedures in the past and the probability that it will be incorporated into performance appraisal.

Locke states, in response, that one's view of a utopian society depends on one's moral code; he believes that rational self-interest is moral and that altruism is immoral. He reiterates his belief that rights are inherent in the individual's nature as a rational being.

Performance evaluation is a key element of personnel management and is essential to organizational efficiency. However, the process of performance evaluation is profoundly affected by the political–economic system in which it occurs. In this paper I contrast performance evaluation or performance appraisal under three economic systems: capitalism, socialism, and the mixed economy.

For this purpose I make no attempt to distinguish between performance evaluation and job evaluation. In personnel management the former refers to the effectiveness with which an individual performs a specified job whereas the latter refers to the value of the job itself to the organization. These concepts, although distinguishable, represent two sides of the same coin. Both pertain to an appraisal of the value of work performed in an organization.

CAPITALISM

Let me begin by defining my terms. According to Rand (1967), *"Capitalism is a social system based on the recognition of individual rights, including property rights, in which all property is privately owned* [p. 19]." Observe that this definition is based on the concept of individual rights (Rand, 1967):

> A "right" is a moral principle defining and sanctioning a man's freedom of action in a social context. . . . *Rights* are conditions of existence required by man's nature for his proper survival. . . . The right to life is the source of all rights—and the right to property is their only implementation. Without property rights, no other rights are possible. Since man has to sustain his life by his own effort, the man who has no right to the product of his effort has no means to sustain his life. The man who produces while others dispose of his product, is a slave [pp. 321–323].

The need for the concept of rights stems from the individual's nature as a rational being. Individuals survive by the use of their minds, or more precisely, by acting on the judgment of their minds. To prevent people from acting on their own judgment is to negate their minds—that is, their reason.

Reason can only be negated by force, by interposing a gun between peoples' judgments and their actions. The use or threat of physical force does not literally stop people from thinking; it stops them from acting on the basis of their thinking—which amounts to the same thing.

The concept of rights prohibits the initiation of physical force or threat of force in social relationships. Rights are a moral concept. Because individuals have rights, it is wrong to initiate force against them. Force is wrong because it negates their means of survival.

Under capitalism all transactions between individuals are by voluntary consent and mutual agreement. Individuals deal with one another through trade rather than through force. For example, with respect to employment, both management and the employee have to agree before an employment contract is made. The government has no right to intervene in hiring or firing decisions or any other labor–management issue, (peaceful) dispute, or transaction. Unions are free to try to organize or to strike and companies are free to deal or not deal with the unions. Only the use of force (or fraud, which is a form of force) is prohibited. Neither side is free to use or threaten to use violence.

It is often asserted by critics of capitalism that the worker is at an unfair disadvantage in dealing with management because the worker is less wealthy, does not own any means of production, and may be in desperate need of a job; to use the common slogan, ''A hungry worker is not free.''

There are numerous errors implicit in this slogan. First, there is the implication that workers under capitalism will always be underemployed and on the verge of starvation. Under capitalism, no one who is willing to work will be without a job for long. Even when jobs are lost in one industry or area, they are created in others. If there is a temporary oversupply of labor, the price of labor will drop, leading towards full employment. Second is the implication that workers can be forced to take any job any employer wants to offer. Because no one has a monopoly on jobs, a worker who does not like what one employer offers can go to another. The prospective employee is free to shop around for the best possible deal. Third is the implication that capitalist employers will pay starvation wages. Actually, in a free labor market, it is in an employer's self-interest not to pay any less than the market wage. An employer who pays less will be unable to hire or retain employees; they will go to employers willing to pay the market wage. Fourth is the implication that real freedom means a guaranteed job. Freedom under capitalism does not mean and could not mean the guarantee of a job (or of job satisfaction; on the latter issue, see Locke, 1976). The right to property does not mean the right to force someone else to provide it. That would be slavery. Property rights refer to the right to *seek* property and to keep what is earned. In this respect the rights and risks of employer and employee are fundamentally alike. There is no guarantee that the employer will be able to find the needed employees, or that the product will sell, or that the company will make enough money to stay in business. The employer whose judgment is wrong may lose everything he or she owns.

Now consider the issue of racism. What if certain employers conspired (for economic reasons or due to shared prejudices) to give blacks only menial jobs despite better qualifications, and/or paid them lower wages than whites for doing the same type and quality of work? What would happen under a capitalist system?

As Dr. George Reisman (1982) has shown, the first result would be that companies who hired substantial numbers of black employees initially would make higher profits than companies that did not. Because they could get the same amount and quality of work done at less cost, they could price their product lower and sell more of it. The result would be that companies with few black employees would be forced to hire more black employees in order to become competitive. This would increase the demand for black labor, thus driving up its price. Ultimately the price differential for black labor would disappear to the degree that work quality was equal.

The identical argument could be made for discrimination against women under capitalism. To take an extreme example, suppose that women's wages were 20% below those of men doing the same work in a certain field. Any clever entrepreneur who decided to hire only women would immediately have 20% lower labor costs and would be able to make substantially higher profits than competitors who hired only men. This advantage would soon increase the demand for female employees in this field, thus driving up their wages. Eventually, if the quality of work were the same, women's wages would equal those of men.

It might then be asked why, in view of the preceding arguments, blacks and women have not achieved wages equal to those of white males in this country. A major reason is that blacks and females have simply not been available in very large quantities at the higher skill levels. Most blacks traditionally have not placed a very high value on education and most women, until recently, did not put a high premium on having careers. A second reason is that in the United States we do not have capitalism but rather a mixed economy. There are numerous ways in which the regulations and economic consequences of a mixed economy discourage upward mobility—for example, the public education system, which does more to destroy than to educate young minds; chronic inflation, which makes savings and long-range financial and career planning almost impossible; extensive regulation of business, which stunts economic growth; and high taxation, which inhibits investment, to name but a few.

The government has now tried to substitute force for the free market in hiring and wage determination through EEOC and other regulations. These are discussed in more detail in the *Mixed Economy* section of this paper.

The keys to understanding the relationship of capitalism and performance appraisal or performance evaluation are the price system and the profit system. Under capitalism the prices of goods and services, including the price of labor, are determined by supply and demand. For example, at the lowest skill levels (i.e., unskilled labor), the potential supply of labor is largest, because everyone in the labor force could perform such jobs. In contrast, only a small number of people can perform successfully at the professional level (e.g., law, medicine, Chief

Executive Officer). Because the supply of such people is limited, the wage level is higher than for jobs requiring less skill.

Because most people value money, they try to get the best salary they can, other things being equal (e.g., location, intrinsic satisfactions, etc.). Thus an employee who feels underpaid as a result of an unfair performance appraisal will tend to seek a better-paying job. The opportunity to change jobs provides a protection for the employee against unfair appraisals.

Now consider the same issue from the employer's (owner's, manager's) standpoint. To survive under capitalism companies must make a profit. That is, their income or revenue must exceed their costs of production. If a company fails to make a profit, it is prevented from expanding, because there will be no money for capital expenditures. Furthermore bank loans are hard to come by when a firm is losing money. Eventually, a firm running at a loss will not be able to meet day-to-day expenses and will go bankrupt.

To survive in the free market a company must control its costs. If a company overpays its employees in relation to their quality and quantity of production, compared to the market wage, its costs of production will rise above those of competitors. This will necessitate higher prices, which will result in lower profits and even losses. Thus firms have a vested interest in not paying above the market wage.

If, on the other hand, an organization underpays its employees in relation to the market wage, this will tend to lower the employees' motivation to produce and will increase the likelihood that they will quit and find other jobs. The owner or manager will then be faced with the cost of recruiting and training new employees. During this time the owner will have lower production from those remaining and from those who are new to the job. Furthermore it will be impossible to hire the most competent employees because they will prefer to take jobs with employers who pay more. All this will decrease work efficiency, increase costs, and lower profits. Thus companies also have a vested interest in not paying below the market wage.

It should be stressed that the effect of underpayment on profits will be especially serious when the employees being lost (or not hired) are highly competent ones. Highly competent employees produce more than less competent ones and are more difficult to replace because they are scarcer. It is also easier for them to find other jobs than the less competent employees, because they are capable of performing jobs that require less skill as well as those jobs that require more skill. Furthermore other employers prefer to hire more competent employees for a given job.

Thus there is a built-in incentive for objective performance evaluation on the part of owners and managers. It is in their self-interest to pay wages that are neither too high nor too low in relation to the market price. It is *their* profitability and *their* survival that is jeopardized if they make errors in evaluating their employees.

To quote economist Ludwig Von Mises (1944/1969):

No man is infallible. It often happens that a superior errs in judging a subordinate. One of the qualifications required for any higher position is precisely the ability to judge people correctly. He who fails in this regard jeopardizes his chances of success. He hurts his own interests no less than those of the men whose efficiency he has underrated. Things being so, there is no need to look for special protection for the employees against arbitrariness on the part of their employers. . . . Arbitrariness in dealing with personnel is, under the unhampered profit system, an offense that strikes home to its author [p. 37].

It should be added that the same principle applies to middle managers as to owners and top managers. Middle managers, like top managers, depend on their subordinates to help them perform their jobs. If they have incompetents working for them, their own performance will suffer, as will the evaluations that their bosses make of their performance.

Thus with respect to performance evaluation, under capitalism the employees' interests are protected in two different ways. From the employers' perspective there is a strong incentive to make fair evaluations; and from the employees' perspective, there exists a means of self-protection if their opinions about their work differ from those of their employers. It is in the employers' rational self-interest to pay the market wage and in the employees' rational self-interest to demand it.

It should be noted that it is in the interest of less competent and less skilled employees to be paid the market wage and not in their interest to be paid above it. If less competent or unskilled employees were paid the same or more than more competent or skilled ones, the costs of goods and services would be higher and the company would suffer losses. They would then have to cut costs, probably by laying off some less skilled employees. At the same time the less competent employees would suffer as consumers. If ability were not rewarded, they would be deprived of the things that more able employees might produce if they were motivated, and they would be prevented from buying goods at the lowest possible cost.

Consider, for example, the consequences of General Motors' janitors and other low skill employees' receiving the same salary as the company president and top executives. First, the Chief Executive Officer (CEO) and top executives would not be highly motivated to work (or to try to become CEO) because they could do just as well by being janitors. Second, the quality of leadership would suffer, as would product quality, so that the janitor would not even want to own a GM car. GM's competitors would be able to undersell GM, because their costs would be lower, thus causing GM to suffer greatly reduced profits and probably losses. In the end, the janitors would have to be laid off. Furthermore they would find it virtually impossible to find other jobs, because at this wage level nobody could afford to hire them; anyone who did hire at such wage levels would take a GM executive in preference to the janitors because the executive would do a better job. If this method of wage determination were applied throughout society, the cost of goods would skyrocket while the quantity and quality of production would plummet. Thus janitors who demanded and received CEO's salary for themselves and for every other janitor and unskilled worker in society would actually be hurting their own interests.

If this seems somehow unfair, consider the following from Rand (1967):

> In proportion to the mental energy he spent, the man who creates a new invention receives but a small percentage of his value in terms of material payment, no matter what fortune he makes, no matter what millions he earns. But the man who works as a janitor in the factory producing that invention, receives an enormous payment in proportion to the mental effort that his job requires of *him*. And the same is true of all men between, on all levels of ambition and ability. The man at the top of the intellectual pyramid contributes the most to all those below him, but gets nothing except his material payment, receiving no intellectual bonus from others to add to the value of his time. The man at the bottom who, left to himself, would starve in his hopeless ineptitude, contributes nothing to those above him, but receives the bonus of all of their brains. Such is the nature of the "competition" between the strong and the weak of the intellect [p.28].

Capitalism is a merit system from top to bottom. It rewards ability as demonstrated in action based on market value. Under capitalism errors in performance evaluation can and do occur, of course. A manager may be a poor observer of subordinate performance; or may not have sufficient information or may have unreliable information about subordinates; or may fail to recall all relevant facts pertinent to an employee's overall performance; or may not understand what good performance actually consists of; or may be riddled with envy and self-doubts and therefore threatened by subordinates with ability; or may be reeking with prejudices, stereotypes, and subconscious biases.

Such errors, however, are eventually self-correcting or at least self-limiting. Companies that have poor performance evaluation at all levels will suffer financially and will eventually fold. Those with mediocre evaluation systems (other things being equal) will be hard pressed by competitors with better systems, and will be forced to change or suffer further declines. To quote Von Mises (1944/1969), "The employer is not in a position to indulge in favoritism or in prejudice with regard to personnel. As far as he does, the deed itself brings about its own penalty [p.38]."

There are numerous historical examples of employees with creative and potentially profitable ideas whose abilities have been seriously underestimated by their employers. Many of them have quit their jobs and have taken their ideas to a competitors or even started their own companies. In some cases they have put their previous employers out of business (Collins & Moore, 1970).

As noted earlier, individual managers who are poor judges of other people's capabilities will find their own careers threatened. They are less likely to be promoted (and more likely to be fired) than those who are better judges of ability. This is an incentive for them to evaluate subordinates fairly if they are able and willing to do so, and limits the harm they can do if they are not.

It must be stressed that while under Capitalism there is an incentive to reward good performance, no employee can expect to receive perfectly objective performance appraisals effortlessly and automatically. Capitalism does not reward passivity, either on the part of the business owner or on the part of the employee. While employers need to appraise their employees, employees need to appraise their appraisers. If employees believe the appraisals to be unfair, they have to take steps to correct them or to change jobs or organizations in order to protect their own interests.

Observe that I have said nothing about the *rights* of employers and employees with respect to performance appraisal. This omission was deliberate. There are no special rights that apply to performance evaluation as such. Any rights involved are simply applications of property rights. This means that the employer may evaluate employees in any manner he or she so chooses, including the choice not to evaluate them at all. Similarly, employees may leave a job anytime they choose regardless of whether they agree with their bosses' appraisals or not. (In both cases I am assuming no breach of contract occurred.) Employment is by mutual consent. Neither side has the right to force the other to comply with their wishes on the matter. If either is in error, each must suffer the consequences.

SOCIALISM

Socialism, according to Reisman (1979), is *"an economic system based on government ownership of the means of production* [p. 147, based on Von Mises, 1966, p. 716–719]." All property is owned by the state. Individuals may or may not have the use of certain property, but only by permission; under socialism there are no property rights. The individual citizen exists only to serve the state. In return, the state claims or implies that it will provide for the needs and welfare of the citizens.

It should be noted that there are two different types or forms of socialism, what Von Mises (1962, 1966) calls the German or Nazi version and the Russian version (described also in Reisman [1979] based on Von Mises). The Nazi version (called National Socialism) allowed nominal ownership of property in the sense that there was no outright confiscation. But ownership was in name only, because the Nazis totally regulated the use of property. Extending the principles already accepted in the Weimar republic (Peikoff, 1982), the Nazis told business owners, for example, what to produce, how much to produce, where to send their production, whom to hire, how much to pay, what hours to work, and so on. Because the right to property means the right of disposal, clearly property ownership was completely absent under Nazism.

The Russian version of socialism involves direct seizure of all private property by the state. Individual citizens may be allowed to keep small items of personal property such as clothing and books but only by permission—not by right. The individual is totally dependent on the state for every need from food, to medical care, to education, to travel, to entertainment, to services such as plumbing, and to jobs and career.

It should be stressed that the difference between Nazism and socialism is one of form rather than of substance. In both cases property rights are totally abrogated, and so therefore is the right to life. (The appalling record of Nazi Germany and Soviet Russia with respect to mass murder is ample testimony to the fact the human life is considered of no importance under socialism.)

It should be noted that it is an error to call countries such as Israel, Sweden, England, and France socialist, as is sometimes done. These are all mixed economies—that is, mixtures of private enterprise and government controls, albeit with more government controls than in the United States. All genuinely socialist countries today are communist countries (Reisman, 1979).

Economically, socialism eliminates at the outset the foundations on which objective performance evaluation is based—namely, the price system and its free market corollary, the profit system. (For a detailed discussion on the inability of socialism to produce or to rationally allocate goods and services, see Reisman, 1979, and Von Mises, 1962).

Because people are not free to own and trade property under socialism, the laws of supply and demand are not permitted to function. Thus there is no objective way to set prices for goods and services. Prices including wages must be set arbitrarily based on the whim of the bureaucrats. Prices set in this manner no longer reflect the sum total of the transactions between buyer and seller on the free market[1].

Similarly, under socialism the concept of profit is meaningless. Because there is no objective pricing system, there is no means of calculating profit and loss. There is no way to determine if a factory is utilizing its resources efficiently or wasting them. There is no means of calculating whether a firm is manufacturing the right goods, paying the right wages, or selling at the right price, or whether it should even be in business at all. No rational allocation of resources or investment capital is possible because, in the absence of a market system, there is no

---

[1]Socialist societies, in practice, may attempt to copy or use as guidelines the prices of goods and labor in capitalist societies. Thus they try to tack on capitalist concepts (including, for example, incentive pay) in order to salvage socialism from utter chaos. However, because this is done rigidly (by edict) and because it is not connected to a profit system, it does not save socialism from its inherent irrationality; moreover, the incentives serve only the values of the rulers, not those of the citizens (see Reisman [1979] for a further discussion of this issue).

way to determine what people want or need. The rational, free-market process of planning (including price setting, investment, and production), which is based on feedback in the form of millions of purchase decisions made by consumers each day, is destroyed by socialism. All such ''planning'' must be done arbitrarily by the socialist bureaucracy. In practice this means that under socialism, products, prices, and wages are based on the desires of the top government officials and their underlings.

Consider now how socialism affects the performance appraisal process. First note that under socialism there is no market wage. Thus it is impossible to claim, according to any objective standard, that a given wage (set by a bureaucrat) is either too high or too low. A ''fair'' wage is whatever the top bureaucrats say it is.

Nor is there any economic standard by which a socialist enterprise can judge the effectiveness of its performance evaluation system, because there is no ultimate measure of economic performance for the enterprise at all. The concepts of profit and loss are meaningless under socialism.

In addition to being *unable* to judge the efficiency of its operations, the socialist enterprise has no incentive to do so. Its managers have no financial stake in its economic efficiency and there are no stockholders demanding profits. There is no danger that the enterprise will go out of business because it is state supported and there are no competitors to whom its customers can turn. Nor is there a danger of losing its best employees because the state owns the means of production and can assign workers wherever it wants. Employees are literally resources like rocks and trees to be disposed of as the state sees fit.

From the workers' standpoint, there is no means of protecting themselves against mistreatment. There is no market wage; nor would the enterprise have any financial stake in paying a fair wage if there were a means of determining it. And the employees have nowhere to turn if their employer is being fair 'because the state is the only employer. Thus the state's capacity to harm employees is literally unlimited. Under socialism the employee is reduced to the status of a slave.[2]

It is not denied that employee performance can be evaluated under socialism. *Some* standard can always be found to evaluate people. But because there is no objective standard, what do socialist bureaucrats use as a substitute?

The answer is obvious once one recognizes the economic and political consequences of socialism. Under socialism there can be no rational economic planning, because there is no price system and no profit system to allocate resources and motivate efficiency. To quote economist George Reisman (1979), socialism is not a method of economic planning and economic production; it is *''an act of*

---

[2]Soviet workers may be allowed to change jobs but only by the permission of the state, not by right. In addition they are subject to the forced draft and can be sent to forced labor camps for exercising freedom of speech or earning money in private (black market) transactions (see Reisman [1979] for a further discussion of forced labor in Russia).

destruction [p. 151]." It results in economic chaos and mass poverty. (For theoretical proof, see Reisman [1979] and Von Mises [1962]; for historical proof, see Soviet Russia: Smith [1976]; for a recent example, see Communist Poland: Ball [1981].

However, recall that socialist governments promise the people that they will guarantee the welfare and well-being of every citizen. Because they cannot deliver on this promise, there is a genuine danger that the people will try to revolt. Such revolts are prevented or avoided in socialist states by terror. Protesters, complainers, and critics are threatened, put in mental hospitals, jailed, or shot. Free trade unions are prohibited; strikes are considered criminal acts. Those who wish to leave the country are strongly discouraged or forcibly prevented from doing so. Those dissenters who wish to stay may be exiled.

What then would a socialist government consider to be the best type of employee? Necessarily one who obeys, who follows orders blindly, who does political favors for his or her bosses, who helps to fudge production figures (in order to appear to meet arbitrary quotas), who does not rock the boat or challenge the status quo, who does not complain about even the worst injustices, who is politically reliable because of having memorized all the party slogans, and who sacrifices values, ambition, integrity, and self-esteem to the government. To quote Hedrick Smith (1976) "If one doctor in a . . . clinic gets a reputation for good conscientious work, she winds up with extra patients and a lot of overtime work but she cannot be paid for overtime. . . . those who get ahead are usually doctors who speak up in Party meetings and curry favor with Party officials." (p.295)

Ability under socialism is not a commodity to be traded in the marketplace to the mutual benefit of buyer and seller, but something to be exploited for the benefit of the state. Although it is true that no socialist state consistently practices the Marxist slogan, "To each according to his needs, from each according to his abilities," the reason is simply that they know they cannot get away with it. Under such a policy, ability would be a detriment, a capacity to be used for the benefit of those who have less at the expense of those who have more. Under such terms any rational person would do everything possible to hide his or her ability. In practice, socialist states do attempt to reward individual ability in some cases, but only insofar as it serves the purposes of the state. For example, socialist countries often choose to reward good athletes because athletic feats have propaganda value for the state. On the other hand, they virutally never choose to reward good writers, social critics, honest newspaper reporters, or judges with integrity because they would be a threat to the state.

Nor is there any protection under socialism for various "minorities" such as blacks and Jews. It is significant that both the Nazis and the Russians were and/or are ferociously racist and anti-Semitic. In both cases the discrimination was originated and was (or is) actively and forcibly promoted by the government. Such minorities, of course, are convenient scapegoats (along with "capitalist roaders") for socialist governments who need a means of diverting attention from their own inevitable failures. The minorities have few options except to leave the country (if they can), because they are not free to trade with other citizens on the basis of their abilities.

According to a United States military attaché, (Smith, 1976), the rules in Russia are:

> "Don't buck the system," "Don't make any waves," "Don't go looking for extra work," "Don't push for reforms because that means changing the way of doing things," just "Cover you ass" [p. 305].

For those who want to climb to the top, additional qualities are needed—above all, political deviousness, pull, and amoral ruthlessness. Reisman (1979), based on Hayek) calls it "Socialist natural selection: the selection of the worst [p. 179]."

THE MIXED ECONOMY

The mixed economy (or the welfare state as it is sometimes called) is not, as is commonly asserted, a third type of system that combines the alleged advantages of both capitalism and socialism while avoiding the alleged disadvantages of both. It is an unstable mixture of the two with the advantages of capitalism and the weaknesses of socialism. I say unstable because the trend of every mixed economy is in the direction of greater and greater controls. I do not go into the reasons for this [3] but history leaves no doubt about the direction of the trend, given the existing premises of supporters of the mixed economy.

The United States is a mixture of capitalism and the Nazi version of socialism. The right to hold property is recognized, but increasingly the use of property is being regulated by the state. For example, business owners and managers are regulated as to: where they can build (zoning), whom and how to hire (EEOC), how much to pay (EEOC and minimum-wage laws), how to design the work

---

[3]Ethically, the reason is the morality of altruism accepted by welfare state advocates, which asserts that man is not an end in himself but a sacrificial victim for the ends of others (see Rand [1967] for details). Economically, welfare-state policies undermine the efficient working of the market system—for example, minimum-wage laws and monopoly labor unions increase unemployment. The free market is then blamed as being inadequate, thus justifying further interventions designed to eliminate the consequences of the previous interventions. These additional interventions lead to still more problems and justify further interventions. The interventionist climate eventually encourages every special-interest group to pass laws to protect itself from other groups, always at the expense of the individual citizen—for example, occupational licensing, which restricts competition and increases costs to the consumers all in the name of protecting the consumer, who never asked for it in the first place.

environment (OSHA), what hours the employees can work at a given pay rate (overtime laws), when they can be open (Blue Laws), what prices they can charge and how successful they can be in terms of growth (antitrust laws and price controls), how to write a customer contract (FTC), how to negotiate with unions (Labor Department and NLRB), what insects and fish can be destroyed in the course of doing business (ecology laws), what products they can sell and who can perform what jobs (occupational licensing laws), what amount of profit they can keep (IRS), what they can say to stockholders (SEC), how company mail is to be sent (postal regulations), how to design bathrooms and parking spaces (laws for disabled), and even how big the signs in front of their office building can be and what to plant around the parking lot. And this only scratches the surface. A given firm may have to deal with government agencies at four different levels: municipal, county, state, and federal, and the various regulations may even contradict each other, be changed and applied retroactively, be uninterpretable, be totally arbitrary, and cost millions of dollars to implement and hundreds of thousands to protest. And all this must be faced in the context of continuous government-caused inflation, which makes rational financial planning nearly impossible.

The cost of these regulations in terms of lost production, lost jobs, higher costs and prices, investments and entire businesses foregone, plants closed, and ability wasted is incalculable. In the drug industry, regulations may have even allowed people to die because potentially life-saving drugs, which did not meet the FDA'S arbitrary standards of approval, could not be sold.

The difference between the mixed economy and socialism is that there is still some degree of freedom left in a mixed economy. After obeying all the regulations and paying taxes, citizens are allowed to keep whatever (if anything) is left. People are still free to quit their jobs and look for others. And performance evaluation in the private sector to some extent is still based on merit.

There is somewhat more similarity between the public sector in the United States and socialism in that public agencies, which Von Mises (1944/1969) calls bureaucracies, do not work on the profit system. The standard of success in bureaucracies is not making money but obedience to rules and regulations. According to Von Mises (1944/1969), the bureaucrat's "main task cannot be efficiency as such, but efficiency within the limits of subservience to the regulations [p. 63]."

Running at a deficit is not necessarily a mark of failure and may even be used to justify a larger budget the next year. Bureaucracies have a strong tendency to expand and to demand more and more money from the taxpayers as more and more categories of "essential" services are concocted by the bureaucrats. Many categories of employees, such as air traffic controllers, are considerably overpaid (Feldstein, 1981).

Fringe benefits tend to be generous in bureaucracies and job security is generally very high. As a result, security-minded people are drawn to such jobs. In fact, it is virtually impossible to fire even the most incompetent employee under the civil-service system. At the same time, there is a marked tendency to resist change and innovation because the bureaucrat has much to lose and little to gain by "rocking the boat."

The essential feature of performance evaluation in the public sector is that evaluations are based less on merit and more on other factors as compared to private business. These factors include: seniority, age, experience, scores on examinations, and personal factors such as being liked by the boss and political pull. In many bureaucracies all employees get the highest possible ratings as a matter of course.

Even though both socialism and the public sector under the mixed economy do not work on a profit system, there are important differences between the two systems. Public agencies exist in the context of a market economy and therefore operate within a price system. Thus, for example, wages can be (but are not always) kept reasonably in line by using the private sector as a guide. Further, the agencies have to compete with the private sector for employees, and thus cannot mistreat their employees too much. The costs of services can be calculated because prices can be calculated; goods have to be bought from the private sector.

Furthermore, even the degree of inefficiency and incompetence of certain agencies can be determined because for certain agencies there are private organizations that can serve as a standard, since they perform the same or similar services as those in the public sector. This is the case, for example, with respect to education, transportation, communications, medicine, fire protection, and trash collection. The incompetence and wastefulness of the public sector in all these areas is easily shown and this may act to a small extent as a brake on further deterioration, especially because there is always the possibility that some of the public-sector services could be turned over to the private sector (as has happened, for example, with fire protection and trash collection). Culturally, there is a general resentment of waste and inefficiency due to the obvious contrast between the public and private sectors. Limited innovation is made in the public sector as a result of innovations made in private organizations and pressures from the citizenry.

Another important difference between economic activity in the United States versus under socialism is that there is as yet no terror apparatus here. In Russia, violating economic regulations, such as black market activity, may be punishable by death. Even creative innovation, which is very disruptive of the rigid and arbitrary plans developed by the state bureaucracy and therefore severely resisted, may be punished when it occurs (c.f. Smith, 1976). Economic order in Russia, in the sense of obedience to rules, is ultimately assured by the KGB

In the United States, we do not have a terror apparatus like the KGB. Instead we have agencies like EEOC; death and imprisonment are replaced by harrassment and fines.

I choose to discuss EEOC because it is most relevant to the issue of performance evaluation. Although EEOC is primarily focused on selection (and promotion), both activities require estimates of employee capability. Thus EEOC has also developed guidelines for performance appraisal as well as for selection.

The alleged purpose of EEOC guidelines is to prevent unfair discrimination in employment (i.e., discrimination not based on ability). In practice it has achieved and actively promotes the very things it was designed to prohibit. It has divided people into various arbitrarily chosen collectives—for example, blacks, whites, Indians, Asians, men, women—and has then *forced* employers to use quotas in hiring and promoting people in these groups in order to match the percentage of each type in the community.[4] (Other collectives such as the fat, the disabled, the old, alcoholics, criminals and homosexuals are now clamoring for the same special treatment.) In an attempt to disguise the real nature of this forced discrimination, EEOC and its apologists have resorted to incredible verbal subterfuges in order to evade the real nature of their policies. Forced discrimination, for example, is called Affirmative Action.

The result has been the hiring and promoting of people who are not qualified or who are less qualified than people who are passed over. It has fostered blatant discrimination against white males.

As a result of EEOC regulations, performance evaluation either must be done according to merit and then ignored or done according to race and sex, and so on, at the outset. Like all mixed-economy regulations, the effect is to undermine the inherent rationality, justice, and efficiency of the market system.

What is especially significant about EEOC policies is that they do not consider *individuals* to be real. They are only interested in the number of people in various collectives. For example, they do not care if an *individual* black was treated justly or not but only in the number of people with black skin who are hired or promoted. Preferential treatment must be given to blacks where there is a history of racial discrimination even at the expense of whites who had no part in causing it. The effect on the individual white poeple who are treated unjustly (and on the individual blacks who are not sure why they were hired or promoted) is ignored. In denigrating the importance of the individual in deference to the collective, EEOC philosophically is very much socialist.

Another EEOC policy, now being pushed strongly be various women's groups, is the concept of "equal pay for comparable work." This doctrine asserts that if a given job requires the same amount of skill as another job, the

---

[4]The EEOC 80% rule for deciding whether or not a group has suffered "adverse impact" as a result of a particular selection device does not contradict what is stated here. In cases in which too small a proportion of a minority group is hired, it does not matter whether the selection device is valid or not. EEOC will demand that other (not yet invented) selection devices be used, or that the jobs be redesigned to require less skill, or that minorities receive special training at company expense. Such demands will cease only when enough minority members have been hired to meet the quota.

pay should be the same. In this view, for example, it is not "fair" that a plumber make more than a nurse because nursing requires an equal or even greater amount of technical training than plumbing.

One government official claims that this doctrine is "so simple one can only wonder what has taken it so long to catch hold." (quoted in Schwartz, 1981, p. 1) Perhaps the reason that it has taken so long is that the doctrine is wrong. It demonstrates a total and fundamental failure to understand the price system. Under the unhampered price system, wages are determined by supply and demand. The reason, for example, that nurses get lower wages than plumbers is that more people are willing to work as nurses than as plumbers in relation to the demand for each. If large numbers of nurses or nursing students changed their minds, left the nursing field, and became plumbers, the wages of nurses would rapidly increase while the earnings of plumbers would rapidly decrease. Until this occurs, however, the wages of nurses will remain lower than those of plumbers.

The philosophical–economic fallacy involved in the "equal pay for comparable work" doctrine is the *intrinsic fallacy*—the notion that value resides *in* things (like jobs) as such, independent of any context. According to Rand (1967), "It is a theory that divorces the concept of 'good' from beneficiaries, and the concept of 'value' from valuer and purpose [p. 21]." Actually *no value resides in any job as such.* A job is only a value to someone for a specific purpose. For example, if nobody wants the services of a saddle maker, then the value of the saddle maker's job is zero, regardless of the degree of skill involved and the years of study it took to master it.

Ordinarily, wage levels are roughly proportional to skill level, but there are exceptions (see Reisman [1979] for a further discussion of this issue). For example, research scientists make less money than businesspeople because sufficient numbers of scientists are willing to take less money in return for special nonmaterial incentives such as freedom and intrinsic satisfaction. On the other hand, certain singers and rock stars make a great deal of money in relation to their skill level because large numbers of people want to hear them and only them. Thus there is no guaranteed connection between pay and skill. Any attempt to impose a given wage on the basis of skill or any other aspect of the job represents the intrinsic fallacy. Because, in fact, there is no way to determine the value of a job by looking just at the job itself, in practice the intrinsic fallacy simply leads to setting wages by fiat based on the personal opinion of some bureaucrat. In this respect, consistent application of the intrinsic fallacy leads to socialism.

THE MILITARY

A word is in order about performance appraisal in the military. In both a capitalist and a mixed economy, the military is part of the public sector. It operates under a price system but not under a profit system and faces all the usual problems of public-sector performance appraisal.

An especially difficult and unique problem in evaluating military personnel is that the military is designed to perform a function that is not performed very often (fight wars) as compared, for example, to business or even civilian bureaucratic tasks. The ultimate source of feedback, winning or losing the war, often occurs too late to prevent what could be catastrophic consequences. Thus performance has to be evaluated to a great extent hypothetically—for example, through substitute measures such as readiness indices, war games, and computer simulations. To complicate matters further, most military personnel play supporting rather than combat roles, thus making it difficult to judge their contributions to the overall mission.

In addition, in free countries the military is firmly (and properly) under civilian control, which means that political factors enter continually into the decision-making process (e.g., Will developing this weapon offend the Russians? Will closing this base put people out of work in Paduka and thus upset Senator Smithers?).

All of these problems would exist to a degree even in a fully capitalist society because the military is necessarily a government function. (If it were in the private sector, it would constitute anarchy.) However, the problems are undoubtedly exacerbated in a mixed economy because of the greater intrusion of government into all spheres.

To take the most blatant example, most mixed economies endorse the military draft. Under capitalism, the draft would be outlawed in principle, because it is a clear violation of the individual's right to his or her own life; the draft constitutes involuntary servitude. In this respect the draft is based on socialist premises because it implies that, at least in respects that the state considers important, individuals exist to serve the state and can be forced to do certain work against their will.

Like the civilian sector, in the mixed economy, the military in addition to being politicized, is typically overstaffed and inundated by rules and regulations.

I do not attempt here to offer a technical solution to the problem of military performance appraisal. This problem has been the subject of a great deal of study by many competent people over the years. I would only suggest that the problems the military is facing today are much more than military problems. Many are cultural in nature. The decline in our military capability has paralleled in an interesting way the decline in our economic health and vitality and in the increasingly negative attitudes of our young people towards authority, hard work, and political–economic freedom. These economic and cultural problems stem in turn from a decline in the quality of the major ideas promulgated by the field of philosophy. I refer particularly to the precipitous decline in respect for and use of reason that can be seen everywhere throughout the culture and the parallel increase in the worship of the irrational (Rand, 1971). In this respect, there are ominous philosophical parallels between America today and the Weimar republic, the precursor to Nazi Germany (For details, see Peikoff, 1982).

Let us hope that this trend can be reversed before it is too late.

ACKNOWLEDGMENT

The author is greatly indebted to Dr. George Reisman for his helpful and astute comments on this paper.

REFERENCES

Ball, R. Poland's economic disaster. *Fortune,* September 7, 1981, 42–48.

Collins, O., & Moore, D. G. *The organization makers.* New York: Appleton-Century-Crofts, 1970.

Feldstein, M. The job of controlling public sector pay. *Wall Street Journal,* October 1, 1981.

Locke, E. A. The case against legislating the quality of work life. *The Personnel Administrator,* May 1976, pp. 19–21.

Peikoff, L. *The ominous parallels: The end of freedom in America.* New York: Stein & Day, 1982.

Rand, A. *Capitalism: The unknown ideal.* New York: New American Library (Signet), 1967.

Rand, A. *The anti-industrial revolution.* New York: New American Library (Signet), 1971.

Reisman, G. *The government against the economy.* Ottawa, Ill.: Caroline House, 1979.

Reisman, G. Capitalism: The cure for racism. *The Intellectual Activist,* 1982, *2,* (Nos. 15–18).

Schwartz, P. The wages of sex. *The Intellectual Activist,* September 1, 1981, *2*(9), pp. 1–3, 6–7.

Smith, H. *The Russians.* New York: Ballantine, 1976.

Von Mises, L. *Socialism.* New Haven, Ct. Yale University Press, 1962. (Originally published in 1951.)

Von Mises, L. *Human action.* Chicago: Henry Regnery, 1966.

Von Mises, L. *Bureaucracy.* New Rochelle, N. Y.: Arlington House, 1969. (Originally published in 1944.)

Reality, Utopia, and Performance Appraisal: Another View

Barbara Lerner

Professor Locke and I have two things in common: We both prefer capitalist marketplaces to planned economies and we both believe that without property rights, all other human rights are jeopardized. As a spate of recent books on what Ernest van den Haag (1979) calls "Sources of hostility to capitalism" amply documents (Kristol, 1978; Silk & Vogel, 1976; van den Haag, 1979), that makes us part of a small minority among intellectuals in the west today and in the third world as well. Those facts make me wish it were possible to make common cause with Professor Locke, but I find that I cannot.

His paper troubles me in a number of ways, perhaps most fundamentally because he presents capitalism as a system based on utopian assumptions about human nature and human rights, in contrast to the allegedly antiutopian assumptions underlying socialist systems—a view he supports by citing a variety of secondary and tertiary sources. Primary sources (Marx, 1857–58/1973, 1875/1978; Smith, 1776/1974) suggest that the exact opposite is true: Utopian assumptions and absolute conceptions are intrinsic features of socialism, not of capitalism.

Utopian assumptions about human nature are most clearly reflected in beliefs about human motivation and human intellectual capacities. As an illustration of the former, consider the notion that human beings will use their productive capacities to the fullest extent possible—or at least to the extent necessary to create and maintain an adequate standard of living for all—without hope of differential external rewards. Karl Marx believed that; Adam Smith did not. As an illustration of the latter, consider the notion that rational planning can provide an adequate substitute for the impersonal and still largely inscrutable forces of the marketplace. Again, Karl Marx believed that; Adam Smith did not. Adam

327

Smith saw selfishness, greed, and ignorance as intrinsic to the human condition, not to any particular social system, and his enthusiasm for the marketplace was a direct outgrowth of his understanding of it as a mechanism capable of channeling those potentially destructive human impulses in socially productive ways. That hardly reflects an exalted view of human nature and the claim that it does looks especially dubious when Smith's views are contrasted with those of Karl Marx.

Marx saw human selfishness, greed, and ignorance as artificial byproducts of capitalist environments—as distortions of the human heart, not Smithian reflections of it—and envisioned the destruction of those systems as an apocalyptic event, ushering in a millenium in which human altruism and rationality would emerge in full glory and reign supreme forever after. All things considered, the claim that capitalism incorporates a utopian view of human nature—in contrast to a more cynical view of people attributable to socialists—does not seem tenable.

Professor Locke's view of capitalism as a source of absolute human rights is even more troubling, suggesting as it does that political systems are reducible to economic ones—again, a belief that can fairly be attributed to Karl Marx, not to Adam Smith. With regard to property rights, in particular, contemporary Anglo–American legal scholars generally follow Jeremy Bentham (1782/1945) in understanding them as creations of the state, not of capitalism or any other economic system, and in making careful distinctions between moral principles and legal ones, distinctions that are obliterated in the formulation Professor Locke quotes.

Property law is the oldest body of law in the western world and the relationship between it and the evolving social and political arrangements of modern states is far too complex to allow for even superficial summarization here. Two very basic points of maximum relevance to Professor Locke's argument can, however, be made. First, property rights are not absolute in any democratic state. They never have been and never will be because if they were, there would be no legal way of resolving disputes, such as those that arise between owners of adjacent lands devoted to incompatible uses. Absolute rights are the province of absolute rulers. In a democratic state, no one's rule is absolute, and no one's rights are either.

Democracy depends for its existence on limited and dispersed forms of power and control. Private ownership of property facilitates that sort of dispersion in the economic sphere but it does not, in and of itself, guarantee similar sorts of dispersion in other spheres. That is why capitalism is probably a necessary but hardly a sufficient condition for the evolution and maintenance of democratic states. The historical record, thus far, seems adequate to support that limited claim; it is not adequate to support the more sweeping one put forth by Professor Locke and the sources he cites, a claim that is explicitly rejected by conservative economists like Milton Friedman (1962) as well as by neoconservative ones like Irving Kristol (1978).

To all of the foregoing, only one response from this audience seems appropriate: So what? What has all this—or any of it, for that matter—got to do with performance evaluation? Professor Locke offers one answer, suggesting that objective performance evaluation is easy in a capitalist society, impossible in a socialist one. My own working hypothesis is that objective performance evaluation is difficult in any complex modern society, impossible in one in which utopian assumptions hold sway.

The problem, in the latter case, is that utopian assumptions conflict with reality and, as a consequence, with the results of valid, objective performance evaluations. In the ensuing clash, if the utopian assumptions are to be maintained, performance evaluations must somehow shift to accommodate them—a shift that moves performance evaluation away from reality, or at least from some significant aspects of it.

In struggling to understand where and how such shifts into unreality take place, it is a mistake to begin by assuming that there is any automatic or invariant relationship between the assumptions that are built into a society and the actual beliefs of its citizens. Indoctrination is, as yet, an imperfect process, and socialization is still a frequently surprising one. Thus, socialism may incorporate utopian assumptions about the innate altruism and wisdom of people in general and of central planners in particular but empirical evidence suggests that many socialist citizens do not, as the people of Poland are currently demonstrating.

Similarly, the fact that the antiutopian assumptions of Adam Smith were shared by the men who drafted the Constitution of the United States and were thus built into the structure of our government (Hamilton, 1787–88/1961; Madison, 1787–88/1961) as well as into our economic system did not provide American citizens with any permanent immunization against the competing assumptions of the utopians. Utopian assumptions are, in fact, very popular in America today, especially in intellectual circles, a circumstance that helps to explain why capitalism is so unpopular in those circles and why extreme egalitarianism—the most common modern form of utopianism—is so seductive and so prevalent there.

Extreme egalitarians believe in equality of distribution, not just for material rewards but for attributions of merit as well. Thus, they tend to deny the reality and/or the magnitude and impact of individual and group differences in developed abilities and character traits. Typically, they see positive cognitive and affective traits as natural, intrinsic characteristics of human beings; negative ones as temporary aberrations produced by defective environments, aberrations that can be quickly and easily eliminated by appropriate environmental alterations at any point in time, either before the fact or afterwards. Their basic, underlying asumption is that human beings are all pretty much alike; apparent differences are not seen as a function of relatively stable and moderately broad cognitive and affective personality traits but of differences in the external situation people happen to be in at the moment of measurement.

Does reality really contradict those views as I suggested earlier? As long as measurement was a crude affair, producing little more than masses of unaggregated data from a host of studies with small, inadequate samples, the answer seemed to be no. Available empirical data seemed, in many ways, at least as compatible with the assumptions of extreme egalitarians as it did with older sets of assumptions about the relative stablity and importance of individual differences in ability and character over time and across situations.

More recently, however, new techniques for aggregating data across studies through metaanalysis (Glass, 1976; Pearlman, Schmidt, & Hunter, 1980; Schmidt, Gast-Rosenberg, & Hunter, 1980; Schmidt, & Hunter, 1977; Schmidt, Hunter, Pearlman,& Shane, 1979) and for correcting or compensating for inadequate samples in old but too-often neglected ways (Epstein, 1979, 1980) have come to the fore, making the gap between empirical reality and the assumptions of extreme egalitarians increasingly clear.

This is most obvious with regard to cognitive traits, although the recent work of personality researchers like Seymour Epstein (1979, 1980) provides some initial evidence that it may be true for at least a few commonly recognized noncognitive personality traits as well. In that domain, however, the basic problem is still as much conceptual as it is methodological, and there Epstein's work thus far has been less helpful. Still, he has, at the very least, laid the groundwork for more meaningful studies of the importance of currently conceptualized noncognitive personality traits by showing that the apparent instability of some of these traits was more a reflection of inadequate sampling than of reality.

In the cognitive domain, this milestone was passed long ago. Test data clearly show that individual differences in at least two moderately broad cognitive traits, verbal and mathematical reasoning ability, are relatively stable over time. Evidence demonstrating this is overwhelming and comes from at least three main sources: (1) from the results of longitudinal studies of intellectual development like Hilton's study of academic prediction and growth (Hilton, 1979); (2) from the routinely high reliabilities achieved with most professionally developed cognitive tests measuring those abilities; and (3) from the power of those tests to predict educational and occupational outcomes over relatively long time spans.

Social scientists have known about the stability of these cognitive differences for a long time, but many of us have tended to underestimate the importance of their effects and implications. One common way of doing that was to argue that these differences were of importance, if at all, only or mainly in school settings. Out there in what extreme egalitarians liked to call "the real world"—the world of nonacademic work—they argued that these differences were rarely, if ever, of more than trivial importance, except perhaps at the extremes.

Until recently, developments in industrial psychology best illustrated, perhaps, by the work of Ghiselli (1963, 1966) seemed to give that argument some plausibility. At least in the occupational sphere, evidence for the general importance of moderately broad and relatively stable cognitive characteristics seemed inconsistent at best. Situational factors, on the other hand, appeared to be almost as important as extreme egalitarians claimed that they were.

The work of Frank Schmidt, John Hunter, and their colleagues (Hunter, 1980; Hunter & Schmidt, in press; Schmidt & Hunter, 1981; Schmidt, Hunter, & Caplan, 1981; Schmidt, Hunter, McKenzie, & Muldrow, 1979; Schmidt, Hunter, & Pearlman, 1981) has pretty well destroyed whatever plausibility that argument had. Using new techniques for aggregating data across studies to correct for deficiencies in sample size, in restriction of range, and in criterion unreliability, they have provided us with a series of convincing demonstrations of the fact that tests of verbal and mathematical reasoning ability are at least as powerful in the occupational sphere as they are in the educational arena. These tests predict worker productivity in a very wide array of occupations at a very wide range of levels and across a very wide variety of occupational settings. In utopia, differences in the abilities these tests measure may not matter much; in reality, they do, and the cost of underestimating their importance for the success of individual agencies and companies, for the national economy as a whole, and for the military as well, is very high.

Plausible or not, the utopian assumptions of extreme egalitarians were built into many of our selection systems in the last decade, not because extreme egalitarians ever succeeded in convincing all or even most employers—let alone most industrial psychologists—that they were right, but because they convinced many lawyers and judges already predisposed towards extreme egalitarianism that they were, and the resultant legal pressures forced many firms and agencies to hire significant numbers of low-scoring applicants in order to avoid charges of discrimination against women, blacks, Hispanics, and others (Lerner, 1977, 1979a, 1979b, 1980).

Many of these employees have now been on the job long enough to be eligible for promotions, but their job performances frequently show a closer correspondence to their entry-level test scores than to utopian assumptions about the implications of those scores. As a result, the same presures that were applied to entry-level tests are likely to be applied to performance evaluations. Inevitably, some extreme egalitarians will try to force changes in the standards for those evaluations, arguing, once again, that the evaluations are inadequate, not the workers, and that any differences in the number of positive performance evaluations and consequent promotion rates between workers of different races, sexes, ethnic groups, and ages reflect old prejudices rather than current realities.

Inevitably, too, some lawyers and judges will buy that argument and try to use the power of the state, once again, to force employers to make employment decisions on the basis of utopian assumptions at variance with reality. If they succeed, the already evident decline in American productivity is likely to grow larger, and our already troubled economy to grow more troubled, threatening the standard of living millions of Americans have come to regard as their birthright, and increasing the risk of civil discord and strife.

Friedrich Hayek, a philosopher and a Nobel Prize winner in Economics, whom Professor Locke and I both respect, shares my concern about the harmful potential of utopian pressures, particularly when they emanate from government sources. He opens Chapter 2 of his classic study *The Road to Serfdom* (1944/1976) with a quote from Hoelderlin, showing that the idea was not original with him either, and I would like to close with it: "What has always made *the State* a hell on earth has been precisely that man has tried to make it his Heaven [p. 24] (emphasis added).

REFERENCES

Bentham, J. In C. W. Everett (Ed.), *The limits of jurisprudence defined.* New York: Columbia University Press, 1945. (Originally written, 1782.)

Epstein, S. The stability of behavior I: On predicting most of the people much of the time. *Journal of Personality and Social Psychology,* 1979, *37,* 1097–1126.

Epstein, S. The stability of behavior II. Implications for psychological research. *American Psychologist,* 1980, *35,* 790–806.

Friedman, M. *Capitalism and freedom.* Chicago: University of Chicago Press, 1962.

Ghiselli, E. E. Moderating effects and differential reliability and validity. *Journal of Applied Psychology,* 1963, *47,* 81–86.

Ghiselli, E. E. *The validity of occupational aptitude tests.* New York: Wiley, 1966.

Glass, G. V. Primary, secondary, and meta-analysis of research. *Educational Researcher,* 1976, *5,* 3–8.

Hamilton, A. Papers No. 1, 31, and 85. In B. F. Wright (Ed.), *The Federalist.* Cambridge, Mass.: John Harvard Library ed., 1961. (Originally published, 1787–88.)

Hayek, F. A. *The road to serfdom.* Chicago: University of Chicago Press, 1976. (Originally published, 1944.)

Hilton, T. L. ETS study of academic prediction and growth. *New Directions for Testing and Measurement,* 1979, *2,* 27–44.

Hunter, J. E. *Validity generalization for 12,000 jobs: An application of synthetic validity and validity generalization to the General Aptitude Test Battery (GATB).* Washington, D.C.: U.S. Employment Service, U.S. Department of Labor, 1980.

Hunter, J. E., & Schmidt, F. L. Fitting people to jobs: The impact of personnel selection on national productivity. In M. E. Dunnette & E. A. Fleishman (Eds.), *Human performance and productivity: Human capability and assessment.* Hillside, N.J.: Lawrence Erlbaum Associates in press.

Kristol, I. *Two cheers for capitalism.* New York: Basic Books, 1978.

Lerner, B. Washington v. Davis: Quantity, quality, and equality in employment testing. In P. B. Kurland (Ed.), *1976 Supreme Court Review.* Chicago: University of Chicago Press, 1977.

Lerner, B. Employment discrimination: Adverse impact, validity, and equality. In P. B. Kurland & G. Casper (Eds.), *1979 Supreme Court Review.* Chicago: University of Chicago Press, 1979. (a)

Lerner, B. Tests and standards today: Attacks, counterattacks, and responses. *New Directions for Testing and Measurement,* 1979, *3,* 15–31. (b)

Lerner, B. The war on testing: David, Goliath, and Gallup. *The Public Interest,* 1980, *60,* 119–147.

Madison, J. Papers No. 51 and 55. In B. F. Wright (Ed.), *The Federalist.* Cambridge, Mass.: John Harvard Library ed., 1961. (Originally published, 1787–88.)

Marx, K. *Grundrisse: Foundations of the critique of political economy* (M. Nicolaus, trans.). New York: Vintage, 1973. (Oringinally published, 1857–58.)

Marx, K. Critique of the Gotha program. In R. C. Tucker (Ed.), *The Marx–Engels Reader* (2nd ed.). New York: Norton, 1978. (Originally published, 1875.)

Pearlman, K., Schmidt, F. L., & Hunter, J. E. Validity generalization results for tests used to predict training success and job proficiency in clerical occupations. *Journal of Applied Psychology*, 1980, *65*, 373–406.

Schmidt, F. L., Gast-Rosenberg, I., & Hunter, J. E. Validity generalization results for computer programmers. *Journal of Applied Psychology*, 1980, *65*, 643–661.

Schmidt, F. L., & Hunter, J. E. Development of a general solution to the problem of validity generalization. *Journal of Applied Psychology*, 1977, *62*, 529–540.

Schmidt, F. L., & Hunter, J. E. Employment testing: Old theories and new research findings. *American Psychologist*, 1981, *36*, 1128–1137.

Schmidt, F. L., Hunter, J. E., & Caplan, J. R. Validity generalization results for two jobs in the petroleum industry. *Journal of Applied Psychology*, 1981, *66*, 261–273.

Schmidt, F. L., Hunter, J. E., McKenzie, R. C., & Muldrow, T. W. The impact of a valid selection procedure on worker productivity. *Journal of Applied Psychology*, 1979, *64*, 609–626.

Schmidt, F. L., Hunter, J. E., & Pearlman, K. Task differences and validity of aptitude tests in selection: A red herring. *Journal of Applied Psychology*, 1981, *66*, 166–185.

Schmidt, F. L., Hunter, J. E., Pearlman, K., & Shane, G. S. Further tests of the Schmidt–Hunter Bayesian validity generalization procedure. *Personnel Psychology*, 1979, *32*, 257–281.

Silk, L., & Vogel, D. *Ethics and profits: The crisis of confidence in American business*. New York: Simon and Schuster, 1976.

Smith, A. *The wealth of nations, Books I–III, 1776*. Harmondsworth, Eng.: Penguin Books, 1974.

van den Haag, E. (Ed.). *Capitalism: Sources of hostility*. New Rochelle, N.Y.: Epoch Books, Heritage Foundation, 1979.

Reply to Lerner

Edwin A. Locke

It is regrettable that Dr. Lerner confined nearly all of her remarks to issues which I never raised; nevertheless, I will answer her points.

Dr. Lerner's thesis appears to be as follows: in the name of utopia (i.e. idealism) modern intellectuals advocate socialism, altruism and absolutism; believe that rational socialist economic planning is possible; and assert that all people are innately equal in intellectual capacity. However, the facts of reality contradict these claims since: socialism (socialist planning) does not work; people are actually greedy, selfish, and often ignorant; rights are only contingent; and individuals differ fundamentally in their intellectual capacities.

Dr. Lerner's thesis is based on a Platonic, soul-body dichotomy, that is, the world of ideas versus the real world, the moral versus the practical, the good versus the possible, theory versus research, the absolute versus the contingent. I disagree both with this dichotomy and with many (though not all) of the specific assertions made by Dr. Lerner. There are so many different issues involved, however, that I will only be able to highlight some key ideas here.

First, it is both dangerous and wrong to concede the realm of morality to socialists, that is, to grant that they stand for what's right and good—for utopian ideals—even though the ideas do not work in practice; the implication is that what works is immoral (or at best amoral). This dichotomy sets up an impossible conflict: either you can do what's right or do what works (what is efficacious and successful), but you can't do both. Whenever one is faced with such a dichotomy, it is imperative to question the premises behind it (e.g., see Binswanger, 1981). In this case a key error is the premise that altruism is moral. It is not.

Rand (1957, 1964) has demonstrated that rational self-interest is the only code of morality consistent with man's nature as a rational being (and the code which

334

is implicit in the concept of individual rights) and that altruism represents the antithesis of a rational morality. Altruism requires that man sacrifice his mind, his ego, his values, his happiness and the products of his efforts to others (the state, the party, the race, the neighbors, etc.). A more anti-life morality could not be imagined. Contrary to the conventional view that socialism is a moral theory which somehow does not work out in practice, while capitalism is an immoral but practical system, socialism is an immoral theory which leads to exactly what one would expect: poverty, suffering and (for many) death. It appeals to the worst in man: his desire for power over other men (in the case of the leaders) and the desire for the unearned (in the case of the followers). In contrast, capitalism appeals to the best in man: the desire to achieve his own happiness by the productive use of his mind. Capitalism works *because* it is based on a rational code of morality, that is, rational self-interest. I would change the quote from Hayek cited by Lerner, as follows: "What has always made the State a hell on earth is the concept that man exists to serve the state." The United States of America was the first country to reverse this premise and declare that the state (the government) exists to serve man, i.e., to protect rights.

Second, rights are not creations of the state or favors from rulers, but are inherent in man's nature as a rational being. Man lives by the use of his mind; to survive he must be free to act on the basis of his judgment (providing he does not violate the rights of others). To violate a man's rights means to initiate force against him, thus preventing free action. While the above view (Rand, 1967) disagrees with the views both of conservatives (who have never defended rights consistently) and of the Founding Fathers (who saw rights as coming from God, thereby implying that they could not be justified by rational argument), this does not make it wrong. The issue must be decided based on the merits of the arguments in each case, not on appeals to authority, i.e., "primary sources."

To claim that rights are not absolute but are gifts or permissions granted or withdrawn at will by the state or the majority is to claim, in effect, that there are no inalienable rights (which is the view held most consistenly by socialists). Once this premise is granted, it is only a matter of time before all of our rights are abridged. Our Constitution, including the Bill of Rights, was designed specifically so that rights could *not* be voted away by a majority. The Bill of Rights, however, did not sufficiently specify man's economic rights, and these allegedly "non-absolute" rights have been the very ones to be eroded. (We are not, incidentally, a democracy but a republic.) The relation between rights and absolute rule is precisely the opposite of that stated by Lerner. When rights are absolute, there can be no absolute (i.e., dictatorial) ruler. (The issue of land disputes alluded to by Lerner is an issue of application, not one of fundamental principle.)

Third, I agree with Lerner's criticisms of egalitarianism (the notion that all are entitled to the same rewards regardless of performance). However, I do not agree with her explanation for it. She implies that it is a result of lack of knowledge about individual differences on the part of egalitarians. This is an extremely benevolent interpretation, and I doubt very much if it is correct. For example, the new research evidence about individual differences has not made egalitarians today less numerous or less militant than in the past; if anything, the opposite has been the case.

I believe that the real motive is *hatred of ability*—hatred of competence, of achievement, of values. Since men are not equal in ability, it is not possible to raise those with less to the level of those with more. One can only penalize the more able for the benefit of the less able. Since the result of this will be to harm everyone (see my paper), the motive can only be hatred of ability for being ability-hatred of the good for being good (Rand, 1971). So much for the premise that socialists are motivated by noble (utopian) ideals.

Tying all the above issues together, the actual dichotomy is not utopia versus pragmatism, but: a rational code of morality which serves to faciliate man's survival and well-being on this earth versus an irrational, anti-life code of morality which leads to misery and destruction, or: rational egoism and its corollaries, individual rights and capitalism, versus altruism, collectivism and socialism.

A final footnote regarding Dr. Lerner's comment on the "difficulty" of performance evaluation. I never discussed the issue of whether performance appraisal was easy (or hard) under capitalism. In fact, it is under capitalism that performance evaluation is most intellectually demanding: the appraiser must integrate a broad range of observations, make highly complex inferences, and reach a conclusion based on his own independent judgment. In contrast, under Socialism judgment is replaced by politics; under the mixed economy it is gradually replaced by seniority and arbitrary regulations.

REFERENCES

Binswanger, H. The possible dream. *The Objectivist Forum*, 1981, *2*, (Nos. 1 and 2)

Rand, A. *Atlas shrugged*. New York: Random House, 1957.

Rand, A. *Capitalism: The unknown ideal*. New York: New American Library (Signet), 1967.

Rand, A. *The virtue of selfishness*. New York: New American Library (Signet), 1964.

Rand, A. The age of envy. *The Objectivist*, 1971, *10* (Nos. 7 and 8)

13

A Sociohistorical Perspective on Performance Assessment

Paul Goldman

Dr. Goldman presents the Marxist orientation to Industrial-Organizational psychology, the work setting, and performance evaluation. He asserted that the worker's performance is treated as a commodity for both the superiors and the organization.

From the Marxist point of view, capitalism is a system in which worker gains (better pay, working environment) represent losses for capitalists or for management. The relationship between management and workers is viewed as a conflict relationship. Scientific management and other technological advances are interpreted within the Marxist view as politically motivated by capitalists in order to increase worker dependence on the organization and to make workers more dispensable or interchangeble. In Goldman's view, America's business moved from ''paternalistic entrepreneurism to corporate capitalism.'' Goldman proposes three forces that are leading managers to a more cynical view of workers.

Performance evaluation for Goldman is an attempt to establish an individual relationship between the employee and the firm. Thus employers will welcome advances in performance-assessment techniques that stress the individual nature of the employee to the organization because by increasing employee productivity, organizations should become more profitable or effective. However, organizational success may or may not mean individual success.

Dr. Schmidt's discussion argues against propositions stated in the Goldman paper. First, Schmidt argues that it is in the interests of workers to cooperate with management in increasing productivity; there are goods to be obtained, and govern-

---

*The author begs indulgence for the sexist language in this chapter. The account of World War I era basic industry refers to a world that was virtually all male and it seemed appropriate to use the language of that period.

ment data suggest that real income has increased for all classes. He also argues against an increase in management interest in performance appraisal, suggesting that management deficiencies may be a more important reason for United States economic setbacks than any changes in the work force. He presents an alternate theory to Marxism based on individual differences in ability, motivation, and interest, and suggests that inequalities in a democratic society may be due to individual differences in combination with economic freedom and individual choice rather than to a continual conflict between management and labor.

In response to Schmidt, Goldman expresses doubt on the accuracy of the government statistics and argues that Schmidt errs when he blames management for the decline in United States' productivity.

What can students of performance assessment, or industrial and organizational psychologists in general, learn from the recent body of Marxist literature on the sociology of organizations? Although most would assume that any relationship between these two scholarly traditions would be contradictory, each deals with similar intellectual issues. They share a deep concern for what Marx called the "relations of production"—that is, the interaction between worker and manager and, to a lesser extent, among fellow workers and between managerial colleagues. Moreover, adherents of both disciplines would agree that productivity is almost always problematic and that differing definitions of what is productive labor or, more colloquially, what constitutes a "fair day's work" hold far-reaching implications, and that they partially explain organizational conflict. Finally, they would agree, if for different reasons, that worker involvement and commitment are important aspects of the work setting.

Similarities between the two traditions should not, however, be overstated. Although resting on a firm conceptual foundation and incorporating a variety of intellectual concerns, many organizational psychologists have a strong applied orientation with the corresponding tendency to narrow their focus. Landy and Farr's (1980) review of the performance-rating literature suggests that this may be a problem. By contrast, Marxist sociology is sweeping and highly theoretical. It may provide clues to the understanding of organizational dynamics, but offers few solutions or strategies, even to workers who wish to change the systems in which they find themselves. Allen (1978) and Mills (1952, 1970), however, suggest that managers can benefit from an understanding of the Marxist approach. Organizational psychology, particularly its application, is geared to the needs of management. Within it we see an assumption that the requirements of management and the needs of workers can be made compatible. Marxists reject the assumption, believing instead that the interests of capital and labor are sharply opposed to one another. A third difference is that organizational psychology deals with the present and the near-term future whereas Marxism has an historical orientation that attempts to unify past, present, and future civilization.

I note the issue of historicism here because it is particularly relevant to my own immediate concerns.

In this paper I discuss the Marxist analysis of work organizations as it has been elaborated by a new generation of industrial sociologists. The argument is developed in four sections. First, I argue that situations of workers differ so fundamentally from those of managers that entirely different analytic approaches are required. Second, I review the Marxist literature on organizations. Third, I describe my own research as a way of illustrating the Marxist approach (Goldman, 1981). Finally, the paper concludes with some speculations about the relationship between managerial ideology and performance assessment.

UNITS OF ANALYSIS

Employee evaluation and performance appraisal are crucial, if elusive, aspects of all organizational practice. Perhaps Latham and Wexley (1981) go too far in arguing that appraisal is the *most* important system for managing human resources within organizations, but its centrality should be clear to students of organizational process. The significance of performance evaluation is that it ties together many of the key concepts of organizational psychology, including productivity, motivation, evaluation, feedback, the work ethic, and distributive justice. However, students of performance assessment often ignore important questions involving the appropriate unit of analysis.

There are at least two general performance-appraisal situations. In oversimplified form, they correspond to the two primary castes that exist in most organizations: managers and workers. Mobility chains for the former theoretically can take them to or near the very top of an organizational hierarchy (or allow recruitment at the top levels by other organizations). The latter group has clearly understood ceilings on occupational achievement, usually peaking at the level of first-line supervisor. This dichotomous categorization corresponds to most empirical realities even though many staff positions fit neither pattern comfortably and a number of corporations do make an effort to find latent executive talent among operational personnel. Performance appraisals serve different functions for each caste because supervisors and raters have different concerns depending on whether the employee to be evaluated is a potential peer or a perpetual subaltern. Much of the difference stems from evaluators' tendency to empathize and identify with managers, while regarding workers as subordinates to be viewed instrumentally. Thus "soft" criteria for managerial evaluation may include interpersonal style and even general social adjustment, whereas the "hard" assessments of worker productivity generally focus on clear, easily measurable output.

The problems of appraising individual managers' performance are probably far more complex than those of evaluating routine workers. Managers work with less specific job descriptions and performance is often difficult to quantify. Moreover, executive evaluation inevitably involves some degree of organizational politics, and sponsorship patterns frequently blur the lines between universalistic and particularistic evaluation. Assessments of managerial personnel have a competitive aspect whenever rewards—such as promotions, new assignments, or pay raises—are finite. Finally, there may be limits to how far managerial performance appraisal may be rationalized. Regardless of whether or not standardized instruments are used, jobs are unique and rating systems cannot be as refined as when dozens or even hundreds of employees are performing essentially the same task. These are thorny issues and most performance-evaluation literature has addressed them in their emphasis on assessing those who do nonroutine jobs, usually with great sophistication. However, these concerns are not central to this paper, as its central focus is on workers in nonmanagerial positions.

The problems of evaluating workers are quite different from those of measuring managers. Social scientists generally see working-class work as routine and the measurement of performance as relatively easily quantifiable. In fact, many factory workers are paid by one or another form of piece rates, particularly in the garment trades, electronic component assembly facilities, or in machine shops. Others are so enmeshed in a productive process-automotive assembly lines for instance—that evaluations of individual workers may be quite difficult even when the individual(s) responsible for uncompleted work or defects can be identified. Evaluating individual performance in these settings is often handicapped by limitations written into union contracts. The overall picture is complex and changing, however, and more and more working-class jobs are now in service, retail, and clerical occupations, and/or in nonunionized firms or agencies. Many of these relatively new jobs have features that are difficult to quantify and these may require performance-appraisal systems that would more closely approximate the types long used for managers. Evaluations of subordinate personnel, however, continue to have quite a different texture than those of managers. Workers' labor is often treated as a commodity by both superiors and by the institutions employing them. A theoretical understanding of this systemic instrumentalism in both the production and service sectors can be facilitated by an approach that includes the recent research on the labor process, which incorporates a general Marxist perspective.

MARXISM AND ORGANIZATIONS

From one of his earliest writings, *The Economic and Philosophical Manuscripts of 1844*, Marx (1962) concerned himself with the alienation of factory workers under the then emerging industrial capitalism. He noted the objectification of the relationship between entrepreneur and worker as the former succeeded in appropriating the latter's labor through ownership of the means of production: the tools, plant, and raw materials. Workers thereby lost their former control over their laboring activity because decisions about product and process, as well as the power to market finished goods, passed to capitalist entrepreneurs. Two decades later, in *Capital,* Marx (1967) described the effect of the detailed division of labor that gradually came to characterize capitalist production:

> While simple cooperation leaves the mode of working by the individual for the most part unchanged, manufacture thoroughly revolutionizes it, and seizes labour power by its very roots. It converts the labourer into a crippled monstrosity, by forcing his detail dexterity at the expense of a world of productive capabilities and instincts. . . . Not only is the detail work distributed to different individuals, but the individual himself is made the automatic motor of a fractional operation [p. 325].

Marx's fundamental point is that under the capitalist organization of production, the worker is transformed from an individual into a commodity and management necessarily develops an instrumental orientation, asking only "How much can we effectively exploit the labor power that we have under our control?"

Marxist writings during the past decade have edited, amplified, and documented Marx's basic propositions in a number of settings, and have relied on empirical research in both historical and contemporary contexts. Most of this writing has been influenced by Harry Braverman's (1974) monumental work, *Labor and Monopoly Capital,* which argued that both the immediate and the long-term impact of scientific management has been vastly underestimated by current students of work and organizations. Braverman claimed that appropriation of workers' knowledge by management and the separation of conception from execution in industrial work altered that work fundamentally, and that this process continued in technology's subsequent invasion of clerical, retail, and sales sectors. A complete review of the literature spawned by Braverman's work is available elsewhere (Goldman, 1983), but several points are sufficiently critical to bring forth here. Perhaps most important is Marxists' belief that capitalism is a zero-sum game. What workers gain by way of better wages and benefits or improved working conditions, capitalists lose in terms of actual or potential profits, even though some firms, those with monopoly pricing power, can recoup their losses by raising prices. The firm's constant push to enhance capital accumulation and workers' efforts (often through their unions) to gain a fuller and more secure piece of the action can and often do lead to conflict. Occasionally this is very broad in scope, as in the Seattle and San Francisco general strikes. More frequently conflict is limited to strikes in one firm or industry. But most of the time it is represented by hostility or apathy among rank-and-file workers without dramatic battle lines or discernible consequences. Capturing the texture of these struggles has become one of the goals of Marxists studying the organizational context of labor relations. This has led to a deep interest in labor history with particular emphasis on those periods in which change is both rapid and extensive. Thus, Thompson (1963), Hobsbawm (1964), and Marglin (1974) studied the English Industrial Revolution, and Stone (1974), Montgomery

(1979), and Clawson (1980) studied the United States during its period of rapid change around 1900.

The main metaphor of Marxist industrial sociology is *politics*, for the always-latent conflict of organizational settings most often engenders the type of maneuver we normally think of as political process. Each desired or actual change, and these are usually but not always initiated by management, is considered in terms of potential reactions to it. Thus, the issue of political control is as important as economic efficiency to the change process. Answering who will control the shop floor and determine how work will be done and how fast then has a political meaning. David Montgomery's (1979) analysis of industrial strikes suggests that in some periods, control issues were as important as economic gains for many unions. Montgomery provides convincing evidence that between 1900 and 1920 unions were more interested than management in developing stable and demanding standards to guide their labor, but that employers were more interested in acquiring the power to manipulate standards frequently. Dan Clawson (1980) also uses historical data to show that nineteenth-century crafts production characterized by the inside contracting system was widespread, existed in diverse industries, involved up to several hundred workers in a single shop, and, most important, was as efficient and as innovative as the competing bureaucratic system that operated in the same industries and sometimes in the same companies. According to Clawson, the system ended not because of internal inadequacies, but because managers wanted to assure themselves of a central place in the production process and to garner the monetary rewards that they felt should come with their organizational status. Marglin (1974) makes much the same point in describing early nineteenth-century English employers.

Other Marxist scholars take the argument a bit further, suggesting that even mechanization and other technological innovations partially reflect managers' perceived needs to control workers. The application of science to industry achieved three ends. First of all, it made production so complicated that the typical skilled craftsman had difficulty learning the start-to-finish knowledge that had characterized the crafts tradition for centuries. Second, it generally reduced tightly coupled, interdependent relations between workers and correspondingly tended to isolate and atomize individuals on the job. Finally, because skills and cooperation are the backbone of trade unionism, it served to reduce or break the substantial power of the crafts unions. David Noble (1979) documents the decision-making process by which the metal-working industry moved towards numerical control in the machining process and concludes that it represents one example of management's efforts to wrest control from shop floor workers. Moble's description comes from the period just after World War II. Burawoy (1979) describes the changes between then and 1974, in the machine shop where he worked:

> fixtures and machines have improved and become more standardized . . . , and the
> skill required in setting up has therefore declined. Moreover . . . there was [thirty

years ago] greater diversity in the operations any one machine could perform, and it therefore took operators much longer to master all the jobs they would have to run [p. 55].

The research of Zimbalist (1979) on the newspaper printing industry and of Mills (1979) on the longshore industry reveal that the desire to curb the power of strong unions was part of management's rationale for developing and implementing radical new technologies that transformed basic production processes in those industries. In both cases, the changeover was only accomplished after intense and prolonged resistence of workers and their unions.

The deskilling of workers enables management to create and take advantage of favorable labor-market conditions. The use of operatives instead of skilled workers reduces employers' dependence on specific individuals, because new workers may be trained and broken in over a period of days or weeks rather than months or years. Marxists have noted recently, however, that this situation does not allow managers to disregard totally the question of worker loyalty. In large firms, differentiation between jobs and the creation of job ladders creates an internal labor market so firms can reward those employees who stay on the job with easier, better-paid jobs. This practice has a long history, as we see from Stone's (1974) study of the pre-1900 steel industry. Burawoy's (1979) study of a metal-working department of a large conglomerate and Edwards' (1979) study of General Electric indicates that this is a continuing pattern.

Manipulation of the labor market raises an even more complex aspect of the Marxist approach. Several authors suggest that bureaucracy itself developed not because of rational imperatives but rather because it was *the* means by which management was able to control workers. It is true that the enormous growth in the numbers of technicians, record keepers, supervisors, and clerical personnel necessitated bureaucratic structure. The more fundamental cause, however, was that employers needed bureaucrats to control a labor force made recalcitrant by deskilling, union busting, and exploitation (Edwards, 1979; Goldman & Van Houten, 1980a). Clawson (1980) suggests that bureaucracy and scientific management were prerequisites to full-scale mechanization, claiming thus that the organizational revolution preceded the technical revolution.

The Marxist sociology of capitalism is not without some ambiguities and one of these bears directly to the issue at hand. Two notions of "control" can often be confused with one another (Gartman, 1978; Goldman & Van Houten, 1977; Gordon, 1976). One form of control is technical and relates directly to management's concerns for improving and maintaining productivity. The other refers to social control, and management's implicit desire to minimize conflict and win workers' loyalty. These may be positively or negatively correlated. For example, a mechanization process that cuts unit labor costs by a micro division of labor may increase social control by isolating individual workers from one another, make them more replaceable and thus more politically timid, facilitate individual evaluation and with it a breakdown of class solidarity, and/or make unionization more difficult. Conversely, demands for immediate increases in productivity resulting in a speedup of one kind or another may have the desired short-term benefits, particularly if jobs are scarce and workers cannot afford to quit, but this may come at the cost of worsening labor–management relations over the long run. It is difficult to assess the overall success or failure of these efforts. Burawoy, whose 1979 book is, along with Braverman's (1974), one of the two landmarks of the Marxist genre, notes that contemporary labor processes may have the tendency to "manufacture consent," and channel workers' energies towards "making out," at least in work places with relatively high wages and an internal labor market. Consent is more grudging in highly exploitative, minimum-wage situations that provide no prospects for workers, but anger seldom expresses itself in collective action. A fair tallying up of the score would probably show that employers are well ahead, although the game's fortunes have in the past turned suddenly in times of war and depression. In any event, further exploration of management designs and intentions can help us understand past and present trends almost as much as observable relationships between management and worker.

This interest in managerial intentionality and instrumentality dovetails with another trend in Marxist social science, that of the "revisionist" historians. This intellectual connection is particularly interesting because a number of these scholars—G. William Domhoff (1969), Gabriel Kolko (1963), and James Weinstein (1968)—studied the early decades of this century. They argued that by the turn-of-the-century at least some segments of the business elite had constituted a self-conscious upper class and had begun to take a sophisticated and increasingly unified view of economic and political processes. This group accepted, and even encouraged, many of the reforms—for example, worker compensation and government regulation—so vigorously advocated by progessives of the time. Revisionist historians suggest that this political direction resulted from a "corporate liberal" philosophy that sought to cool out working-class discontent by acceding to relatively inexpensive ameliorations of the social conditions that fostered revolt. This analysis argues that businessmen had a far-sighted and well thought out view of the future and that they were willing to sacrifice some short-term gains for long-term stability. Such strategy in the political arena was an obvious counterpart of many efforts to transform the work place, where conflict was both more direct and more intense. In order to add to the research on this question, it is important to examine not only what corporate elites tried to do, but to look at how they thought, and especially how they conceptualized the labor-relations situation.

EMPLOYER AND WORKER, 1916–1922

The period during and just after World War I seems particularly appropriate for pursuing this question. It was a chaotic epoch, characterized by the boom of the war years (when labor was in short supply) *and* the bust of the postwar period (when unemployment was high). It marked the end of a decade of extremely bitter strikes. Moreover, the basic *structural* changes in American manufacturing had already been more-or-less completed by the time the United States entered the war. Merger and economic concentration, mechanization, and a general Taylorist philosophy all dominated the world of the larger firms as America's business moved from paternalistic entrepreneurism to corporate capitalism.

Managerial awareness, then as now, was reflected and even abetted by the development of the business press during the late nineteenth century. Virtually every industry sector had at least one trade journal that communicated information and ideas about both the specific technical concerns of its readers and also general business practices. Labor problems were given considerable coverage, indicating how important and problematic they were to readers. At the same time, more general popular business periodicals also grew in circulation. The most prominent examples were *Factory, Industrial Management,* and *System.* This type of source is widely used by business historians who have interested themselves in the ideas held by American businessmen (Krooss, 1970; Sutton, 1956). A page-by-page reading of each number of these journals between 1916 and 1922 provided the primary data base for this research.

Articles in the business press probably provide a better representation of executive thought 60 years ago than they do now. Virtually all articles were written by, or ghost written for, prominent executives or were verbatim interviews. This contrasts with the committee approach popular in contemporary weekly or monthly journalism. Managers were willing, even eager, to share their plans and experiences with peers in other firms and industries, and they often demonstrated an almost evangelical fervor. The corporate presidents, plant managers, and employment managers, even those from the largest firms, appeared unworried that their words would be read by competitors or labor activists. Labor relations apparently did not have the status of a trade secret. Although these writings were probably intended to have a public-relations impact and to show the authors' and their firms' progressive and humane natures, their validity is reinforced by the fact that most of the articles were descriptions of actual programs. Competition between magazines and trade journals also encouraged accurate information and a high circulation implies that these periodicals did not express views that were incompatible with their readers' personal philosophies. It is also possible that trade journals were both intended and received as a means by which a more self-conscious and class-conscious elite in the center communicated with those on the periphery. However, we must also keep in mind that successful programs will always be overrepresented in such literature and that failure will generally be underrepresented.

How, then, did management view labor? First of all, most corporate executives were keenly aware of differences between themselves and those who labored in shop, factory, and mine. John D. Rockefeller, Jr. (1916) distinguished between "the man of money and the man of muscle [p. 115]." James Logan

(1916) of U.S. Envelope betrayed the fact that nineteenth-century paternalism was far from dead during the war years: "I prefer the old-fashioned word 'help' to 'operative,' 'worker,' or 'employee' for they are our helpers [p. 561]." Other employers' remarks implied that workers, although not necessarily unintelligent, had weak characters and were easily led astray by outside agitators. Colorado Fuel and Iron's E. S. Cowdrick (1921) asserted that: "the laboring man can think; he wants to think, and he is going to think, whatever his employer may do or say. But he does not always think straight. . . . Sometimes he harbors distorted ideas of anarchy and sabotage and class hatred [p. 33]."

Many employers saw personal communication as one method for improving industrial relations. Meyer Bloomfield (1917) wrote that "there is such general acceptance among large employers that contact, real contact, between management and men that the only open question is . . . the best ways of getting such contact [p. 282]." Thomas Wilson (1918), president of a packing company, claimed that "any one of my 25,000 or 30,000 employees may come to see me whenever he likes—my door is never closed [p. 347]." Managers valued sincerity, honesty, and fair play in dealings with employees. As one employer put it (Borchard, 1921), "if the attitude of your executive is just and on the square, the great majority of your men will show their appreciation [p. 61]." As much as they valued forthright communications, these men were rationalists who believed in the "Facts" even more. They were convinced that worker miscomprehension and resistance occurred only because employees simply did not understand truths that had universal validity. Many companies even had classes to educate workers in the "facts." President Gary (1919) of Browning reported that: "during my talk I could see by the men's knitted brows that they were all taking it in. When it was over, I think that it was entirely evident to them that the executive end of a business is involved in more than merely taking in profits [p. 919]."

The information presented does not show that influential business executives displayed a nakedly instrumental view towards those they employed. Their writings suggest the implied hope, however tentative and naive, of creating a harmonious industrial community with a sense of partnership between management and labor. As James Farrell (1916) of U.S. Steel explained it, management wanted to show the worker that "his welfare and the welfare of the employer were identical [p. 228]." That belief, of course, however self-deluding or self-serving, has been a staple of managerial thought for at least the past century. World War I era businessmen recognized, though, that their idealized community had been severely flawed in earlier years. Although it was easy for them to limit their acknowledgment of injustices and exploitation to the past, their sensitivity to the problem is revealing. ARMCO President George Verity (1918) argued that "the workman's condition fifteen or twenty years ago was often so bad, he was often given so little reason to trust his employer and so many reasons to distrust [p. 707)."

There were, however, powerful forces leading many businessmen to an instrumental, even cynical view of their employees. The growth of organizations was one such force. By war's end, most managers came to realize that direct communication, whether of fact or feeling, was hampered by the increasingly large size of many firms. It was also clear, at least to John Calder (1920) and to International Harvestor's Arthur Young (1920), that the foreman would have to play a more positive role in labor relations. James Logan (1922) of U.S. Envelope wrote that "we must take for granted . . . that the help . . . can never know about the management. But they can know the people immediately over them. . . . It is by these men . . . that the larger management is appraised [p. 124]." Evidently it was at about this period that the foreman came to assume the ambiguous and oft-conflicted position that has been described in recent literature.

A second barrier to whatever hopes employers had for strengthening industrial community was their own view of unions. Most employers felt they already paid adequate and fair wages—the highest they could afford—and they believed that decent wages attracted good workers and committed effort. Employers felt unions unnecessarily intervened with this straightforward relationship between employer and employee and most agreed with GE's Richard Rice (1919) that "no means has been devised of dealing with employees through labor unions which has shown any efficiency [p. 418]." Employers' commitment to the concept of individualism meant to them that they should have the right to negotiate singly with each employee and evaluate the individual's worth to the firm. This issue is still problematic and must be considered when studying performance-appraisal systems as they apply to working-class occupations.

A third problem employers faced in creating industrial community was their own capitalistic instincts. Businessmen are necessarily situational and opportunistic. During the postwar recession their behavior and rhetoric changed sharply from what it had been when they were desperate for labor. It was easy for them to reinterpret the past and forget their apparently idealistic pronouncements. *System* correspondent Samuel Crowther (1919) felt that wage cuts were necessary and that "employees need a great deal of instruction on the subjects of wages, output, and employers' profits, sympathetic strikes, and other questions on which they now have false notions [p. 1059]."

SOME CURRENT PARALLELS

Historical comparisons are always difficult, frequently intellectually dangerous, and often unconvincing. Nevertheless, surface similarities between the period just following World War I and in the several years after the end of the Vietnam War are suggestive (Goldman & Van Houten, 1980b, 1980c). These probably represent recurring issues and uncertainties in labor relations within the American capitalist economy rather than any historical coincidence. Most striking is the apparent lack of consensus on so many of the same questions that troubled managers 60 years earlier. For example, there is still debate about whether material rewards or nonmaterial incentives (mainly job enrichment) motivate best. On the other hand, many managers share the same concern as their fore-bears that routine, repetitive work is deadening and saps both human potential and worker motivation. Although humanistic management, job enlargement, flextime, quality-control circles, and even work place democratization may be only "so much window dressing" as one critic claims, enough programs have been begun that we would be justified in concluding that a substantial proportion of managers think (or hope) these are viable options (Lederer, 1978).

In some respects, contemporary businesspeople seem less concerned with community for its own sake and more interested in how "good human relations" can contribute to union avoidance and hence profitability than did the World War I generation. Good pay and fair play, especially in administering work rules, contribute to a union-free environment (Kilgour, 1978). Some managers, howev-er, do believe that such an environment is a desirable way of improving human relations (Curley, 1978) "since there is an absence of an adversary relationship between company management and . . . union officials. . . . In this non-union atmosphere, management invariably has a sincere concern for employees [p. 69]." It is also ironic that managers are still worried about the ability and training of first-line supervisors to carry out effective human relations.

A final parallel is many businesspeople's opportunistic approach to unions. For a generation, most commentators have felt that management and labor had wrought a mutually beneficial accommodation and settlement from one another whereby business accepted a democratic, nonradical trade union movement in turn for labor's support of the free enterprise. Conflict was routinized and usually not traumatic for either side, except perhaps in organizing campaigns. The trade union movement's political weaknesses and its failure to grow during the 1970s created a climate in which employers could go on the offensive, much as they did in the 1919 to 1922 period. Although managers no longer believe that organizing drives are fomented by "reds" or "outside agitators," they are no less deter-mined to stop new campaigns and to explore the possibility of decertifying currently recognized unions. Their willingness to hire labor-relations consultants who gain reputations for union busting, to provoke strikes, to violate labor laws, and generally to engage in preventive labor relations shows how fragile and situational labor–management accord has been. Industrial psychology plays a latent and minor role because its tenets reinforce some of the systemic tendencies of the capitalist order. Although one can cite instances in which psychological and attitudinal testing are administered in order to screen out workers with prounion sympathies, such efforts are rare and probably ineffective (Kilgour, 1978). At the same time, because some techniques, including performance as-sessment, are methods to evaluate and compare *individuals,* they conflict with the goals and preferred practices of most unions.

The foregoing analysis suggests that we should locate the present interest in performance evaluation within a broad historical and sociological framework. Its roots lie not only in present concerns about individual and organizational productivity but also in features built into the structure of capitalist economies. Put most simply, managers act on the belief that workers are not sufficiently motivated, and in some cases are unable, to maximize on-the-job productivity individually or collectively. Correctly or incorrectly, this assumption is widely held. The historical evidence presented here suggests that employers have been concerned about worker effort and performance at least since the turn of the century. One of several justifications for Taylorism was the perceived tendency of workers to "systematically soldier" on the job.

Managers and management though should not, however, be underrated. Many businesspeople, then as now, have developed a sophisticated understanding of the obstacles to worker motivation. They have recognized that overly routinized work, arbitrary supervision, poor communication between management and employee sap energy and ingenuity. Proposed solutions have strong similarities that cut across the decades. Performance assessment carries on a tradition that began with scientific management, continued with management's efforts to improve personal communication, and even incorpoates more recent incentive plans and job enlargement schemes. These programs attempt to establish an *individual* relationship between employee and firm. During the early years of this century, these techniques carried with them a belief, or at least a hope, that they would help return labor relations to its mid- to late-nineteenth-century epoch of paternalistic community when the troubles of the turn-of-the-century period had not yet upset the relative tranquility.

Individualism and rationalism in management thought, along with vastly increased organizational size, very easily led to a view of workers that has become instrumental, quantitative, and ultimately a bit moralistic. Individualism and competitiveness in personal and professional life have served most managers well. For them department or company success has often resulted in advancement. This experience, as well as the expectation that workers should believe and behave similarly, constitutes a crucial part of the cultural system of most managers. Most employers are likely to welcome innovations in labor-relations technique—sophisticated performance—assessment schemes, for instance—that stress the individuation of the employee's relationship to the firm.

Employees locked into a lower organizational caste within the organizations will not share these views. Organizational success may or may not spell individual success. Potentially increased earnings may only constitute a marginal motivating factor, particularly if relations with coworkers provide a major source of work satisfaction. The competitiveness that goes with individualized evaluation is only worth the effort if the company can offer a reasonable chance to jump to more demanding and responsible positions. Perhaps more important, systemic demands make it easy for firms to act cynically and take unfair advantage of workers. The changing industrial-relations strategies of the post-1919 years and the current attack on organized labor are one example. The moving of business to locations with less expensive labor is another. The current enthusiasm for performance assessment as a tool to increase productivity, whatever its benefits in formalizing expectations and providing concrete feedback, should contend with these issues if it is to become an effective, long-lasting practice and not a passing fashion.

I would like to conclude this essay by returning to the question posed at its outset: Are there lessons from recent Marxist industrial sociology and from its interpretation of the hisotrical past that can be applied to current practices of performance assessment? Probably not. The capitalist system has not been able to coopt the personal commitments workers have to one another and to transcend the conflicts that result from hierarchical inequalities and from the likelihood that corporate strategies to maximize returns will conflict with workers' perceived and real needs. Community depends on solidarity, reciprocity, and on differences in place of inequalities. Performance-appraisal systems in which peer evaluation plays a major role, in which the unit of analysis is the work group and not the individual, and in which worker evaluations of supervisors carry as much weight as evaluations of subordinates fit these requirements. Equitable sharing of organizational success and failure (as well as a diminution of the differential between executive salaries and worker wages) also might contribute to an organizational climate that approaches an industrial community. Worker belief that productivity gains will be shared and that wage reductions and/or layoffs will fall as heavily on executives as on them should have a similar impact. These practices are incompatible with either the capitalist impulse or private ownership of the means of production. They could hardly be implemented in an open system where, among other considerations, labor market demand for executives, technical experts, skilled workers, and operatives fluctuates in an unsyncronized fashion and in a world dominated by multinational corporations.

ACKNOWLEDGMENTS

I would like to acknowledge the University of Oregon Graduate School for a summer grant that enabled me to collect the data for this paper. Some of the findings were presented at the 1981 American Sociological Association Meetings. I appreciate the assistance of Mimi Goldman, Don Van Houten, Nancy DiTomaso, Roslyn Feldberg, Jack Hammond, Glenn Goodwin, Daniel Pope, and Frank Landy, who read and critiqued either that version or earlier versions of this one, as well as typists Vicki Van Nortwick, Robin Mendoza, and Stella Vlastos.

REFERENCES

Allen, V. L. Marxism and the personnel manager. *Personnel Management*, 1978, *8*, 18–122.
Bloomfield, M. The new profession of handling men. *Industrial Management*, 1917, *52*, 441–446.

Borchard, J. E. Attitude. *Industrial Management*, 1921, *61*, 140.

Braverman, H. *Labor and monopoly capital: The degradation of work in the twentieth century*. New York: Monthly Review, 1974.

Burawoy, M. *Manufacturing consent: Changes in the labor process under monopoly capitalism*. Chicago: University of Chicago Press, 1979.

Calder, J. Training foremen. *Factory*, 1920, *25*, 355–358.

Clawson, D. *Bureaucracy and the labor process: The transformation of U.S. industry, 1860–1920*. New York: Monthly Review, 1980.

Cowdrick, E. S. Some results of cooperation between management and men. *Industrial Management*, 1921, *62*, 32–33.

Crowther, S. Why men strike. *System*, 1919, *36*, 620–621, 670–676.

Curley, D. O. Employee sounding boards: Answering the participative need. *Personnel Administration*, 1978, *23*, 69–73.

Domhoff, G. *The higher circles: The governing class in America*. New York: Random House, 1969.

Edwards, R. *Contested terrain: The transformation of the workplace in the twentieth century*. New York: Basic, 1979.

Farrell, J. A. Profit sharing. When? Why? How? *System*, 1916, *29*, 227–232.

Gartman, D. Marx and labor process: An interpretation. *The Insurgent Sociologist*, Fall 1978, *8*, 109–125.

Gary, S. How my men help me to manage. *Factory*, 1919, *22*, 917–919.

Goldman, P. *Managerial ideology and labor in the aftermath of World War I*. Paper presented at the annual meetings of the Society for the Study of Social Problems, Toronto, 1981.

Goldman, P. The labor process and the sociology of organizations. *Perspectives in Organizational Sociology: Theory and Research*, 1983, *2*.

Goldman, P., & Van Houten, D. R. Managerial strategies and the worker: A Marxist analysis of bureaucracy. *Sociological Quarterly*, 1977, *18*, 108–125.

Goldman, P., & Van Houten, D. R. Bureaucracy and domination: Managerial strategy in turn-of-the-century American industry. *1979 International Yearbook of Organizational Studies*, 1980, *1*, 108–141. (a)

Goldman, P., & Van Houten, D. R. Uncertainty, conflict, and labor relations in the modern firm I: Productivity and capitalism's 'human face.' *Economic and Industrial Democracy: An International Journal*, 1980, *1*, 63–98. (b)

Goldman, P., & Van Houten, D. R. Uncertainty, conflict, and labor relations in the modern firm II: The war on labor. *Economic and Industrial Democracy: An International Journal*, 1980, *1*, 263–287. (c)

Gordon, M. Capitalist efficiency and socialist efficiency. *Monthly Review*, July–August 1976, *28*, 19–39.

Hobsbawm, E. J. *Labouring men*. New York: Basic, 1964.

Kilgour, J. Before the union knocks. *Personnel Journal* 1978, 57, 186–192.

Kolko, G. *The triumph of conservatism: A reinterpretation of American history, 1900–1916*. New York: Free Press, 1963.

Krooss, E. *Executive opinion: What business leaders said and thought about economic issues. 1920's–1960's*. Garden City, N.J.: Doubleday, 1970.

Landy, F., & Farr, J. L. Performance rating. *Psychological Bulletin*, 1980, *87*, 72–107.

Latham, G., & Wexley, K. *Increasing productivity through performance appraisal*. Reading, Mass.: Addison-Wesley, 1981.

Lederer, V. Decision-making: Should employees get in on the act? *Administrative Management*, Spetember 1978, *39*, 51–52. 58–62.

Logan, J. Men—the biggest problem in business. *System*, 1916, *31*, 559–566.

Logan, J. What to do today about tomorrow's labor problems. *Factory*, 1922, *29*, 123–125, 156.

Marglin, S. What the bosses do?: The origins and functions of hierarchy in capitalist production. *The Review of Radical Political Economics*, Summer 1974, *6*, 33–60.

Marx, K. The economic and philosophical manuscripts of 1844. In E. Fromm (Ed.), *Marx's concept of man*. New York: Ungar, 1962.

Marx, K. *Capital*. New York: International, 1967.

Mills, C. W. A Marx for the managers. In Robert K. Merton, (Eds.), *Reader in bureaucracy*. New York: Free Press, 1952.

Mills, C. W. The contribution of sociology to studies of industrial relations. *Berkeley Journal of Sociology*, 1970, *15*, 11–32.

Mills, H. The San Francisco waterfront: The social consequences of industrial modernization. In A. Zimbalist (Ed.), *Case studies on the labor process*. New York: Monthly Review, 1979.

Montgomery, D. *Workers' control in America*. New York: Oxford University Press, 1979.

Noble, D. Social choice in machine design: The case of automatically controlled machine tools. In A. Zimbalist (Ed.), *Case studies on the labor process*. New York: Monthly Review, 1979.

Rice, R. Improving relations of employer and employee. *Electrical World*, 1919, *73*, 418–419.

Rockefeller, J. D., Jr. There's a solution for labor troubles. *System*, 1916, *30*, 115–121.

Stone, K. The origins of job structures in the steel industry. *Review of Radical Political Economics*, Summer 1974, *6*, 61–97.

Sutton, F. X., S. Harrison, C. Kayson, J. Tobin *The American business creed*. N. Y.: Schocken, 1956.

Thompson, E. P. *The making of the English working class*. New York: Pantheon, 1963.

Verity, M. Why we have no trouble with our men. *System*, 1918, *33*, 707–710.

Weinstein, J. *The corporate ideal in the liberal state*. Boston: Beacon, 1968.

Wilson, E. How I deal with men. *System*, 1918, *33*, 347–350.

Young, H. Some experiences in industrial relations. *Factory*, 1920, *24*, 259–264.

Zimbalist, A. Technology and the labor process in the printing industry. In A. Zimbalist (Ed.), *Case studies on the labor process*. New York: Monthly Review, 1979.

Alternative Theories:
Comments on Goldman

Frank L. Schmidt

Paul Goldman is not exactly the stereotypical raving, fist-shaking, morally out-raged Marxist. His paper fails to conjure up mental images of revolutionary flames consuming America. He tends to suggest or imply his propositions rather than to boldly state them, and therefore he impresses me as a tentative, doubting, and perhaps reluctant Marxist. Neverthess, he does advance propositions, and I try here to identify and address the major ones:

1. Goldman maintains that it is not in the interests of workers to cooperate with management in increasing productivity. I argue that it is.

2. Goldman maintains that the current increase in management interest in performance appraisal is part of a war by management on labor. I contend that such increased interest may not even exist. But if it does, it may be part of a process of shifting the blame for our current economic troubles from the shoulders of management to labor. I argue that management deficiencies are a more important cause of our economic setbacks than any changes that have taken place in the work force.

3. Goldman offers Marxist theory as the explanation of economic behavior in the United States and other capitalist countries. I offer an alternative theory that I believe is more consistent with both everyday observation and with cumulative research knowledge in psychology.

4. Finally, I discuss some more specific points of disagreement.

---

[1]The opinions expressed in this paper are those of the author and do not necessarily reflect the policies of George Washington University or any other organization.

ALTERNATIVE THEORY OF WORKER INTEREST

Goldman maintains that employee resistance to performance appraisal is based on a fundamental fact: It is not in the interests of workers to cooperate with management to increase production and productivity. As Goldman points out, this proposition is based on the assumption that capitalism is by its nature a zero-sum gaem. I believe he means this only metaphorically, because if capitalism were a zero-sum game, there would be no fruits of increased productivity for workers and management to fight over. Yet he clearly believes that such fruits exist, because his position is that management will appropriate all such gains to itself. It is management's failure to share these gains that Goldman believes is the basis for worker resistance to productiviey-improvement efforts. His position is clearly consistent with Marxist theory. Marx predicted that capitalism, by its very nature, would inexorably lead to progressively greater relative and absolute impoverishment of workers.

What does the evidence on this point indicate? The economic record shows that over the last 40 years, the increases in wealth resulting from increased productivity have not gone entirely to the wealthy. This additional wealth has been distributed across all income classes, and therefore real income has increased for all classes, even though the *relative* distribution of income has been changed only slightly in the direction of less inequality. This has been true not only in the United States, but in all other industrialized democracies. This pattern of distribution of new wealth is due in part to government programs for income redistribution of new wealth and to the success unions have had in increasing wages in many important segments of the economy. Without government programs and union activities, lower-income classes may not have received their proportionate share of the new wealth. But we must remember that Marx predicted increasing relative and absolute impoverishment of workers with no qualifications attached. Clearly he was wrong, and therefore Goldman is also wrong. In the past, workers have shared proportionately (or better) in the fruits of increased productivity, and I know of no reason—and Goldman presents no reason—why this state of affairs will not be maintained. It is therefore clearly in the interests of workers in general—both blue- and white-collar employees—to cooperate with management in efforts to improve productivity. Such improvements mean a better life for all.

ALTERNATIVE THEORY OF MANAGEMENT INTEREST
IN PERFORMANCE APPRAISAL

Is the increased interest on the part of management in performance appraisal part of an attack on labor and workers? It is not clear that there is such an increased emphasis; this conference was sponsored not by industry but by government. There has been a tremendous emphasis on performance appraisal in government recently. It is one of the few things on which former President Carter and President Reagan agree. Goldman maintains that the high unemployment associated with bad economic times weakens the market position of labor, making labor vulnerable to pressures and attacks from management. Management is unable to resist this opportunity to weaken labor and make workers more compliant, and so it attacks. One form this attack takes is an increased emphasis on performance appraisal; such an emphasis will intimidate workers. This is the Goldman theory.

My theory may seem stranger to many of you than the Goldman theory. My theory holds that if management is increasing the emphasis on performance appraisal, the purpose is not to weaken labor but to shift the blame for economic failures from management to workers.

As everyone is aware, the 1970s was a decade of slowing productivity growth, high inflation, and slow economic growth. United States economic competitiveness relative to foreign competitors such as Japan and Germany declined. Increased emphasis on performance appraisal is, in part, an attempt by managers to lay the blame for these economic failures on the doorstep of labor— labor broadly defined as all employees not part of upper management. And indeed part of the responsibility probably does belong there. There have been declines in work values, motivation, and perhaps performance. But my theory— which is not original with me[2]—holds that changes in the behavior of top management are a far more important cause of our economic troubles.

Specifically, upper management in many large companies now consists not of production-oriented engineering types or marketing types, but mostly of financial and accounting people and lawyers. The earlier production and marketing types tended to identify with the company product and were committed to long-term product-development activities; their major goal was to capture as large a share of the market as possible by successfully competing on quality and price. These characteristics are still dominant in Japanese upper management. The financial and legal people in upper management in the United States today, by contrast, know little of production process and do not identify with the company product. They have little interest in investing in long-term development of new products, because they are not interested in either in the products or in the long term. Their focus is on short-term profits attainable through financial manipulations—for example, currency exchange trading and speculation, identification and exploitation of tax loopholes in mergers and acquisitions, and so on. This sort of orientation by upper management may produce rosy short-term profitability pictures for the company in question, but it contributes little to growth in national productivity and wealth. In fact it is my belief that it leads directly to the

---

[2] I first heard this theory explicated five years ago by John Hunter. More recently I have seen it advanced in several articles in newspapers and magazines. I have never seen any treatment of it in the psychological literature.

kind of economic slippage we have seen over the last decade. American management has, it seems, been eager to blame our economic failures on changes in the work force. But it has shown no inclination to even recognize its own failures, much less to remedy them. Any increased emphasis on performance appraisal for employees below the top management level could be part of an attempt to shift the blame. Of course management may be unaware that it is the major cause of our economic problems, and therefore may not be *consciously* shifting the blame. But if so, this lack of awareness indicates the scope of the problem.

This is a conference on performance appraisal. Goldman and I differ on the performance-appraisal rating we would give to upper management in America. He seems to feel that upper management is almost diabolically efficient and clever in fulfilling the role assigned to it by capitalism—a role that is morally repugnant to him. He feels management is performing very well. My assessment is that upper management is failing the American economy and the American people.

This disagreement illustrates an important point about performance appraisal: In order to evaluate performance, one must have a theory of performance. Such a theory specifies what desirable performance is. If one's theory of performance is faulty, one's performance appraisals will be faulty. I believe this is the ultimate problem underlying our current economic problems.

Why did American corporations allow the financial–legal elite to become dominant in upper managemet? I believe the answer lies in the pressures that exist in this country for immediate profitability. Investors today seem to respond mostly to current and near-future profit-and-loss pictures, making it difficult for firms with good long-range profit prospects but mediocre or poor short-term prospects to raise capital. The change in investor behavior, in turn, may be due to the fact that a large proportion of available investment funds today are managed by professional stock-fund managers (again, financial people). Such managers are themselves evaluated on the basis of the year-to-year or even month-to-month profitability of their investment decisions. So again the problem may be one of faulty performance appraisal. From the point of view of long-term economic growth and success, investment managers are being evaluated on the wrong performance dimensions. They are being rewarded for the wrong kind of "performance."

I am told by colleagues in economics that their discipline has not yet given much attention to this change in American managements. If the theory presented here is correct, it is clear that industrial-organizational psychologists and other social scientists concerned with organizational behavior should consider what role research can play in examining this problem.

ALTERNATIVE THEORY OF ECONOMIC BEHAVIOR

Today, only those with a true religious faith believe that Marxism is or could still be a valid scientific theory. Most of us view Marxist theory as we do Freudian theory: as a set of postulates that can explain anything and everything ex post facto but can predict nothing. Given the flexibility and imaginativeness of ex post facto Marxian interpretations, Marxian theory is immune to any real test and thus immune to falsification. Marxist theoreticians are probably busily at work at this very moment concocting ex post facto explanations for the worker rebellion directed against socialist communism in Poland. That task may challenge even their accomplished imaginations. Nevertheless, we must recognize that some so-called Marxists do not view Marxist theory as a scientific theory but merely as a potential source of interesting hypotheses to be tested. Such poeple should not be called Marxists.

As an alternative to Marxism, I offer a theory of economic behavior in modern capitalist democracies that I believe is much more consistent with the facts, including the facts revealed by psychological research. My theory consists of the following postulates:

1. Because of both genetic and environmental influences, people differ tremendously from each other in the traits and abilities that promote and retard economic growth and productivity. These traits include intelligence and subsidiary mental abilities, physical strength and stamina, motivational dispositions, drive, personality, and self-discipline.

2. Modern industrialized societies stimulate strong acquisitive drives in many people simply as a result of producing a large number of alluring products and services that can be acquired. Further, because of its emphasis on individualism and individual accomplishment, democratic capitalism stimulates not only acquisitiveness but also high achievement motivation, often in the same individuals. But even those who are achievement oriented but not acquisitive often wind up with relatively high incomes as a consequence of their achievements.

3. Under these circumstances if people have economic freedom, the individual differences just mentioned *inevitably* create large differences in income.

4. Equality of economic opportunity, even when created and policed by the government, does not eliminate inequalities in income. Equality of economic opportunity merely allows individual differences to translate themselves directly and fairly into income differences. This is true even though government-provided equality of opportunity in education, health and so on, is itself a form on income redistribution.

5. In societies with democratic governments and egalitarian traditions, the public will force the government to introduce income-redistribution programs that prevent inequalities in income from becoming "too great." We have hundreds of such programs in this country today (such as Medicaid, AFDC, etc.), and we are told by economists that it is because of such programs that the distribution of national income has become less unequal since the 1930s.

Thus economic inequalities are not due to an historically determined exploitation of workers by an evil capitalist class. Most such inequalities are due simply to the natural operation in democratic industrial societies of individual differences in combination with economic freedom. Further, this process does not eliminate individual choice. There are always individuals who choose not to maximize, or even to emphasize, economic success. The fact that these processes are quite "natural" does not mean they are always harmless. Without government intervention, economic inequality might reach levels that are morally unacceptable to most people. There is, of course, much debate about how far government should go in attempting to reduce economic inequality.

ADDITIONAL POINTS OF DISPUTE

Goldman discusses economic behavior of capitalist countries only. He never mentions events in socialist or communist countries. The implication is that such problems as, for example, worker resistance to productivity-improvement efforts do not exist in such economies. Do workers in the USSR, for example, really show higher levels of job involvement, work commitment, and performance than in capitalist countries? All the evidence that exists points in the opposite direction. Even Russian social scientists admit that work motivation is a serious problem in the USSR and that American workers work harder. In Time magazine recently, a Polish worker described worker–management relations as follows: "We pretend to work and they pretend to pay us." The current poor economic status of Poland is a matter of general knowledge.

Likewise, Goldman leaves out all reference to public-sector employees, the worker group that grew the fastest during the 1970s. In the public sector the profit motive—the churning engine of Goldman's theory—is not operative, and so his theory does not apply. Yet research has shown that there is increasing convergence between the properties of public and private-sector bureaucracies. Could it possibly be that processes other than those postulated in Marxian theory are operating?

Goldman contends that technological innovations in industry are primarily politically, rather than economically, motivated. For example, one important purpose of the assembly line was, he would hold, to make workers feel less independent and more replaceable and interchangeable. The technological innovations he has in mind reduce levels of required worker skill. More recent technological innovations have typically had the opposite effect: They have increased management's reliance on highly trained and skilled employees. Computerized data-processing systems are one example. If work technology is really an arena of political warfare, this must be one war the capitalist class is losing.

Goldman contends that management has accepted and encouraged government social-welfare programs as a means of "cooling out" working-class discontent and thereby short-circuiting worker rebellion. However, such government programs as unemployment compensation, food stamps, and welfare payments make workers less dependent on employers and thus potentially much more difficult to control. Certainly, businesspeople frequently complain that growing numbers of people no longer want to work because welfare programs are more attractive than wages from work. If so, this clearly represents a reduction in management control over labor.

Goldman refers to managers and workers as "castes." Castes do not allow for mobility into or out of their ranks, yet we know from extensive research that there is substantial upward and downward occupational mobility in the United States and other industrialized capitalist countries—both intergenerational *and* intragenerational. This has been known at least since the extensive research of Lipset and Bendix during the 1950s. We also know that one of the strongest correlates of upward and downward occupational mobility is one of the individual difference traits mentioned earlier—mental ability. In some cases, upward mobility might require the worker to leave and go to another employer or to school for additional training. But such cases still represent upward mobility within the capitalist system.

Goldman maintains that workers tend to be evaluated by "hard" criteria of job performance, whereas managers are evaluated by "soft" criteria of subjective judgment. In fact, most employees at all levels are evaluated using soft criteria. This allegation by Goldman is related to his belief that workers are viewed instrumentally merely as commodities, whereas this is not the case for managers. He should present this theory to the chief executives of television networks who are fired whenever the Nielsen ratings for their shows fail to attain some predetermined level. Hard criteria of performance are not applied to managers? A major consequence of the development of corporations in the nineteenth century is that managers became employees. They were no longer owners, and, as a result, were very often treated as commodities. Actually, there are very few people in the United States today who are not employees and who cannot therefore be treated as "commodities."

Reply to Schmidt

Paul Goldman

Frank Schmidt's comments reveal the inherent limitations of a microsociological perspective that views the American political economy as a closed system and judges its success or failure primarily from an economic frame of reference. One example may serve to illustrate the problems of a closed-system approach that so offhandedly dismisses Marxian propositions. Schmidt cites the current distribution of income in the United States as evidence that capitalism does not inevitably lead to progressive impoverishment of workers. Those statistics, however, are glaringly incomplete if, not unreasonably, we wish to include *all* employees of American-owned firms regardless of whether they work here or in the Third World.

Schmidt errs when he gives American managers poor marks for their recent performance. Although capitalism is by no means an irresistible force, a comparative approach suggests that the American version has been unusually successful in its stability and its resistance to calls for radical redistribution of income and nationalization of industry and banking. Moreover, compared to Western European countries and Japan, we have low individual and corporate taxes and no political party or social movement has mounted a credible challenge to private ownership of the means of production since the end of World War I. American capitalists were successful in taming one of the world's most militant trade-union movements through propoganda, repression, cooptation, and individuation of work. Current efforts to blame workers for the nation's lagging productivity indicates only that management looks at the war on labor as an on-going struggle.

Finally, although I agree with Schmidt's contention that top managers have failed to invest in productivity and job creation, I think the reasons have less to do with their poor judgment than with capitalism's systemic contradictions. Capitalist firms have *always* been oriented towards maximizing profits and growth, not to serving the economy in general or the people. Presently this end is best served not by more productive capacity but by acquisition and conglomeration and by foreign investment. What results is a gigantic prisoner's dilemma: Rational behavior for each individual corporation may be irrational for the system as a whole. Although we will continue to measure individual performance, these conditions make it possible that the task will come to resemble trying to weigh an elephant with a Guttman scale.

14 Concluding Remarks

Sheldon Zedeck

Frank Landy

As indicated in the Introduction to this book, the purpose of this conference was to generate a series of original papers and discussions on the topic of performance appraisal. The contributors represented the areas of Industrial-Organizational psychology, social psychology, developmental psychology, psychometrics, sociology, law, and anthropology. The goal was to stimulate, guide, and expand the research horizons for Industrial-Organizational psychologists by identifying basic problems and issues in performance appraisal and fostering examination of traditional concepts in new formulations.

This chapter summarizes the presentations and discussions, highlights the overlap or commonality among the presentations, and provides a set of propositions derived from the presentations and comments that have potential value for future research in the area of performance appraisal.

SUMMARY OF PRESENTATIONS

The 12 papers were initially categorized as: (1) organizational issues (impact of the organization on the individual); (2) individaul issues (impact of the individual on the organization); (3) methodological and measurement issues; and (4) sociopolitical issues. This categorization was a useful scheme for assigning topics, but the products do not fall neatly or exclusively into categories; instead, there is considerable overlap. Nevertheless, this summary follows the categorization adopted in the planning stages.

Organizational Issues

This section focuses on the organizational factors and characteristics that influence the performance-appraisal process and its participants, the rater and ratee.

The paper by Hall deals with the ways in which an individual can influence an organization's behavior and performance. In particular, Hall describes the possible effects that individuals at different levels within an organization have on organizational decisions (outcomes) through their strategic power and influence. The implications for performance measurement concern the administration of rewards. In particular, Hall recommends that performance-based reward systems should be less formal so that the occurrence of unintended consequences is minimized, and that reward emphasis should be shifted from short-term to long-term performance. Hall's 12 implications reflect a preference for a performance-appraisal system that recognizes differences within individuals on different aspects of performance, and over an extended period of time. In essence, the type of performance system recommended is one that is flexible and adaptable both from the organizational and individual perspective. This emphasis is consistent with suggestions by Mitchell and Guion, who argue that analysis should be at the individual level with the implication that aggregation over people, jobs, and organizations be minimized until we have a better understanding of the performance process.

Staw's comments address two issues that are relevant to all of the presentations. First, there may be an implied assumption among all the discussants that we know what good performance is. This assumption requires an elaboration of a theory of performance, which was not proposed. Second, Staw discusses the situation in which group performance is the central concern. Several participants (e.g., Mitchell, Mohrman and Lawler, and Lerner) noted the difficulty in determining individual contribution to group performance. Future research should address the issues of how to measure group performance and how to determine the contribution of a single individual to group performance.

Mitchell's paper describes the way in which the links in the arousal $\rightarrow$ motivation $\rightarrow$ behavior $\rightarrow$ performance $\rightarrow$ appraisal $\rightarrow$ feedback chain may be influenced by social, task, and situational factors. In particular, such factors as task characteristics, social cues, norms, social facilitation, administrative technology, environment, and group characteristics are suggested as factors that directly influence the links or, as indicated by Goodman and Fichman in their comments, that may moderate relationships. Some interesting questions emerge from the paper: Is the motivational model the same for the rater and the ratee? Is evaluation a motivating task for the rater? Does the evaluation task per se motivate the ratee? Mohrman and Lawler, who are concerned with individual issues, suggest that raters' motivation is a function of the perceived consequences of particular ratings—specifically, how they will be used, who will see them, the anticipated reactions of the ratee, and the performance–reward link established in the organization.

There are some points in Mitchell's paper that are reinforced by other participants. In particular, Mitchell sees motivation as an individual phenomenon that would suggest that a policy-capturing approach may be appropriate for its study (Zedeck, 1977). The notion of individual analysis of motivation can be extended to the individual analysis of performance behaviors as suggested by Guion, Hall, and Palermo. This latter approach is consistent with Guion's specific call for a policy-capturing approach to the study of performance issues. If such an approach is used, the problem cited by Mitchell regarding the aggregation of people over time, jobs, or settings can be subsequently studied by clustering those with similar motivation to rate and, in addition, performance policies.

Goodman and Fichman are critical of the lack of specificity in definition and direction provided by Mitchell. Consequently, they offer an additional and alternative set of concepts and propositions to be examined in future research—namely, labor, technology, organizational arrangements, and environment. To some, these concepts may appear to be similar to Mitchell's social and organizational factors, and equally nonspecific. Nevertheless, the debate highlights the need for increased research in taxonomies of individual, task, social, and organizational factors. Such research should lead to increased precision in variable specification and definition as well as finer and more reliable distinctions within and between sets of factors.

The paper by Steers and Lee focuses on the role of employee commitment and organizational climate as facilitators of effective performance appraisals. This paper is in the "organizational" section because the intention was for organizational climate to be perceived as an organizational characteristic that affects performance-assessment issues.

According to Steers and Lee, effective performance-appraisal systems are ones that yield information relevant to evaluation (individual assessment), guidance and development, and motivation. This assertion requires a specification of how organizational effectiveness is defined, conceptually and operationally. Steers and Lee further offer several propositions: for example, the more information that flows between the supervisor and subordinate, the greater the likelihood that desired outcomes will be achieved. The concept of "more information" could be part of an operational definition of "effectiveness"—that is, more information might yield opportunities for better choices and decision. On the other hand, more information might result in confusion, distortion, and in discounting of some information of potential value. In the long run, individual effectiveness may in fact be reduced rather than enhanced. The point is that though Steers and Lee suggest that their hypotheses are adequate to guide subsequent research, they presume a better understanding and measurement of organizational effectiveness than now exists.

Steers and Lee also call for an examination of the degree to which employee commitment influences the conditions that facilitate effective performance-appraisal systems, and further, how performance appraisal influences organizationally desired outcomes. Likewise, they suggest looking at the role of organizational-psychological climate. Other organizational properties or characteristics that might facilitate effective performance-appraisal systems are the incumbent's power (suggested by Hall) and the task, social, and organizational cues (suggested by Mitchell).

As suggested by Steers and Lee, the reciprocity of the direction of links and feedback from one variable to another, need to be examined. For example, Steers and Lee propose that employee commitment (reflected by increased tenure), influences employee participation, a condition that facilitates effective performance-appraisal systems. (The effect could also appear if the direction was from employee participation to increased retention and tenure.) In addition, some possible links not specified by Steers and Lee should also be examined. For example, it may be assumed that organizational goal support results in clear job standards and expectations but only in a nonambiguous environment. This latter hypothesis looks at the impact of an employee commitment variable on a facilitating condition as moderated by a psychological-climate construct.

Cummings' comments on the Steers and Lee paper basically focus on the distinction between trust, climate, and commitment and how they are substitute terms for psychometrically sound performance-appraisal systems. Cummings' comments also point up the uses for which performance appraisals are sought—in particular, control and development and direction. Though commitment/climate may be substituted for appraisals, when appraisals are replaced or eliminated, there is no relatively objective check on the maintenance of the assumed positive commitment/climate within the organization. In other words, though it is suggested that research that examines the relationship between commitment and acceptance of ratings may be fruitful and may identify conditions that facilitate acceptance, the replacement of an evaluation system is questionable. Keep in mind, though, that the proposal assumes that there is a psychometrically sound appraisal form, the need for which is highlighted by Bartlett's comments.

Individual Issues

The concern within this section is whether a cognitive, personality, or social-research perspective might be used to study the performance-appraisal process. The key to these orientations is a particular emphasis on the study of individual differences.

A particular point raised by several participants (e.g., Campbell, Staw, and Bartlett) was the lack of a theory of performance. Palermo's paper attempts to provide a theory but one that is more abstract than those with which industrial and organizational psychologists are familiar. Palermo provides the perspective of a cognitive psychologist. The theory is a conceptual framework for synthesizing the performance-evaluation situation. In particular, Palermo argues that each person has a "theory of the world" and that events, contexts, and stimuli have different meanings for each individual depending on the theory held by each person. Variations in theories among individuals are due, in part, to specific individual experiences. As part of the explication of this theory, Palermo introduces notions of classification of ambiguous behaviors within schemas. In essence, he is suggesting that performance appraisal involves one's rationalization of his or her decisions by categorizing people according to an abstract system of rules that operate at a tacit level.

Palermo's framework does not suggest specific testable hypotheses. Its value is that it provides us with a conceptual framework that emphasizes the study of the individual and a determination of how he or she makes decisions, recalls information, and views the world. Again, this interest in the individual was stressed by Mitchell, Hall, and Guion.

Higgins' comments support the position of Palermo. From the perspective of social cognition, social stimuli are often considered to be ambiguous and are susceptible to different interpretations by the same individual at different points in time and by different individuals at the same point in time. In other words, it depends on your "theory of the world."

Higgins extends Palermo's arguments by elaborating on two aspects of the performance-appraisal process. First, Higgins proposes that evaluations should be more "holistic" and that they are not necessarily composed of individual elements that sum to a whole. He suggests that supervisors should not rely on a strategy that involves simply combining the independent value of each of the worker's different attributes. Analysis of one's overall or total performance cannot be detected by summing up performances on separate domains because of the interrelationships among these domains—interrelationships that are true or illusory due to covariation theories held by others (Cooper, 1981). Thus, behaviorally oriented performance-appraisal methods that require as many evaluations as there are domains or dimensions of performance and that avoid the use of "overall" evaluations may not provide us with a total assessment of the ratee.

In addition, Higgins discusses "similarity error," which occurs when evaluators infer interrelationships among particular attributes, or, in performance-evaluation terms, the problem of halo. Higgins' solution for this problem is to rely on behavioral evidence as much as possible and to control the urge to go beyond the information available or given. Such a strategy is the essence of behaviorally anchored rating scales (BARS) but there is evidence that BARS have not accomplished their objectives (Jacobs, Kafry, & Zedeck, 1980).

Second, Higgins discusses questionnaires as evaluation instruments. The points raised regarding long-term memory, stored information, and recall in communications contexts are crucial to an understanding of the performance-appraisal process and need to be studied in an appraisal context (Cooper, 1981;

Feldman, 1981). Not only may there be a limitation to questionnaire forms for obtaining performance-appraisal data per se, but questionnaires on "paper people" may be a problem, as suggested by Guion and Ilgen, for studying the performance-appraisal process.

Borman's paper examines several areas within personality psychology that have relevance for performance-appraisal problems and issues. Though the review is based on the personality literature, there is, in part, a social-cognitive bias as evidenced by the topics of information processing, perceptual judgment, memory impression, memory decay, and the like. These concerns are introduced and integrated within personality constructs. In particular, Borman presents: (1) implicit personality theory as an explanation for halo biases and systematic distortion in ratings; (2) personal-contruct theory as an explanation of the content–behavior–situation context upon which an evaluator focuses; and (3) trait–situation considerations as a basis for understanding and studying variability in an individual's performance within a dimension over time and situations. In addition, Borman proposes new models and strategies for measuring, recording, and interpreting evaluations.

The emphasis on situations is strongly reinforced by Shweder's comments. Shweder distinguishes between abstract structures or theoretical aspects and surface structures or content aspects of performance. Shweder pushes for greater attention to details of a task or situation, which in turn may yield finer analysis and distinction in performance. Performance is best assessed when the situation is taken into account, and when definition of situation may entail task and organizational characteristics such as those suggested by Mitchell. These orientations to situations call, again, for more work on taxonomies of situations as well as tasks and behaviors.

Whereas the Mitchell paper addresses the organizational factors that affect the motivation links from arousal through appraisal, the Mohrman and Lawler paper addresses the special issue of an individual's motivation to appraise. In particular, the argument is made that motivation is affected by the meaning the individual gives to the components of the performance-appraisal situation, by the organizational context, and by the formal appraisal system. (The significance of "meaning" is also addressed by Palermo.) Appropriate performance-appraisal behaviors will result if supervisors and subordinates have a shared social definition that is consistent with the intent of performance appraisal. An expectancy model is postulated such that motivated behavior occurs when there is a perceived ability to effect certain appraisal behaviors, there is an appropriate understanding of the appraisal role in which one finds oneself, there is a likelihood that certain outcomes will occur because of certain behaviors, and there are outcomes that the individual values.

The Mohrman and Lawler motivation model is discussed in the context of performance-appraisal functions and organizational settings. The implications for the contribution of these two considerations to the understanding of the performance-appraisal process has also been made by Cummings, who discusses control and direction purposes, by Steers and Lee, who discuss organizational climate, and by Mitchell, who discusses specific task and organizational influences on the performance-appraisal process.

Bartlett's critique of the Mohrman and Lawler paper focuses on measurement problems. Putting aside the specific criticisms, some of Bartlett's concerns were echoed by others at the conference. In particular, Bartlett saw a need for better operational definitions of performance, or as others refer to the issue, a need for a performance theory. Bartlett stressed the need for providing training in the observation of behavior. He also suggested the possibility of differences in evaluation as a function of purpose of rating.

We must acknowledge that Bartlett was one of the few to comment on the importance of appraisal methods in the process. In general, recommendations for the use of specific methodologies for performance appraisal were absent from the discussions and this was by design. Much of the literature on performance appraisal has focused on methodologies, formats, response biases, and the like. In setting up the topics for discussion at the conference, we believed that we had gone as far as possible with methodology and that future enhancement would require a better understanding of the more general aspects of the process. Bartlett's comments, however, keep us attuned to the need for methodological rigor, both in developing a performance methodology as well as in studying the process. All of the variables, constructs, and conditions that have been espoused and identified are useful for understanding the performance-appraisal process only if studied with reliable and accurate appraisal devices.

The O'Leary and Hansen paper focuses on the contributions that social-cognition theories can make to the understanding of the performance-appraisal process. In particular, they review the literature in the area of self-fulfilling prophecies and perceptions of cause (attribution theory) in an attempt to generalize to performance-appraisal contexts. Their premise is that biased expectations based on category membership (gender) affect perceptions of, and behavior towards, persons in those categories, and can result in those persons' behavioral confirmation of the erroneous expectations.

Ilgen's comments support the importance of the social-cognition theories while at the same time being critical of the paradigms used, the limited external validity of the results for the performance-appraisal context, and the overconcentration on sex differences. In addition, Ilgen concentrates on factors that directly affect performance-appraisal accuracy. These factors are objectivity of performance, appraiser's knowledge of performance dimensions, observational opportunities, and appraiser expectations for appraisee performance.

The O'Leary/Hansen and Ilgen papers provide us with a social-cognitive perspective from which to view the performance-appraisal process. Perhaps most important, however, is the need to look at the social-cognition literature not as a source of post hoc explanations of particular performance but rather as a source for a predictive model. Are effort and luck real factors causing differences or are they reasonable rationalizations for outcomes? One gets the feeling that social-cognition theories can explain all of behavior after the fact. However their predictive value may be limited. Attribution theory may be useful as a heuristic device but more limited as a theory of behavior. Different and better paradigms than those traditionally used will need to be developed in order to shed more light on whether sex differences have the direct or indirect effects, as predicted by Ilgen, on performance.

Ilgen's paper also reviews the specific issue of opportunity to observe and its impact on appraisal accuracy. Because Ilgen's paper deals with social cognition, it is relevant to note at this point the work of Newtson (1973) who has studied fine versus gross units of behavior and their implications for attribution processes. Newtson found that the size of the perceived unit of behavior is variable. That is, perceivers of human behavior, or observors, can vary the level at which they analyze observed behavior. Behavior can be broken down into fine, detailed units with each unit representing meaningful actions, or it can be assessed in terms of large units of behavior. Specific results showed that those who employ fine units of analysis are more confident and have more differentiations in their ratings than those utilizing gross units. In addition, of particular relevance here, is the tendency for fine-unit perceivers to perceive behavior as more personally caused whereas gross-unit perceivers are more situational in their attributions. Such research may reveal the degree (fineness) to which behavior can be observed, recorded, and analyzed by evaluators, and the types of dimensions (global versus specific, general versus anchored) needed to evaluate behavior.

Methodological and Measurement Issues

This section focuses on methodological and measurement issues such as theory development, operationalization of variables, specificity, and modeling. They are issues that are germane to testing any of the specific propositions generated by the papers in this conference.

The Vineberg and Joyner paper on performance evaluations in the military focuses on evaluations of technical performance and overall suitability ratings. Particular attention is given to the applied methodological issue of "hands-on" or simulated tests of job-performance proficiency in contrast to paper-and-pencil tests. Their presentation highlights some basic research questions. As one example, they raise the issue of measuring performance at several points in time and across various dimensions. Little research has been conducted along these lines, the possible exception being the AT&T Management Progress Study (Bray, Campbell, & Grant, 1974). How much stability in performance, on specific or overall dimensions, is there as one moves across jobs, when jobs are within the same family (or career ladder), or when the jobs may be only randomly related? A good illustration of this issue is the stability of one's performance as he or she moves, for example, from, a sales position in which salary is based on commissions into a fixed salaried supervisory position. Some of the performance dimensions for sales and supervisory positions are similar or overlapping—is performance similar for this candidate in the two positions? The example, however, also highlights other research issues, one of which is consideration for a manager's ability to evaluate performance. That is, if prior perforamnce (sales success) is used to promote one into a higher-level position (the supervisory position), then it is unlikely that one of the domains of the new position—the task of evaluating and providing feedback to others—was considered when the promotion was made. The point is that promotional decisions should perhaps be based in part on one's ability to evaluate and develop others. Simulation exercises, such as those called for by Vineberg and Joyner and by Curran, should be developed to tap one's ability to evaluate others.

The notion of simulation exercises, introduced by Vineberg and Joyner, and expanded upon by Curran, is an interesting one, especially when actual criteria are not available. However, use of these exercises can be extended to positions for which supervisors have no opportunity to observe or for positions in which supervisors have little familiarity with the work of the persons they are responsible for evaluating. The obvious limitation of such simulations is the degree to which the exercise appears "contrived" or the extent to which cues from the environment influence performance. Furthermore, it is conceivable that such simulations may yield increased response bias due to inconsistency between the exercise and the actual context.

The issue of feedback loops, touched on by Curran is one that needs more research. In addition, examining the feedback loop between current and future ratings, we need to look at the impact of social, individual, and organizational variables on current and future ratings. The relationship between current and future ratings could be moderated by such factors as commitment, trust, and power. This interest may require a more dynamic study of the evaluation process than we have typically undertaken. We need to study performance appraisal in a longitudinal fashion taking into account interactions and feedback between all factors and conditions that impinge on performance and its appraisal. It is unlikely that there is a direct chain of links but more likely that there is a "wheel" or "all-channel" type of network. Such research will benefit from the development of rules and taxonomies of behaviors, tasks, and format as called for by Vineberg and Joyner, as well as from rules and taxonomies for classifying organizational and situational constructs. That is, certain behaviors drawn from certain tasks may be most appropriately tested by a particular format but only in an organizational entity that has a particular structure or communication network. Taxonomy research that was begun by Frederiksen, Jensen, and Beaton (1972) and Fleishman (1975) may be a good point from which to start.

Hunter's paper introduces meta analyses into the domain of performance assessments. Hunter tested alternative explanations of the composition of supervisory ratings. In particular, he asked if supervisory ratings were a direct function of a worker's performance (as assessed by a work-sample test) or if they were formed on the basis of the supervisor's judgment of a worker's job knowledge rather than direct observation of performance per se. Results indicate that ratings are a function of both performance per se and job knowledge, with the latter having twice as much contribution to the determination of the ratings. However, as Hunter acknowledges, much of the variability in supervisory ratings is still unexplained after taking into account cognitive ability, job knowledge, and perforamnce. It is suggested here that the source of the unaccounted variance may be found in the individual, social, and organizational factors cited by the participants in the conference. The truly disturbing fact is that these factors may account for more of the variance than is accounted for by the ability, knowledge, and performance factors represented in the 14 studies analyzed by Hunter.

Guion's search for these additional factors led him to enlarge the model proposed by Hunter. Although he disucsses factors along the lines of ratee, rater, and context categories, these obviously relate to the broader individual, social, and organizational categories. Also, though Guion suggests that most of his variables have a direct effect on supervisory ratings, it is suggested here that they may also affect job knowledge and performance per se. For example, the reaction of a supervisor to the "annoyance syndrome" cited by Guion can result in the implementation of a developmental plan for the worker that involves special training. That worker's job knowledge is subsequently affected and differs from prior knowledge. In turn, performance and ratings are affected.

We want to stress Guion's point, also made by others, that more research be conducted on the individual rater. Such research will facilitate our understanding of the rating process and contribute to the development of a theory of performance.

The Campbell paper, as well as the comments by Naylor, present a discouraging view of the contribution that modeling has made to the understanding of the performance process. In fact, both participants suggest that modeling cannot contribute to an understanding of a process, and may not even necessarily accurately describe it; rather, modeling is a parsimonious fit of data. One reason for Campbell's assessment of the state of affairs may be found in Hunter's presentation. His analysis revealed a relatively inconsistent set of relationships between performance and other variables. Perhaps these data support the conclusion that the performance construct cannot be modeled, or that performance is not a unitary construct and represents a complex model.

In spite of the Campbell and Naylor modeling conclusions, their presentations steer us into directions for better understanding of the process though from a less mathematically derived perspective. Campbell and Naylor both suggest that the process can be understood by asking evaluators to explain their behaviors (ratings) and the factors leading to the evaluations. Thus, in-depth interviews might shed some light on the process as well as on an increased understanding of what performance is.

Many at the conference called for such a "theory of performance." Campbell suggests that an a priori theory can be investigated by latent trait and causal modeling. Results of such analyses that show that proficiency on a latent domain such as "motivating subordinates" may be caused by "proficiency at setting goals and planning work" would be useful in personnel functions such as developing training programs for those in supervisory positions. Perhaps error-avoidance training, which is now typically provided, should be replaced with training on how to do what is required in one's job; that is, supervisors would be taught how to set goals and plan work for their subordinates.

The notion of criterion-referenced measurement is one that also should receive more attention. The simulations called for by Vineberg, Joyner, and Curran can be based on the notion of mastery of concept where performance on the test would correspond to a specific objective that is to be achieved by the worker. This is one area in which BARS may be useful in that it identifies different levels of performance; we can assume that the mid-range of the scale represents typical or minimally acceptable performance (Jacobs et al., 1980). Furthermore, the identification of "errors in performance" would be useful for development of training programs.

An important distinction made by Campbell is that of modeling the rater's behavior (i.e., how he or she combines and uses performance information) and that of modeling the ratee's behavior (i.e., how the worker performs his or her tasks). An analysis of the differences may reveal which of the behaviors are important to the rater, the sequence in which data are used and combined, and the form of the equation. But how will this information help the ratee? Are we traveling down separate paths?

Sociopolitical Issues

Given that we gain a better understanding of performance and its evaluation, how does it fit into a larger system? This section contrasts the role of performance appraisal in two political systems, capitalistic and socialistic.

The Locke and Lerner "debate" centers on capitalistic versus socialistic societies and their implicit assumptions, and concerns for the impact of the political system on performance assessments. This philosophical exchange raises some interesting research questions. Though Lerner acknowledges the difficulty of objective performance appraisal in any complex modern society, her discussion of egalitarianism and equality of distributions has implications for evaluations of group performance, a notion that has inherently different problems than evaluation of individuals. Perhaps the work of Shapira and Shirom (1980) regarding BARS for the evaluation of tank crews can be extended to organizational units or groups. Shapira and Shirom followed the typical BARS procedure for identifying behaviors but instead of focusing on individual behaviors, they identified group behaviors that defined dimensions such as "teamwork" (extent to which the crew performed its activities with full coordination and cooperation among its members) and "proficiency in maneuver" (extent to which the crew displayed professional skills in performing the right maneuvers while moving or stationed in the field).

Locke's paper is related to some of the recent cognitive approaches to performance appraisal (Cooper, 1981; Feldman, 1981). Locke mentions problems of recall when an evaluation is called for, although he describes this as an error. What is "accurate" about the behavior recalled if the process begins with observation and procedes through such stages as encoding, storage, recall, and judgment? Where does distortion take place? Another error cited by Locke is a result of poor observation. Here training techniques (Bernardin, 1978; Borman, 1975; Latham, Wexley, & Pursell, 1975) may be useful, though Spool's (1978) review suggests that much research is still needed in order to have a better understanding of the observation process. Related to this research aspect is the problem of one's ability as an observor, or evaluator. Few attempts (Zedeck & Kafry, 1977b) have been made to identify the individual-difference variables associated with ability to accurately evaluate others. Perhaps the real issue is opportunity to observe—it is acknowledged by several participants in this conference (e.g., Locke, Vineberg and Joyner, Hunter, and Guion) that many jobs are situated such that the supervisor's own duties do not require or involve direct observation of his or her subordinates' performances. These questions are germane to any society in which formal or informal evaluations are required.

The Goldman and Schmidt exchange regarding Marxist versus capitalistic virtues and explanations for the current state of the economy is interesting and provocative. The debate will obviously continue, and other explanations and theories will be offered. Nevertheless, there are points made by Goldman and Schmidt that have immediate implications for research in the area of performance appraisal.

Goldman stresses the situational differences between manager and worker. Though his orientation is philosophical, historical, and sociological, his comments have practical implications. For example, regardless of whether a caste system exists or not, more and more recognition is being given to the notion that performance appraisals serve different functions (Jacobs et al., 1980: Landy & Farr, 1980; Zedeck & Cascio, 1981; Zedeck & Kafry, 1977a). More research is needed to delineate the relationships between purpose of rating, method of rating, and the types of criteria used in ratings such as the soft–hard distinction made by Goldman.

Both Goldman and Schmidt point out the influence of such organizational and individual factors as politics, interpersonal relations, and need for achievement and acquisitiveness on performance measurement, which is consistent with the types of factors mentioned by the other presenters.

Goldman suggests that a performance-appraisal system is designed in part to enhance a unique relationship between an individual employee and his or her firm, which fosters personal and professional competition. The process by which people differentiate themselves from others, including perhaps the organization, and make themselves singular or unique may have negative consequences. It is possible that the performance-appraisal process that includes evaluation and feedback isolates that individual from his or her peers and creates a competitive environment that results in negative consequences for the individual and organization. This process, which appears to be related to the concept of organizational commitment as espoused by Steers and Lee, has not been studied by Industrial Organizational psychologists, though our social-psychology colleagues have emphasized conformity and deviance constructs (Maslach, 1974).

Schmidt's comments accentuate the need for a theory of perforamnce, particularly for managerial performance. Future research should be directed along the lines of that initiated by Tornow and Pinto (1976) who have developed a managerial taxonomy that leads to a system of describing, classifying, and evaluating upper managerial positions. Meta analyses, as suggested by Lerner and demonstrated by Hunter, and consortium approaches to the study of managerial performance may overcome problems cited by Goldman such as evaluating positions with few incumbents. In sum, the Goldman and Schmidt exchange, though philosophically, sociologically, and politically oriented, suggests a number of avenues for future research that have implications for the practitioners.

OVERLAPPING ISSUES

A cursory content analysis of the presentations and comments reveals six overlapping themes. First, a number of presenters bemoaned the fact that there is no theory of performance; some suggested that a theory, if represented as a model, is not useful; and still others postualted general abstract theories that related to individual analysis of meaning of the context. Second, the remarks of several participants revealed the need for a taxonomy of tasks, situations, behaviors, people, and organizations. Such work would contribute to a more parsimonious theory. Third, there were suggestions for increased attention to an individual analysis of one's performance and less emphasis on aggregation of people, jobs, and tasks. Fourth, several comments called for research on group performance in situations in which task performance required interdependence. Fifth, there was more recognition of the role played by the purpose of evaluation in the appraisal process than has appeared in the literature to date. Essentially, theory and research are suggesting that appraisal processes are influenced by the purpose for which the evaluation is made. Sixth, some comments stressed the problems in opportunity to observe behavior; some stressed the problems in observation. One suggestion was to do away with observation and rely on self-monitoring. Observation is the crux of evaluation and much research is needed on the relationship of observation to one's cognitive-processing mechanisms. These six themes can generate many hypotheses for future research.

PROPOSITIONS

As previously indicated, the purpose of this conference was to guide research. Each paper explored a general theme related to performance appraisal. Following, we present sets of propositions, that were extracted from the presentations and discussions. There are four such sets, corresponding to the four major groupings of papers. The sets are obviously not exhaustive. Some of the propositions are very specific, others are general; some may even be inconsistent with others. After proper operational specification of the concepts, research should yield results that reduce the amount of unexplained variance found by Hunter's meta analysis, which in turn should generate new research. It is our hope that these propositions will stimulate such research.

Organizational Issues

1. The impact of a single person's behavior on organizational outcomes and characteristics is a function of individual formal/strategic power and the organizational level occupied by that person; the impact is greater as a result of strategic position than as a result of specific performance (assuming assessment of performance is comparable at the different levels).

2. The impact of rewards on performance is influenced by whether long- or short-term performance is stressed by the organization.

3. Managerial impact on performance varies as a function of the type of organization (public versus privately owned).

4. The assessment and subsequent impact of performance varies as a function of whether the worker works alone or in an interdependent group; the definition of performance changes as one changes the level of aggregation (individual versus group). Though individual performance can be assessed, the group performance is not necessarily a sum of individual performances.

5. Performance of individuals affects the type of style, decision-making strategy, and communications system adopted by supervisors.

6. Variations among workers' work values, norms, and expectations require the organizations's adoption of particular performance–reward systems, management styles, job structure, and job conditions.

7. The emphasis on assessment of outcome measures may result in inappropriate or counterproductive behaviors on the part of the individual.

8. The reward system for performance varies as a function of the organizational level and nature of work performed by the worker.

9. Social cues given by supervisors and coworkers influence the type of behavior emitted and outcome produced by a particular worker.

10. An individual's behavior and performance outcome is dependent on the degree to which he or she is identifiable and accountable.

11. The evaluation process per se is assumed to be a motivating task for the rater and ratee.

12. Requiring the supervisor to evaluate the subordinate results in increased motivated behavior for the supervisor in his or her own position.

13. Performance assessments are affected more by organizational constraints such as administrative technology, machine technology, and environment than by personal factors such as ability, role perception, and effort.

14. Organizational constraints such as administrative technology, machine technology, and environment interfere with and inhibit one's ability and effort; that is, performance is affected by individually controllable and organizationally controllable factors.

15. Performance assessments of a worker are a function of the evaluator's perception of task characteristics such as autonomy and feedback and group characteristics such as interdependence and sociometric properties.

16. Effective performance-appraisal systems facilitate employee evaluation, guidance and development, and motivation; however, a single system may not be equally effective for every purpose and may in some instances be counterproductive.

17. An organization with a positive climate and employees with strong commitment can replace a performance-appraisal system that monitors and controls employee performance.

18. Conditions that facilitate effective performance appraisal, such as adequate communications networks, clear job standards, and involvment of employers in the appraisal design and implementation, may be counterproductive to motivation to perform because the task environment may become too structured.

Individual Issues

1. The assessment of behavior is a function of the "theory" and "meaning" attached by an individual to that behavior and situation. Variability of "theory" between individuals leads to variability among raters within groups (e.g., supervisors) and between groups (e.g., supervisors versus incumbents) regarding the interpretation and evaluation of a given performance, which in turn leads to low interrater agreement.

2. Modeling of decisions and evaluation behaviors requires awareness of "theories of the world."

3. Inconsistencies within one's "theory of the world" and interpretation of events leads to a reliance on response biases such as halo, leniency, and central tendency when forming judgments about others.

4. The effectiveness of a performance-appraisal system is a function of a rater's/ratee's perception of the use to which the evaluation will be put.

5. Evaluation of past performance is a function of the degree to which performance had been adequately coded and stored in categories.

6. Observed behaviors for which there is no storage category or that have been classified into a category other than the one for which evaluation is requested are not used in evaluations by the evaluator.

7. "Overall" performance evaluation is a function of the evaluation of the individual components of performance; or, the whole equals the sum of the parts.

8. Evaluations are based on an "implicit personality theory" regarding the degree to which behavioral categories are interrelated and consistent with each other; inconsistent behaviors are ignored, distorted, or discounted.

9. The longer the interval between observation and evaluation, the greater the likelihood that "implicit personality theory" will affect evaluations.

10. Effectiveness of performance appraisal may depend on having observation and recording by one "evaluator" and evaluation per se by an independent evaluator; this is in contrast to having one person observe, record, *and* evaluate.

11. Raters vary in the degree to which they note cues or behaviors as relevant to their evaluations of performance dimensions.

12. A person's rating style, or the way in which he or she uses cues, varies as a function of the situation (e.g., self, peer, or subordinate evaluation) and the purpose of the evaluation (e.g., control, direction, or development).

13. There is more consistency in the behavior of an "average" performer than there is in the behaviors of "very good" or "very poor" performers.

14. A rater's personal constructs influence the behaviors that are noted, recorded, and evaluated; behaviors that are not part of, or are inconsistent with, one's personal construct theory are ignored, distorted, or discounted.

15. A rater's evaluation of a ratee is composed of his or her assessment of that ratee's variability in performance across different situations and his or her own theory of the cooccurrence of events.

16. Private, internal appraisals may be inconsistent with social, overtly expressed appraisals because the latter are more functional in that they can lead to desired outcomes or changes in behavior (they direct and control behavior); thus, there may be intentional distortion in order to "motivate" the ratee.

17. Differences between rater and ratee in perception of the use of a performance evaluation lead to negative consequences for the rater, ratee, and organization.

18. The accuracy of a rater's evaluation reflects the rater's own performance; the more accurate the ratings that he or she provides, the better evaluations he or she will receive from his or her supervisor.

19. Rater's evaluations are a function of self-fulfilling prophecies that are based on the rater's assessment of the ratee's job knowledge determined at the time of hire; self-fulfilling prophecies can also be based on a desire to support one's own initial decision to hire the ratee.

20. Evaluation of observed events is more a function of the attributed cause of the event than the actual evaluative component of the event.

21. Attributions of causes of behavior are a function of the ratee's similarity

to others, stability of performance over time, and consistency of performance within a performance domain.

Methodological and Measurement Issues

1. A performance-appraisal system suited for certification may not be suited for uncovering individual differences in performance above some minimal level.

2. In situations in which important behaviors are called for on an infrequent basis, performance measurement may benefit from simulating the performance situation.

3. When a particular behavior is infrequently required, ratings of that behavior may be contaminated by the ratee's perceived performance in other, more frequent behaviors.

4. Measuring the same aspect of behavior with different methodologies may yield different results depending on the level of abstraction or separation between the job behavior and the method of measurement (e.g., hands-on testing versus paper-and-pencil testing for mechanical proficiency).

5. The use of simulated exercises may be more appropriate for evaluating those with whom the rater is less familiar.

6. The amount of information processed and the way in which it is combined may be a function of the degree to which the rater has had an opportunity to observe the ratee or the degree to which the rater is familiar with the ratee.

7. Evaluations may be influenced by the amount of time in position for the ratee and the amount of information accumulated over time on the ratee.

8. Job knowledge seems to be more important than job performance in influencing supervisory ratings.

9. Large portions of variance in supervisory ratings are unrelated to job knowledge or job performance of incumbents.

10. Supervisory ratings provide information about "typical" performance but may provide less information about potential levels of "maximum" performance for a given ratee.

11. There is a figure–ground relationship between the performance of a "target person" and the performance of others in the target person's work group or peer group.

12. Individuals who work alone may be evaluated less reliably than those who work with others.

13. Performance-measurement systems can only be effective if there is a clear definition of expected or acceptable levels of performance.

14. Performance measurement might be more effective if a set of "errors to avoid" could be constructed and a person's behavior scanned for instances of those errors.

15. The integrity of performance assessment might be augmented by forcing the evaluators to use more information when making judgments.

Sociopolitical Issues

1. With respect to administrative decisions regarding the distribution of monetary rewards, it is difficult to separate the worth of the job from the worth of the person.

2. The perceived value of a person's efforts is moderated by the value of the job title that the person occupies.

3. A predictor of managerial success might be a measure of the "ability to judge people." Such a predictor might be included as a component in a selection or promotion system.

4. "Performance" evaluation in the public sector depends more on factors such as seniority, age, experience, test scores, and personal factors than on merit.

5. Variance in rating distributions is much lower in public-sector settings than in private-sector settings.

6. Managers are evaluated using more benevolent (soft) criteria than workers, who are evaluated using more objective and demanding criteria.

7. The process of performance evaluation isolates workers, breaking down common bonds that they may have with peers.

REFERENCES

Bernardin, H. J. Effects of rater training on leniency and halo errors in student ratings of instructors. *Journal of Applied Psychology*, 1978, *63*, 301–308.

Borman, W. C. Effect of instructions to avoid halo error on reliability and validity of performance evaluation ratings. *Journal of Applied Psychology*, 1975, *60*, 556–560.

Bray, D. W., Campbell, R. J., & Grant, D. L. *Formative years in business: A long-term AT&T study of managerial lives.* New York: Wiley, 1974.

Cooper, W. H. Ubiquitous halo. *Psychological Bulletin*, 1981, *90*, 218–244.

Feldman, J. Beyond attribution theory: Cognitive processes in performance appraisal. *Journal of Applied Psychology*, 1981, *66*, 127–148.

Fleishman, E. A. Toward a taxonomy of human performance. *American Psychologist*, 1975, *30*, 1127–1149.

Frederiksen, N., Jensen, O., & Beaton, A. E. *Prediction of organizational behavior.* New York: Pergamon Press, 1972.

Jacobs, R., Kafry, D., & Zedeck, S. Expectations of behaviorally anchored rating scales. *Personnel Psychology*, 1980, *33*, 595–640.

Landy, F. J., & Farr, J. L. Performance rating. *Psychological Bulletin*, 1980, *87*, 72–107.

Latham, G. P., Wexley, K. N., & Pursell, E. D. Training managers to minimize rating errors in the observation of behavior. *Journal of Applied Psychology*, 1975, *60*, 550–555.

Maslach, C. Social and personal biases of individuation. *Journal of Personality and Social Psychology*, 1974, *29*, 411–425.

Newtson, D. Attribution and the unit of perception of on-going behavior. *Journal of Personality and Social Psychology*, 1973, *28*, 28–38.

Shapira, Z., & Shirom, A. New issues in the use of behaviorally anchored rating scales: Level of analysis, the effects of incident frequency, and external validation. *Journal of Applied Psychology*, 1980, *65*, 517–523.

Spool, M. D. Training programs for observors of behavior: A review. *Personnel Psychology*, 1978, *31*, 853–888.

Tornow, W. W., & Pinto, P. R. The development of a managerial job taxonomy: A system for describing, classifying, and evaluating executive positions. *Journal of Applied Psychology*, 1976, *61*, 410–418.

Zedeck, S. An information processing model and approach to the study of motivation. *Organizational Behavior and Human Performance*, 1977, *18*, 47–77.

Zedeck, S., & Cascio, W. F. *Performance appraisal decisions as a function of rater training and purpose of the appraisal. Journal of Applied Psychology*, in press.

Zedeck, S., & Kafry, D. Capturing rater policies for processing evaluation data. *Organizational Behavior and Human Performance*, 1977, *18*, 269–294. (a)

Zedeck, S., & Kafry, D. Evaluations of the developers of behavioral expectation evaluation scales. *Journal Supplement Abstract Service*, 1977, *7*, 123 (MS. 1618). (b)

Author Index

Subject Index